Shattered Spaces

Shattered Spaces

ENCOUNTERING JEWISH RUINS
IN POSTWAR GERMANY
AND POLAND

Michael Meng

HARVARD UNIVERSITY PRESS

Cambridge, Massachusetts, and London, England · 2011

Publication of this book was supported by a grant from the Graham Foundation for Advanced Studies in the Fine Arts.

Library of Congress Cataloging-in-Publication Data
Meng, Michael.
    Shattered spaces : encountering Jewish ruins in postwar Germany and Poland / Michael Meng.
        p. cm.
    Includes bibliographical references and index.
    ISBN 978-0-674-05303-8 (alk. paper)
  1. Jews—Germany—History—1945–1990.   2. Jews—Germany—History—1990–
3. Jews—Poland—History—20th century.   4. Jews—Poland—History—21st
century.   5. Collective memory and city planning—Germany.   6. Collective memory and
city planning—Poland.   7. Memory—Social aspects—Germany.   8. Memory—Social
aspects—Poland.   9. Memorialization—Germany.   10. Memorialization—Poland.
I. Title.
    DS134.26M46 2011
    305.892′404309045—dc22   2011012096

Contents

Illustrations

Preface

In 2001, I happened upon a small book in Potsdam's library, a reprint of a publication marking the unveiling of the city's synagogue in 1903. A short chronology of the building's history listed its destruction in 1958. "That's late," I thought. To be sure, I had already been thinking about urban reconstruction. The summer before arriving in Potsdam—fresh out of undergraduate studies on a Fulbright—I was reading any book I could find on urban space, historic preservation, and memory, feeling liberated to explore a new topic after my senior thesis and keeping my mind awake during a sleepy summer job. I checked out the book, walked downstairs, and looked for where the synagogue once stood. I happened upon a block apartment building, constructed in the late 1950s like many across the Soviet bloc in the wake of de-Stalinization. I suspected this was the spot but was not certain; I had the synagogue's prewar address but no prewar map. But it did not take long before a small plaque, erected in 1979, as I discovered later, caught my eye: "The synagogue of the Potsdam Jewish community stood at this location. It was plundered and destroyed by the fascists in the night of November 9–10, 1938." No mention of the wrecking ball in 1958, I noted curiously.

Several months later, I traveled to Kraków. I had studied Eastern European history, but was more of a "Germanist" at the time—a few phrases were all the Polish I knew. Like just about every American in Kraków, I was a tourist, but walked through the city's preserved "Jewish district" with interest as a budding urban historian. I was struck that after decades of neglect this area was now being refurbished in a city of few Jews. Although Kraków never became one of "my" cities—a decision I wondered about while walking through the snowy sludge of a dark, cold Warsaw winter several years later when I returned to Poland to do research for this book—it first got me thinking comparatively. Indeed, when I arrived back in the United States after my Fulbright year, I had a topic in hand, and now I just had to learn Polish and figure out how to frame it. The Polish would come, and I knew that I wanted to think broadly across space and time: I wanted to connect my Potsdam and Kraków discoveries, to think about the destruction and preservation of Jewish spaces across national, political, and local borders. This book is the outcome of my efforts to do that. It is a study of the material traces of Jewish life in Berlin, Warsaw, Potsdam, Essen, and Wrocław over the past sixty years (I decided against Kraków because it is an exceptional case in Poland, and in Europe, for that matter). It pursues two main questions over six decades: What happened to Jewish sites after the Holocaust? How have Germans, Poles, and Jews encountered them since 1945?

When I began this project, I thought my answers to these questions would involve arguments about memory, but once I started my research, I realized that they entailed much more. They meant thinking about block apartment buildings as much as debates about the Holocaust. My research also made me realize that I was writing about more than just Polish, German, and Jewish history. At its core, the postwar history of Jewish sites is about German-Polish-Jewish relations, but it is also about democracy, Communism, the Cold War, tourism, urban space, and cosmopolitanism. And it is a history centered in Europe, but one that radiates out to other parts of the world, especially the United States and Israel. Finally, my research challenged the main assumption I had going into this project. Like many historians who rely on the nation-state and the Cold War to tell their stories, I thought that the handling of Jewish sites would fall distinctly along the lines of the Oder-Neisse border and the Iron Curtain. But the deeper I probed, the more I realized that national, political, and local differences shaped what in many ways was a parallel history across a diverse region. National and political differences mattered, but not always as sharply as one might expect. My aim became to explain the parallels as much as the divergences.

In so doing, I decided to focus on Poland and Germany. I selected these two countries not just because I happen to be more familiar with their histories, not just because they caught my traveling eye or because the Fulbright commission wisely placed me in Potsdam rather than my first choice of Berlin. I chose them for the empirical factors that bring these two cases together into a sensible comparison of, as the historian Marc Bloch put it, "differing and, at the same time, related realities": the history of Jewish-gentile relations, the legacies of the Holocaust, the international interest in both countries, and the postwar history of Jewish sites. Yet, no matter what my reasons, I know that my comparison will be jarring to a few. Several years ago, a colleague came up to me after I had delivered a paper and objected to my comparison of the "victims" to the "perpetrators." To be sure, the differences in how the Holocaust unfolded in Nazi Germany and occupied Poland remain central, but they do not always amount to such simplistic dichotomies. The connections that link these two countries make this hardly a comparison of two completely distinct cases.

I suspect, though, that it was not just the comparison that triggered criticism but the subject that I was discussing. Germany and Poland have received international scrutiny like no other European countries for how well or how poorly they appear to be dealing with the legacies of the Holocaust. Whatever they might be doing, they are acting either rightly or wrongly: either Germans have "mastered" the past or they have fallen short; either Poles are slowly reaching the implicit German standard of monuments, speeches, and debates or they are lagging far behind it. My aim is to avoid falling into this success/failure dichotomy without giving up my critical charge as a scholar. I uncover many tensions in encountering Jewish sites, but I also critically examine why some changes did take place. While I find in these changes many dilemmas, I also see at times self-reflective and historically conscious thinking among some Germans, Poles, and Jews, cosmopolitical claims that challenge us to consider our own provincialism. I compare and analyze as a historian and writer, but also as a person interested in how two societies have encountered ethnic hatred and violence and how the long, contradictory experiences of those societies can challenge more of us to think critically about our own pasts and presents.

This brings me, then, to one final point—my title. This book is about shifting encounters with physical spaces, mostly shattered sites that for most of the postwar years were traces of the past left in the wake of genocide. Ruins, though, are hardly static; they have histories that change as people perceive and deal with them in different ways—neglecting, destroying, altering, transforming, preserving, restoring, and reusing them. Sometimes they cease to be ruins altogether when they become fully functioning buildings again: the restored synagogue in Wrocław, today a prayer house and cultural center, is one example. In writing "encountering Jewish ruins" in my subtitle, I mean precisely this shifting history of meanings, perceptions, and interpretations of physical spaces.

Shattered Spaces

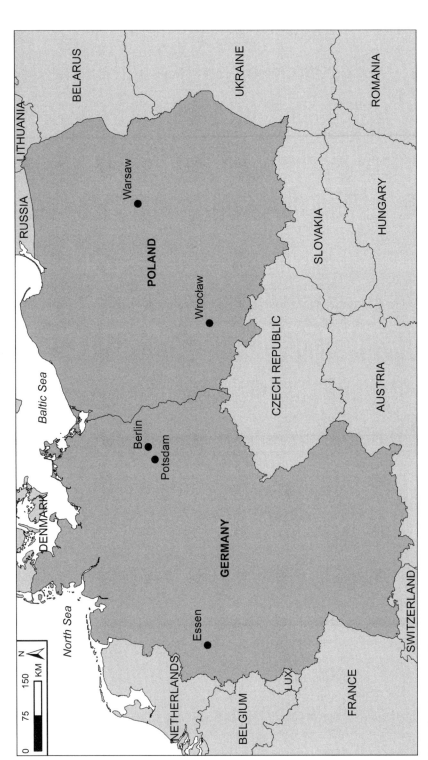

Map of contemporary Europe

Introduction

In 1945, many Polish and German cities amounted to little more than mounds of shattered stone. Berlin, the epicenter of Hitler's empire, which caused much of the damage, had 75 million cubic meters of rubble after 52,000 tons of aerial bombs and street-by-street fighting in the last throes of the war. Dust covered Berliners as they came out of their cellars to brave the streets. "This Sahara of ruins," the *New York Times* declared with a tinge of triumphalism, "is doomed to revert almost to the level of the modest fourteenth-century fishing village from which this pride of a long line of German emperors grew."[1] And Berlin hardly stood as the most damaged capital. That unfortunate distinction went to Warsaw, which the Nazis demolished as part of their deadly occupation of Poland. Warsaw's destruction made "Berlin and Prague look like garden spots by comparison." After touring the city, General Eisenhower said simply, "Warsaw is far more tragic than anything I have seen."[2] Warsaw and Berlin, however, were not alone in 1945. They reflected the postwar norm across the region of East Central Europe. Wrocław, Potsdam, and Essen—the other cities whose urban stories unfold in these pages—were not much more than piles of ruins either.

Rubble defined the postwar landscape, but not all of it was caused in the same way. Aerial bombs and street fighting created much of the debris, but substantial parts were produced by deliberate acts of violence, especially against Jewish property. The Nazis demolished Jewish sites across Europe, targeting in particular sacred spaces such as synagogues and Jewish cemeteries. Genocide has long involved attacks against culturally symbolic sites, from the destruction of Carthage in 146 BCE to the demolishment of mosques in Sarajevo in 1992, but never on this scale.[3] Indeed, few could imagine the enormity of the destruction. In July 1944, the Yiddish novelist Isaac Bashevis

Singer looked back on the Jewish life that had once existed in the capital of his native Poland. A year earlier, the Nazis had crushed the Warsaw Ghetto Uprising and leveled the area where most Jews lived before the war. Singer could barely grasp what this meant:

> On Saturday morning the streets were full of the scent of cholent and kugel. The sound of Sabbath songs rang out from all windows. Here was the Land of Israel.... "Those" streets included the following: Dzielna, Pawia, Gęsia, Miła, Niska, Stawki, Muranowski Square and first and foremost Nalewki and Franciszkańska. Those Jews traded before the First World War with Vladivostok, Petropavlovsk and even China. They had their stores packed up to the rafters with merchandise.... It is hard to imagine that all of that pulsating and glittering life has been extinguished, that this gigantic collection of human singularities was wiped off the face of the earth.[4]

In 1938, about 370,000 Jews lived in Warsaw. In 1945, fewer than several thousand did.[5] Most Jews lived in the city's northern part with the largest number in the district of Muranów. In 1943, the Nazis torched the district street by street, burning to the ground Muranów's streets, homes, and synagogues. After the war, few Poles mourned this massive destruction. City workers sifted through the rubble for bricks to rebuild Warsaw, while nearby residents searched for a find. "In our childhood, we practiced a strange, secret archeology in the ruins," the Polish actor Marek Kondrat recalled in 2003. "We dug up various things—pots, toys, fragments of household items. When we found something, we said, 'What the Jews left behind.'"[6] A similar disregard for Jewish ruins existed in postwar Germany. In the West German city of Essen, fewer than 200 Jews survived the Holocaust. Their towering stone synagogue remained abandoned for over two decades. In 1961, city officials turned the building into the House of Industrial Design to display mixers, plates, and washing machines, among other wonders of the German economic miracle. In Potsdam, the city's synagogue, located right in the center of town, stood in bombed-out form until 1958, when the East German regime decided to tear it down. An apartment building was built in its place.

Such destruction and disregard for Jewish sites are not exactly new to Jewish history. The Roman emperor Vespasian reportedly destroyed the

Aerial view of the destroyed Warsaw Ghetto on May 16, 1943. (National Archives and Records Administration, College Park, Maryland, courtesy of the United States Holocaust Memorial Museum)

synagogue in Antioch to build a theater in its place. "From the spoils of Judea," he had inscribed on the new building. Numerous Jewish sites remain deserted in Arab countries after the migration of Jews in the years following the creation of the Israeli state; a synagogue in the Algerian town of Miliana serves as a gymnasium.[7] Still, Jewish ruins in postwar Europe were unique. They reflected the results of an enormous genocide. Shards of broken stone—abandoned streets, homes, synagogues, cemeteries, and communal spaces—became the main traces of Jewish life after the Holocaust.[8] Since so few Jews survived Nazi Germany's "Final Solution" and many of those who did left for Canada, Latin America, the United States, or Israel, empty spaces were all that were left in many villages, towns, and cities. A region that once had 3.6 million Jews had by the early 1950s a mere 90,000. Germany and Poland, two countries with deep histories of Jews, became after 1945 landscapes of Jewish ruins. Writing some fifty years after Singer, the Polish author Agata Tuszyńska told of her own mournful search for the "world of Polish Jewry" through "shattered symbols"—those found in the pages of Singer's novels and those located on the streets of her hometown "in the remnants of synagogues, the remnants of traces." "My movie theater—severe, cold, devoid, to be sure, of the particular melody of prayerful voices, but obviously wiser than any ordinary movie house—was a Jewish synagogue."[9]

What now should be done with all these ruins? "Neither the expulsion of the Jewish population from Spain nor Babylon offers any relevant clues," wrote West Germany's main Jewish newspaper in 1951.[10] The scale of the problem overwhelmed Jewish leaders, but they clearly knew what ideally should happen. Jewish sites should be preserved. While Germany and Poland's official Jewish communities were small for most of the postwar period, they had active Jewish leaders who tried to shape the handling of Jewish property. In 1951, a group of American and German rabbis demanded the preservation of synagogues and Jewish cemeteries in the Federal Republic of Germany (FRG). In the Communist East, Jewish leaders made similar appeals to officials in the German Democratic Republic (GDR) and the Polish People's Republic (PPR). The American Jewish Joint Distribution Committee (JDC), a relief agency founded in 1914, worked from abroad to preserve Jewish sites in Europe.

But Jewish organizations could only do so much. "The full JDC global budget would not be sufficient," an official noted in 1963, to restore the "hundreds of Jewish cemeteries" in Poland.[11] But most of all, local Jewish leaders had little control over what happened to Jewish sites. In the two Germanys and Poland, municipal officials owned and controlled most communal property for different legal reasons across the Iron Curtain. In West Germany, most Jewish communal property was returned to newly created Jewish successor organizations, which often ended up selling it to local governments in order to distribute the profits as quickly as possible to Holocaust survivors. In East Germany and Poland, both Communist parties rejected restitution altogether and seized all Jewish property. Although the reasons differed along

Cold War lines, the effect was the same. In most cases, local officials were the ones who had the power to decide what to do with Jewish sites, not local Jewish leaders.

The decisions of local officials often proved disastrous. In the 1950s and 1960s, urban planners, historic preservationists, and local political leaders demolished numerous damaged Jewish sites or allowed them to fall to ruin by neglect. In some cases, such as in Warsaw, almost every last fragment of the Jewish past—its streets, shops, prayer houses—vanished from the urban landscape. A sprawling housing complex emerged from the ruins of Muranów. "What is it?" asked a reporter in 1965. "It was the ghetto," a young Polish writer answered.[12] As Poles and Germans rebuilt their bombed-out cities, towns, and villages, they expelled the traces of the Jewish past. The few Jewish sites that escaped the wrecking ball gradually decayed by neglect or were turned into movie theaters, storage houses, swimming pools, libraries, and exhibition halls. Urban modernism and Stalinist socialist realism dominated urban reconstruction at this time in divided Germany and Communist Poland. Both approaches had little regard for preserving much of anything, but certain historic sites were reconstructed. Germans and Poles made deliberate choices about what to rebuild and preserve from the rubble of the war. In selecting what was culturally valuable, they were also making choices about what was not. In the 1950s and 1960s, they rarely perceived Jewish sites to be part of the national or local heritage worthy of maintaining. Jewish sites also reflected a deeply discomforting, abject past that few Germans and Poles wished to encounter in the early postwar decades.[13]

The bulldozer, though, did not reach every Jewish site. In fact, Jewish sites were some of the war's last ruins on otherwise reconstructed streets. In 1957, a London traveler walked through the broken tombstones of East Berlin's Jewish cemetery on Schönhauser Avenue and remarked that "the 'Third Reich' has left behind its unmistakable traces."[14] Years later, that was still the case. Crumbling synagogues stood in the centers of East Berlin and Warsaw, while in Essen, West Germans began to question whether the synagogue should house an exhibition of industrial products. Some forty years after the war, Jewish sites still continued to stir and perplex.

But they did so in increasingly new and different ways. By the late 1970s, a dramatic change started to unfold across this diverse region. Jewish ruins began to trigger interest, curiosity, nostalgia, recollection, and melancholia. In

Even late into postwar reconstruction, Jewish ruins remained standing, like these on Levetzow Street in West Berlin in 1955. (Landesarchiv Berlin)

Jewish ruins existed some sixty years after the war, such as this synagogue in Rymanów in 2001. (Photo by Krzysztof Kobus)

one of the most surprising and little-studied developments of postwar European history, Germans and Poles started to restore the historic traces of prewar Jewish life in both democratic and Communist societies. This shift emerged first on the local level as church groups, city leaders, political dissidents, and ordinary residents became concerned about the neglect and erasure of Jewish sites since 1945. Over the years, recovering the material traces of Jewish life then expanded to involve national politicians, tourists, and international Jewish leaders. By the late 1980s, Jewish sites were attracting local, national, and international attention. They were becoming transnational spaces of multiple encounters with the Jewish past, and a number of reconstruction efforts soon followed. In Warsaw, the state rebuilt its only surviving synagogue in 1983, while in 1988 East Germany's Communist Party announced the restoration of East Berlin's main bombed-out synagogue. In Essen, the synagogue's interior was restored to its prewar design. In a region of few Jews, a spatial presence of Jews started to reemerge in the built environment.

Berlin's New Synagogue being restored in 1990. Beginning in the late 1970s, Germans and Poles began to perceive Jewish sites as evocative ruins of the past that had to be restored, preserved, and commemorated. (Bundesarchiv Bild 183–1990–1018–027)

Since the collapse of Communism in 1989, interest in Jewish sites has increased at an almost dizzying rate. Tourists in the tens of thousands from the United States, Israel, Canada, and the United Kingdom have traveled to Poland and increasingly Germany in search of the Jewish past, while some Germans and Poles have continued to be attracted to almost anything perceived to be Jewish. People both far and near have become drawn to Jewish spaces for a variety of reasons—heritage tourism, growing discussions about the Holocaust, postmodern fascinations with the historic, nostalgia for a lost past, longings for cosmopolitanism in a globalizing world, and quests for new meaning and identity. While the motivations may vary widely, the effect has become clear. "Jewishness" has now become something to be photographed, preserved, displayed, and mediated. Jewish sites have become what they were not just a few decades earlier: pieces of heritage that must be saved for their historical importance and perceived authenticity; they have become historic monuments, valuable ruins of the past that evoke curiosity, nostalgia, memory, intrigue, melancholia, and critique.

This intense interest in the Jewish past stems partly from sentimental longings for a lost multiethnic past, but it cannot just be reduced to mere kitsch. Rather, Germans, Poles, and Jews imbue Jewish sites with new meanings and uses. Some mourn them as markers of an irretrievable past, becoming stranded in the ruins like nineteenth-century romantic artists as they snap pictures of Jewish traces to be displayed in books or on the Internet. Others seek to retrieve what has been lost through restoration efforts or the building of Jewish museums. In these and other ways, "Jewishness" often becomes something to be recalled, restored, commemorated, and harnessed—an artifact of the past that can be displayed, observed, and celebrated. At a moment when Jewish life in both countries has been growing, Poland and Germany have become more than ever the "museum keepers of world Jewry," landscapes to view a "static and finalized pre-Holocaust heritage."[15] Jewishness stays frozen in time for many Jews traveling to Europe who rarely conceive of Germany and Poland as anything but "traces of a vanished world."[16] For them, going to Europe has become a secular ritual to encounter the Holocaust. Similarly, non-Jewish Poles and Germans often relegate Jewishness to the past, but to different ends. Encountering Jewish sites has provoked some to think critically and deeply about their pasts in order to build stronger pluralist, democratic futures, but more commonly Germans and Poles embrace

Jewish sites as self-congratulatory symbols of an already secured demo-cratic tolerance and pluralism. Reconstructed or newly built Jewish sites create a restored sense of diversity that seeks to fill the void left by the Holo-caust. In a postfascist and post-Communist world, Jewish sites become spaces of what I call redemptive cosmopolitanism, a commemorative dis-play of multiethnicity that celebrates the cathartic, redemptive transforma-tion of Germans and Poles into tolerant democratic citizens. Restoring a synagogue or Jewish cemetery rarely involves thinking deeply about the shattered histories that these spaces reflect: their destruction during the war and their neglect and erasure after 1945. In reconstructing multiethnicity from the ruins of multiethnicity, this commemorative cosmopolitanism ex-hibits comforting, soothing flourishes of tolerance and difference for all to see, but deflects critical engagement with liberal democracy's collapse in the past and its failures in the present.

This shifting history of Jewish sites lies at the center of this book. *Shattered Spaces* is about changing encounters with ruins in the postwar urban land-scape. Broken fragments of stone become evocative ruins when someone gazes upon them and imbues them with significance; otherwise they linger on as worthless rubble to be swept away or ignored. Shattered buildings can be protected, preserved, altered, restored, neglected, or destroyed. How they are dealt with depends on how they are perceived at a specific moment in time and space by a particular person or collective group.[17] Once swept away as worthless rubble, Jewish sites have since the mid-1970s been preserved as valuable ruins. This changing history of Jewish sites—from rubble to ruin, from destruction to preservation—is distinctive to Poland and Germany. To be sure, practically every corner of Europe has some kind of Jewish festi-val, museum, or reconstructed Jewish district where before no Jewish pres-ence existed for decades. Similar elements of this story can also be found outside Europe. New York's Lower East Side became the wholesome Jewish space of contemporary imaginations after World War II, and Jewish traces are now being rediscovered in North Africa as heritage tourism expands into the region.[18] But few societies have faced the burden of the Holocaust—encountering those empty synagogues, streets, and cemeteries—quite as intensely as Germans and Poles have. It was, after all, in Germany that the

Final Solution originated and in Poland that it unfolded with the greatest brutality in the midst of the Nazi occupation. Poland and Germany also had small Jewish communities after the war, making the problem of empty Jewish spaces greater than in other countries, such as France or Hungary, where larger Jewish populations lived. And no other European countries have received the kind of international attention that Germany and Poland have from the earliest postwar years to this day: Germany because of Nazism, Poland because it was once home to the world's largest Jewish population killed almost entirely by the Nazis.

This book excavates these Polish and German stories from documents culled from over thirty archives in the United States, Germany, Poland, and Israel. It reconstructs from 1945 to the present the shifting history of Jewish sites—mostly synagogues and Jewish cemeteries—in the cities of Warsaw, Berlin, Potsdam, Essen, and Wrocław. It focuses mainly on sacred sites rather than, say, private homes or other communal sites such as Jewish schools and hospitals, because sacred sites are the spaces that have captured the most interest since 1945. Poles, Germans, and Jews have long perceived synagogues and cemeteries as the most salient traces of the prewar Jewish past. These five cities have been selected for what they reveal about the postwar history of Jewish sites and for the important features that they share. All five cities were heavily destroyed during World War II, contained prominent Jewish sites in their city centers, had small Jewish communities for most of the postwar period, and confronted the issue of Jewish sites over the past sixty years. The choice of Warsaw and Berlin is perhaps most obvious because they were the cultural centers of Polish and German Jewry before the Holocaust. The three medium-sized cities of Potsdam, Essen, and Wrocław had less-celebrated traditions of Jewish life, but this difference makes them compelling choices to add breadth and variation. They provide different glimpses into the postwar history of Jewish sites than would otherwise be offered by focusing simply on the two metropolises. These three cities also faced after the war the shared question of how best to fashion new urban identities from their common Prussian pasts, showing in particularly rich ways how Jewish sites fit into local discussions about historic preservation and urban space. But while these five cities have been chosen for these reasons, they have not been selected as "independent" case studies to be compared systematically with each other.[19] Although this book offers comparative and parallel readings, it brings these five cities together to form a kind of analytical kaleidoscope—a shifting analytical gaze that moves from city to city to reveal multiple perspectives on the common themes of memory, urban space, tourism, cosmopolitanism, the Cold War, and postwar Jewish life. This book unearths similarities and differences, but to develop an understanding of historical themes that lie below, across, and within the national boundaries of Poland and Germany and the political regimes of democracy and Communism. In short, it reconstructs a transnational history of Jewish sites.[20]

In so doing, *Shattered Spaces* enriches a range of interdisciplinary discussions in German, Slavic, Jewish, Holocaust, and urban studies. In the past several years, scholars in anthropology, history, cultural geography, museum studies, and architectural history have become interested in Jewish spaces. Studies have recently appeared on the destruction of ghettos, the building of museums, the revitalization of Jewish quarters, and the return of confiscated property.[21] Most of these works have focused on Europe since 1989, as popular interest in Jewish culture, memory, and tourism seems far from abating. Well-known writers such as Omer Bartov, Svetlana Boym, Ruth Ellen Gruber, Michel Laguerre, Marianne Hirsch, and Leo Spitzer have brought popular attention to Jewish sites and districts in contemporary Europe.[22] Their works have explored in rich detail the cultural politics of Jewish spaces, but this book is distinct in the breadth of its focus and interests. It is the first transnational, comparative history of Jewish sites that spans from 1945 to the present. Moreover, *Shattered Spaces* deals with a wide variety of scholarly themes and questions. It sheds light on the postwar history of Jewish life over some sixty years and analyzes the politics of cultural difference in the urban landscapes of democratic and Communist societies. It examines the destructive logic of urban modernism and selective historic preservation during the early postwar years, and then shows how conceptions of historic preservation broadened to include ethnic minority sites by the 1980s. I argue that this change took place in large part because of the growing transnationalization of Jewish sites: heritage tourism, discussions about the Holocaust across parts of the world, and international disputes about Jewish sites shaped the local politics of space. Finally, in reflecting on the contemporary fascination with "Jewishness," I engage in discussions about authenticity, nostalgia, and cosmopolitanism in a globalizing Europe. Rather than arguing that tourism and nostalgia have simply produced kitschy, inauthentic spaces, I unearth the deeper political and cultural meanings of restoring the Jewish past in the urban environment. Some Poles and Germans have celebrated Jewish sites as cosmopolitan symbols of redemption from ethnic hatred, while others have reflected on them to think critically about what it means to be German and Polish after the Holocaust. Engaging in ongoing discussions about cosmopolitanism, I analyze the paradoxes and possibilities of thinking beyond the nation in its redemptive and self-reflective modalities.[23]

Shattered Spaces also enhances the field of memory studies, even though it is not solely about memory. In fact, one of its aims is to show that the postwar history of Jewish sites cannot be reduced to memory alone. In 1958, Potsdam's synagogue was torn down in part because East German historic preservationists at the time, not unlike their counterparts in Poland and West Germany, rarely fought for the preservation of buildings constructed in the twentieth century (the synagogue was built in 1903). In 1983, Poland's Communist Party restored Warsaw's only synagogue to counteract opposition to its long-standing anti-Zionist policies, not to reflect upon the past. Still, memory is important and the body of literature on it is large. In terms of the Holocaust, historians have typically examined the most obvious, intentional forms of memory—memorials, trials, films, debates, and museums—with the assumption that a historical controversy or a memorial reflects a broadly held national memory. Of course, this focus makes sense because these media are central vectors of cultural memory, but examining them alone restricts discussion to political leaders, intellectuals, writers, artists, architects, and historians. Broader social histories of memory continue to be the exception. Most studies also focus only on the nation-state and its ethnic majority. In writing about "German" and "Polish" memories, historians often ignore voices both outside and within the nation. Few historians have paid close attention to Jews living in Germany and Poland and even fewer have analyzed how memories interact across national borders.[24] Finally, most historians tend to describe memory in terms of successful recollection or failed suppression. This dichotomy produces grand narratives about memory lapses and booms, rather than analyzing the meanings of what is actually recalled and forgotten at a particular moment in time.[25]

This book strives to overcome these limitations by examining shifting, multiple interpretations of the past in the urban landscape. It understands memory as an encounter with the past by individuals, groups, and societies, which becomes entangled in broader cultural meanings, identities, and narratives that change over time and space. Drawing on the work of other urban scholars, this book studies the city as a particularly rich container of multiple memories.[26] Jewish sites were located on ordinary streets and engaged different groups of people from different parts of the world—politicians, church leaders, dissidents, ordinary citizens, Jewish leaders, and tourists. Lastly, *Shattered Spaces* looks at multiple memories of multiple pasts. Historians often conceive of time as either linear or circular, but here I think of it in terms of layers that have varying degrees of depth, width, length, and origin.[27] Many pasts overlap, intermingle, and collide in Jewish sites, some surfacing more powerfully than others at different points in time and space. The Holocaust stretches wide and deep, but it exists alongside many other pasts. Indeed, Jewish sites reflect Europe's twentieth century—its histories of emancipation, expulsion, violence, war, genocide, destruction, restoration, democracy, fascism, and Communism.

In taking this multilayered approach, this book ultimately challenges some basic assumptions about the legacies of the Holocaust in East Central Europe. Europe divided into "Western" and "Eastern" parts continues to dominate the mental mapping of the continent as it long has.[28] As common perceptions would have it, the pattern of Holocaust remembrance fell along the continent's east-west axis. While remembrance gradually emerged in the democratic West, so the argument goes, a deep silence shrouded the Soviet bloc until democracy triumphantly lifted it in 1989. The historian Tony Judt, for example, suggests that in Eastern Europe "there was of course never much question of recognizing Jewish suffering."[29] Likewise, Omer Bartov watches interest in the Holocaust fade ever more away as he travels from Berlin to Kiev. As he goes from town to town in Ukraine, the German historian in him looks in frustration for the kind of memorials found across reunited Germany as he stumbles upon only "neglected and suppressed" sites of nonmemory—"disappearing ruined synagogues and overgrown cemeteries." While he does find a few restored spaces in Eastern Europe—mostly in Kraków—he sees them as cryptic, trumpery objects of a "virtual," "exoticized" revival.[30] Germany's eventually successful, seemingly more authentic encounter with the Holocaust stands as the part for the European whole, the progressive teleology of sober recollection that rarely can be found in other areas of the continent, not least of all in its less affluent, less urbane eastern margins.

Shattered Spaces complicates this mental mapping of memory and un-settles Germany as the successful model of postwar repair. The Cold War was certainly important. It deeply shaped the postwar history of Jewish sites, but in often unpredictable and contradictory ways. In the 1980s, Po-land experienced one of the more searing debates about the Holocaust in Europe partially in reaction to the Communist Party's anti-Jewish cam-paign of 1967–68. A comparable, if more muted, response emerged in East Germany as church groups, dissidents, and ordinary citizens grew tired of the state's demonization of "Zionists." West Germany never pursued such overtly anti-Jewish policies. Its intellectual, cultural, and political elite even-tually embraced the Holocaust as a central part of German identity, but of-ten with the belief that remembrance would engender the redemption of Germanness.[31] The contradictory impulses of redemptive cosmopolitanism have their deepest origins and most powerful echoes in the Federal Republic. In unearthing these tensions, I am not attempting to blur three distinct cases. The differences are important. The postwar history of Jewish sites var-ied strikingly at times from nation to nation and city to city. And yet encoun-ters with Jewish sites unfolded in related ways across local, national, and political borders. This book takes seriously both the parallels and the diver-gences of the history it tells. It analyzes how distinct local, national, politi-cal, and international contexts shaped different directions along what turned out to be a similar path from destroying Jewish rubble to preserving Jewish ruins. In this sense, *Shattered Spaces* both reinforces and challenges the centrality of the Cold War to narrating postwar European history. It shows how the divergent political cultures of democracy and Communism varied in importance depending on the time and the place.[32]

Finally, this book argues that the postwar handling of Jewish sites re-mained deeply embedded in the national histories of German-Jewish and Polish-Jewish relations, no matter how transnational Jewish spaces became over the postwar decades. For encounters with Jewish sites above all in-volved Germans and Poles confronting their historical relationship with Jews. This was not an easy past to encounter. Jewish sites conjured up deeply discomforting memories. The Holocaust marked the most tragic period in the history of Jewish-gentile relations in Germany, Poland, and for that matter

most of Europe. Nazi Germany stood out above all the rest, for sure, but interwar Poland was moving in alarming directions on the eve of the war. By
the late 1930s, many Poles and Germans excluded Jews from their national
and local communities. Exclusive ideas of collective belonging had been
developing since the late nineteenth century, but became widespread in
both countries during the politically and economically unstable interwar
years. The road to nationalism took different turns, but in the end led down
a violent, hateful path.[33] Of course, the wartime murder of the Jews unfolded
differently in Germany and Poland. Germany was where the Nazis conceived
of the Final Solution, while Poland was where the Nazis implemented the
genocide during their brutal occupation of the country. Although the Holocaust did not determine postwar encounters with the ruins of Jewish life, it
did deeply shape them. Before moving on to the postwar period, then, I
want to discuss briefly the similar and different dynamics of Jewish-gentile
relations in the region just before and during the Holocaust, especially for
the lesser-known case of Poland, which will receive more attention.[34] How
did ordinary Germans respond to and become involved in the Nazi persecution of the Jews before and during World War II? How did Poles react to and
become entangled in the murder of their Jewish neighbors in the midst of a
devastating occupation?

In the years before World War II, Europe's democratic states collapsed one
after another. An era that was supposed to be one of parliamentary elections
turned out to be one of dictatorial decrees as democracy receded in Hungary, Italy, Poland, Portugal, Germany, Austria, Estonia, Greece, Romania,
and Spain. Democracy collapsed for a number of economic, social, and political reasons, but authoritarian movements, mostly from the right wing of
the political spectrum, actively destroyed it. Most of these antidemocratic
movements embraced an exclusive understanding of the nation that persecuted minorities. This ethnic hatred, however, varied across Europe. The
worst case was Nazi Germany, which persecuted its Jewish population like
no other European state. But Germany was hardly alone. Anti-Jewish hatred
existed practically everywhere on the continent, although most virulently in
Eastern Europe, where the "minority problem" dominated national politics
after the breakup of the German, Russian, Austro-Hungarian, and Ottoman

empires. In the late 1930s, Hungary led the way among Eastern European states in passing two major laws that restricted Jewish involvement in the economy, but antisemitism also proved widespread in Romania, Lithuania, Latvia, and Estonia. The Czech lands were the main exception where Jews stayed relatively secure. Poland was more complicated. It never revoked Jewish emancipation like Hungary did, and some Polish leftist politicians, writers, and academics opposed anti-Jewish persecution. Yet Poland's main leader, Józef Piłsudski, was not as strong a defender of Jews as the Czech leader Tomáš Masaryk was. Although Piłsudski kept the extreme antisemites at bay until his death in 1935, he did little to improve the conditions of Polish Jews. In fact, their everyday life worsened over the course of the interwar period. Polish Jews suffered from economic pauperization, boycotts, and social exclusion like Jews throughout Central and Eastern Europe.[35]

Nothing, though, of course quite resembled what German Jews experienced. Their plight began immediately when the Nazis came to power. In 1933–34, Nazi Germany excluded Jews from German cultural, intellectual, and political life before stripping them of most of their citizenship rights in 1935. In these years, the Nazi solution to the "Jewish question" was segregation inside Germany, but by 1938 it had radicalized to forced removal from Germany. In the wake of the *Kristallnacht* pogrom and the final confiscation of Jewish property, the regime settled on forced emigration to rid Germany of its Jews. In explaining these prewar years of persecution, historian Saul Friedländer has developed the notion of "redemptive antisemitism" to capture the ideological obsession that Hitler and his closest allies had with the "Jewish question." Believing that the German nation could be redeemed only through the removal of the Jews, the Nazis strove to eliminate the Jewish community from German society because the very survival of the nation was at stake. Friedländer argues that this "redemptive antisemitism" shaped the attitudes of the Nazi elite, suggesting that most ordinary Germans, although holding anti-Jewish prejudices, did not adhere to such an extreme, obsessive form of hatred against Jews.[36]

But while the prejudices of German society might not have been as radical as those of the Nazi elite, most Germans accepted the persecution of their Jewish neighbors. The Nazi campaign against German Jewry hardly developed in isolation from German society as simply the chaotic functioning of the Nazi state or the ideological intentions of a few Hitler henchmen. Local officials pushed for the exclusion of Jews from German society often ahead of orders from Berlin, and ordinary Germans became involved in violence against Jews and their property. They were more than just "indifferent" to the plight of their Jewish neighbors. Germans actively participated in their exclusion and persecution. Some acted against Jews to advance their own self-interests; some went along with the Nazi system as the easiest way to get on with daily life; some felt pressure to conform; some found the policies of the Nazis attractive. The motivations varied, but the effect did not. The Nazi persecution of Jews gradually became an ordinary, accepted part of daily life. It became deeply integrated into German society. In the words of historian Carolyn Dean, Nazi anti-Jewish policy became a "normalized prejudice."[37]

This normalization of anti-Jewish bias took on many different forms, but was often small and ordinary in the years before the war: shopkeepers showing hostility to Jewish consumers; landlords ending rental agreements with their Jewish tenants; strangers on trams harassing those who "looked" Jewish; friends or acquaintances severing ties with their Jewish neighbors; local citizens taking over Jewish businesses, homes, and possessions. Of course, some Germans responded in kindness to their Jewish neighbors and some opposed the regime's anti-Jewish policies, although exactly how many is difficult to know because those who did usually kept quiet in a dictatorship that persecuted opposition. But a dominant pattern has become clear after extensive research on popular opinion in Nazi Germany. As Marion Kaplan has put it, most Germans became "deeply implicated" in the gradual process of isolating and impoverishing Jews, becoming involved in their "social death every day."[38]

The Nazi assault on German Jewry in the 1930s was exceptionally intense, but anti-Jewish prejudices also became a normalized part of interwar Polish society. After World War I, Poland regained its independence from German, Russian, and Austro-Hungarian control, which had partitioned the country in the late eighteenth century. Poland reemerged as a relatively poor country with agriculture dominating the economy. It was ethnically diverse with about 65 percent Poles, 16 percent Ukrainians, 10 percent Jews, 6 percent Belorussians, and 3 percent Germans.[39] A democratic system initially took hold in Poland, but it proved short-lived as successive governments failed to secure a parliamentary majority. In 1926, Piłsudski carried out a military coup that ousted the far right, which had briefly formed a coalition government, from political power. He established an authoritarian state that lasted until 1939 when the Nazis and Soviets invaded Poland. The regime, known as *Sanacja,* emphasized loyalty to the state, anticorruption, discipline, and restoration of "health" to the political system.[40] It had a mixed approach to Poland's large minority population. Minorities, including Jews, were much relieved when Piłsudski triumphed over the right, but Piłsudski was no progressive. Although he had played a leading role in the Polish Socialist Party during the partition era, he was interested more in national liberation than in socialist revolution. As he put it, his coup had carried out a "revolution without revolutionary consequences."[41] Still, much to his credit, Piłsudski succeeded in saving Poland from fascism, something his counterpart Paul von Hindenburg tragically failed to do in the Weimar Republic.

But, in the end, Piłsudski's regime did little to alleviate the economic, political, and cultural exclusion of Jews, which increased over the interwar years with the rise in anti-Jewish biases, prejudices, and attacks. Four major waves of anti-Jewish aggression marked interwar Poland. The first phase broke out in 1918 during the Polish-Ukrainian War, which left over 200 Jews dead (the worst attack was in Lwów in November 1918); the second wave took place in 1930–33 at universities, where students staged anti-Jewish riots and protests; the third, organized by the newly founded National Radical Camp (ONR), involved anti-Jewish violence in the summer of 1934; and the fourth, occurring between 1934 and 1937, erupted on university campuses when the ONR and student groups such as the All-Polish Youth developed "ghetto benches" as the first step in the "dejudaization" of Polish higher education. As these waves of assaults unfolded, anti-Jewish sentiments were becoming a normalized part of Polish Catholicism. By the 1920s, a number of Catholic leaders embraced the ideological language and concepts of racial antisemitism that saw Jews as one of the church's central enemies. Most importantly, though, Polish Jews were threatened by National Democracy. Founded by Roman Dmowski in 1897, National Democracy became a powerful movement after the war that deeply disdained Piłsudski's government and hated Jews. Piłsudski embraced the multiethnic past of the Polish-Lithuanian Commonwealth. Dmowski wanted the very opposite—a Poland made up only of Catholic Poles. Although Dmowski never succeeded in forming a government during the Second Republic, his movement helped shape the state's policy toward Jews, especially after 1935 when Piłsudski died and no other strong moderate took his place. In 1937–39, the Polish government curtailed the economic, educational, and political life of Jews and endorsed Dmowski's position that Jews should emigrate from Poland. On the eve of the war, the majority of Poland's political elites, except for those on the left, believed that the best way to solve the country's "Jewish problem" was for Jews to emigrate.[42]

World War II exacerbated this already tense relationship between Poles and Jews. In September 1939, the Nazis and Soviets divided Poland in half. In the territory controlled by the Nazis, the Germans dismantled the Polish government almost entirely except for minor bureaucrats who were kept to aid the administration. The Nazis then incorporated the western part of Poland into the Third Reich and turned the rest of the country into the General Government. In pursuit of grand visions of empire, the Nazis established a brutal colonial regime in Poland. They sought to make the incorporated territories as ethnically "German" as possible through a massive program of population transfer and mass murder. After pushing Jews and Poles from this area into the "dumping ground" of the General Government, the Nazis transported thousands of ethnic Germans from across northeastern Europe into the homes, businesses, and farms left behind. In the process, the Nazis killed tens of thousands of non-Jewish Poles, deported at least 1.5 million Poles to Nazi Germany for forced labor, kidnapped as many as 50,000 Polish children, destroyed at least 300 villages, and ruthlessly attacked the Polish opposition. In 1944, the Germans brutally crushed the Warsaw uprising. Some 170,000 Varsovians died and 150,000 were expelled from the city. The Nazis unleashed such brutality on no other part of Europe except Ukraine and Belarus.[43] But while non-Jewish Poles suffered immensely, Polish Jews were targeted above all others. Forced into newly created ghettos across Poland, they were then systematically murdered from 1941 to 1945. By the end of the war, the Nazis had killed about 3 million Polish Jews, or about 90 percent of Poland's Jewish population. The number of non-Jewish Poles killed was about 2 million, or about 10 percent of Poland's population.[44] While most Poles could be "tolerated" as slave laborers, no room existed for any Jews within the Nazi empire.

In the midst of this engulfing terror that tragically affected their own lives, how did Poles react to the plight of their Jewish neighbors? Poles responded in various ways. As part of the Polish underground state, the organization Żegota (code name for *Rada Pomocy Żydom,* or the Council for Aid to Jews) helped Jews with locating housing, forging documents, medical assistance, and financial support from the fall of 1942 to the end of the war. The extent of and the motivations for rescuing Jews are difficult to know. In Warsaw, around 27,000 Jews escaped from the ghetto, and perhaps as many as 11,500 survived through the aid of many Poles (the exact numbers await further research).[45] The individuals helping Jews varied from antisemites to blackmailers to extortionists to good Samaritans. And yet whatever the individual reasons, the fact is that rescuing Jews was not widespread in Poland (like in much of Europe). Poles undertook other illegal acts against the German enemy more often than they did saving Jews. They also made survival on the "Aryan" side all the more risky with all too many blackmailers and denouncers roaming the streets. As one Holocaust survivor put it, "hiding Jews was a very dangerous activity and no-one could expect from people such heroism. Nevertheless, there was no need for denunciation of one's neighbor because he was hiding a Jew."[46]

In some cases, Poles went further than identifying or exploiting Jews on the "Aryan" side of the ghetto walls. A small number of Poles became directly involved in mass murder. Brought into the open by Jan Gross's *Neighbors,* a startling book about the massacre of Jews in the small town of Jedwabne, the role of Poles as perpetrators challenges commonly held notions of Polish victimization, martyrdom, and resistance during World War II. It is a particularly emotive topic that provokes suspicion and anger, but it is one that recently has benefited from careful research by historians. Although Jedwabne was by far the most deadly incident, with somewhere between 1,000 and 1,600 Jews perishing, it was not an isolated case. In over twenty other towns, Poles carried out violence against Jews during the summer of 1941. These massacres occurred in the *kresy,* or eastern borderlands that the Soviets had occupied until June 1941 when the Nazis invaded Russia. Poles murdered Jews for a variety of reasons. Some killed because the German soldiers in the area encouraged them to do so, others sought material gain through the seizure of Jewish property, others wanted to settle old scores, and still others imagined that Jews had collaborated with the Soviets against Poland.[47]

But what appears central is that those who became involved in mass murder did not perceive the people they were beating with a club or shoving into a burning barn as human beings like themselves. Prejudice against Jews had become so normalized that the division between "us" and "them" had become integrated into everyday life. This normalized prejudice took hold over years of increased persecution, violence, bias, and separation during the 1920s and 1930s, but became murderous in the *kresy* during June–July 1941 for concrete reasons. The *kresy* had just endured twenty-one months of Soviet occupation that ushered in swift changes in Polish society.[48] One change involved a sliver of the Jewish population that became attracted to the equality granted by the Soviets. Ethnic minorities could now fill jobs, for example, as teachers and public officials, that had long been denied them by the Polish state. A very small number of Jews benefited from the Soviet occupation, while the vast majority endured the harshness of occupation, war, economic restructuring, death, and deportation like everyone else.[49] But Poles perceived the condition of Jews differently, believing that Jews had collaborated with the Soviets en masse. Refracted through the powerful anti-Jewish stereotype of "Judeo-Communism" *(żydokomuna),* the reality of the Soviet occupation became twisted to conform to the broad fears of Polish society that Jews had destroyed the Polish state. Jews were often forced to sing Russian songs and bury statues of Lenin during the massacres of June–July 1941. This antisemitic fantasy became murderous precisely when eastern Poland switched from Soviet to Nazi occupation in June 1941. By late June and early July 1941, Nazi special military and police units started to carry out extensive shootings of Jews. Just as the Nazis began to move closer to the Final Solution, pogroms and massacres in eastern Poland broke out, encouraged by the Germans on Reinhard Heydrich's orders for "self-cleansing actions" in the area. It is within these broader contexts—of *żydokomuna,* of the Soviet occupation, and of the Final Solution—that the violence in Jedwabne and in some twenty other towns in the *kresy* erupted.[50]

But such direct participation in mass murder was exceptional. Nazi officials in Berlin and German perpetrators in Poland were the main killers of Polish Jews. If on a spectrum of social behavior killing Jews is on one end and saving them is on the other, one can safely say that the overwhelming majority of Poles were neither heroic rescuers nor cold-blooded murderers. Most Poles became drawn into, took advantage of, or benefited from the persecution of their Jewish neighbors in much more everyday and less clear-cut ways. It was not just that Poles and their government officials in exile observed the Holocaust with hardened indifference; many governments and societies did the same, including those that possibly could have done something, such as Britain, the United States, and particularly the Soviet Union.[51] Terms like "indifference" and "passive complicity" do not fully capture how entangled Poles became in the Holocaust. In a country where Jews made up 10 percent of the overall population and where in many small villages Jews constituted nearly half of the population, the persecution, ghettoization, deportation, and mass murder of 3 million people over five years intersected with the lives of numerous ordinary Poles in countless ways.

This involvement in the Holocaust took on many different forms, from identifying Jews to the Nazis to blackmailing Jews living on the "Aryan" side to moving into the enormous number of Jewish homes now suddenly abandoned.[52] One could cite many instances to illuminate the everyday nature of these interactions, but the Polish-Jewish writer and literary critic Michał Głowiński provides one remarkable example in his memoir. He recalls an experience at a café in Warsaw on the "Aryan" side. While his aunt, who looked "Aryan," went to make a phone call, the young Głowiński, sitting by himself, sparked the interest of the women surrounding him, who became increasingly anxious about his presence:

> In the beginning, it seemed to me that all was calm. . . . Yet after a while I couldn't escape the realization that the scene was playing out otherwise. It was difficult to harbor any doubts that I had become the center of attention. . . . The women stared at me as if I were an extraordinary monster, whose very existence called into question the laws of nature, and as if they would have to decide what to do with me that very moment, for things could not remain as they were. . . . I heard "A Jew, there's no question, a Jew. She certainly isn't, but him—he's a Jew." . . . I heard one of them say, "We have to let the police know." . . . Most often they spit out the threatening word "Jew," but also, most terrifying, they kept repeating, "We have to let the police know." I was aware that this was the equivalent to a death sentence. If I'd then known something about Mediterranean mythology, I would doubtlessly have thought I'd landed in the possession of the Erinyes, the Furies, desirous of mutilating me. Yet would such an analogy be appropriate? For those women were not possessed by an uncontrollable hatred. . . . These were normal, ordinary women, in their own way decent and resourceful, hardworking,

undoubtedly scrambling to take care of their families in the difficult conditions of the occupation. . . . They had found themselves in a situation that felt to them trying and threatening, and they wished to confront it directly. They only did not think at what price. Perhaps this transcended their imaginations—although they must have known how it would end if they were to "let them know"—or perhaps such thoughts were simply not within the boundaries of moral reflection accessible to them.[53]

One might be tempted to consider these interactions with the Holocaust to be forms of "collaboration." They do, of course, reinforce Nazi rule, but such labels overlook the perceptions of these actions in the minds of those carrying them out. Poles who took over Jewish apartments, blackmailed Jews on the tram, or threatened to call the police did not necessarily, in their own moral universe, see these actions as forms of cooperation with the German enemy. In a country with the greatest resistance to the Nazis, had Poles perceived persecution against Jews as collaboration, then denunciations, seizing property, blackmailing, and murder would likely have occurred less often.[54]

All of this is, though, by no means to take away from the crucial role of the Nazis and more broadly of ordinary Germans in the Holocaust. The conditions that shaped German behavior clearly differed from those of Poles. Polish society was terrorized by the occupation, war, and mass murder that Germans had designed and implemented. The unequivocal responsibility of Nazi Germany for the Holocaust meant that German society became involved in the mass murder of Jews on a much greater scale. A broad range of Germans became complicit in the genocide, from bureaucrats in Berlin to soldiers on the frontline to women at home to foreign ministry officials scattered across the globe. The Holocaust did not emerge simply from the functioning of a massive bureaucracy, which once set into motion took on a life of its own. It hinged on the active and deliberate participation of many different segments of German society from church leaders to industrial barons to ordinary men and women.[55] It simply would not have happened without them. Nevertheless, most Germans, apart from those designing, perpetrating, and assisting Nazi policy, faced less often the kind of up-close encounters with Jews that characterized Polish-Jewish relations during the war. The number of Jews who still lived in Germany was tiny when the Nazi state decided on mass murder in the fall of 1941. Because Germany was not the geographic space where the Holocaust took place, the reaction and behavior of German society took on different forms. Issues crucial to the Polish case—for example, the dynamics of gentile-Jewish relations on the "Aryan" side of the ghetto or the generally low societal approval for saving Jews—are not as central to the German situation. Different questions apply. What did ordinary Germans know about what was happening in Eastern Europe? How did they react to this knowledge? Did it affect their support for the regime?

The popular postwar refrain that ordinary Germans knew nothing about the Holocaust has been shattered by historical research. Although Germans did not know the full scope and method of the Final Solution, particularly the precise details of assembly-line mass murder in the death camps, they did have access to information about the mass exterminations. In fact, anyone who wanted to know at least generally about the Nazi plan to destroy European Jewry merely had to turn to the Nazi media.[56] Germans also heard about the Holocaust through letters from the front, soldiers returning from duty, and press coverage by news organizations such as the BBC. Ordinary Germans challenged Hitler's policies when they directly impacted their own lives, whether it was against the Nazi euthanasia program, the taking down of crucifixes, or the deportation of Jews married to non-Jews in Berlin.[57] But when circumstances were otherwise, the majority of Germans went along with the genocidal policies of the Third Reich with only a few noble exceptions of opposition.

This acceptance largely stemmed from the basic fact that most Germans generally supported the Nazi regime and its anti-Jewish policies. In November 1938, the Nazi Party carried out a massive attack on Jewish property that has long been interpreted by historians as the one instance when the bourgeois sensibilities of German society became frazzled by Nazi anti-Jewish policy. Piles of broken glass littered Germany's clean and orderly streets. The day after the pogrom, someone snapped a photo of Potsdam's lightly damaged synagogue. A sizeable crowd, dressed in long overcoats and top hats, gathers in front of the building, some leaning close to each other as if in conversation, while others stand by themselves, perhaps just stopping by for a quick look before moving on with their day's schedule. Their bicycles are, in fact, nearby to ride away. A small group of children, perhaps eight in total, perch on the sills of the synagogue's two large bottom windows as they peer through the glassless frames. One of the large doors, held ajar, allows some a closer glimpse inside. No single face can be seen as the crowd gazes at the synagogue. Is this crowd shocked? Concerned? Curious? Mesmerized by the spectacle of broken windows, burning rooftops, and spectators? One can only imagine what this particular crowd's reaction might have been, but one point seems clear: while the Jewish community clearly interpreted *Kristallnacht* as the last sign that it was now utterly urgent for them to flee, few Germans protested against the purpose of the pogrom as one more attack against the Jews. After some six years of Nazi rule, the persecution of Jews had become so normalized that those staring at Potsdam's synagogue did not stop to think about what it meant for their Jewish neighbors. Germans did not face during the Holocaust intimate encounters with Jews as often as Poles did—running into them in the pastry shops of their capital city or in the forests of their smallest village. But on this day they certainly did. Potsdamers probably decided to pass by the synagogue perhaps with some concern but generally not worried about what was happening to a minority group they no longer considered part of their local and national community. Some Germans opposed the aims of *Kristallnacht*—Berlin's towering, domed New Synagogue stands today thanks to a policeman who rushed to save it—but a sizeable number participated in, jeered at, and watched the violence explode in their villages, towns, and cities. This was up-front, local violence that almost no Germans could have missed right along their neighborhood streets. "Torah scrolls, altar cloths, prayer books, and top hats lay on the streets, all destroyed and dirtied," an eyewitness in Berlin wrote about the synagogue on Pestalozzi Street. "Christian children are walking around with the hats."[58]

The normalization of anti-Jewish hatred in the years before 1945 is crucial to understanding the postwar history of Jewish sites. The Holocaust became after 1945 a kind of collective "abject"—a discomforting, polluted, and disdained part of the self. The abject is neither self nor other. It is an unwanted part of the self that shatters one's sense of identity and meaning because it lies outside the self but is still part of it. The abject is "a weight of meaninglessness" that "crushes."[59] As a deeply unsettling, abject past, the Holocaust laid bare the traumatic condition of European modernity and

Potsdam's synagogue after *Kristallnacht* in 1938. (Potsdam Museum)

the fragility of human empathy; it shattered fantasies of progress, democracy, tolerance, and plurality. It provoked profound anxiety and fear.[60] Indeed, Germans and Poles have attempted to contain the Holocaust's nauseating effects over the past sixty years through a number of management strategies—denial, suppression, disavowal, acknowledgment, commemoration, and recall. These reactions have unfolded in similar and different ways in Poland and Germany. In Poland, the Holocaust has often been inflected through the perspective of the colonized. Poles have a long list of nationally mythologized moments of suffering at the hand of others; victimization is at the very core of what it means to be Polish.[61] World War II understandably reinforced this collective identity. Walking along the ruined streets of Warsaw after imprisonment in Auschwitz and Dachau, Tadeusz Borowski described what was now left of Poland: "I enjoy inhaling deep into my lungs the stale, crumbling dust of the ruins. . . . I watch the peasant women squatting near their wares against the walls of the bombed-out houses, the dirty children running between the puddles, chasing their rag ball, and the dust-covered, sweaty workmen who from dawn till dusk hammer at trolley-bus rails along the deserted street."[62] As Poles remembered their ruined cities along with all the other tragedies of the German occupation, they justifiably recalled their own victimization. But they often did so in ways that excluded the suffering of Jews and in ways that rarely confronted their moments of complicity in the Holocaust. In the early postwar decades in particular, the bonding memories of ethnic nationalism omitted the memories of Jews. Some Poles even perceived Jewish suffering as a direct threat to their constructed identity as a nation of eternal victims, drawing on deeply rooted tropes of Jews as the "threatening Other."[63] Since the 1970s, a number of Poles have been challenging this exclusive form of memory in remarkable ways, but it has endured.

To be sure, Germans had plenty of rubble to write about as well. They crafted narratives of suffering that captured real experiences and hardships but that elided their role in supporting a regime of war, occupation, and genocide.[64] But the differences between Germany and Poland are crucial. Victimization has not been as historically central to German identity as it has been for Poland. Germany was not colonized since the late eighteenth century; 5 million of its citizens were not murdered; its capital was not torched street by street. Germany was the imperial power that dominated and destroyed. Moreover, the dynamic of competitive victimization between Jews and non-Jews has not been nearly as intense in the German case as it has been in the Polish one. But while these differences are key, the Holocaust provoked for Poles and Germans shared anxieties about their traumatic relationship with Jews. As Poles and Germans emerged from their basements to their rubble-lined streets, they confronted spaces of a similarly abject past. Their first encounter with Jewish ruins began just after the war as they confronted what to do with all the confiscated properties of their now largely absent Jewish communities.

1

Confronting the Spoils of Genocide

The first encounter Germans and Poles had with Jewish sites happened right after the war, when they confronted what they should now do with the spoils of genocide. As Nazi Germany implemented the Final Solution, it carried out a massive seizure of property throughout Europe that fell into the hands of the Nazi state, European governments, and local residents. Already during the war, Jewish leaders in the United States, Great Britain, and Palestine became concerned about what would happen to this stolen property once the conflict ended. Needless to say, they did not want it to stay in the hands of the German state or its accomplices across the European continent. In 1944, the World Jewish Congress called for "*uniform* laws" to be enacted "in all territories formerly occupied, annexed, dominated, or influenced by Axis powers."[1] In that same year, the jurists Siegfried Moses and Nehemiah Robinson articulated the need for reparations and the return of Jewish property in two separate books.[2] Their works provided initial shape and inspiration to Jewish demands for restitution, which the World Jewish Congress, the Jewish Agency, and the American Jewish Joint Distribution Committee made just after 1945. These organizations pushed the allies to make returning Jewish property and restitution central to Europe's postwar reconstruction. Although Germany naturally became the primary focus of their attention, other countries, such as Poland, were important given the enormous amount of property that had been seized during the war throughout Europe. Indeed, the Polish government received intense pressure, especially from local Jewish leaders in Poland, to return Jewish property. In 1946, the Central Committee of Jews in Poland, the most important Jewish organization at the time, wrote that giving Jewish property back to its rightful owners does "not require any justification given that they emerge behind the backdrop of the murder of 95 percent of the Jewish community by the occupiers, an exceptional barbarity in the history of mankind."[3]

Yet, no matter how justified the claims, restitution encountered numerous obstacles in postwar Europe. Few Europeans rushed to the courthouse to return what they had taken during the war. Perhaps this was to be expected: Jewish property was robbed by people, states, businesses, and organizations that hardly winced when they were taking it in the first place.[4] The Cold War also complicated matters. Pushed by American military authorities, West Germany adopted an extensive restitution program, but the Soviet bloc states, including the German Democratic Republic (GDR) and the Polish People's Republic (PPR), opposed any form of returning Jewish property. Restitution became a political tool of the Cold War, especially between the two German states. The Federal Republic of Germany (FRG) brandished its restitution laws as proof of its moral superiority over the "totalitarian" dictatorship just next door. The GDR countered that it was the true antifascist Germany because it had removed the real source of fascism to begin with—capitalist property rights. This Cold War divergence is perhaps not surprising, but it could not have been completely predicted at the time that West Germany, dominated by a conservative government of Christian Democrats, would implement a restitution program, while the GDR and PPR, drawing on Communist and socialist movements that before the war had supported or at least not overtly opposed Jewish rights, would pursue policies that oscillated between benign neglect of and outright hostility toward Jews.

What is more, this Cold War divide was not nearly as clear-cut as it might seem at first glance. In the FRG, GDR, and PPR, a series of laws and state actions declared Jewish communal property "abandoned" and "heirless." The legal justification differed greatly across the Iron Curtain, but the effect was the same: most Jewish communal property—synagogues, cemeteries, schools, and the like—ended up falling into the ownership of local municipal authorities, save those that the local Jewish communities owned or managed. Jewish leaders in the two Germanys and Poland strongly protested these legal moves, arguing that the postwar Jewish communities were the legal heirs to prewar Jewish communal property, but they ran up against an intractable series of bureaucratic moves.

Why Implement Victor's Justice?

Just after the war ended, Jewish leaders urged the four powers controlling Germany to pass restitution laws in each of their occupation zones. The Americans and more grudgingly the British tended to be receptive to their pleas. U.S. military and civilian leaders believed that the security of Germany's Jewish population was important to democratization. There were important exceptions, such as the strained relationship between the American military and Jewish refugees who settled in occupied Germany after the war, but the United States stressed the importance of fighting antisemitism and promoting restitution more than any other occupying power. As John J. McCloy, the U.S. high commissioner for Germany, put it in 1952: "I have always had a deep conviction that unless Germany dealt with the problems of restitution we had little hope for the future of Germany."[5] The Americans moved quickly to return Jewish property. In May 1945, the U.S. military placed all stolen property under allied control for it to be returned through a restitution law.[6] The Americans hoped to pass a unified law for occupied Germany, but this proved impossible. The four occupying powers could not agree on one. The Soviets were the most unpredictable because Stalin wavered until 1947–48 on whether to include Germany in his emerging empire in Eastern Europe. He seemed to prefer that the state take over property rather than give it back, although in 1948 the Soviet Military Administration drafted a law for the return of some property that had been confiscated by the Nazis.[7] The French were the least powerful occupying force and generally followed the American-British lead, but in this case insisted on a broader nondenominational law rather than one specifically focused on Jews. The British were in the most complicated position. Although they recognized the need for returning Jewish property, they preferred the "indirect rule" of letting German courts handle the issue. The British also were reluctant to give up their colonial possession in Palestine. The White Paper of 1939, a British document that restricted Jewish emigration to Palestine, remained in effect until the British left in 1948 with the creation of Israel. The British feared that money gained from the sale of returned Jewish property would be directed toward illegal emigration to Palestine.[8]

Isolated by its allies, the U.S. military decided to act alone and issued a restitution law for its occupation zone in November 1947. Pressure from

Jewish organizations on the State Department and support from U.S. military governor Lucius D. Clay, who personally pledged his commitment to restitution to Jewish leaders, ensured passage of the law after months of debate.[9] The French soon followed with a similar measure, but it took the British two years to come around with their version. Although it took time for the allies to create a unified policy, they stayed committed to restitution in the long run. They did not scale it back like they did with other occupation policies such as denazification. Without the allies' continued support, the return of Jewish property probably would not have taken place on the scale that it did in the early FRG. It is certainly true that the occupying powers needed support from West German politicians. Chancellor Konrad Adenauer understood the political importance of restitution, while Theodor Heuss, Ernst Reuter, and Kurt Schumacher spoke poignantly at times about the need for recognizing German complicity in the Holocaust.[10] But the role of the occupying forces in pushing restitution in the first place was crucial.

The restitution laws governed both individual and communal property, but handled them differently. While individual Jews could reclaim their property, German-Jewish communities could not because the laws technically declared all communal property heirless and created Jewish successor organizations to take it over. The assumption was that the small postwar Jewish communities would not be able to manage all the property and that they might not exist for that long. The last thing Jewish leaders wanted was for the German state to keep unclaimed synagogues, community centers, and Jewish cemeteries. Ironically, though, this is exactly what happened in many cases because the Jewish successor organizations typically sold the properties back to the state. Their aim was to get the property back as quickly as possible and then sell it to help Holocaust survivors throughout the world. This meant that much of West Germany's Jewish communal property was sold to state or city governments after officially being returned. In Essen, for example, the district court returned the city's synagogue to the Jewish Trust Corporation, the successor organization for the British zone, which then sold it to the city. Essen's local Jewish community of 145 members, too small for the enormous structure, expressed no interest in owning the building.[11]

Some German-Jewish leaders, however, did not acquiesce so easily to these legal arrangements. A handful of them opposed the Jewish successor organizations, especially the Jewish Restitution Successor Organization

(JRSO), the largest and most powerful agency that was responsible for the American zone. They argued that West Germany's postwar communities were the rightful successor to prewar Jewish communal property. As Philipp Auerbach put it, the postwar communities were a "continuation of the former (pre-Nazi) communities [and] therefore there could be no discussion about 'successor' to communal property."[12] The JRSO hoped early on to reach a compromise. In 1949, it suggested that any property the Jewish communities needed be returned to them, while the rest be handed over to the JRSO.[13] In the early 1950s, the JRSO reached individual agreements along these lines with most Jewish communities in West Germany. Yet this compromise did not satisfy West Germany's most vocal Jewish leaders, notably Karl Marx, Heinz Galinski, and Hendrik George van Dam. As the general secretary of the Central Council of Jews, van Dam had a particularly important platform from which to voice his discontent, which he did often. One clearly frustrated JRSO official referred to the entire problem with the Jewish communities as "this van Dam (or should I say damn) issue."[14]

Van Dam claimed that the JRSO was "dictating" its interests with the "complete exclusion" of the Jewish community in Germany.[15] In 1952, he launched a public attack against the JRSO in West Germany's most important Jewish paper, the *Allgemeine Wochenzeitung der Juden in Deutschland*. While repeating many of the points he had expressed in countless letters to the JRSO, he now went so far as to suggest that the JRSO was committing an "act of one-sided seizure." "This property has been transferred to the successor organizations by military government law," he wrote; "it is the heirless estate of German Jewry, which above all is to be used for Jews from Germany who are still alive and for those living in Germany."[16] This attack startled the JRSO. Benjamin Ferencz, one of the JRSO's negotiators, responded immediately. In a spirited letter, he criticized van Dam's "nationalistic principle that German property should be used only for German Jews" and noted that without the occupying powers, restitution would be severely limited, as German state officials "have persistently been trying to undermine" it. "Perhaps one day," he continued, "you will have an opportunity for a free hand in trying to convince the German officials about German restitution problems without the interference of Americans. I would not be surprised if our actions up to now would be regarded as an 'usurpation,' as you call it, but I expected such criticism to come from the Germans and not from the Central Council of Jews in Germany."[17]

Ferencz's response, while perhaps understandable, failed to acknowledge the source of the problem. The unease Jewish leaders in Germany had with the JRSO stemmed from the deeper issue of whether Jews should live in the "land of the perpetrators" in the first place. Most German Jews decided neither to stay in nor to return to Germany, but those who did, especially their community leaders, became strongly committed to rebuilding Jewish life in the country. They resented the disapproval of Jews outside Germany for their choice to stay in or return to the country. The JRSO, no matter how good the cause it served, insinuated by its existence that Jewish life in Germany had ended, or at the very least that it would end soon. In 1952, Karl Marx, editor of the *Allgemeine Wochenzeitung,* pointed precisely to this underlying tension in his response to Ferencz's reply, which van Dam had forwarded to him. Marx urged Ferencz to recognize that Jewish life in Germany "no longer can be denied" and that all Jews "must support with all their heart the task of strengthening these communities." He ended with the hope that Jews in Germany will soon have the "feeling that they are not being treated as if they could not manage their own affairs, but are regarded as having equal rights."[18]

Resentment toward the JRSO reached its peak in the early 1950s when Jewish leaders in Germany decided to fight for their "equal rights" in court. In towns and cities throughout West Germany, Jewish communities registered claims for the return of the same property that the JRSO did. In some cases, German courts or local officials upheld the rights of the local community in clear contradiction of American military law. Such was the case in the southern German city of Augsburg, where a postwar community of thirty-five Jews successfully regained its property. The JRSO appealed the decision. The first two German courts ruled in favor of the Jewish community in a stunning rebuke of American restitution law. The appeal then went to the Court of Restitution Appeals, the highest arbiter of restitution matters in the U.S. zone, made up of American jurists and run by the U.S. High Commission. In 1954, the Court of Restitution Appeals overturned the earlier rulings of the German courts. Although it recognized the needs of the local Jewish community, it sided with the JRSO and proclaimed that the JRSO was the legal successor to Jewish communal property. This ruling finally settled the legal dispute between the JRSO and the Jewish communities.[19]

The JRSO's problems, though, were hardly over. By the early 1950s, the JRSO faced another and potentially more serious obstacle to its work as opposition to restitution increased in West Germany. Local, grass-roots antirestitution organizations were emerging across the country, emphasizing the hardship of Germans who "bought" Jewish property during the Third Reich. Antisemitic attacks about Jewish revenge became frequent as these antirestitution groups sought to uncover the "real" intentions behind restitution. As one organization founded in West Berlin put it, restitution created "new injustices" because the "purchase" of Jewish property occurred in good faith out of concern for Jews.[20] The confiscation of Jewish property was simply a consequence of the war that had no right to be repaid then. The real victims were the German "buyers" of Jewish property. Nothing less than a denial of Nazi anti-Jewish policy underpinned these brazen assaults. As the West Berlin antirestitution organization continued, "the sacrifices that the Jewish population had to make between 1933 and 1945 were losses of the war."[21] Similar attacks became increasingly common in West Germany. In 1950, the U.S. military noted that "a large part of the German population considers the restitution law unjust" because the transactions were conducted in "'good faith' for 'good money.'"[22] On May 4, 1950, many of the organizations representing "persons injured by restitution" formed an umbrella organization to advance their cause, while a new journal, *Die Restitution,* began publishing articles about the injustices of the restitution laws. These groups targeted the Jewish successor organizations in particular, attacking them as large, anonymous apparatuses out to harm the German economy.[23]

With some 150,000 claims that still needed to be settled, the JRSO grew concerned that this opposition would complicate its work. In 1950, it suggested to John McCloy, a long-standing supporter of restitution, that it complete its restitution work more quickly by settling all outstanding claims with each German state for one lump sum of money. McCloy supported the idea and put pressure on the German states to negotiate with the JRSO. But state officials balked at the idea, not least of all because under the deal the property claims were to be transferred to them, making them responsible for forcing the "buyers" during the Third Reich to either pay for the property or give it up. Needless to say, the German states did not want to become claimants against their own citizens. They stalled as much as they could, but eventually relented after much haggling and intense pressure from McCloy. By 1951–52, four out of the five states in the U.S. zone had reached a settlement with the JRSO.[24]

The lone holdout was West Berlin. Controlled by three different foreign powers, West Berlin started the restitution process late. It was not until 1949 that West Berlin enacted a citywide measure after the British finally passed a restitution law for its zone of occupation. Initially, all three Jewish successor organizations in the French, American, and British zones filed claims for heirless property, but in 1950 the JRSO took over as the sole representative for the city and became the central negotiator for a bulk agreement with West Berlin. Negotiations dragged on for years. West Berlin had the largest Jewish community in the FRG, with about 6,000 members, and was led by the energetic Heinz Galinski. Sharing the ambivalence of van Dam and Marx toward the JRSO, Galinski filed his own restitution claims for the Jewish community and turned to his contacts in the city to look after the community's interests in negotiations with the JRSO, which they did.[25] Berlin officials sided with Galinski probably out of solidarity with the local community but also for purely financial reasons: more money allotted to the community from a JRSO agreement meant less money the city had to pay out overall. This alliance between Galinski and the city strained relations with the JRSO, which knew that each side was pushing the other to force concessions from the organization.[26]

Most of all, though, the West Berlin government seemed plainly disinterested in brokering a fair agreement. In negotiations that stretched over three years, the JRSO essentially had to cut its losses and sign an agreement of 9 million marks, a paltry sum for assets estimated at 75 million marks.[27] This stunning defeat stemmed from a combination of bad fortune and ill will. In 1952–53, the JRSO developed a good relationship with Mayor Ernst Reuter of the Social Democratic Party, who seemed interested in reaching a fair agreement. But in September 1953, Reuter died. The person whom the JRSO considered to be "one of the few friends we might count on in Berlin" was now gone and chances of a settlement seemed grim.[28] As one JRSO official summed up the situation, "it appears that the JRSO global settlement with Berlin is out the window—if not forever then at least for a long time to come—for Reuter was the only one with the prestige and the apparent desire to do something in connection with a global settlement for Berlin restitution and compensation."[29]

West Berlin's new mayor, the Christian Democrat Walther Schreiber, expressed deep unease about reaching an agreement. In 1953, he insisted that
the entire idea of restitution relied on outdated legislation that the allies had
imposed on Germany. He reportedly went on to stress that Germans had
suffered from the war and that no one spoke of restitution for them.[30] Two
months later, Schreiber followed up these remarks with a letter to the JRSO
that challenged the organization's claims and came close to rejecting restitution altogether. He noted that the city's "permanent concern" lies with
"helping Berlin's economy with every power" and that Berlin's "economic
weakness" meant that it could not cover all restitution claims. Settling all
claims in bulk would lead to "unfair treatment" toward the current owners
of the property because the city would de facto be forced to prosecute them.
As for those pieces of property that had already been returned to the JRSO,
the mayor said that the city was not "indisposed" to purchasing them provided that they serve a "public interest."[31] In short, Schreiber had all but relieved Berlin of responsibility for restitution claims except those for which it
was "directly liable under the law."[32]

This letter rattled JRSO officials. They appealed to Chancellor Konrad
Adenauer, whom they tended to see as sympathetic to their cause. The chancellor reportedly said that his fellow Christian Democrats were "fools" and
that he would talk to them. In a private meeting with the mayor, Adenauer
apparently urged Schreiber to conclude an agreement with the JRSO.[33] The
JRSO and West Berlin officials verbally agreed on 20–25 million marks, but
in the spring of 1955, the finance department came back with a much
smaller amount of 12–13 million marks. The JRSO's main negotiator, Benjamin Ferencz, was furious. "After 2.5 years of intensive negotiations and firm
promises by three mayors," he exclaimed, "we are, in a thinly disguised form,
being told to accept a crumb for our bother or go to hell."[34] On June 23, 1955,
the West Berlin senate passed the official offer with only a slightly higher
proposal of 13.5 million marks. The JRSO realized that it had virtually little
choice other than to accept it. Ferencz wrote:

> We have been negotiating this bulk settlement for over three years. We
> have had negotiations with Berlin's last three mayors. We have brought
> to bear political pressures ranging from Adenauer to Conant to Dulles,
> and the major political parties inside Germany. . . . Nevertheless, the

history of these negotiations has been the history of broken promises by the German authorities and continuous concessions by the successor organizations. The failure to conclude an agreement has been a clear indication that there never has been a strong desire to reach an agreement. All this is clear evidence of the lack of public interest and the general hostility to the restitution program. In Berlin we have, step by step, been beaten back into retreat since we lacked the power or the possibility to do anything else. Our back is now against the wall. . . . In the face of the existing and increasing hostility I cannot say with certainty that if we go on we will, within the next few years, be successful in meeting more than Berlin now offers.[35]

Ferencz's analysis sums up well the weak position of restitution in West Germany. Forced into an agreement with the JRSO, Berlin paid out a pity sum for the property of its once large Jewish community. In comparison to East Germany and Poland, West Germany seems like an impressive, triumphant case of rectitude and justice. Some historians and commentators have viewed restitution as a positive step in Germany's successful return to Western, democratic civilization after its plunge into barbaric Nazism. "A German has the right to be proud of the work of restitution," concluded the well-known restitution lawyer Walter Schwarz. But serious conflicts complicated restitution in practice.[36] Although the existence of restitution was never in doubt—American backing made that certain—the lack of complete West German support for it made its implementation difficult. West Germans dismissed and some outright opposed the return of Jewish property in the early postwar years. This opposition emerged partly from the dominant narratives of victimization and redemptive survival that emerged in the early FRG. Jewish claims for property appeared as only further evidence that Germans were being victimized, and not just by the allies but also by Jews. Some Germans associated with the antirestitution movement called themselves "people injured by Jews" *(Judengeschädigte)*.[37] In short, antisemitism played a role in creating opposition to restitution, if less overtly so than in East Germany and Poland.

In 1949, the staff of the Jewish Restitution Successor Organization poses for a portrait. Benjamin Ferencz, a tireless advocate of restitution, stands in front with the lighter jacket. Without the efforts of the JRSO, restitution likely would not have been implemented as fully in West Germany. (United States Holocaust Memorial Museum, courtesy of Benjamin Ferencz)

Why Help "Jewish Capitalists"?

Indeed, the situation in East Germany was clearly worse, as Julius Meyer, head of the State Association of Jewish Communities in the GDR, knew. In 1950, he sent a letter to the finance ministry, inquiring about the current state of Jewish communal property in the GDR. In the immediate postwar years, he and other Jewish leaders had requested the return of Jewish property but to little avail. With the occupation now over, Meyer perhaps hoped that the newly formed East German state might be more reasonable and change its position. He noted that the Jewish community had "still not acquired its own property," as most of it remained "under the control of the state" or in the hands of those who had seized it during the Nazi program of "Aryanization." "We ask," he explained, "that you take into consideration the fact that the Jewish community, because of the extermination policy of the fascist state, finds itself in a situation like no other religious community."[38] Meyer's plea had no effect, and it points to a key problem that East Germany faced, debated, and pushed aside for over four decades: what to do with confiscated Jewish communal property? It was a problem created entirely by the East German state in the earliest years of its existence. When the GDR was created in 1949, its ruling Communist Party of Socialist Unity—known by its abbreviation, SED—rejected calls to develop a wide-ranging policy of restitution.

The SED, though, clearly had a choice on restitution, and at times it looked as if it might move in a different direction. A number of restitution efforts emerged just after the war in the Soviet zone. In September 1945, the state of Thuringia issued the first restitution law of postwar Germany. Although the law was drafted when the United States briefly controlled the territory, it had the support of Soviet and German Communist officials, who enacted it. In Brandenburg and Saxony, state officials attempted to preclude the selling of confiscated Jewish property in the hope of later passing a restitution law.[39] In 1946, the Soviet-created German Central Finance Administration drafted a law for the return of property confiscated by the Nazi regime.[40] And in 1948, Paul Merker and Helmut Lehmann, both members of the powerful SED Central Committee, wrote another restitution law. Merker seemed optimistic about its passage, writing that Walter Ulbricht and Franz Dahlem were in "agreement" with its basic principles.[41]

All of these measures were admittedly limited in scope. Merker's restitution law, the one most seriously considered by the SED, only allowed claims to be made by Jews living in Germany and did not apply to any property already under Soviet military control. Jewish leaders Leo Löwenkopf and Julius Meyer strongly protested this second provision, noting that Jews must not be "disposed by the law for a second time."[42] Still, a less-than-ideal law would have been better than no law at all. In the end, though, the SED flatly rejected any restitution program just days before the formation of the GDR in 1949. It refused to supply payments to Israel, return Jewish property, or provide reparations to East German Jews. Part of the reason was simply Cold War politics. As Adenauer's Germany embraced the American demand for restitution and close ties with Israel, East Germany followed the growing anti-Zionist line of Moscow. The SED also claimed that returning Jewish property made no sense in a system where property rights did not exist, and it argued that the issue of reparations had already been settled in the form of payments to the Soviet Union. Finally, it understood restitution in a distinctly socialist way. In 1949, the SED agreed to give assistance for health, housing, and employment to those recognized as persecuted by the Nazi regime, although it made an unequal distinction between Communist, antifascist fighters, and Jewish victims.[43]

The only partial exception to these broader developments was the issue of Jewish communal property. On April 29, 1948, the Soviets decreed the "return of property confiscated by the Nazi state to democratic organizations." While designed mainly for Communist groups, this order allowed "church or humanitarian" institutions to get their property back.[44] For the first and what proved to be the only time in the history of the Soviet zone and later the GDR, Jewish communities could reclaim their confiscated property. But the order had limitations. It required that all organizations submit their claims within two months. Since most Jewish communities lacked the organizational resources to file the paperwork themselves, responsibility for doing so fell to the newly formed State Association of Jewish Communities in the Soviet Zone. Although this organization tried to recover as much communal property as possible, it simply did not have the resources to track down in such a short time all the holdings that the Nazis had confiscated. Still, it was able to recover about 122 pieces of property, such as synagogues, Jewish cemeteries, and community centers, although the level of success varied greatly by region.[45] The state of Brandenburg, where Potsdam was located, fared by far the worst. With no Jewish community in Brandenburg to help out, the state association found it especially difficult there to gather all the necessary information to file the claims. It recovered a mere four properties in the entire state. In 1949, it petitioned for this to be changed. Its director, Julius Meyer, asked Brandenburg's state president to return thirty-seven pieces of Jewish communal property that had not been placed on its original list. The state urged that Meyer's request be granted given that the association's "members had been treated especially hard by the measures of the National Socialist leadership."[46] In 1950, the Interior Ministry of the newly formed GDR authorized the return of some property, but Potsdam's synagogue and Jewish cemetery were not among those given back, probably because no postwar Jewish community existed to use them.[47]

The situation in eastern Berlin was more complicated. Although it had an active Jewish community fighting for its legal rights, the city was quickly becoming divided along the lines of the Cold War. While theoretically Britain, France, the Soviet Union, and the United States were supposed to cooperate with each other through the Allied Command for Berlin, in practice they conflicted on almost every policy, with the return of Jewish property being no exception. By 1949–50, the Berlin community made some progress in the western zones, but negotiations with the Soviets had yielded no results regarding the release of property located in eastern Berlin (about seventy to eighty pieces). The Soviet order on communal property had no legal jurisdiction in eastern Berlin because the city remained under the control of all four powers.

In 1947, Berlin's city council moved to change this situation. Proposed first by the SED, the council suggested drafting a citywide restitution law that included the return of Jewish property. During the debate on the matter, members of the council argued that the city must give back what had been stolen from the Jews. One member in particular—a SED party member—suggested that the Nazi persecution of the Jews demanded passage of a citywide restitution law. While opposition to returning Jewish property was growing among the SED's ranks, it had not yet taken hold over all German Communists:

> Ladies and Gentlemen. The proposal brought before us signifies the moral and political need to make justice out of injustice. . . . No one would ever claim that Jewish property was legally acquired, given that the Jews were already being subject to persecution at the time. . . . I don't need to recount the details of *Kristallnacht* of 1938, but allow me to go through a few numbers that show the horrible havoc that persecution and destruction wreaked on German and Berlin Jewry. Before 1933, 186,000 Jews lived in Berlin. Of these 186,000 about 40,000 Jews emigrated. Of the 146,000 Jews that were still in Berlin before *Kristallnacht*

only 7,400 returned, which means that around 138,000 fell victim to annihilation by the Nazis.[48]

The city council passed the proposal and requested that a law be prepared for the "prompt return of formerly owned Jewish property located in the city of Berlin."[49] Two months later, the city council started debating the law, but it ultimately came too late.[50] On June 24, 1948, Stalin responded to the introduction of the new mark in the western zones by cutting off all road, rail, and water routes into the city. The Berlin Blockade and the city's subsequent division shattered the law's prospects. Just two months later, even as local SED leaders were still debating the law, the Soviets ordered that all Jewish property in their zone be placed under their direct control (it had been located in a citywide trust). Headed by a city official named Otto Stockfish, this new trust held somewhere between 1,400 and 2,800 pieces of property, of which about 70 belonged to the Jewish community.[51] Since the Soviets had already established a policy of confiscating property in eastern Berlin, this decision did not bode well for the Jewish community's chances of getting its property back.

But the community did not stop trying. From 1949 until roughly 1953, Julius Meyer and Heinz Galinski sent a number of requests to the newly formed city government in East Berlin.[52] Although the city's finance department initially expressed little interest in shifting course, it eventually came around to the idea of settling some of the Jewish community's claims. After discussing the issue with East Berlin mayor Friedrich Ebert, the department suggested giving back those properties that the Jewish community needed provided that the city was not already using them. The draft proposal involved returning forty-four buildings for a community no larger than 2,000 at the time.[53] But just as the earlier restitution law had fallen victim to wider political changes, so, too, did this measure. The proposal appeared just as opposition toward Jews in East Germany started to increase. Beginning in 1951, showing support for Jews became a political liability in the GDR, like throughout much of the Soviet bloc, which at the time was in turmoil after Josip Tito, the Communist leader of Yugoslavia, split from Stalin in 1948. By 1950–51, the purge of "deviants" that followed the Tito-Stalin feud had shifted to alleged "Jewish cosmopolitans." As Cold War tensions intensified and Ulbricht centralized the East German state along the lines of Stalin's dictatorship, Jews became targets of SED attacks. Drawing on the show trial against Rudolf Slansky, a Jewish functionary in the Czechoslovak Communist Party, the SED initiated a purge of "cosmopolitanism" that went after veteran Communists of largely Jewish origin. One of the highest government officials targeted was Paul Merker. While he himself was not Jewish, his alleged connections with the capitalist West and his plans to return Jewish property became the main reason for the SED's campaign against him.[54]

The purge of cosmopolitanism was a pivotal moment in East German history. Just six years after the collapse of Nazism, the SED portrayed Jews as ideological enemies. Jews symbolized what the party hated at the dawn of the Cold War. East German antisemitism became a "cultural code," a symbol of the SED's fight against U.S. imperialism, capitalism, and increasingly the state of Israel.[55] Jews were neither the source of the SED's greatest apprehensions nor at the center of its politics, but they became highly visible symbols of the party's broader fears and dislikes. This strand of antisemitism was not violent as earlier outbursts of Jewish hatred often were and certainly was not genocidal as in the case of the Third Reich. In fact, it opposed these earlier forms of anti-Jewish hatred. The SED claimed that it had eliminated all forms of prejudice against Jews by building a socialist, antifascist Germany. But in reality the SED attacked Jews in the name of antifascism and anticapitalism: Jews were seen as the carriers of bourgeois culture, cosmopolitanism, capitalism, and American imperialism—precisely what the GDR believed had to be removed and opposed in order to build a socialist, antifascist state.

The core elements of this antifascist, anticapitalist antisemitism appeared in a key document of the purge. On January 4, 1953, the SED published in its main newspaper, *Neues Deutschland,* an article entitled "Lessons from the Trial against the Slansky Conspiracy Center." Written by Hermann Matern of the SED's Central Party Control Commission, it went after Paul Merker and his proposal for restitution, charging that he harbored suspicious ties to American imperialism and Zionism. Merker's call for the return of Jewish property was merely an attempt to enrich his "rich Jewish émigrés" and to "allow U.S.A. finance capital to penetrate into Germany." Matern argued that Merker's close affiliation with Jews and Zionist organizations had become a grave danger to East Germany. Zionism had infected the working class with the "poison" of "chauvinism," "cosmopolitanism," and "reactionary bourgeois ideology." The Zionist movement stood in direct opposition to the ideological aims of Communism: "[it] has nothing in common with the goals of humanity. It is ruled, directed, and commanded by USA-Imperialism, serving exclusively its interests and the interests of Jewish capitalists."[56]

What caused such anti-Jewish hatred to take hold in East Germany less than a decade after the collapse of Nazism? Stalin's paranoia about Jews and his growing antipathy toward Israel triggered it, but he alone does not explain why the SED carried out the campaign with the zeal that it did. Although a vigorous purge of "cosmopolitanism" also erupted in Czechoslovakia and other Communist states removed Jews from their ranks, the campaign's intensity varied across the Soviet bloc. No major stir unfolded in Poland.[57] The SED had a choice on this one. In the early 1950s, the GDR was hardly stable. Agricultural collectivization forced thousands to flee to the West, significant challenges to Ulbricht's power still existed, and growing mass discontent erupted onto the streets in June 1953. The Cold War, which the East German leadership experienced acutely with West Germany so close, exacerbated these internal tensions. As the SED looked to remove perceived internal and external threats to the GDR's security, it turned to Jews with their alleged ties to the West as highly public symbols to attack and in doing so to shore up political support. This targeting of Jews during political and social instability represents a classic example of a "xenophobic assertion"—the tendency to project onto the Jewish minority the broader fears and anxieties of the majority.[58]

This antisemitic campaign derailed any further attempts to return Jewish communal property. In East Berlin, the proposal to give some property back to the Jewish community was shelved for good. In the spring of 1953, East Berlin ceased negotiations with the Jewish community, even going so far as to refuse to supply a simple list of its property.[59] Two years later, it started drafting a general policy toward Jewish property that effectively precluded any future negotiations with the Jewish community. After three years of internal debate in which some SED members feared that Jews tied to "international Zionist organizations" might find out about the decision, the city passed an unpublished measure that allowed Jewish property currently held by the city to be returned to those who "bought" the property in Nazi Germany, provided that they were still legally listed as the owner.[60] Since administering the holdings proved to be an unexpected drain on the city's budget, the city wanted to see the property given back to someone, just not to Jews. Reflecting a mix of Cold War antagonism and outright prejudice, the city argued that returning the property to its original owners would follow the undesirable West German model of supporting "Israeli capitalists" through a policy of "restitution."[61] As the principal owner of the Jewish community's property, East Berlin now retained control over all its property with the exception of five pieces that it allowed the community to use as if it were the owner. This policy remained in effect for the next four decades. Precisely what Jewish leaders had feared happened in the "antifascist" GDR—Jewish property was confiscated "for a second time."[62] But few in the SED seemed to recognize the paradox or the problem. "Well, we were always against the Jewish capitalists just like we were against the non-Jewish capitalists. Had Hitler not disposed them, we would have done it after the seizure of power," Walter Ulbricht is reported to have said.[63]

Why Return "Formerly Jewish" Property?

The handling of confiscated Jewish property in postwar Poland overlapped in several ways with developments in the two Germanys, but was refracted through the very different historical condition that Poland found itself in after the war. Postwar Poland emerged not as a successor state or even an ally of Hitler but as the first European country that defiantly said no to him. It developed the strongest resistance movement against Nazism on the continent. Poles thus remembered the war as a lofty time of heroic sacrifice and patriotic duty, not one of collusion and collaboration for which they had to make amends after the war. The reality on the ground was, of course, more complicated. The Nazis created the opportunity for taking Jewish property, but many Poles seized the chance when given it. Indeed, few other issues expose the participation of Poles (and Europeans, more largely) in the Holocaust more starkly than that of Jewish property.[64]

Polish involvement in the Nazi confiscation of Jewish property differed across the western, central, and eastern parts of the country. The Nazis directly incorporated western Poland into the Third Reich. In these "incorporated territories," they created the Main Trusteeship for the East, which confiscated any property that could be used for the resettlement of ethnic Germans and the general benefit of the Third Reich. The trust was charged with expropriating all Polish private and state property as part of Himmler's grand designs to Germanize this area. Although these utopian plans soon proved impractical and fell to the wayside as Hitler prepared for war against the Soviet Union, they involved the forced deportation of no fewer than 500,000 Poles and Jews to the "dumping ground" of the nearby General Government. All of those deported—mostly non-Jewish Poles at this point—lost their possessions, homes, businesses, and farms as they were forced to make room for incoming ethnic Germans. The situation in central Poland was different. The Nazis turned this part of Poland into a colony ruled by Hans Frank. The German occupiers took whatever Polish property they wanted, but focused mostly on confiscating Jewish property in central Poland, where most of the ghettos were created. In a process that was both regulated and ad hoc, a variety of different owners took over Jewish property left behind as the Nazis forced Jews into the ghettos. Some of the property went directly to the Nazi state, some was stolen by German soldiers who wanted their share of the war loot, and some was controlled by Nazi-created trusteeships in Poland. Numerous Poles became drawn into this process not just as owners but also as administrators. In the General Government, the Nazis created trusteeships that included Poles as managers. The Nazis preferred to have Germans fill these posts, but often settled for Poles because they needed someone to do the job. Poles made up 30 percent of the trustees in the district of Warsaw. Smaller cities had an even higher percentage because local Polish mayors were often the ones who suggested names of potential trustees to the German occupiers.[65]

In eastern Poland, Polish participation in the seizure of Jewish property was even more direct. As the Nazis pushed the Soviets out of this area in June 1941, local Poles moved into the homes, apartments, and shops left behind by Jews killed on the spot by the Germans or later deported to the death camps. In some cases, Jews handed their possessions over to Polish friends, but typically this involved Poles grabbing what they could for material gain. "The dregs of society poured out into the city," the physician Zygmunt Klukowski wrote in his diary, "with their wagons from the countryside as they stood waiting the entire day for the moment when they could start looting. News is coming from all directions about the scandalous behavior of segments of the Polish population who are robbing abandoned Jewish apartments."[66] More tragically, the plunder of Jewish property was one of the motivating factors for the wave of pogroms and massacres that erupted in over twenty towns in the eastern regions of Łomża and Białystok during the summer of 1941.[67]

What happened to all this confiscated property once the war ended? Were there ever calls from Polish society or initiatives by the Communist-dominated government taking hold in Poland to give Jewish property back to surviving heirs or to Jewish successor organizations? The issue of Jewish property emerged at an especially precarious time for Poland and its Jewish population. War, occupation, and genocide had ravaged the country. No other geographic space in Europe with the exception of Soviet Ukraine and Belarus experienced such massive destruction and upheaval. Cities, industries, roads, and bridges lay in ruins; an astounding 5 million Polish citizens had died; the country's prewar minorities, once making up one third of the population, were gone after the Holocaust and the forced removal of Germans, Ukrainians, Lemkos, Belorussians, and Lithuanians after the war. Poland's border shifted westward as it lost large swaths of its prewar territory in the east to the Soviet Union. In the midst of all these changes, property across Poland was lost, transferred, and seized. The very notion that a home, an apartment, or a farm belonged to a particular individual collapsed as many Poles went on a looting frenzy just after the war, taking whatever they needed and wanted in a time of great scarcity.[68]

The early postwar years were also a particularly fragile moment in Polish-Jewish relations. In June 1946, the Jewish population in Poland reached its postwar height of 240,000 after thousands of Polish Jews returned from the Soviet Union, where they had survived the Holocaust. By 1949, the number had dropped to 98,000.[69] Some Jews left for Palestine, but most fled Poland after the outbreak of extreme postwar violence. In 1945–46, Poles killed perhaps as many as 1,500 Jews in villages and towns across their country.[70] The Kielce pogrom in July 1946, first triggered by accusations of blood libel after a Christian boy went missing, was the most tragic when forty-two Jews were killed. The second deadliest attack occurred a year earlier in the southeastern town of Leżajsk, when sixteen Jews died from a bomb that exploded under their home.[71] This violence erupted for a variety of reasons—charges of blood libel, disputes over property, complicity in the Holocaust that provoked "fear" of returning Jews who reminded Poles of their wartime guilt, and antisemitic accusations of Judeo-Communism (*żydokomuna*) that intensified as Communism was taking hold in Poland. Many of the perpetrators were involved in the anti-Communist underground, which was made up mainly of right-wing groups whose greatest problem with Jews was probably that they were "simply *not Poles*."[72] Believing that Poland must be ethnically pure, they attacked Jews as minorities who did not belong in their country and who threatened claims to material goods at a time of immense scarcity.

These attacks against Jews affected the issue of confiscated Jewish property in several ways. The violence itself stemmed partially from property claims. Some ethnic Poles attacked Jews in order to dissuade them from reclaiming their possessions.[73] But above all, the violence diverted precious attention away from the issue among both Jews and Poles. As Jewish organizations in Germany concentrated on restitution, those in Poland had to worry about security and could focus on little else. Non-Jewish Poles who expressed concern about Jews—mostly intellectuals writing in left-wing social and literary journals—also focused on condemning the carnage unfolding before them rather than on the importance of returning Jewish property.[74] Moreover, the violence sent a clear signal to Polish Communists about the prevailing mood among parts of society. In a country where the antisemitic stereotype of Judeo-Communism (*żydokomuna*) was common, Communist officials feared that any overt association with Jews could be politically toxic. Fighting for the rights of such a minuscule minority group was clearly going to yield many more political losses than gains. Put simply, Jews in Poland lacked political allies willing to press for their needs in a sustained and vigorous manner.[75] They were abandoned from almost all sides: the Soviets appeared oblivious to their plight; Polish Communists, even if they wanted to help, were running away from them in their grab for political power; and the main political opposition—the Polish Peasant Party and the militia bands made up mainly of right-wing groups—either were generally silent about Jewish matters or embraced an ethnocentric vision of a future Polish state that did not include Jews.[76]

Indeed, few other issues reflect Poland's abandonment of its Jewish population more starkly than that of Jewish property. No social, legal, moral, or political pressure existed that called for returning it. There were, of course, a few exceptions. In 1945, a member of the Council for Aid to Jews demanded that Poles "go after at last all of those who took over Jewish property from the hands of the occupiers and made a fortune; for it is precisely they who today are most interested in the extermination of the remaining Jewish survivors."[77] In 1945–46, the state also allowed for a tiny amount of individual property to be returned. But few Poles seemed remotely interested in rectifying the wartime robbery of Jewish property. Poles did not want to give up what they had gained; they accepted and sanctioned the confiscation of Jewish property. Poles declared, perceived, and marked Jewish property as "abandoned," something that could now just be taken over and used without much thought or discussion. They invented an entirely new linguistic device—*mienie pożydowskie*—that legitimized its seizure. The Polish prefix "po" indicates the leaving behind of something that is now gone; the expression translates as "formerly Jewish property," but the English hardly captures the discursive power of the Polish. The phrase reflected and produced a moral economy that justified the wartime and postwar taking of Jewish property. In March 1946, the Marxist literary journal *Odrodzenie* republished a poem by the writer Zuzanna Ginczanka that brilliantly captured this linguistic and physical possession of *mienie pożydowskie*. Beginning with a line from one of Horace's odes about his own eternity, *Non omnis moriar* (Not all of me will die), she writes bitterly and sardonically about what will survive her destruction—the material objects that now remain in the hands of those who took them, goods that cling to their fingers by her blood. Ginczanka might be gone, but her possessions—these "J things," now declared to be "formerly Jewish"—drip with memories of guilt, collusion, and murder.

> Non omnis moriar—my proud estate,
> Meadows of my tablecloths, fortresses of indomitable wardrobes,
> Spacious sheets, precious bedding
> And dresses, light dresses will be left after me.
> I did not leave any heir here,
> So let your hand ferret out the J things,
> Chominowa, of Lwów, brave wife of a snitch,
> Sly informer, mother of Volksdeutsch.
> Let them serve you and yours, why should they serve strangers.
> My dear ones—not a lute, not an empty name.
> I remember you, and you, when the Schupo were coming,

You also remembered me. Recalled also me.
Let my friends sit down with a goblet
And toast my funeral and their riches:
Kilims and tapestries, serving dishes, candlesticks—
Let them drink the night through, and at first light's dawning
Let them search for precious stones and gold
In couches, mattresses, comforters and carpets.
O, how they will work, like a house on fire,
Skeins of horsehair and sea grass,
Clouds from torn pillows and feather beds apart
Will cling to their hands, will change both hands into wings;
My blood will glue the oakum with fresh down
And will suddenly transform the winged to angels.[78]

Avoiding a thorough return of individual Jewish property meant looking the other way and forgetting about what happened during the war in the service of building a new postwar society. To embark upon a complete return of Jewish property would have opened up and interrogated just how involved Polish society became in the Holocaust; it would have meant looking into when, how, and why Jewish property was confiscated in the first place. It also would have entailed depriving Poles of precious goods during a time of dire need. The Communist regime knew a thing or two about material objects and the power of the state to provide or withhold them. It was not about to disrupt the Nazi-created wartime redistribution of wealth that the plunder of Jewish property enabled.

Indeed, the physical, cultural, and linguistic seizure of *mienie pożydowskie* became coded into postwar law. In May 1945, the Communist-influenced provisional government passed a law on "abandoned and deserted properties" that declared Jewish property "abandoned" and "heirless."[79] In 1946, the state issued a slightly changed decree on "abandoned and formerly German property" to include more specifically the possessions of the expelled German population of western Poland.[80] This law dealt with both individual and communal property, but treated them differently. It allowed direct heirs of individual property—children, parents, spouses, brothers, and sisters— the chance to reclaim their property by going through the magistrate or small claims courts, except for any land or businesses subject to nationalization. It is impossible to guess how many Jews actually filed claims and of them how many then got their property back; the Polish government seemed interested in giving them the chance to do so, even extending the original submission deadline by an entire year at the request of the World Jewish Congress. But there is little doubt that the number was extremely small for several reasons. First, the number of Polish Jews was itself small, as only 10 percent survived and those who did were fleeing Poland by the thousands. Second, a large number of Jews who stayed resettled in western Poland, taking over "former German property" rather than lodging claims for their homes located elsewhere in the country. Third, the legal process of going through the courts took time and money from a population that had neither, while corruption and opposition to giving the property back lowered the number of successful cases even more.[81]

Finally and crucially, the law deliberately restricted claims to only close relatives, which disadvantaged Jews who had lost so many direct heirs. When the measure was first discussed, Jewish leader Emil Sommerstein pleaded that the line of heirs be broadened to family members, such as cousins, aunts, and uncles, but his suggestion was rejected on the grounds that extending it would place too much property in the hands of a small group of Jews and could trigger antisemitic attacks.[82] But there were other reasons. Returning all individual Jewish property would have meant repealing the wartime and postwar spoilage of genocide. If the line of heirs were extended, or if a Jewish successor organization were to take control of heirless property, a sizeable number of Poles would have been forced to give up what they had acquired.[83] In its restricted scope, then, the law sanctioned the postwar norm of confiscating "formerly Jewish property." Moreover, returning all Jewish property would have conflicted with the ideological demands of Communism. As the American Jewish Joint Distribution Committee admitted, if all Jewish property in Poland "was restituted, either to individual Jews or to a successor organization, Jews would be the largest property holders other than the state."[84] In February 1945, Władysław Gomułka, at the time Central Committee chairman of the Polish Workers' Party, made clear that this was simply not going to happen: "It is also common knowledge that part of the capital before 1939 rested in Jewish hands and that [now] this capital is ownerless because the Germans killed the Jews. This capital must again pass on, pass into the hands of the state."[85]

But these important reasons do not fully account for the opposition to returning Jewish communal property. Giving back synagogues, cemeteries, schools, and other communal buildings would not have displaced tens of thousands of people, nor would it have created an enormous nonstate property owner, because so much of the Jewish community's property was destroyed. In Warsaw and Wrocław, for example, the number of claims would have been tiny. And yet Communist Poland, like East Germany, never officially returned one single piece of property to its postwar Jewish community. The reason, though, was not for lack of a law. The justification—cited throughout the regime's history as late as the 1980s—came from a single document published in 1945 by the Ministry for Public Administration, known as MAP, the abbreviation of its name in Polish. In a measure on "provisionally regulating matters of the Jewish religious population," MAP declared that ten or more Jews could establish a "Jewish religious congregation" *(kongregacja)*. This "congregation" was deemed to be an entirely new legal entity with no ties to the prewar "community" *(gmina)*. The measure allowed congregations to use some prewar property, but prohibited them from officially owning it because they were not legal heirs to the *gmina*.[86]

As these regulations were supposedly provisional, Jewish leaders in Poland pleaded for them to be changed. In October 1946, the Organizing Committee of Jewish Religious Congregations requested that all "abandoned property of former Jewish religious communities, foundations, and other organizations" be returned.[87] Jewish organizations justified their claims on moral and practical grounds. The Central Committee of Jews in Poland (CKŻP) argued that restitution was a "partial undoing of the moral injustice committed against the Jews by the occupiers."[88] It also suggested that returning property to Jewish organizations was essential to ending the defilement, misuse, and neglect of Jewish sites that was occurring across Poland after the war.

Polish officials at times seemed willing to consider these concerns. In 1946, MAP noted that the CKŻP's status as the only legally recognized Jewish organization could justify its "claims to take over the property of the former Jewish religious communities and Jewish foundations."[89] But for the most part, MAP blocked the return of Jewish communal property. It turned a "provisional" regulation into a permanent one. Its 1945 measure stated that Jewish communal property would "provisionally remain in control of the state until the introduction of a law on abandoned property."[90] But such a measure came into existence a mere three months later, when the law on abandoned and deserted property was announced. The law included, though, an important provision. Article thirteen stated that abandoned property could be "used and managed" by public associations, including "help organizations for groups of people who were particularly persecuted by the Germans."[91] At first glance, this would seem to grant Jewish organizations the right to reclaim their property, and in fact numerous local Polish officials thought as much. In 1945, the Białystok regional government wrote to Warsaw asking if Jewish communal property was "abandoned" and, if so, whether the Jewish religious congregations could reclaim it as "organizations continuing with the legal recognition of the former religious communities."[92] Warsaw responded that Jewish communal property was abandoned, but that the postwar congregations could not claim any of it because they were not its legal heirs. The Jewish congregations could only use properties that they needed for religious purposes. The state could confiscate all others, which Warsaw officials knew would lead to the seizure of Jewish communal property across Poland, for they knew the facts on the ground. The amount of property that Jewish congregations needed was dwindling by the day as the few Jews who survived the Holocaust were fleeing from Poland.[93] In places where no Jewish congregation existed—hundreds of towns and villages across Poland—various parties took over the property.[94] Although in theory local authorities were supposed to consult with Warsaw to find appropriate uses for Jewish sites, this rarely happened, and synagogues were turned into storage houses, museums, movie theaters, libraries, factories, cafeterias, archives, and schools.[95]

As this transfer of property took place in town after town throughout Poland, Jewish leaders did not simply sit idly by and watch it unfold. They opposed it as vigorously as they could. In the late 1940s, the CKŻP pressed officials to approach the issue with some flexibility, holding out hope that the authorities might change the law.[96] Poland's Jewish congregations also fought back in numerous letters to authorities in Warsaw. Opposition lessened by the early 1950s, but then resumed a few years later. The political unrest of 1956 probably explains the timing. In June 1956, mass crowds in Poznań gathered in protest of low wages and lack of goods. Polish Communism was in deep crisis. Poland's Communist party, the Polish United Workers' Party (PZPR), responded by bringing Gomułka back, who in 1948 had been dismissed from his leadership of the party for alleged "nationalist" deviation during the Stalin-Tito split. Gomułka introduced reforms that moderated the worst excesses of Stalinism and briefly gained support from the Polish population. Sensing perhaps an opportune moment, Jewish leaders petitioned state authorities to change the state's policy toward Jewish communal property, triggering the most significant and drawn-out dispute over the issue in the history of Communist Poland.

Although the conflict involved just one specific case—the Jewish congregation in Kraków—it had potentially wide-ranging implications for the entire country. The dispute began in early January 1956, when municipal authorities in Kraków became the owners of the Jewish congregation's property and attempted to transfer some of it to another party. The law on abandoned and formerly German property stipulated that the state would officially become the owner of any "abandoned" property after ten years of managing it. This was mere confirmation of what had already taken place in the late 1940s. Still, the Jewish congregation in Kraków was furious, not least because it had been using some of the buildings that the state now owned. Maciej Jakubowicz, the congregation's chairman from 1945 to 1979, sent a series of long, impassioned, and angry letters to some of the state's highest officials. "All property belonging to the Jewish Religious Community," he wrote tersely in underlined letters, "should be returned to the congregations without any exceptions."[97] Jakubowicz argued that Poland's Jewish congregations were the legal heirs of the Jewish communities, and flatly rejected the notion that Jewish communal property was "abandoned."[98] Jakubowicz also pleaded that "every piece of property" be returned as the "only way to avoid the desecration of religious sites."[99] The Department for Religious Affairs responded by simply restating the regime's now long-standing approach toward Jewish communal property. Since the Jewish congregation was a "completely new religious organization" with no legal ties to the prewar Jewish community, the property had rightfully been declared "abandoned" and escheated to the state. As for the ongoing destruction of Jewish sites, the department explained that local officials were doing everything possible to protect them, but that "time and the effects of the weather were above all contributing" to their ruin.[100]

But such bureaucratic obstinacy did not deter Jakubowicz. He took the issue to the courts and succeeded to a certain extent. In December 1958, the local court in Kraków sided with the Jewish congregation and ordered that its name be placed on the city's property deed as the owner of fourteen pieces of property that had formerly belonged to the Jewish community. The court based its decision on correspondence written by municipal authorities in 1946–47 that declared the postwar congregation "the appointed institution" of the prewar Jewish community "for religious and social purposes."[101] This statement implied that the Jewish congregation was the legal successor to the Jewish community. Officials in Warsaw were hardly enthused. They turned to Poland's Supreme Court, which heard an appeal regarding one of the properties—Kraków's Old Synagogue. In a cautiously written decision, the Supreme Court upheld the state's position that the Jewish congregation had no legal right to the property. But then, in an intriguing twist from the strictures of the law, it added that "in this concrete case" the state had "abused the law" by "demanding" to own the property. The court came to this view in light of the "notorious destruction of the Kraków Jewish population by the German invaders" and the "indisputable cultural-historical character" of the synagogue. "It is the opinion of the Supreme Court that the People's Republic has a moral responsibility to respect the above-mentioned emotions of its citizens."[102] It ordered that the Jewish congregation be allowed to manage the synagogue. Bound by a series of legal maneuvers set after the war, the court's decision changed nothing in terms of the legal state of Jewish communal property. It did not challenge the premise that the property was abandoned, and it only gave the Jewish congregation the right to manage the synagogue. But the decision did show that at least some jurists in Poland—and no less than those sitting on its Supreme Court—recognized the limitations of a law that declared a synagogue abandoned in a city with a Jewish congregation.

This decision infuriated the Department for Religious Affairs in Warsaw. In numerous letters sent to Kraków officials, the courts, and the justice department, the department criticized the decision for making it "very difficult to take up legal action in the matter" of Jewish communal property.[103] The department also emphasized that the Kraków case had no legal precedent and that local Jewish congregations had no legal basis for filing motions before the courts.[104] In 1961, it reinforced this point by officially recognizing as a legal entity the Religious Association of the Jewish Faith, an umbrella organization of the local Jewish congregations. This move allowed only this association to represent the legal interests of Poland's religious Jewish population and thereby prevented local Jewish organizations from turning to the courts to oppose the confiscation of their property. This policy lasted until 1989.

Cold War Divides and Parallels

Just as in the case of the GDR, this early postwar story of opposing the return of Jewish communal property in Poland is puzzling on some levels. To be sure, Poland's Communist regime discriminated against Jews and avoided any pretense of treating them preferentially in a society where the antisemitic stereotype of Judeo-Communism remained strong. The PZPR sought to legitimize its rule by embracing an ethnically exclusive notion of the nation that had long been the hallmark of the political right in Poland and Europe. This included doing as little as possible about returning Jewish individual property so as not to disrupt the wartime redistribution of material wealth that it engendered. Still, all told, the PPR before 1967–68 represented a dramatic shift from its interwar predecessor, which persecuted Jews with a flood of discriminatory measures. In the 1950s and early 1960s, the PZPR went out of its way neither to support Jews nor to harm them. In these early years, it maintained ambivalent, yet at times moderately amicable, relations with Israel. In 1950, a government promotional piece published in New York claimed that Poland had changed for the better: "The wall of nationalism and antisemitic prejudices erected by Polish reactionaries has been torn down." Perhaps this was just written for an American audience, but perhaps it was written out of genuine conviction and belief that Communism had created a different Poland. Perhaps the Jewish sociologist Lucjan Blit had good reason to believe that the one thing Jews in Poland could count on was "that as long as a Communist regime was in power, official antisemitism would be out of the question."[105]

Blit was, alas, wrong in the end, but his point raises key questions: What happened to Communism in Europe after the Holocaust? Why did such opposition to Jews emerge in East Germany and Poland? It is certainly true that anti-Jewish biases and attitudes existed among socialists and Communists from the very beginning; critiques of capitalism, industrialization, and the middle class could easily slip into antisemitic attacks. On balance, however, no other political movements in Europe defended Jews more consistently before the war than those on the left. But Communists in Eastern Europe found themselves in a different position after the war. Seizing power in societies that generally did not want them, they had to choose their battles wisely. Since the 1930s, the situation for Jews had deteriorated in almost all parts of Europe, but especially in Central and Eastern Europe, which later made up the Soviet bloc. This part of the continent was the geographic epicenter of the Holocaust, and by 1945 anti-Jewish hatred had become a normalized part of politics and society. Any Communist official with even an ounce of political acumen doubtlessly knew that fighting for the rights of Jews simply made no sense. Turning away from Jews and even directly attacking them were an "implicit 'give' for the 'take' of power," as sociologist Jan Gross put it.[106] One could go even further to say that doing so was a way of strengthening power.

It is not surprising, then, that Polish and East German Communists gave little priority to returning Jewish property. They had little reason to do so and few people suggested that they act differently. The Soviet Union did not push East Germans or Poles to return Jewish property, and no Jewish successor organization formed in either country to force the issue. The only main advocates for restitution came from local Jewish leaders, who fought strongly for returning confiscated property but who had little power. Polish and East German authorities cared little about their pleas, save some SED members who were later silenced in 1951–53. Although some Polish and East German intellectuals, writers, and politicians wrote at times passionately about the need to fight antisemitism in 1945–50, they hardly formed a broad swell of societal concern about Jewish property.[107] In this sense, West Germany was different. Pressure did exist in the FRG that forced German authorities to deal with confiscated Jewish property. But it tellingly came from the outside. The JRSO provoked resentment among Jewish leaders in Germany, but it fought tirelessly for restitution in the face of growing opposition in West German society and politics by the late 1940s. Without the continued presence of outside pressure groups like it, even more problems with restitution would probably have emerged, if not even an eventual scaling back of the restitution laws.

It was, though, the very presence of such outside organizations that made restitution difficult to implement in West Germany. The impetus for returning Jewish property did not stem from a deep, societal reflection on German complicity in the persecution of the Jews. With the exception of a few politicians motivated by a variety of different concerns, most German intellectuals, church leaders, writers, journalists, and ordinary citizens were not pushing their political leaders to confront the problem of confiscated Jewish property.[108] Such social pressure simply did not exist in the early FRG; restitution never became assimilated and normalized into West German politics and society during the 1950s. The very opposite occurred to a certain extent. In dismissing restitution as victor's justice, West Germans could distance themselves from the entire issue or interpret it as yet another form of victimization. Some even went further to believe that restitution was just another way that Jews were out to harm Germany. In some ways, this lack of acceptance for restitution just after the war is not surprising. After all, it was not long ago that Germans had watched, lived through, and participated in twelve years of persecution against Jews.

It is on this level of societal norms that the seemingly clear-cut Cold War trajectories of East-West become blurred. In the FRG, GDR, and PPR, no social norm existed that called for and sanctioned the return of Jewish property. Few Germans and Poles wanted to give up the goods of genocide. In the immediate postwar years, it admittedly must have been difficult to initiate a dialogue about what just had happened and how possibly to repair broken relationships with no food on the tables, no lights on in the bombed-out houses, no water running through the pipes. But a basic recognition of complicity and the need for reconciling wrongs had to exist in the first place, no matter what conditions were like on the ground. Some exceptions, of course, stand out. A few members from the Social Democratic Party of Germany (SPD) and the SED believed strongly in restitution as a constituent part of building a postfascist Germany. Such voices emerged less often in Poland, where restitution became refracted through the perspective of the colonized. The Nazis confiscated a large amount of Polish property, deported hundreds of thousands of Poles into forced labor, and killed nearly 2 million of them. Poles could easily dismiss or simply not even think about restituting crimes committed by someone else during a brutal occupation that they had opposed and experienced. But the Nazi occupation of Poland, while horrific, did involve collusion from Poles. Possibly hundreds of thousands became involved in the management, seizure, and use of Jewish property. Returning this now "formerly Jewish property" would involve a material loss and would require confronting Polish complicity in crimes more comfortably thought to have been carried out exclusively by someone else.

2

Clearing Jewish Rubble

In 1945, Warsaw and Berlin, two of Europe's largest centers of Jewish life, were cities of Jewish rubble. The Nazis destroyed the Jewish communities in both cities, and afterward many Jews who survived emigrated to North America, Latin America, or the Middle East. Only a small number of Jews decided to rebuild their lives in either capital. In the early 1950s, Warsaw's official Jewish community totaled fewer than 200 members. Although more Jews resided in Warsaw and several active secular cultural institutions existed in the city, including a Yiddish theater, a Yiddish publishing house, and the headquarters of the Socio-Cultural Association of Jews in Poland, Jewish life in the capital had declined dramatically. "I know that the Jews have disappeared from Warsaw," Isaac Bashevis Singer wrote, "but I cannot truly imagine it. . . . I cannot present Warsaw *judenrein* nor Jewish streets as heaps of rubble."[1] Berlin, too, had become a landscape of Jewish ruins. Once a city of 160,000 Jews in 1933, it had in the early 1950s no more than 6,000 in the west and 1,000 in the east.[2] In 1956, a Protestant minister called on Berliners to protect the city's abandoned Jewish sites. "The once flourishing Jewish community," he wrote, "was exterminated almost entirely. A cemetery of 113,500 tombstones remains behind and is not being preserved because its members died, were murdered, or have emigrated."[3] A complicated question thus emerged in these former Jewish cities: What now was to be done with the ruins of Jewish life?

Germans and Poles confronted this question just as they began to rebuild their war-ravaged capitals. In 1945, Berlin and Warsaw lay in ruins after enduring military attacks with fundamentally different aims. The Nazis destroyed the Polish capital by quashing the Warsaw Ghetto Uprising of 1943 and the citywide Warsaw Uprising of 1944. These two acts of demolition were different even if the destructive results were the same. Whereas the Nazis intended to destroy the ghetto before the uprising broke out, the devastation of the rest of the city came in response to the rebellion of 1944. In both cases, the Nazis clearly had no strategic reason for engaging in such massive destruction. They pursued a murderous campaign against the Jews left in the ghetto and then a year later expelled the city's population as revenge for the Warsaw Uprising. These campaigns against Warsaw's population reflected the overall brutality of the Nazi occupation of Poland that left 90 percent of its Jewish population and 10 percent of its non-Jewish population dead. The destruction of Berlin was different. It occurred primarily as a consequence of military operations—allied air raids and Soviet ground assaults—intended to defeat Hitler and ceased once victory had been achieved. In short, the allied military attacks against German cities were means to achieve the end of victory and the cessation of hostilities, while the Nazi attacks on the civilian populations of Polish and other Eastern European cities were postvictory war aims of genocide and imperialism implemented only after military resistance had been crushed.

These differences, though, mattered little to postwar planners who had to rebuild divided Berlin and Warsaw. They confronted shared questions. How should the city be rebuilt? Should it be reconstructed in an entirely new way, or should the city's historic buildings and layout be rescued from smoldering ruins? At a surprisingly early stage, a general framework for rebuilding the two Berlins and Warsaw emerged. An impulse to build a new, modern city defined the basic contours of planning in all three cities. Urban planners hoped to reorder the urban landscape based on the guiding principles of urban modernism, which stressed dividing cities into functional parts for housing, work, and recreation separated by green space and linked by an efficient transportation system.[4] Architects and urban planners relished the task before them. In 1946, the architect Hans Scharoun spoke of a unique opportunity to turn Berlin's notoriously disorganized layout into "distinct and modest parts, and to order and fashion these parts together into a beautiful landscape, like the forest, meadow, mountain, and lake."[5] In the early 1950s, such utopianism took on different forms in East Germany and Poland during the height of Stalinism as socialist realist architecture spread across the Soviet bloc. With its monumental buildings, wide boulevards, and sprawling squares, at least in theory socialist realism rejected the decentralized,

functional designs of urban modernism, but in practice it continued many
of its basic tenets, such as the use of green space and efficient transportation
schemes. Like urban modernism, socialist realism also aimed to transform
the city from the disorganized layout and cramped, dark tenement housing
of the derided industrial metropolis. Whether in socialist or capitalist ways,
then, postwar urban planners hoped to secure a more progressive future by
changing the city in form, layout, function, and style.[6]

This reformist impulse strongly animated discussions about urban planning in Berlin and Warsaw, which reflected like few other capitals in Europe
the perceived ills of the industrial city. Warsaw became an industrial metropolis over the nineteenth century, but almost no municipal government
existed to plan for its massive growth. After the failed Polish uprising of 1863–
64, tsarist Russia limited the power of local officials who could not develop a
unified approach to managing Warsaw's exploding population, which went
from 260,000 residents in 1870 to 884,000 in 1914.[7] Berlin was certainly better off than Warsaw as one of the three imperial capitals that had colonized
Poland, but it, too, had expanded rapidly over the nineteenth century. Berlin
increased from 180,000 people in 1800 to over 4 million in the mid-1920s,
becoming one of world's largest cities in a little over a century. Managing
this growth and providing enough housing went unresolved for decades. In
1900, 50 percent of all Berlin families lived in tenement housing with merely
one small room and a tiny kitchen.[8]

This urban past provoked both similar and different responses from municipal officials in postwar Berlin and Warsaw. Urban planners in the two
Berlins staked out the most radical position as they competed with each
other to construct the best urban landscape for postwar life. Large parts of
Berlin's historic core were cleared away as urban modernism and socialist
realism reigned supreme. In contrast, urban planners in Warsaw developed
an exceptional blend of urban modernism, historic reconstruction, and socialist realism. Warsaw became the symbol for Poland's renewal from the
destructiveness of Nazism—its martyr city that epitomized the country's
wartime suffering and postwar resurrection. Historic preservationists rebuilt Warsaw's old town, while urban planners constructed the rest of the
city on the basic principles of modernism with strong influences from socialist realism in the early 1950s during the peak of Stalinism. This embrace
of the modern and the socialist might appear like a flight into the future, but

it remained deeply entangled in the past. As the wrecking ball moved from street to street in divided Berlin and Warsaw, it cleared away numerous historic buildings. Urban renewal—its dueling impulse for reconstruction and destruction—paved over the particular, historic form of the urban landscape.

Jewish sites fell victim to this ruinous dialectic. By the early 1960s, only a few traces of Jewish life could be found in Warsaw, West Berlin, and East Berlin. Germans and Poles perceived Jewish sites as little more than rubble that could be swept away for the building of something better. Such disregard for the past is perhaps not surprising; it is, in fact, hardly new. In the 1890s, municipal officials in Prague razed the Jewish ghetto in the euphoric embrace of the "modern." In the 1950s and 1960s, urban renewal demolished the "blight" of poor and minority neighborhoods across the United States.[9] Still, the post-1945 period is distinctive for the extent of destruction in the wake of genocide. The built environment of Warsaw and divided Berlin came to reflect the homogeneous makeup of their postwar populations as nearly all the spatial markers of the Jewish minority vanished throughout the 1950s. Of course, the Holocaust and wartime destruction account for much of this erasure, but postwar urban reconstruction played its own important role. After all, it cleared away not just any kind of broken stone. Jewish sites were hardly ordinary ruins—ragged stone that had aged over years of natural decay, evoking wonder, awe, beauty, mystery, strangeness, and nostalgia. Their untimely, sudden thrust into existence—created in minutes rather than decades—hauntingly captured the destructiveness of modern life. Jewish sites provoked fear and anxiety. To be sure, Jewish spaces were hardly the only ruins created by violence in postwar Europe; the wreckage upon wreckage really did seem to reach the sky. Violence against the built environment produced across the continent, in the words of the Spanish writer Juan Goytisolo, "rage and decrepitude: ruined buildings, burned-out tanks, skeleton roofs, hanging beams, entire districts abandoned by their inhabitants."[10] Yet, for Poles and Germans, Jewish sites were some of the most haunting wreckage. They conjured up memories of a deeply anxious past that few wanted to encounter. In building their new cities, Germans and Poles found it much easier to erase these reminders of the past than to mourn the catastrophe behind their shattered condition.[11]

Cities of Jews

As Berlin and Warsaw grew economically over the nineteenth century, they became cities with substantial Jewish populations. In 1840, about 6,456 Jews lived in Berlin. That number grew in a short thirty years to 36,326 in 1871, and by 1933 the community had reached its height of 160,564 Jews. Since the 1700s, Jews had lived in Berlin Mitte, the central district of the old town, where they made up 10.1 percent of the population in 1890. This district came closest to being Berlin's "Jewish district." The Jewish community's oldest cemetery on Great Hamburger Street, its main synagogue on Heidereuter Lane, and the Jewish hospital on August Street were all located in Mitte, as were numerous Jewish bakeries, butchers, schools, and bookstores. Although a mixed neighborhood hardly dominated by Jews, Mitte was Berlin's center of Jewish life for most of the nineteenth century. In 1866, this standing reached its architectural zenith with the unveiling of the massive prayer house on Oranienburger Street known as the New Synagogue. Located on one of Mitte's main streets, the building signaled the expansion, strength, and vitality of the Jewish community like no other building project before or after it. Plans for the synagogue first surfaced in 1846, but stalled as Prussian officials initially rejected the location of Mitte and as Jewish leaders debated over what kind of synagogue should be built for the increasingly diverse community of Orthodox, moderately Liberal, and Reform believers. By a decade later, these issues, if not resolved, were at least settled enough to launch an architectural competition after the community had purchased a plot of land on Oranienburger Street. The Protestant architect Eduard Knoblauch created the winning design of a Moorish-style building that seated 3,200 people. Towering 120 feet and topped by a majestic golden dome, the synagogue immediately became the most prominent architectural marker of Jewish life in Berlin.[12]

And yet, just shortly after the New Synagogue was unveiled, Mitte started to decline in importance as Berlin's center of Jewish life. Jewish immigrants from Eastern Europe continued to settle in the district, but by the interwar years a large number of Jews also lived in western Berlin. In 1925, Wilmersdorf was 13 percent Jewish and Charlottenburg 8.9.[13] The construction of synagogues in the west soon followed. The erection of the liberal synagogue on Fasanen Street in Charlottenburg marked this spatial diversification

Berlin's New Synagogue in 1883. (Bildarchiv Preussischer Kulturbesitz/Art Resource, New York)

most clearly. What the New Synagogue was for the east, the Fasanen Street synagogue was for the west. Designed by Ehrenfried Hessel in 1912, the massive building rivaled the monumentality of the New Synagogue, but departed from it in architectural style. Romanesque elements found in German churches dominated its exterior in a departure from the seemingly exotic Moorish flourishes of the New Synagogue.

The situation was considerably different in Warsaw. Warsaw's Jewish population lived more compactly in one area than was the case in Berlin. This spatial concentration occurred gradually over the course of the nineteenth century, when Warsaw was located in the Kingdom of Poland, a semiautonomous region under Russian rule during Poland's partition. In 1792, 6,750 Jews lived in the city; a century later, 320,000 did. Warsaw's Jewish population had increased by 46.4 percent. A distinct "Jewish" area did not fully develop until the mid-nineteenth century, when Jews living in the Kingdom of Poland were granted more legal rights than their fellow Jews in the Pale of Settlement. From that point on, Jews could live wherever they wished, and large numbers gradually gravitated to the city's northwestern section. Jews lived in all parts of Warsaw, with large numbers around Grzybowski Square, in the old town, and in the Praga district, but its northern parts, especially the district of Muranów, became the cultural, economic, social, and religious hub of Jewish life.[14]

Muranów reflected Warsaw's chaotic growth over the nineteenth century like few other areas. It was one of Warsaw's most overcrowded districts, with 590 people living to the hectare. Filled with shops, small factories, and markets, Muranów had a bustling economy of craftsmen and retailers that provided the city with many of its basic consumer goods and services; Warsaw's residents bought half of their clothing and linen from its shops. The district's Jewish population was generally poor, but it produced an exceptionally rich intellectual, political, cultural, and religious life that made Warsaw one of the world's most vibrant Jewish cities. Speaking mostly Yiddish and largely Orthodox in religious belief, Jews living in Muranów distinguished themselves from non-Jewish Poles living in the rest of the capital. The district became a city within a city that was clearly "Jewish" to the general population and to itself. As Poland transitioned from a rural to an industrial society, Muranów reflected the important role Jews played in Poland's industrialization and elicited a mixture of reactions from some Poles who saw it as a place of bustling energy to others who derided it as an area of disease and crime.[15]

But Muranów was not the only part of "Jewish Warsaw." A small group of wealthier Jews also lived in the city, and they acculturated into Polish society and supported the Jewish Enlightenment. They lived farther south on Marszałkowska, Królewska, and Nowy Świat Streets, and their greatest mark on the urban landscape came with the construction of the Great Synagogue in 1878. The Italian architect Leandro Marconi designed the building, which was constructed on Tłomackie Street next to Bank Square. Located in Warsaw's economic center, which Antonio Corazzi grandly redesigned in the 1830s, the synagogue signaled the arrival of Jews in the capital. But its singular presence underscored how marginal the Jewish Enlightenment was

Warsaw's Great Synagogue. (United States Holocaust Memorial Museum, courtesy of Bruce Tapper)

in Warsaw. In contrast to Berlin, which had more monumental synagogues, Warsaw had few other architecturally prominent houses of Jewish worship. Exceptions were the unique, two-story rotunda building in Praga erected in 1839 and the Nożyk synagogue on Grzybowski Square completed in 1901 mainly in Romanesque style. But the vast majority of the city's synagogues—totaling perhaps 300 by the interwar years—were simple prayer houses scattered in the areas where Jews lived and worked.[16] In short, for all its grandeur, the Great Synagogue reflected the religious orientation of only a sliver of the city's Jewish population. Warsaw Jews—and for that matter most Polish Jews—expressed little interest in acculturating into Polish society, with Zionism, socialism, and Orthodoxy offering more attractive ways of life and the rise of antisemitism lessening their attraction to Polishness.[17] The spatial effect was clear. Just as the Great Synagogue brought the Jews out of the ghetto, Muranów kept them back in: "The ghetto had been abolished long ago," the Polish-Jewish journalist Bernard Singer wrote about Muranów, "but there still existed an invisible wall that separated the district from the rest of the city."[18]

But the ultimate separation of Muranów came with the Nazi invasion of Poland. On November 15, 1940, the Nazis created the Warsaw Ghetto,

Ruins of Warsaw's Great Synagogue after the Nazis demolished the building in 1943. (Bildarchiv
Preussischer Kulturbesitz/Art Resource, New York)

which held at its height 460,000 Jews. It became the largest ghetto in Nazi-
occupied Europe. Ten-foot walls imprisoned Jews in central Warsaw, bor-
dering the old town in the east, including the entire area of Muranów in the
north, and stretching all the way down to Jerozolimskie Avenue in the
south. After the deportation of 280,000 Jews to Treblinka in July–August
1942, the ghetto shrank in size and came to a tragic end with the outbreak of
the Warsaw Ghetto Uprising in April 1943. The Nazis leveled the entire
northernmost part of the ghetto following a month of fighting and left in
their wake a field of ruins. In one final act, the Nazis demolished the Great
Synagogue on May 16, 1943. Jewish Warsaw was no more.

Resurrecting Warsaw among Sacred Ruins

A year later, in August 1944, the Home Army, the military arm of Poland's wartime opposition movement, initiated the city's second rebellion—the Warsaw Uprising—against the few German troops still stationed in the capital. Poles briefly regained control of Warsaw within a short three days, but the Nazis sent in reinforcements and launched aerial bombardments over the next sixty-three days before fighting ceased when Polish supplies ran out. As the Red Army sat idle on the east bank of the Vistula River, the Nazis destroyed the Polish opposition and set the city ablaze. Since Stalin wanted to extend control of the provisional Communist state that he had just established in Poland, he refused to help the Home Army and prevented allied aircraft from using Soviet-controlled airfields to bring in desperately needed supplies. He simply waited for the Nazis to do him the favor of crushing the Home Army, one of the last nuisances to his rule in Poland. The result was catastrophic. One hundred fifty thousand civilians and 16,000 soldiers died in the uprising, bringing the total number of Varsovians who perished during the Nazi occupation to around 685,000.[19]

In 1945, Warsaw stood eerily silent—a ghost town of desolate streets among burnt-out ruins. The Nazis had killed close to its entire Jewish population, expelled what was left of its civilian population, and torched its landscape. Of 25,498 buildings, 11,229 were totally destroyed and 3,879 partially so. The total destruction in Warsaw amounted to 21.9 billion złoty, which today would be about $54.6 billion.[20] Recovering from this disaster became a pressing task for the newly formed Communist state. In comparison to divided Berlin, Warsaw's rebuilding moved at an astonishingly quick pace. The PZPR realized that it could use the reconstruction of the capital to gain support among a population that had historically shown little interest in Communism. Publishing two newspapers about the rebuilding effort, *Stolica* and *Skarpa Warszawska,* the regime tactfully turned Warsaw into Poland's martyr city whose reconstruction from the rubble symbolized the nation's resurrection from the death of Nazism.

Poland's Communist provisional government wasted no time in crafting this narrative from Warsaw's ruins. In 1945, it created the Office for the Rebuilding of the Capital, which oversaw Warsaw's reconstruction. In one of its first acts, the agency organized an exhibition called "Warsaw Accuses" that displayed the capital's recovery from destruction. The exhibition appeared in Poland's National Museum before traveling to the United States. It included two sections of photographs. In a series of before-and-after photos, the first section documented the ruined "symbols" of Poland's "national civilization"—the Royal Castle, Theatre Square, St. John's Cathedral, and the Old Town Market Square. It framed Warsaw as the "modern Pompeii" and lodged a metaphorical accusation "before the tribunal of nations" against the Nazis for aiming to "kill culture and the nation."[21] The second part showcased images of the rebuilding effort already underway to display, literally and symbolically, Poland's determination to pick up from the ruins of the war.

Warsaw's rebuilding office faced the daunting task of carrying out this nearly sacred act of recovery. The agency was filled with left-wing, avant-garde architects who had formed the backbone of Poland's interwar urban modernist movement. Urban modernists hoped to overcome the perceived spatial ills of the late industrial city by radically altering the urban landscape. They called for creating distinct areas in the city for work, housing, and recreation that would be separated by greenery and linked by an efficient, rational transportation system. In 1933, the International Congress of Modern Architecture codified these basic principles in what came to be known as the Athens Charter. As participants in these international discussions, Poland's modernist architects hoped to apply functional designs to Warsaw's notoriously chaotic, cramped urban layout.[22] Plans for the new Warsaw came mainly from architects associated with the Warsaw Polytechnic School of Architecture, such as Roman Piotrowski, Helena and Szymon Syrkus, Barbara and Stanisław Brukalski, Bohdan Lachert, and Józef Szanajca. These architects now had the unprecedented opportunity to carry out in practice what before they had only imagined on paper.

In 1946, the first major plan for Warsaw emerged after months of discussion among Polish architects. Strongly influenced by urban modernism, it envisioned a "functional pattern" that organized the capital into separate parts for housing, industry, leisure, and green space.[23] The design received enthusiastic praise. In the United States, it appeared in an exhibition called "Warsaw Lives Again."[24] The pioneering modernist architect Walter Gropius and the architectural historian Lewis Mumford praised the creativity of the design, and Wacław Ostrowski, head of Warsaw's Division for Urban

Planning, noted the significance of the work: "Poland has today the possibility of building a capital that fully satisfies the needs of the state and the nation. If we seize this opportunity, Warsaw will come back to life from catastrophe better and more beautiful. If we miss this only chance, it will be a new catastrophe for the capital."[25]

Ostrowski had little reason to fear. In 1949, the PZPR announced the Six-Year Plan for the Reconstruction of Warsaw, which guided the capital's rebuilding. The plan kept the modernist, functional design of the 1946 proposal, but now called for building a distinctly socialist city.[26] With power fully in hand by 1948, the PZPR now turned to changing Poland's social, cultural, and economic life. Its revolutionary vision included reshaping the built environment. The Six-Year Plan stressed the development of industrial production as befitting a "city of workers" and the construction of new, bright housing complexes that transcended the dark, cramped tenement houses of the capitalist past, which had deprived workers of "greenery, recreation grounds, and cultural facilities."[27] The plan also called for the building of wide avenues and squares that could be used for parades and demonstrations. The new socialist Warsaw would transcend the economic injustices of the prewar capital by creating a rational, organized urban layout and including housing for workers right in the city center.[28]

But as much as the Six-Year Plan embraced socialist realism at the height of Stalinism, it continued many of the plans drawn up for Warsaw just after the war. The most important one was the massive re-creation of Warsaw's old town, which had been underway since 1945. Just after the war ended, historic preservationists from Warsaw's rebuilding office started reconstructing Warsaw's heavily damaged old town. Although some experts opposed reconstructing buildings that no longer existed, most agreed that select parts of Warsaw's past must be preserved.[29] The opening essay to the first issue of *Stolica* put it clearly: there were "no two ways about it among Polish society that the monuments of cultural and architectural value in Warsaw" must be "resurrected." Surrounded by prewar pictures of Warsaw's Royal Castle, medieval cathedral, and Market Square, the article claimed that Warsaw's "own eternal, living beauty" had to be rescued from the sea of rubble. "The resurrected walls of the old town will not be a lifeless creation, but will stand as a living link connecting the past to the present and the future."[30] Resurrecting Warsaw's architectural monuments involved more than just rebuilding broken stone. It involved a symbolic, performative act that displayed the survival of the nation after the Nazi occupation. As the newspaper article continued, "we are not a nation whose history began in January 1945 at the moment when the barbarians from the west were chased away. Our history dates back to the tenth century of the Christian era."[31] Such religious casting of Warsaw's reconstruction drew on deeply rooted national myths about Polish martyrdom that stretched back to Poland's imperial conquest by Prussia, Austria, and Russia in the 1790s. Although no longer a state from 1795 to 1918, Poland endured as a mental construct among poets, writers, and intellectuals who imagined it as the "Christ among the Nations"—the country crucified for the sins of the world that someday would return to rescue humanity. In both a real and an imagined sense, Warsaw became the symbol of Poland's wartime and postwar condition; destroyed and broken, yet resilient and invincible, its "sacred ruins" represented Poland's tragically heroic past and its "resurrection" from nearly total destruction. The reconstruction of the old town was no flight into a lost, romanticized past. A teleological, sacrosanct sense of time underpinned its logic as the past was possessed and utilized for a redemptive imagining of national recovery. The Six-Year Plan openly embraced this redemptive memory politics. The PZPR used the symbolism of the old town to underscore the basic point that the party was preserving the nation's past and identity.

The main person charged with putting this sacred task into practice was the historic preservationist Jan Zachwatowicz, who became Poland's general conservator for historic monuments in 1945. As smoke still billowed from the ruins of his beloved Warsaw, he formulated a new approach to historic preservation that rejected the long-standing predilection among preservationists for conserving an architectural site in its current state. Instead, he advocated for reconstructing buildings that no longer existed from the ground up. He argued that reconstructing historic buildings was necessary for Poland's revival after World War II: "The experiences of recent years—when Germany wanted to destroy us as a nation and demolished our historic monuments—have brought into dramatic clarity the significance of the monuments of the past for the nation. For the nation and its cultural monuments are one."[32] Zachwatowicz expressed little patience with previous concepts of historic preservation, especially the romantic, melancholic reflection on ruins. He harnessed the past for the present and the future; he

Jan Zachwatowicz, the architect of Poland's historic reconstruction program, oversaw the meticulous rebuilding of Warsaw's old town. (Narodowe Archiwum Cyfrowe)

had no time for melancholy, no time for reflecting on what had been lost, no time for wallowing in the past. Zachwatowicz saw historic preservation as key to "defending our culture, about fighting for one of the most fundamental elements of our immortal nation. It is not about sentimental affections, oldness, or longings, about that sort of song 'about old Warsaw.' "[33] He appreciated Poland's war-damaged monuments for their utility—they were to be rebuilt, re-created, and reconstructed. And rebuilt they were. Zachwatowicz encouraged the reconstruction of historic monuments across Poland, but his most important project was the rebuilding of Warsaw's old town. Lasting into the 1960s (and with some buildings into the 1980s), the effort entailed re-creating hundreds of buildings, based usually on photographs and drawings that Zachwatowicz and others had preserved during the Warsaw Uprising.

The effect became clear. Zachwatowicz turned Warsaw into a city of memory with selectively reconstructed streets. His team erected more than just a few memorials; memory animated their entire task. They transformed the old town into streets of staged historic monuments, which displayed the redemptive survival of the city and the nation. The old town became a space of spectacle and consumption, a space to experience, photograph, and witness national renewal. This restorative nostalgia denied the irreversibility of time by claiming that Warsaw's past had never been lost. It aestheticized the past. Zachwatowicz's preservationists venerated Warsaw's ruins and endowed them with what Walter Benjamin called the "aura" of art—the sense of distance in time and space that underlies claims to uniqueness, authenticity, and tradition. Warsaw's sacred ruins had to be restored because no less than Poland's survival appeared at stake. Warsaw suffered a violent, unnatural catastrophe. The ravages of time did not slowly decay its old town, but rather human violence did. This untimely death seemed arbitrary and haunting, yet also full of redemptive promise: the city's precious ruins could be brought back to life and with them the Polish nation. An acute failure to mourn the war's losses propelled this rescuing of the past from being past.[34]

The Ghetto Space

Brushing up just against the perimeter of the old town, Muranów never fit into this restorative and redemptive harnessing of the past. Historic preservationists did not worship the ghetto rubble as sacred ruins of the nation. The exhibition "Warsaw Accuses" included only one photo of Muranów out of fifty-six about Warsaw's destruction. The emerging narrative about Warsaw's death and rebirth marginalized the ghetto space. In an essay about postwar Warsaw, the sociologist Stanisław Ossowski brilliantly captured this acute absence of Muranów in postwar urban planning. He advocated precisely for the combination of new and old that formed the cornerstone of the Six-Year Plan. Turning to which parts of "old Warsaw" should be rebuilt, he argued that the "sphere of the historic" should mainly include buildings constructed before 1830. Here he followed many historic preservationists in Poland and divided Germany who defined the "historic" in terms of age, but he also argued that only buildings that aspire to "eternity" and fit into the future needs of the city should be preserved. Ossowski did not see the ghetto as

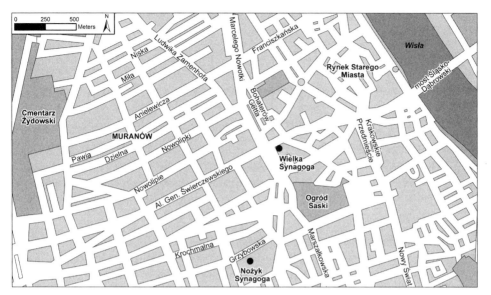

Map of postwar Muranów and the old town in central Warsaw. (Adapted from *Plan dzielnic centralnych miasta stołecznego Warszawy,* Państwowe Przedsiębiorstwo Wydawnictw Kartograficznych, 1955)

valuable under any of these criteria, noting that "Warsaw did not suffer . . . any serious loss of its historic monuments" in the district. He added that the "Jewish question" had "soured the atmosphere of the capital" and that Muranów was "to a considerable extent culturally foreign to Polish society."[35] This disinterest in Muranów as a historic space is not that remarkable; late nineteenth-century tenement houses were rarely defined as historically important cultural monuments in the late 1940s. What is striking, though, is Ossowski's emphasis on the foreignness of Muranów. Ossowski wrote a powerful critique of postwar antisemitism in Poland in 1946, so it would be difficult to read his remarks as overtly prejudicial, but they do reflect how the perception of Jews as culturally different influenced postwar conceptions of historical value and urban space.[36]

It is perhaps not surprising, then, that no Jewish sites appeared on Warsaw's list of historic monuments in 1945, and that one can search in vain through the hundreds of files located in the Warsaw city archive for any discussion of Muranów's historic value.[37] Indeed, urban planners saw the ghetto space as vacant terrain that could be cleared for building the socialist future. As

Zachwatowicz's team waded through the old town's sacred ruins searching for the minutest architectural piece to be saved, city workers plucked through the ghetto rubble and found nothing but bricks to use elsewhere.[38] The old town was preserved as sacrosanct traces of the Polish nation; Muranów was ultimately swept away as detritus. It was turned into a sprawling housing complex in the 1950s.

In 1945, Muranów was little more than a desolate field shaped by rolling hills of broken glass and crushed stone. "The aching eyes devour the scene," a survivor wrote just after the war. "Every stone, every heap of rubble is a reminder of the Holocaust. Here a protruding length of pipe, there a bent iron rail, there a charred sapling—these are what is left of our devastated world." Traveling across Poland just after the war, the Jewish writer Jacob Pat described walking over once familiar streets. "I gaze into the litter of stone, dust and brick: Traces of houses, charred covers of prayer books, a bill marked 'Paid,' a broken fork, a rusted spoon, a housewife's earthen pot, a ragged belt, the sole of a shoe."[39] In the early postwar years, this haunting space provoked attention from some Poles and Jews. In 1946, the first monument to the ghetto uprising was unveiled. Designed by the architect Leon Marek Suzin, it featured a red circular tablet raised above the ground by stone masonry with the following inscription in Hebrew, Yiddish, and Polish: "To those who fell in the unprecedented heroic battle for the dignity and freedom of the Jewish people, for a free Poland and for a man's liberation. From the Polish Jews." Reflecting not a competitive memory between Poles and Jews but a shared one, this plaque framed the uprising as part of both Polish and Jewish history.

Indeed, some non-Jewish Communists and left-wing Jews commemorated the ghetto uprising as a shared heroic moment of fighting against the Nazis. As the Marxist-Zionist leader Adolf Berman proclaimed, "the armed brotherhood of the Polish and Jewish radical workers' movement was not a phrase, but a fact. . . . The uprising in the ghetto, the first massive, revolutionary rebellion in Poland during the occupation, undoubtedly became one of the sparks that triggered the Polish resistance movement." A Communist newspaper wrote similarly: "Our party, the Polish Workers' Party, is proud that its forces, units of the People's Guard, were at the front of those who provided aid to the heroic defenders of the Warsaw ghetto from the 'Polish' side of the ghetto wall."[40] These words crafted a selective

On April 1, 1947, a group of Jewish survivors marches through the ruins of Warsaw, probably in observance of the fourth anniversary of the Warsaw ghetto uprising. Although the district would later be turned into a housing complex during the height of Stalinism, left-leaning Jews and non-Jews commemorated the space just after the war, where in their eyes a shared, heroic moment in Polish and Jewish history took place. (United States Holocaust Memorial Museum, courtesy of Leah Lahav)

memory of brotherhood, but they reflected a unique moment after the war when leftist Jews and Poles converged around a common language, memory, and purpose as they sought to build a better socialist future from the ruins of the past.

But these joint commemorative efforts initially had little impact on the plans, which first appeared in May 1945, to use the ghetto area for a new housing complex.[41] Once dominated by cramped tenement houses, Muranów quickly became one of the main areas in Warsaw for Communist urban planners to display their clearing away of the capitalist past for building the new socialist future. As architect Stanisław Albrecht put it, "the barbaric occupants of the city had destroyed not only assets of national culture, but also some sections which were not a credit to the city, but were the result of chaotic economic and social life in the nineteenth century." Albrecht likely meant here Muranów, or an area like it, which now could be used to build spacious new apartment buildings to display the triumph of socialism over the discredited industrial past. "Now, on the ruins and embers of Warsaw, will be built a new city, adjusted to new ways of life," he concluded.[42] But Muranów presented architects with a particularly difficult task. It was like no other area in the city. Urban planners had to deal not only with its enormous amount of rubble, so thick that most of it was not even removed, but also with its traumatic symbolism. The first designers of the new Muranów simply ignored the district's catastrophic past. Published in 1946–47, the first plans focused only on the technical details of the housing complex.[43]

But in 1948–49, a new architect, Bohdan Lachert, took over the project. As a young, avant-garde architect during the interwar period, Lachert had designed a number of housing complexes for the Warsaw Residential Cooperative. He clearly relished the opportunity now before him. "The task of rebuilding Warsaw is great," he said before a meeting of architects in 1946; "we are standing before the greatest architectural competition of all times in our history."[44] Lachert set out to transform Muranów into a new district of geometrically square, functional, and unadorned apartment buildings erected among ample green space. He was, though, clearly aware that his new project would be sitting on top of the former ghetto. During the war, his home became a refuge for opponents and targets of the Nazi regime, including Jews who had escaped from the ghetto.[45] Partly for practical reasons and partly for symbolic effect, he decided to build the apartments on top of the ruins and to use the rubble mixed with concrete for their foundation, dramatizing the idea of Warsaw reemerging to life from death and destruction. "The building of a new residential district in Muranów for the working class, on a mound of rubble," he wrote, "will testify to the emergence of a new life on the old ruins of social relations, on an area that commemorates the great barbarity of Nazism and the heroism of the Ghetto fighters." Lachert intended for his project to serve as a kind of oblique architectural encounter with the traumatic, abject past. He left the front of the buildings unstuccoed with dark red, rusty brick that would capture the somberness of the ghetto space. As Lachert explained, "the history of the great victory of the nation paid for through a sea of human blood, poured out for the sake of social progress and national liberation, will be commemorated in the Muranów project."[46]

Lachert intended, in fact, for his project to complement the Warsaw Ghetto Monument that had just been erected in 1948 slightly north of his housing complex. The idea for the monument came from the Central Committee of Jews in Poland. The committee settled on a design by the Polish-Jewish sculptor Natan Rapoport that heroically commemorated the Warsaw Ghetto Uprising, depicting on its western side proletarian-looking figures brandishing arms as they almost jump out from the granite in which they are carved. The eastern side shows twelve Jews, their heads slouched, reluctantly moving to their fate. Lachert, who wrote an expert commentary on the monument, praised Rapoport's design and stressed that the "grim atmosphere of this great mausoleum, erected among a cemetery of ruins, soaked with the blood of the Jewish nation" must remain as "new life comes into existence." In a symbolic sense, Lachert's apartment buildings would dramatize Rapoport's monument. "The ruins, in the largest possible amount, should remain in place, remembering the days of terror and resistance, constituting the ground on which a new city, a new life will be raised," Lachert continued. As his project manager put it simply, Muranów was "built from red rubble, as if from the blood of Warsaw."[47] Surrounding the ghetto monument, Lachert's project was the boldest attempt in postwar Warsaw to bring Polish and Jewish suffering together into a single progressive, socialist memory. One suffering did not have to diminish the other, and one memory did not have to belong just to one particular ethnic group; they could flow in distinct yet complementary directions as a way to recall the past in the hope of constructing a better future. Lachert made Jewish suffering central to Warsaw's redemptive narrative of national recovery. This "greatest tragedy ever known to history" is "for Warsaw one of the most valuable elements of homage for those who write the permanent, unforgettable pages of Polish history."[48]

But Lachert's plans proved short lived. In 1949–50, the PZPR moved away from the modernist principles that shaped Lachert's project and much of Warsaw's reconstruction up to that point. The party now embraced the new architectural style spreading across the Soviet bloc with the advent of Stalinism. Socialist realist architecture aimed to document the triumph of Communism over capitalism in the built environment. It hoped to transcend the "bourgeoisie" functionalism of urban modernism by constructing buildings socialist in content and national in form. What this meant in practice

The Warsaw Ghetto Memorial in 2007. (Photo by Michael Meng)

were monumental, ornate buildings across Eastern Europe constructed in a style that supposedly reflected a particular nation's architectural heritage. In 1955, Warsaw saw the completion of its most celebrated socialist realist architectural project—the Joseph Stalin Palace of Culture and Science. Built in grandiose style and towering nearly 800 feet, the building, Stalin's gift to Poland, dominated Warsaw's skyline then and still does today. The other major socialist realist project built in the city center, the Marszałkowska Housing District, involved neoclassical apartment buildings animated by murals and statues of workers.

In the wake of this architectural shift, Lachert's plans encountered stiff criticism for their modernist expression and alleged gloomy representation of the ghetto. In 1953, a stinging rebuke of his project appeared in the journal *Architektura*. The critic Jerzy Wierzbicki concluded bluntly, "Muranów does not attain a fully positive expression." Although Wierzbicki provided a formulaic rejection of previous "errors" at the peak of Stalinism, he also focused on Lachert's architectural representation of the ghetto space. Wierzbicki recognized "the difficult task" Lachert faced: "In 1940, Muranów was included in the ghetto by the Nazis in order to wipe it literally from the face of the earth three years after murdering the Jews enclosed in the ghetto. That once animated and lively part of the city was turned into a wasteland covered with a layer of rubble several meters deep." Yet he then attacked Lachert for attempting to give expression to this past. Wierzbicki criticized the construction of the apartments on top of the ruins, which he claimed had produced "an interesting, flat lay of the land and a monotonous terrain." The buildings themselves were also "monotonous, sad, and grey" with "rubble hallowed brick" creating a somber environment. In response, Lachert defended parts of his project, but conceded that he was mistaken to symbolize the ghastliness and destruction of the ghetto.[49]

The fallout proved decisive. The PZPR decided to stucco Lachert's buildings, painting on the white surface small designs with decorative ornaments implanted on the cornices. Muranów was now to be a cheerful, bright, and colorful place for the working class. The stuccoing had painted over literally and figuratively Lachert's attempt to reflect upon the ghetto space. The party wanted to erase the trauma that lay beneath the Muranów apartment buildings. It wanted pretty apartments to surround the Ghetto Monument that it started using in the 1950s to celebrate the triumphant pages of Polish Communist history with increasingly little focus on Jewish suffering.[50]

This new Muranów, sanitized of its past, now fit into Warsaw's eclectic blend of old and new, although quite differently than how Lachert had imagined it doing so. Historic reconstruction, urban modernism, and socialist realism formed intertwined aspects of Warsaw's rebuilding. The old town's meticulous reconstruction represented Poland's revival from the ruins of war, while Muranów reinforced the importance of the Communist order in that rebirth. "New, bright houses grow on the ruins of the ghetto," the main party newspaper cheerfully wrote; "these houses and the forest of scaffoldings that are rising up throughout all of Warsaw are evidence to the constantly growing power of peace and socialism."[51] Whereas Warsaw's old town appeared as a great national loss that must be restored, its rubble carefully

Ruins of the Warsaw ghetto, undated. (Narodowe Archiwum Cyfrowe)

Postwar Muranów in 1959. While the old town was carefully rebuilt as a massive project to save Poland's national past, Warsaw's center of prewar Jewish life was cleared away to make room for building the socialist future. (Narodowe Archiwum Cyfrowe)

sorted through for the tiniest architectural piece, Muranów was seen as scattered debris, rubble that could be shoveled up for the building of the socialist future. "As much as possible, bricks are being taken out from the remaining ruins, which is saving billions [of złoty] in terms of both money and labor," Warsaw's daily reported.[52] The new, socialist Muranów underscored the redemptive narrative of recovery that the Communist Party crafted from Warsaw's ruined landscape. It did so materially by providing the space for a massive housing complex and mnemonically by burying the ghetto's traumatic traces.

But much was lost in the process—almost every trace of Jewish Warsaw. The Great Synagogue on Tłomackie Street, lying in a pile of ruins on Muranów's southeastern edge, never made it onto the city's historic reconstruction program. The synagogue only rarely and fleetingly entered into discussions about the city's architectural history.[53] Its rubble was cleared away and the space stood empty until as late as the mid-1970s, when the city finally started building a skyscraper on the site. Although this project was approved in the 1950s, work on it languished for decades for reasons unknown (probably a combination of limited funding, worker strikes, and other building priorities). In 1976, the first metal shell of the building started to appear only for it to rust away before work resumed in the late 1980s. Redesigned in a light blue, reflective glass, the skyscraper finally opened its doors in 1991 and now towers over the northern part of central Warsaw.

Warsaw's oldest synagogue faced a similar fate. Constructed in 1836 by the architect Józef Lessel, the building was located in Praga on the eastern side of the Vistula River. Built in the original design of a two-story rotunda, the synagogue was damaged during the war, but not enough to require massive reconstruction. In late 1948, Warsaw officials put the building on the city's list of historic buildings after the Central Committee of Jews indicated that the Jewish community planned to rebuild it. But no restoration work ever followed. In 1951, the city suggested tearing the synagogue down to make room for a parking lot. A few years later, plans surfaced for it to be transformed into a local branch of the Registry Office, but in 1961 city officials demolished the synagogue to make room for a playground for a nearby preschool. Its rubble formed a knoll for children to slide down on snowy winter days.[54] A few Jewish sites did, however, survive both the war and postwar

Former site of Warsaw's Great Synagogue in 2007. (Photo by Michael Meng)

urban reconstruction. The Judaic Library, designed by Edward Eber and adjacent to the Great Synagogue, became the Jewish Historical Institute in 1947, one of the most important Jewish institutions in postwar Warsaw that published a number of studies on Polish-Jewish history. The city's two Jewish cemeteries and the Nożyk Synagogue near Grzybowski Square also remained, but all three fell into severe dilapidation over the 1950s and 1960s.

The Nożyk Synagogue was the only Jewish prayer house left after the Holocaust and subsequent postwar urban reconstruction. (Marian Gadzalski, 1964, ŻIH Photo Collection, ŻIH-III-3244)

Rebuilding Divided Berlin

Like Warsaw, Berlin lay in a pile of ruins in 1945. Although only 19 percent of the city's buildings were totally damaged, in certain parts of the city—above all in old Berlin—the destruction was enormous. Looking out on these ruins from the Brandenburg Gate, one architect could barely hold back his excitement: "I was beaming: what a possibility to plan here a new landscape, and what a possibility to remove this field of ruins and build new, modern houses."[55] But, unlike in Warsaw, such dreams of radical planning proved short-lived. Berlin's reconstruction took on a much more practical shape and lacked the kind of grand, redemptive memory politics that animated Warsaw's rebuilding. To be sure, Berlin's rubble-lined streets symbolized for Germans their own suffering. In film, literature, and photography, rubble became an integral component of German cultural memories of victimization. The "rubble women," who sifted through the city's shattered stone, emerged as iconic figures in the immediate postwar years. As civilians who withstood bombing raids, widowhood, evacuation, and rape, they became ideal figures to recast the Nazi past as a time of innocence, anguish, and hardship. Their tireless efforts to clear away the city's ruins, while struggling to feed their children, made women heroic symbols of sacrifice and strength that endured in both the FRG and the GDR.[56]

But these memories of victimization did not become centrally articulated in Berlin's postwar built environment like in Warsaw. Instead, urban planners opted for more modest designs in Hitler's former capital. The Nazi past complicated Berlin's reconstruction, as urban planners in both cities strove to distance themselves from what they perceived as Nazi architecture ("modernism" in East Berlin and "classical monumentality" in West Berlin). Moreover, Berlin was a divided city where grand building schemes for the entire city were simply not possible. The Cold War deeply shaped Berlin's postwar reconstruction and identity like in few other European cities. Surrounded by the GDR and cut off from the FRG, West Berlin became a city of display, a showcase of "democracy," "capitalism," and "freedom" on Communism's doorstep. East Berlin filled a similarly performative role as the capital of the GDR. Cold War competition between the two cities did produce a few major, symbolic rebuilding projects, but for the most part, hundreds of dull, functional apartment buildings came to dominate the postwar urban landscapes of both Berlins.[57]

The first designs for Berlin, though, emerged before its division. In May 1945, two groups of urban planners put forward ideas for the city's reconstruction. The Collective Plan, designed by the architect Hans Scharoun, envisioned a radical change of the urban landscape that left hardly any of the city's historic form in place. The Zehlendorf plan, conceived by Walter Moest, also called for little reconstruction of Berlin in favor of a new urban layout. These two plans reflected the dominant impulse to build an entirely new Berlin that shaped postwar reconstruction from the beginning, distinguishing it from Warsaw with its eclectic blend of modernism, socialist realism, and historic reconstruction. But these plans quickly proved impractical as Berlin split into two separate governments in late 1948. As Cold War tensions intensified with the Berlin Blockade, East and West Berlin moved in competing directions as both sought to use architecture to legitimize their respective democratic and Communist systems of rule.[58]

East Germany launched the opening salvo. In 1950, East German leader Walter Ulbricht announced the "sixteen principles" for making "cities destroyed by American imperialism more beautiful than ever."[59] At the height of Stalinism, he rejected urban modernism as "cosmopolitan" and advocated for centralized, hierarchical, and monumental designs that incorporated "progressive" national traditions from the German past. As urban planners in Warsaw combined the historic with the socialist, those in East Berlin staked out a more radical position and cleared away numerous war-damaged structures for the building of socialist realist ones. As a song by the Free German Youth went, "Away with the rubble and with erecting what's new. . . . Down with the old remains. Stone for stone then the new. . . . Berlin, you will be more beautiful than ever."[60] The SED's enthusiastic embrace of socialist realism intersected in obvious, if broad, ways with Nazi monumental architecture, but East German urban planners saw urban space as central to building an antifascist society. The Soviet Union provided a model of progressiveness for East German urban planners who believed that socialist realism would change German society after Nazism.[61]

These reformist ideas were implemented most ambitiously in East Berlin's district of Friedrichshain just east of the historic center. In 1949, the SED started construction on a wide, east-west boulevard named in Stalin's honor that became the GDR's most celebrated rebuilding project. The first buildings erected on the street were functional, modernist structures, but in 1950–51, Hermann Hanselmann redesigned the project to reflect the new trend of socialist realism. His long, wide boulevard, framed by ornamental apartment buildings held together on both ends with a pair of towers, became the showpiece of East Germany's new architectural style. The SED billed the project, which the party celebrated in newspapers, placards, and illustrated volumes, as proof of East Germany's supremacy over the West: Germany's future clearly lay in the hands of the SED, which was working tirelessly to rebuild a better, more progressive society.[62]

West Berlin's political leadership hardly sat by as the SED made these claims. In 1949, Mayor Ernst Reuter declared that "Berlin must become a showcase of freedom as well as a showcase of economic prosperity."[63] West Berlin's Department for Building and Housing faced the daunting task of converting these sweeping words into reality. How was Berlin to become a "showcase of freedom"? Did a "democratic" architecture exist to compete with socialist realism? Rolf Schwedler, West Berlin's rebuilding director

during the 1950s, argued for building a "modern Berlin."[64] Urban modernism would reflect West Berlin's development into a transparent, democratic
society. Its decentralized layout and functional, unadorned buildings would
provide a stark contrast to the ornamental, monumental buildings carried
out in East Berlin.[65]

Indeed, urban modernism animated the most celebrated rebuilding project of West Berlin's postwar reconstruction—the reconstruction of the
Hansa Quarter near Berlin's sprawling Tiergarten park. Allied bombs destroyed this traditionally middle-class neighborhood where a sizeable Jewish
population had once lived, and the rubble was cleared away to make room for
a modernist apartment complex. The project aimed to transcend the cramped,
stone structures of the district's past and secure a better future with functional buildings set in harmony with the nearby park. The "city of tomor-
row," as the project was called, would transcend the alleged atomization of
the masses and restore balance to the family. Based on a heterosexual model
of society and patriarchal gender stereotypes, the Hansa Quarter offered an
ideal place for women to raise children and a relaxing setting for men after
work. It removed the "added burden" placed on female wage earners by suggesting that they return to homemaking and allow children once again to
grow up in a "loving and secure" environment.[66]

Initiated in direct response to the Stalin Avenue project, the Hansa Quarter was also unabashedly Cold War theatrics. It showcased the moral superiority of the West by guaranteeing individual freedom through its decentralized layout among ample green space. As the winning architects explained,
"the free person does not want to live in a camp or in houses that are lined
up one after the other like workers' barracks."[67] As if these words were not
enough to provoke East Berlin, West Berlin's leadership went a step further
and launched in 1958 an international architectural competition for rebuilding the entire city. The designs that came out of the competition never
materialized, but West Berlin made its point by staging a competition that
ignored the existence of the east. Mayor Otto Suhr called the plans a "de-
monstrative documentation of freedom" that "proved the achievement of
the Western world."[68]

The SED interpreted this move as the sheer provocation that it was, but
proved unable to respond to it. The party's reconstruction of East Berlin
languished behind that of West Berlin and failed to deliver on its own inces-

sant promises to build a "socialist center" after grandly starting with Stalin Avenue. In 1950, Ulbricht ordered the destruction of Berlin's famous war-damaged castle to make room for a large demonstration square and a central building that was to form the center of East Berlin, but the space then stayed virtually empty for the next twenty-five years. After numerous plans and contesting visions, the SED finally announced an international competition for East Berlin, which the party hastily put together in response to the one in West Berlin. With the aim of turning Berlin into a "showcase of the socialist camp," the design contest was nothing less than a debacle: a mere 124 architects expressed interest in the East Berlin competition, as opposed to 392 for the West Berlin one.[69] The ideas that came out of the competition produced nothing, and the SED ultimately settled on a futuristic, 1,200-foot television tower (*Fernsehturm,* 1965–69) and a glossy, modernist-style "Palace of the Republic" (*Palast der Republik,* 1973–76) to constitute the focal point of its "socialist" city that it had been planning since the late 1940s. Conflict within the party about how best to build a "socialist center" and inconsistent ideas about the GDR's prescribed architectural style delayed consensus for years. The result became clear. As the SED moved away from monumental architecture and returned to practical, industrial modernism by the late 1950s during de-Stalinization, the urban landscape of the two Berlins gradually appeared more alike than different. The ideologically driven urban planning of the early 1950s had waned as both cities focused on practical projects such as roads and housing. The simple, unadorned apartment buildings that emerged throughout West Berlin differed from those in East Berlin in craftsmanship and size, but not much in architectural style and form. Whereas Warsaw combined historic reconstruction, modernism, and socialist realism in a redemptive recasting of the city's rebirth from the ashes of war, urban planners in East and West Berlin embraced a practical form of modernism that ended up demolishing many of the city's historic buildings.

Jewish Spaces in Divided Berlin

This destruction took place across Berlin, but the demolition of Jewish sites stood out in particular as erased symbols of the city's traumatic past. The early postwar history of Jewish sites unfolded differently in divided Berlin than in Warsaw for several reasons. One was the different geographies of prewar Jewish life in the two cities and the extent of their wartime destruction. Unlike in Warsaw, Jews in Berlin were more spread out across the city; the main spatial markers of Jewish Berlin were individual sites rather than a distinct, concentrated area of town. Although these spaces suffered heavy damage during *Kristallnacht* and the war, many more still existed after 1945 than was the case in the demolished district of Muranów. Another difference was that Berlin became the center of postwar Jewish life in divided Germany, whereas Warsaw did not, as the rebuilding of Jewish life in Poland shifted westward to Lower Silesia. The Jewish communities in divided Berlin were small, but they had strong Jewish leaders who contested the handling of Jewish sites, especially in West Berlin.

Jewish life reemerged in Berlin just days after the war ended. The city became a transitory home to tens of thousands of Jewish displaced persons, or DPs. Most eventually left Berlin, but some Jewish DPs stayed, along with several thousand German Jews who survived the Holocaust, to build a new Jewish community in the city. In May 1945, Rabbi Martin Riesenburger held the first Jewish religious service in postwar Berlin, and several months later, six synagogues reopened across the city.[70] As the first occupying power to arrive in Berlin, the Soviets installed Berlin's first postwar government, made up largely of German Communists who recognized early on the needs of the Jewish community. Just two weeks after the war ended, Berlin's municipal government established the Liaison for Jewish Affairs, directed by the Christian Democrat Siegmund Weltlinger. An active member of Berlin's Jewish community during the 1930s, Weltlinger survived the Holocaust and set out to restore Jewish life in the city. He worked to secure financial aid for the Jewish community and combat antisemitism. "An enduring presence of Jewish life can only be built," he wrote in 1946, "when the ideology of racism in Germany is overcome and when the Jews are fully compensated for their injustices."[71] With help from officials such as Weltlinger and with crucial support from the American Jewish Joint Distribution Committee (JDC), Jewish life reemerged in Hitler's former capital. In March 1947, Berlin's Jewish community had 7,807 members.[72]

Still, the challenges of rebuilding Jewish life in postwar Berlin were daunting. With its bank accounts confiscated and its physical possessions sold, burned, destroyed, or bombed, Berlin's Jewish community had lost nearly

In 1946, German, Jewish, and French officials attend the reopening of a synagogue in the French sector of Berlin. The city became home to the largest Jewish community in postwar Germany. (United States Holocaust Memorial Museum, courtesy of Herbert Friedman)

everything and had to rely on city and occupying authorities for almost everything, even requesting in 1946 "a box of small candles" for Chanukah.[73] As late as 1949, the JDC, which had an office in Berlin, concluded that the community is "far from self-supporting."[74] Moreover, antisemitism persisted in Berlin and throughout occupied Germany. The U.S. military concluded in numerous memos that Germans continued to harbor negative views toward Jews, and a government report written in the Soviet zone singled out antisemitism as the most pressing concern among Jews. The Jewish communities "request a vigorous campaign," the memo explained, "to fight back an already resurgent antisemitism. Just recently tombstones at the Jewish cemetery in the district of Weißensee were damaged and knocked over without any prosecution of the perpetrators."[75] In 1947, the Jewish community reported destruction at another Jewish cemetery just outside Berlin.

Notifying the Soviet Military Administration about the incident, the community ended its letter ominously: "We believe that such acts of destruction are the beginning of a new wave of antisemitism."[76] But just how seriously the Soviets took these warnings is unknown. Some of their own soldiers were apparently involved in vandalizing Jewish property. In 1945, the Soviet military used the Jewish cemetery in Weißensee for "military exercises."[77] When the Jewish community complained, Soviet authorities responded that it was not "members of the Soviet army" who were mishandling the cemetery, but rather "bandits who are dressed in Russian uniforms."[78]

It was thus in the midst of this early postwar world—defined by hope, concern, occupation, and scarcity—that Berlin's Jewish community negotiated with city and occupying officials about its property. In 1945, the Soviets allowed the Jewish community to establish the synagogue on Oranienburger Street as its headquarters and the Western powers permitted it to use several other synagogues in each of their sectors, but most Jewish sites remained abandoned and destroyed.[79] Since the community had few funds to rebuild them, it had to rely on assistance from municipal and occupying officials, who rarely seemed eager to help. The U.S. Office of Military Government denied requests to fund repairs on the synagogue on Münchener Street in Schöneberg, and the Berlin government refused to assist in rebuilding the synagogue on Pestalozzi Street in Charlottenburg.[80] Whatever assistance the Jewish community did eventually secure came only after months of repeated requests. In 1947, Jewish community leaders Julius Meyer and Hans-Erich Fabian requested money to restore Berlin's three main Jewish cemeteries. Berlin's mayor, Ferdinand Friedensburg, promised "to do everything in order to bring about a new trust between the Jewish people and the wider populace, and to this end to restitute as much as possible the spiritual, physical, and material injustices of the Jews."[81] But months passed with no action. In July 1947, the city indicated that it would repair select Jewish sites, but it took another eight months for the money to be approved and then months more for the funds finally to reach the Jewish community.[82]

Such haggling for even the smallest amount of assistance became slightly easier with the official split of the Berlin Jewish community into two separate organizations in 1953. The Jewish community stayed unified throughout the city's division in 1948, but broke up just after the SED's attack against "cosmopolitanism." In East Berlin, a tiny community with almost no money emerged in the wake of this antisemitic campaign. The SED now confronted the choice of either supporting the Jewish community or simply allowing it to wither away. Although the SED might have preferred the latter given its antireligious stance, it realized that having no Jewish community in the capital of the antifascist Germany would be paradoxical to say the least. In 1953, the East Berlin government thus agreed to give the Jewish community 300,000 marks to rebuild its synagogue on Ryke Street, which was constructed in classical and local styles inspired by the nearby brick churches of the surrounding region.[83] East Berlin officials decided to assist the community not for any architectural or preservationist reasons—not because the synagogue represented a monument of the German past worthy of protection—but for practical and political reasons. In January 1953, East Berlin's Jewish community had between 45,000 and 52,000 marks in its account.[84] The city supported a project necessary for the Jewish community's religious survival and one with clear political implications. Renamed the "Temple of Peace," the synagogue became home to a Jewish community loyal to the party. Its religious leader, Martin Riesenburger, served the interests of the SED well by often publicly chastising West Germany for its "antisemitism" and clarifying the GDR's critical stance toward Israel. Riesenburger represented a classic example of the handful of German Jews who became attracted to Communism's egalitarian message. Some leading Jewish Marxist politicians, writers, artists, and academics returned to East Germany and reached high positions in the party. Seeing themselves less as Jews and more as Communists, they worked to build an antifascist, Communist state and usually had little interest in religious life, but Riesenburger was exceptional in that he did. His support for the SED proved crucial to the Jewish community's survival. When it came to allocating money, the party often noted his fight against the "antisemitic leadership in West Germany."[85]

This political relationship, though, had limitations. The state's support was not enough to preserve or even keep standing East Berlin's many Jewish sites. In 1956, a SED memo noted that numerous Jewish sites damaged during *Kristallnacht* and World War II had yet to be repaired. The list included some of Berlin's most prominent Jewish relics: the Moorish three-domed synagogue on Oranienburger Street, the city's oldest Jewish cemetery on Great Hamburger Street, and Europe's largest Jewish cemetery in Weißensee.[86] Many of these sites were falling into disrepair or were threatened by new

Martin Riesenburger at the reopening of the Ryke Street Synagogue in East Berlin on August 30, 1955. East Berlin's small Jewish community used the synagogue throughout the history of the GDR. (Bundesarchiv Bild 183–21038–0007)

Ruins of the synagogue on Johannis Street 16 in East Berlin in 1953. (Bildarchiv Pisarek/ akg-images)

building projects. Writing in 1957 about the Jewish cemetery on Schön-hauser Avenue in Prenzlauer Berg, a tourist noted that "most of the tomb-stones have been knocked down or smashed."[87] In the late 1950s and early 1960s, the city wanted to build a sports complex on what was left of Berlin's oldest Jewish cemetery on Great Hamburger Street in Mitte, but resistance from Riesenburger ultimately precluded this from happening.[88]

The Jewish community's heavily damaged synagogues suffered an even severer fate: they were cleared away in the 1950s and 1960s. Built largely in the mid-nineteenth century and clustered mostly in the north central part of Mitte, they included synagogues large and small: Heidereuter Lane 4, Johannis Street 16, Kaiser Street 29, Artillerie Street 40, and Gerlach Street 19. As one of the oldest synagogues in Berlin and the site where thirty-five Jews were hanged in the sixteenth century, the synagogue on Gerlach Street elicited an intriguing exchange between the Jewish community and city officials. In the mid-1950s, the city placed the synagogue under historic preservation at the suggestion of the Jewish community, but changed its position a decade later. In order to make room for the rebuilding of East Berlin's city center, city officials decided to tear down the synagogue. Lacking the power to halt the decision because it did not own the property, the Jewish community agreed with the city's plans, only asking that the plaque remembering the death of the thirty-five Jews be saved.[89]

Berlin's most famous synagogue suffered a similar fate. Although the New Synagogue on Oranienburger Street survived *Kristallnacht* with only minor damage thanks to a Berlin precinct police chief who forced the Nazis out of the building, it sustained severe damage during the war. In 1958, the SED ordered the destruction of its large, bombed-out sanctuary but left the façade standing by request of the East Berlin Jewish community. It is unclear why the SED demolished the 3,200-seat sanctuary. No documents exist on the decision, but the party's general ambivalence toward Jews likely played a role. Indeed, three years after the building's destruction, the East Berlin Jewish community sent a letter to the GDR minister for church affairs requesting that the remnants of the synagogue be restored in order to house a Jewish museum. "There is no more important place than this site," the community wrote, "to build a Jewish museum in the GDR to bear witness to Nazi barbarism, the destruction of Berlin Jewry, and to the Jews who once lived in Germany."[90] The state ignored the request. It apparently did not want to build a Jewish museum in such a highly symbolic and centrally located space. The remnants of the New Synagogue remained damaged for the next four decades.

Such neglect of Jewish sites was, however, hardly limited to East Berlin. Although much of the Jewish community's property existed in the east, a significant amount was also located in West Berlin, where nearly all of it disappeared from the urban landscape over the 1950s. As in East Berlin,

The bombed-out façade of the New Synagogue in East Berlin in 1960. (Landesarchiv-Berlin)

West Berlin's Jewish community had little power to stop this from happening because it did not own all of its property. The Jewish Restitution Successor Organization (JRSO) retained ownership of unused property until 1955, when a settlement turned it over to the state of Berlin. From that point on, just as in East Berlin, the fate of Jewish sites hinged on decisions by municipal

Ruins of the New Synagogue in East Berlin on July 21, 1961. (Associated Press)

officials. As West Berlin officials prolonged negotiations with the JRSO over a settlement, Jewish communal property deteriorated with each passing year. Jewish sites remained virtually in the same damaged condition that they had been in since 1938. They were some of the last ruins along other- wise reconstructed streets.

The synagogue on Fasanen Street in Charlottenburg is a case in point. Designed by Ehrenfried Hessel in 1910–12, the synagogue featured three large cupolas and vaulted tunnel passageways that drew on early Christian Byzantine architecture. The massive stone structure survived the war intact, but the Nazis had destroyed its interior when they set the building on fire in November 1938. After the war, district authorities showed no interest in providing even the most basic forms of protection for the structure after repeated cases of vandalism. By the early 1950s, the synagogue had turned into such a run-down place that the police deemed it a threat to the public. "The site of the ruins," one police report noted, "is being frequented by asocial elements and prostitutes and thus is to be regarded as a danger to public safety."[91] Another report went into more detail: "[The site of the ruins] is very strongly contaminated. An abundant amount of human feces, litter, and underwear were found there among other things. . . . Since residents of the surrounding houses are always complaining of rat infestation . . . not just a quick sanitation of the ruins must take place because they are probably the source of the rats but also the property needs to be fenced in to preclude further defilement."[92]

City officials recommended that the synagogue be enclosed, but demanded that the JRSO pay for it. The JRSO was hardly amused. In a lengthy letter, it argued that Jewish organizations were not responsible for securing buildings destroyed by the Nazis. The JRSO pointed to the participation of the local police during *Kristallnacht* and implied that their actions bore similarity to those of the current force in the supposedly democratic, post-Nazi West Germany:

> The property in question was previously a synagogue, which during *Kristallnacht* was destroyed by unknown persons, but, as you ought to know, this was induced by the Reich government at the time and carried out under the acquiescence of the appropriate security forces. The fact that the building is currently in such a condition that it provides safe haven for asocial elements and prostitutes is not because of wartime destruction but because of *Kristallnacht*. So, from now on, the Jewish Trust Organization is supposed to cover the costs because the security forces cannot protect this once holy site, which was desecrated in such a terrible manner, from further desecration. Money set aside for charitable purposes is supposed to be spent to remove a danger to public safety that arose because the security forces at the time were not able to prevent this danger from happening. We assume that your letter

to us was processed just routinely without taking into consideration the peculiarity of this case.[93]

If the FRG signaled any break with the Nazi past, the JRSO certainly did not think so. It saw the current defilement of the synagogue as a continuation of Nazi attacks against Jewish property. Perhaps not surprisingly, city officials disagreed. Failing to consider the JRSO's point, the Charlottenburg building department noted dryly that "the costs accrued for property owners of damaged or destroyed buildings . . . are part of the losses of the war."[94] Although the district later agreed to cover temporarily the costs of enclosing the synagogue, it insisted on getting reimbursed for the paltry 522 marks that it spent on the fence. In an internal memo, the Charlottenburg district mayor noted that the city's continued demand for the funds was "legally in order—politically unjustifiable!"[95] Still, district officials continued to press their case and even turned to the restitution office for funds. The restitution office concluded that the JRSO was responsible for reimbursing the money in light of the global agreement that it had just signed with West Berlin.[96]

It is unknown if the city ever received its 522 marks, but the global agreement of 1956 proved to be the turning point in the building's postwar fate. Since the city now owned the building, it could do whatever it wanted with it. At first, the department for urban planning suggested demolishing the synagogue to make space for a parking lot in light of "pressing parking problems."[97] But no sooner did it make this suggestion than a radically different proposal surfaced. Aware of both the symbolic importance of the synagogue and its pitiful postwar treatment, West Berlin's political leadership intervened, halted plans to use the space for a parking lot, and decided to build a Jewish center instead. City and Jewish leaders had been discussing the idea for the center since the immediate postwar years, but plans crystallized after a series of high-level meetings among West Berlin Jewish community leader Heinz Galinski, Mayor Otto Suhr (SPD, 1955–57), Mayor Willy Brandt (SPD, 1957–66), and federal president Theodor Heuss (SPD, 1949–59). In 1956, West Berlin's parliament approved of the "erection of a cultural center for the Jewish community." The measure subtly presented the project as a form of restitution: "The Jewish community of Berlin had until 1933 numerous cultural institutions, which all fell victim during the Nazi period and especially during *Kristallnacht*. Since the restitution law does not earmark funds for the reconstruction of such cultural institutions, the parliament sees it as Berlin's honorable duty to make available at the very least the necessary funds from its budget for such a cultural establishment."[98]

On November 10, 1957, hundreds of West Berliners, Jewish leaders from across the world, and leading city and federal officials gathered for the center's groundbreaking in front of the damaged synagogue, a place that only months ago had been a hangout for what the police derisively called asocials.[99] With the Israeli, Berlin, and German flags flying in front of the building, Willy Brandt and Heinz Galinski led the festive occasion, which was as much about the past as it was about the future. Held just a day after the anniversary of *Kristallnacht* in front of the still monumental yet scarred synagogue, the ceremony carried different meanings for Jews and Germans gathered there. Jewish leaders saw the building as a monument to the Holocaust and a functional space for building a permanent community in postwar Germany. The ruins of the synagogue reflected the collective destruction of Germany's Jewish community, which strongly shaped the conflicted identity of the postwar community. Many Jews who survived living in Hitler's capital preferred to leave and saw life in Germany as merely a temporary waiting station on their way to North America, Latin America, or the Middle East. As Rabbi Leo Baeck put it in 1945, "the history of Jews in Germany has found its end."[100]

But some Jews stayed, and West Germany's Jewish leaders, such as Heinz Galinski, Siegmund Weltlinger, Hendryk George van Dam, and Karl Marx, became committed to rebuilding Jewish life in postwar Germany. Similar to Riesenburger's attraction to the liberating power of Communism, they believed that reviving Jewish life was crucial to democratization and proof that Nazism had not made Germany *judenrein*. "I have always held the view," Galinski observed in the early 1990s after serving for over forty years as West Berlin's community leader, "that the Wannsee Conference cannot be the last word in the life of the Jewish community in Germany."[101] This resiliency in full awareness of the Holocaust shaped the basic contours of Jewish identity for the generation of survivors who stayed in Germany. The community center reflected this mix of past and future. The winning design envisioned a simple functional building that included the old building's surviving portal and three glass convex windows on the roof that mimicked the synagogue's three towering cupolas. While the building's modernist design

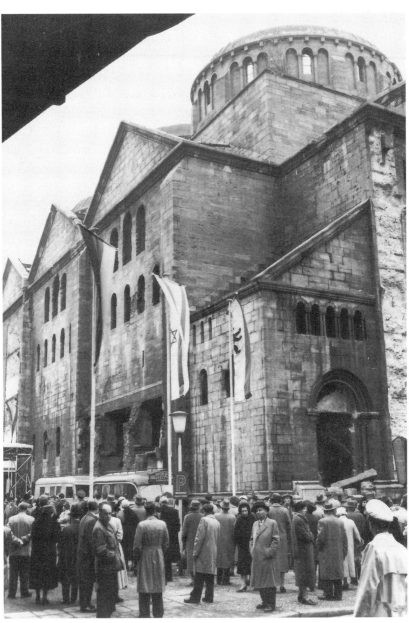

Ceremonial groundbreaking of the Jewish community center in West Berlin on
November 10, 1957. (Landesarchiv Berlin)

Demolition of the synagogue on Fasanen Street in West Berlin in 1958. (The Granger Collection, New York)

expressed the new beginning of Jewish life, the portal and cupolas rein-forced the importance of remembering the past. As the Jewish community put it in a festive book prepared for the occasion, "a piece of the façade of the old synagogue will be incorporated into the new building as a way to re-member both the great times of Jewish life and culture in Berlin as well as the terrible times lived through during the Hitler regime."[102]

If the erection of the center reflected the Jewish community's internal negotiation between remembering catastrophe and rebuilding communal life, its meaning for West Berlin's political elite, dominated by the Social Democrats, was refracted through a qualitatively different set of concerns. In contrast to Adenauer's cautious approach toward dealing with the Holocaust,

Heinz Galinski in front of the Jewish community center on January 20, 1967. He led West Berlin's Jewish community from 1949 to 1992. (Bundesarchiv B 145 Bild-P094007)

some Social Democrats believed that reflecting upon the catastrophe of the past was essential for West Germany's democratic redemption. Remembrance had cathartic effect by producing at least theoretically a less racist citizenry through "enlightened knowledge."[103] In West Berlin, the Social Democrats controlled a majority in parliament for nearly thirty years, and the city's two dominant political leaders of the 1950s—Ernst Reuter and Willy Brandt—reflected more openly on the Holocaust than members of the other mainstream parties did at the time. In 1951, Reuter described *Kristallnacht* as a "day of disgrace for Germany" when "thousands of our fellow citizens and fellow human beings" had their "property destroyed" and their "freedom and life deprived."[104] Reuter spoke vaguely—the word "Jew" never appeared once in his statement—but two years later, on the tenth anniversary of the Warsaw Ghetto Uprising, he remarked directly. "The terrible attack on the ghetto," he remarked, "was only a small link in a large chain in a terrible campaign of destruction against the Jews in Germany and against the Jews in all of occupied Europe that the National Socialist regime undertook and pursued with a scientific-technical precision to the bitter end."[105]

Similarly, Willy Brandt advanced reconciliation between Germans and Jews in the name of democratic renewal during his time as mayor. His genuflection in 1970 as chancellor in front of the Warsaw Ghetto Monument is well known, but already in 1939, while in exile, he wrote about the persecution of the Jews and argued that restitution must be an important component of rebuilding Germany.[106] At the groundbreaking for the new community center, he emphasized the need for recalling Germany's past and stressed the contribution of Jews to Berlin's history. He noted that "the enormous sacrilege and bloody shame of our recent past" could be overcome only "when we do not forget, but courageously deal with" the Nazi past.[107] These words were probably spoken genuinely by a staunch resister to Nazism, but they also carried clear political implications. The erection of the community center displayed the "progressiveness" of the democratic West. The return of Jews to West Berlin produced a redemptive script of German renewal through the liberal, democratic celebration of "cosmopolitan Berlin": the community's visible presence dramatically signaled West Berlin's departure from Hitler's capital.[108] In this sense, the building of the community center likely reflected the concerns of West Berlin's political elite more than those of the city's wider population. Newspapers had limited coverage about the center, and the few articles that did appear only obliquely touched on its significance.[109] In short, the linguistic, mnemonic, and political appropriation of Jewish space as a marker of postfascist rehabilitation—what later I will call redemptive cosmopolitanism—had not yet become embraced by broader segments of German society.

Restored fragment of the synagogue on Fraenkelufer in 2010. In 1959, most of the
building was demolished, but this portion was rebuilt as a prayer house for West Berlin's
Jewish community. (Photo by Daniel Brunet)

Indeed, the building of the community center proved exceptional. More
common was the clearing away of the "blight" of damaged Jewish sites across
West Berlin. In Kreuzberg, for example, the local mayor complained about
the crumbling condition of his district's synagogue, even refusing to walk
foreign visitors by it.[110] Built in 1913–16 to serve the Jewish community's
growing population, this large, neoclassical synagogue stood severely damaged for over twenty years. After the war, the Jewish community used a small
part of the building for religious services, but repairs were badly needed. In
one of its requests, the Jewish community reminded the mayor that the
synagogue had been "completely destroyed," to which either he or one of his
assistants scribbled in the margins "during the war or in 1938?"[111] In 1959,
district officials demolished most of the building, but a small fragment was
restored and was used by the Jewish community as a prayer house.

But the most concentrated erasure of Jewish sites took place around the
Tiergarten, where three damaged synagogues were cleared away: Lützow
Street 16, Levetzow Street 7–8, and Siegmund Court 11. As the largest of the

three buildings, the synagogue on Levetzow Street provoked the most attention. Located in the Hansa Quarter and built in neoclassical style with four large pillars defining its façade, the synagogue was damaged during *Kristallnacht* and the war, but its imposing structure remained intact after 1945. Writing ten years later, city officials complained to the JRSO about the poor condition of the building, to which the JRSO responded tersely: "We would like to point out that the synagogue was not damaged during the war, but was willfully destroyed in November 1938." Citing two paragraphs of the Nazi order that required Jewish organizations to pay for the damages of *Kristallnacht,* the JRSO continued: "Now, in 1955, the building regulation department is going so far as to demand that the owner of a destroyed synagogue pay for clearing away damage caused in 1938." It then repeated in Latin a quip from the Roman satirist Juvenal: "It is difficult not to write satire about that (Difficile est saturam non scribere)."[112] Several months later, the synagogue was torn down and the area was turned into a playground.

As part of the old Hansa Quarter now being transformed into a modernist utopia of green spaces and functional buildings, this synagogue captures particularly well the ambivalent position of historic structures in general and Jewish spaces in particular in West Berlin's postwar reconstruction. In building the new Berlin, urban planners reacted against the compactly built, ornately designed historicist tenement houses that once made up areas such as the Hansa Quarter. This modernist, universalistic aesthetic built over the particularity of the district's previous form and identity. The reordering of urban space showcased West Berlin's transition into a transparent, democratic, and free city. Restoring war-damaged buildings played little role in this recasting of West Berlin's future, but Jewish sites were disregarded like few other historic structures in the city. In the late 1940s, Weltlinger wrote to Berlin's mayor about a synagogue on August Street that recently had been turned into a barn. Pleading that this "holy site" not be "debased any longer," he said: "I am convinced that you will show full understanding for the feelings of the Jewish community; one would probably hardly even think of putting a barn in a Protestant or Catholic church."[113] Berlin's empty Jewish spaces, destroyed during *Kristallnacht* with the participation and awareness of the general population, had become abandoned in the truest sense of the word.

Indeed, perhaps not surprisingly, the main historic structure that was saved in West Berlin was a church. Built in 1895 in neo-romantic style and

damaged in November 1943, the Kaiser Wilhelm Church was initially slated
to be torn down, but a storm of protest from Berliners in the late 1950s, led
by *Der Tagesspiegel*'s "Save the Tower" campaign, saved it from destruction.
Berliners saw the church as an evocative ruin that reflected the tragedy and
suffering of war. Preserved in bombed-out form, it stood out in an area
dominated by shops, tourists, cars, and businesses. Just off the bustling avenue of shoppers on a quiet street stood the Jewish community center on
Fasanen Street, and farther down another synagogue once existed on Pas-
sauer Street. In 1950–51, the synagogue was leveled to make room for a parking garage for West Berlin's *KaDeWe* department store.[114] Unlike the church,
but like so many other Jewish sites across Berlin, this synagogue did not
evoke mourning and concern. Berliners did not perceive it as a valuable ruin
that had to be saved; they saw it as rubble that could be erased for the building of something better.

The Anxiety of the Holocaust

In the ruined landscapes of Berlin and Warsaw, postwar urban renewal
cleared away numerous Jewish sites in the 1950s. In Warsaw, urban planners
combined modernism, socialist realism, and historic reconstruction both to
preserve the nation's cultural remnants and to secure the socialist future. A
less monumental planning scheme shaped Berlin's reconstruction. With the
exception of the Stalin Avenue and the Hansa Quarter projects, urban planners in both Berlins focused on meeting practical needs such as housing and
transportation. Still, a shared reformist belief in progress shaped the rebuilding of all three cities. Urban planners aimed to build a better, more
modern urban landscape that transcended the perceived ills of the late
nineteenth-century industrial city. With renewal, though, came destruction: Jewish rubble was swept away in the euphoria and promise of postwar
urban reconstruction with almost little concern or thought.

But Jewish sites did not just fall victim to the ruinous dialectic of urban
renewal. Urban planners, historic preservationists, city officials, and ordinary citizens also neglected and erased Jewish sites because they conjured
up discomforting memories that unsettled the prospect of building new
postwar societies. Warsaw became a city of carefully constructed temporal
markers that narrated Poland's wartime suffering and postwar redemption.

This deeply symbolic rebuilding scheme delivered a normative future of socialist renewal rooted in a re-created Polish past. It promised repair, recovery, and redemption—all of which the shattered spaces and memories of the ghetto area disrupted, indeed, left potentially unachievable, if they were not somehow normalized into the banality of postwar life. The ghetto space in the heart of Warsaw triggered the anxiety of the Holocaust like few other places in Poland. As one gigantic corpse, it laid bare the revolting finitude of the self. The corpse is the "utmost of abjection"—"it is death infecting life," Julia Kristeva writes. Lachert called Muranów a "cemetery of ruins" soaked with Jewish blood.[115] What is more, Muranów reflected the tragic breakdown of Polishness in the face of human suffering. Why would Poles want to encounter the collapse of their very identity as a nation—the "Christ among the Nations," the "For Our Freedom and Yours," the romantic mythos of the brotherhood of victims—that fell apart before reaching the ghetto walls? Most Poles did not. Instead, they valorized their resistance against the Nazis and recalled their own suffering during the Nazi occupation.[116] If the ghetto space had been where the Nazis imprisoned and killed non-Jewish Poles, who bravely resisted these murderous designs, it might have been handled differently after the war. Perhaps its ruins would have been preserved as a gigantic site of memory as the French did with the martyred village of Oradour-sur-Glane.[117] But the ghetto was never used to narrate Poland's suffering, with the important exception of Lachert's bold, remarkable plans, which were ultimately rejected. Writing in 1952 after visiting Warsaw, W. E. B. Du Bois brilliantly captured the ghetto's exclusion from the rest of postwar Warsaw: "A city and a nation was literally rising from the dead. Then, one afternoon, I was taken out to the former ghetto. . . . Here there was not much to see. There was complete and total waste, and a monument."[118]

Jewish sites provoked a similar anxiety in divided Germany, all the more so given the country's unequivocal responsibility for the Holocaust. Many Germans also wanted to expel the abject past from the urban landscape as they crafted narratives of their own suffering. In the Federal Republic, memories of victimization about the bombing of German cities, the expulsion of Germans from Eastern Europe, the rape of women by Soviet soldiers, and the harshness of allied policies dominated the early postwar years, while in East Germany the SED fashioned an antifascist narrative of Communist resistance and victimization.[119] Of course, West Germany's political elite accepted responsibility for the Holocaust more than the SED ever did, but the differences between the two Germanys appear less sharp when one takes the view from the streets far removed from the corridors of state politics. The handling of Jewish sites, especially Berlin's numerous synagogues, unfolded similarly in West and East Berlin. In both cities, Jewish leaders contested the destruction and neglect of Jewish sites, but to no avail. Few Berliners showed any concern about the material traces of Jewish life and saw them as little more than scattered debris. Such disregard is perhaps not surprising; it happened, after all, in the wake of twelve years of Nazism when anti-Jewish hatred became a normalized, assimilated part of everyday life. Destroyed in plain view in 1938, Berlin's synagogues starkly reflected German involvement in the Nazi assault on the Jews.[120] Few Berliners wanted to confront their complicity in the Holocaust and support for Nazism. By erasing Jewish spaces from the urban landscape, they secured a postwar normality free of the reminders of violence and persecution. For some Berliners, who walked by abandoned Jewish spaces each day well into the 1950s, the destruction of Jewish sites might even have marked the final removal of a lingering Jewish presence—a post-genocidal expunging of the threatening and anxious Jewish abject.

3

Erasing the Jewish Past

In 2007, the German weekly *Die Zeit* published an essay on the destruction of Germany's "architectural monuments." In a country on its way toward "demolition," it reported that a hundred thousand historic buildings had been torn down in just the last few years. "Since 1945, many more architectural monuments have fallen than in the aerial war. Just after the first wave of destruction from the air ended, the second began in the Federal Republic. It was called reconstruction," it concluded with ironic play on the word *"Wiederaufbau."*[1] This indictment of postwar urban planning only includes West Germany, but of course the other Germany added its share to the pile of demolished stone. Although historic preservation was stronger in East Germany than popular assumptions imply, it is certainly true that many more block apartment buildings dotted the GDR's urban landscape than beautifully restored historic buildings. The same, though, cannot be said of its neighbor just to the east. In fact, the exact opposite occurred in Poland, where historic reconstruction became popular after the war. Historic preservationists recreated the old towns of Warsaw, Wrocław, Gdańsk, Poznań, and Lublin like nowhere else in Europe. Indeed, historic re-creation became so dominant that one Polish architectural critic decried Poland's "obsession" with restoring its past.[2] If divided Germany was a country of demolition, Poland was one of restoration.

Germans and Poles encountered their historic landscapes differently largely because of the circumstances they found themselves in after the war. In the two Germanys, urban modernism and socialist realism promised a clean break from the Nazi past. A new urban landscape reflected German hopes of redemption from dictatorship and genocide by building a new, postwar Germany. In Poland, the war and Nazi occupation strongly shaped the country's concept of reconstruction *(odbudowa)* by strengthening ties to the nation and its spatial markers of the past. Although the PZPR promised a better, more prosperous future through new building projects, it restored historic buildings as both an actual and a symbolic act of preserving the Polish nation after Nazism. "Entire pages of our history, written in the stones of architecture, were deliberately ripped out," wrote the historic preservationist Jan Zachwatowicz in 1946. "We cannot stand for that. The sense of responsibility for future generations demands the rebuilding of that which was destroyed."[3] The concepts of *odbudowa* and *Wiederaufbau* could not have diverged more sharply. If the year 1945 signaled for Germans hope for a new beginning, it represented for Poles a sacrosanct moment to restore the past.

In light of these differences, one might assume that the early postwar history of Jewish sites would differ starkly across the Oder-Neisse border. But in all three countries, historic preservationists did nothing to maintain Jewish sites and voiced no concern when they were torn down, neglected, or transformed. Although this silence is most surprising in the Polish case, given its strong historic reconstruction program, it is also notable in the two Germanys, where historic preservationists, politicians, and ordinary citizens often vigorously opposed the demolition of other historic buildings, just not Jewish ones. Germans and Poles carefully selected what to restore from the rubble, preserving what they believed reflected their national pasts and excluding what they perceived did not. As in previous decades, narrow, nationalistic conceptions of cultural heritage deeply shaped the practice of historic preservation.[4]

But the erasure of Jewish sites is not just another story about the exclusionary practices of nationalism. It is also—and more importantly—a story about the exclusionary power of local urban politics. In rebuilding their cities, Germans and Poles were not just repairing broken stone; they were creating new ways of imagining their local urban landscapes. Cities are, however, hardly clean canvases. Layers of time color their streets; memory dirties their stones.[5] Germans and Poles had to confront the shards of the past and decide what to do with them. In Essen, Wrocław, and Potsdam, historic preservationists, urban planners, and local officials sought to reshape their pasts to fit their current ideological needs and norms. Essen's identity had long been tied to Germany's industrial barons, who became complicit with Nazism. After the war, Essen quickly shed its Nazi slogan as the "Armorer of the Reich" and embraced the postwar consumerism of West Germany's economic miracle, stylizing itself as the "shopping city." Wrocław, a city with a shifting history under Piast, Bohemian, Austrian, Prussian, and German rule, became part of Poland in 1945 with the westward shift of the country's border. Portrayed as having eternally "Polish" roots from the medieval period, Wrocław expunged its most recent status as Breslau and became "Polish," complete with the expulsions of Germans and the resettlement of Poles. Potsdam, a Prussian garrison city, had deep military traditions that Hitler exploited in his infamous "Day of Potsdam" in 1933 when he paraded through the city. The East German regime sought to cover over this past by building a new, antifascist Potsdam. In creating these new identities, urban planners adopted different approaches to their historic landscapes. In Essen and Potsdam, little was preserved, while in Wrocław an extensive, if selective, program of reconstruction was carried out. In all three cities, though, Jewish sites were destroyed and neglected like few other traces of the past.

Essen, the Shopping City

At the beginning of the nineteenth century, Essen was a small, agrarian town of 3,500 residents. Located in the Ruhr area not far from Belgium and the Netherlands, it became merely 100 years later a large, industrial city of 118,000 people. Essen benefited from the nearby coal mines of the Ruhr, the technological advances of the steam engine, and the entrepreneurial ingenuity of its most famous family, the Krupps. In 1811, Friedrich Krupp established a steel foundry that became one of Germany's economic powerhouses. The Krupp firm, which produced railroad products and armaments, turned Essen into a major city. Essen became known for its labor movement and worker radicalism, but its rising prominence became expressed in an array of splendid buildings constructed in the historist style favored by the burgeoning middle class at the time. By 1887 a neo-Gothic town hall towered over Essen's center, several years later the industrialist Friedrich Grillo built a neoclassical theater, and in 1913 the architect Edmund Körner unveiled his monumental synagogue in the heart of the old town on Steeler Street, just 200 meters away from the market square and Essen's historic cathedral.

Essen had arrived, and so had its Jewish population. In the 1870s, 832 Jews lived in Essen, but by 1912 the population had reached 2,839. Benefiting from the city's economic boom, the Jewish population entered Essen's middle class and expressed its stature through the building of a new synagogue. The Jewish community and municipal officials selected a design by the local architect Edmund Körner, who used simplified Romanesque and Byzantine elements to create a compact stone structure. While an imposing edifice, the synagogue fit into its surroundings. The extension of a courtyard enclosed by turrets and a metal gate blended the building in by gently bringing it into the street. The choice of this architectural style reflected the changing self-definition of Essen's Jews by the turn of the century. In 1870, the Jewish community built a much different synagogue. Following the general trend of synagogue architecture at the time, it constructed a Moorish-style structure complete with two onion domes. Forty years later, the Jewish community expressed its "Jewishness" more subtly by choosing a building that was at once seemingly distinct and native to the surrounding landscape. The Essen synagogue was intended to be as much "Jewish" as it was "German." At the unveiling, Jewish community member Max Abel noted that the synagogue rested on the "ground" of "our German fatherland." The building expressed the "faithful quest" of Jews to achieve what the emancipation process had allowed—"being citizens of our state."[6] He spoke as a bust of Kaiser Wilhelm II dominated the synagogue's hall and as Essen's mayor toasted the Hohenzollerns. The Essen synagogue captured, as historian Paul Mendes-Flohr has so aptly put it, the "bifurcated soul of the German Jew."[7]

This combination of Germanness and Jewishness received enthusiastic praise in the press. "I am convinced," exclaimed one local in the *Essener Volkszeitung,* "that the entirety of Essen is proud of this noble building, just as Essen's citizenry is with the same right proud of the unprecedented development of our hometown, which now has experienced through this wonderful building such a splendid enhancement that so magnificently fits into the image of our city."[8] The building's monumentality captured the interest of most observers, while others emphasized the synagogue's innovative, modern style. As one review put it, "the building's forms are no longer oriental and are also not copies of some older style, but are the 'beginning of the twentieth century.'"[9] The synagogue received warm praise precisely because its building's "orientalism" was modestly articulated. One of the leading

Essen's synagogue in 1914–15. Located in the center of town, it symbolized the integration of the Jewish community in German society. (Essen Stadtbildstelle)

architectural critics in the Rhineland praised Körner's design for not being too Jewish. "The purely stylistic appropriation of oriental forms," he wrote, "in most locations [is] a foreign object, which annoyingly stands out and has no connection to the surrounding landscape. The preservation of the native, local landscape is also the main precondition for a synagogue, for a 'mosaic Mosque' will always make itself out to be an intrusive troublemaker under German skies, in the environs of north German brick buildings or south German half-timbered structures and stucco buildings."[10] In fin de siècle Germany, experts and locals saw Körner's synagogue as precisely the opposite—an integrated part of Essen's urban landscape that reflected its booming confidence as an economic powerhouse.

The building's monumentality was also—quite literally—the main reason why it survived the Nazi period. Just after midnight on November 9, 1938, local Nazis broke into the synagogue and rolled in barrels of gasoline. "I saw black clouds of smoke rising out from the synagogue," a local firefighter reported; "I determined that two industrial barrels holding about 200 liters of gasoline were lying on the street before the synagogue."[11] The next morning, Esseners gathered in front of the building as smoke still billowed from its windows. Although the Nazis tried to force the Jewish community to pay for the synagogue's demolition, the cost and the risk to nearby houses was too high for it to be carried out. While the synagogue's interior was charred, the building itself survived. The synagogue also escaped the destruction of Essen's old town during World War II. Since the Krupp firm was a central producer of armaments, the allies heavily bombed Essen.[12] The city endured thirteen aerial attacks. By 1945, Essen's old town lay in a pile of ruins. The city's oldest churches, its town hall, its city theater, and nearly 90 percent of its stores were destroyed. Pictures taken just after the war show a field of ruins with virtually no central point of orientation with one exception—the synagogue on Steeler Street. The Nazis had blown out its windows, damaged its cupola, and burned its interior, but there it was. Returning to Essen just after the war ended, one local resident recalled seeing the synagogue amid a field of ruins:

> When in the summer of 1945 I was released from a short stint as a prisoner of war, I had trouble getting my bearings in my hometown. The synagogue was a point of orientation. In the middle of a vast field of

rubble, the unique domed building towered above, damaged, but spared by the war. It reminded me of the day when before our eyes the smoke billowed out. It was in the year before the start of the war. On the way from the "castle," as we called our school, to swimming lessons in the pool on Steeler Street we saw what could not be ignored on the morning of November 10, 1938.[13]

The synagogue stood out not only because it survived the war, but because it reflected the fractured history of German-Jewish relations. It was a stark reminder right in the center of town of the Nazi expulsion of the Jews. It was indeed this traumatic past that local residents and urban planners struggled to make sense of throughout the 1950s as they discussed how to rebuild Essen and what place, if any, historic structures such as the synagogue should have in the city's future. How would a building, once celebrated for its grandness but now sitting empty and damaged in a city of almost no Jews, fit into Essen's reconstruction?

The rebuilding of Essen became closely tied to its economic restructuring. The Krupp firm turned Essen into a major city, but the company no longer could serve as the linchpin of the city's economic vitality and urban identity. Essen's status as the "Armorer of the Reich" made it a target like few other cities of allied measures to dismantle the German wartime economy. Since Krupp had been the largest employer in Essen, city leaders were now forced to diversify the economy. Essen still relied heavily on mining, but attracted new industries in areas such as electronics, automobiles, resale, service, banking, and insurance. In the 1950s, retail in particular became important as hundreds of shops filled the streets of the old town. This economic strategy was not entirely new. In the 1920s, several large department stores had been built in the old town and a number of smaller shops started to fill its streets. As the world economic crisis reached its height in 1929–30, Essen increasingly became known not just as the "Krupp City" but also as the "Shopping City."[14] It was, however, after 1945 that this identity became solidified. In 1950, the city began marketing itself as "Essen, the Shopping City," with a large placard, which still exists, that greeted arriving visitors from the train station. As West Germany experienced its "economic miracle" partly on the backs of cheap "guest worker" labor mainly from Turkey, Essen became one of the country's main places to indulge in the economic growth.

Essen's synagogue on *Kristallnacht,* November 9, 1938. (Essen Stadtbildstelle)

This diversification of Essen's economy shaped the rebuilding of its old town, which urban planners turned into a shopping district. In 1949, Essen's urban planning office announced its plan for the city's reconstruction. Drawing on ideas developed during the Nazi period by urban planner Sturm Kegel, the design divided the city center into two parts.[15] North of the train station became the shopping area, while the south served as the central business district for Essen's emerging service, banking, and insurance industries. A traffic ring encircled the old town to allow easy access for shoppers, and two large squares were built to make the city center less congested. Implemented throughout the 1950s, the plan preserved the old town's medieval, kidney-shaped layout, but involved demolishing many of its historic buildings.[16] In comparison to Potsdam and Wrocław, Essen was by far the most radical in embracing the modernist urge for wide streets, spacious squares, and functional buildings. In the 1950s, urban planners constructed a 14,000-meter square that became the old town's central organizing point, "the commercial center, the heart of the shopping city."[17] Called Kennedy Square after the American president, it became defined by an array of modernist buildings (Amerika-Haus/Kennedy-Haus, 1951; Allbauhaus, 1954–56; Hochhaus am Gildenplatz, 1955; and Heroldhaus, 1954–55).[18] Not far from Kennedy Square, another sprawling square was constructed, Porsche Square, which later was turned into a shopping mall. Two north-south, east-west retail shops linked these two squares, forming the core of Essen's consumerist downtown. By the mid-1950s, most of these plans were carried out, and city leaders proudly looked back upon what they had accomplished. In a 1956 commemorative book, *Essen: From Ruins and Ashes a New City Emerges*, they declared reconstruction a success: "All in all it follows that eleven years after the enormous caesura of the war Essen is on the best path to pursuing a modern urban planning."[19]

A few buildings, though, escaped the modernist wrecking ball. The construction of Kennedy and Porsche squares stood in sharp contrast to the nearby Castle Square that had long been Essen's main point of focus. Located about 400 feet to the south from Kennedy Square, this area became a "tranquil island" anchored by the reconstruction of Essen's most important historic monument—its cathedral.[20] This church, dating back to the ninth century, had long been the focal point of Essen's old town, tying the nineteenth-century industrial city to its medieval, Christian past. A grass-roots effort to reconstruct the damaged church began immediately after the war. Lasting from 1947 to 1958, the reconstruction involved rebuilding most of the structure completely. The cathedral was one of the few historical buildings in Essen's old town to be reconstructed after the war.[21]

The other historic building saved after the war was the synagogue, although hardly for deliberate reasons. Essen's synagogue remained standing after 1945, but became spatially separated from the new Essen. When city

officials and Jewish leaders built the synagogue on Steeler Street, they made
a deliberate statement about its importance in the urban landscape: it faced
the medieval market square and stood east of the cathedral by less than 200
yards. It had become, both visually and spatially, an integral part of the built
environment. The exact opposite occurred after the war. As the city rebuilt
the cathedral, preserved the historic Castle Square as a "tranquil island,"
and constructed Porsche Square, no attempt to integrate the synagogue into
any of these nearby projects ever emerged. Indeed, as the center of the
downtown moved slightly north to the retail area between Kennedy and
Porsche squares, the market square lost its spatial importance and with it
the synagogue.

This spatial separation was reinforced by the wide traffic streets that encircled the downtown. One went in front of the synagogue. A five-lane highway, it divided the downtown into two parts: the major retail center in the
west and the synagogue in the east. For thirty-five years, the synagogue sat
isolated in this area until 1979, when the city's new town hall was erected near
it. This major project had been in the works since the early 1950s, but the
building that was constructed—a dull, twenty-eight-floor glass skyscraper—
hardly fit with the synagogue just down the road. Urban planners certainly
could have imagined a better way to integrate the town hall with the synagogue, but they did not, and the effect today is all too clear for anyone who
visits Essen. The cupola of Körner's structure peaks just slightly above the
tops of department stores, but its monumental stone remains hidden. One
has to walk down to the highway to see it. But there the postwar surroundings eclipse the building as well: the huge parking garage behind it, the busy
intersection of the five-lane highway, the bus terminal underneath the enormous, cavernous passageway to the shopping mall on Porsche Square, and
the dominating, twenty-eight-story skyscraper town hall. Standing there
among the buzz of cars and the nearby chatter of shoppers, one realizes just
how little urban planners thought about the presence of this massive building as they rebuilt the city. One even wonders why the synagogue is still
there. The wrecking ball was, after all, moving at a furious pace along the
streets of Essen's old town, and Sturm Kegel, a leading urban planner in Essen after the war, called for demolishing the synagogue in his first plans for
the city's reconstruction drafted in 1941.[22] So why was the synagogue not
just dynamited to make the parking garage larger for a few more Germans
to reach their stores with ease? City officials, including Kegel, probably

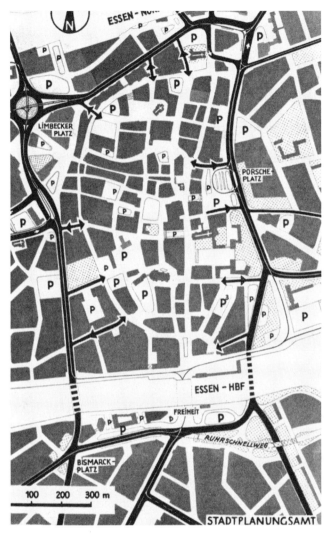

Map showing the streets that circled Essen's downtown and effectively separated the synagogue from the rest of the city's reconstruction. (From *Essen: Aus Trümmern und Schutt wächst eine neue Stadt* [Essen: Die Stadt Essen, 1956], 30)

wanted to avoid the pretense of carrying out what the Nazis had planned in 1938, but that is the short answer to a longer postwar story.

In 1948, a local newspaper asked: "What is to become of the synagogue?" The postwar Jewish community of 145 Jews no longer wanted the building. The synagogue had become a "defiled house of worship" and was too large

Model of Essen's reconstruction, with the synagogue isolated in the eastern part of the city. (From
Essen: Aus Trümmern und Schutt, 31)

for its needs.[23] In 1959, the Jewish community opened a small synagogue on
Ruhr Avenue designed by the architects who built West Berlin's Jewish community center. But the old synagogue was still there, and something had to
be done with it. In 1948, city officials tore down its damaged courtyard so
that "traffic can operate more easily."[24] In place of it, they erected a stone sarcophagus covered with metal plates and topped by a small fixture of the Star
of David. A small plaque adorned the sarcophagus and read: "More than
2,500 Jews had to lose their lives in 1933–1945." Even this vague description
seemed offensive to some Esseners. Soon after the monument was built,
someone desecrated it.[25] After its erection, though, the city abandoned the
synagogue as it rebuilt the rest of the city. This disparity caught the attention
of several journalists. "What the bombs were not capable of doing," one

wrote, "the ravages of time now threaten." Another journalist wondered what was going to happen with the synagogue and endorsed a plan to use it as "a temple of humanity, which will remember the victims of brutality."[26] Still another asked: "Is the Essen Synagogue being left to ruin?" The answer provided was damaging:

> The rebuilding of Essen has taken place rapidly. Even on Steeler Street there are new buildings on the highway: the labor union building, Porsche Square, the complete rearrangement of Castle Square. Only the synagogue seems to have been forgotten. The burned-out walls do not bother anyone. Those who now go by this architectural work probably wonder why one has not let it ruin even more. Grass and even trees are growing out of the rounded cupola and through the holes in the windows. The interior offers an image of desolation. The columns have collapsed and pieces of the ceiling fall down with every vibration from the congested street. Three months ago, the building inspection department prohibited entry into the synagogue. Danger of collapse![27]

As rain was pouring into the synagogue from its damaged roof and pieces of stone were falling onto the nearby street, the city even had to erect a protective fence around the building. The synagogue had fallen into such a dilapidated state that plans for it to be demolished started to surface.[28]

But while destroying the synagogue would perhaps have been the easiest solution, actually doing so proved to be complicated. The abandoned synagogue symbolized the absence of Jewish life, but it also represented another, seemingly less discomforting past that some Esseners did not want to lose. In the 1950s, local residents and city leaders continued to celebrate the building's architecture as an important landmark in Essen. Local journalists, citizens, and municipal officials expressed interest in preserving this "valuable structure," "this most beautiful and impressive Jewish building in Germany," "this proud building," and "this magnificent creation of Professor Körner."[29] Körner's monumental design had yet again helped to save the building. Interest in the synagogue, though, focused only on its architecture as Esseners celebrated the building's pre-Holocaust past. The Nazi destruction of the building and the murder of the city's Jewish population rarely surfaced in postwar accounts; why the synagogue was abandoned in the first place received no reflection. An article published on November 9, 1956, of all days, is a telling example. Although its headline noted that the "synagogue was set on fire seventeen years ago," the article quickly pivoted away from *Kristallnacht*. "That was seventeen years ago. Today not much has changed with the lifeless architectural work. It is really too bad about a building . . . whose design . . . has long been the object of many visitors throughout the world." The only hint of the Nazi period appeared when the article noted that the Jewish community had been so "melted down" that it could not use or maintain the building.[30] Otherwise interest in the synagogue was limited to its architectural legacy and implicitly to the historical period of mythic German-Jewish symbiosis.

But the main reason why the city could not demolish the synagogue was simple. It did not own the building—an obstacle that cities in East Germany and Poland never confronted with the Communist confiscation of Jewish property. Had Essen's synagogue existed on the other side of the Iron Curtain, it might well have been dynamited. But in West Germany, a legal process had to unfold first. In 1953, Essen's district court returned the property to the Jewish Trust Corporation (JTC), the restitution successor organization for the British-occupied zone of which Essen was a part. Since the local Jewish community had no interest in the building, the JTC offered to sell it to the city as a way to get it off its balance sheet.[31] Municipal authorities were reluctant to purchase the synagogue, but came around to doing so as they became more involved in its upkeep over the years. By the mid-1950s, the building, with its crumbling pieces falling off—one so large that it broke the sidewalk down below—posed a danger to pedestrians. The synagogue needed basic repairs, but the JTC refused to supply any money because it believed that restitution funds should not be used to maintain properties destroyed by the Nazis.[32] In 1959, the city put forward 300,000 marks to secure the building. A year later, it decided just to purchase the synagogue with so much invested in it, but now it confronted more than ever what to do with the building. There was no shortage of ideas. The local Jewish community had long proposed turning the building into a memorial for "all the victims of National Socialism," while some Esseners suggested using it to house a regional museum.[33]

But city officials had another idea in mind. The House of Industrial Design, a local association that sponsored an exhibit on designer industrial products, needed a new location after its lease was canceled at the Krupps' historic villa Hügel outside Essen. City officials offered several prime locations in Essen's downtown, but none satisfied the association's leadership, and it began to look for better offers from the nearby cities of Köln and Dusseldorf. City officials were desperate not to lose this "Essen institution."[34] In early November 1959, about a week after the city agreed to purchase the synagogue, city officials suggested putting the exhibit in the building to the association's director, Carl Hundhausen, who immediately took to the idea. Hundhausen believed that this "monumental structure" was the perfect setting for displaying "modern objects."[35] Several months later, the city approved the plan with little debate. When one city council member asked if the local Jewish community "had upon the sale of the synagogue reserved the right to have its say" in its future use, the chief municipal director "unequivocally answered in the negative."[36] No one suggested that the Jewish community should be contacted in advance out of plain decency. The local Jewish community was incensed when it heard the news. "We are astonished to learn about the fate of the synagogue from newspaper clippings," it wrote in a letter to city officials, "especially since at the time we were assured that the Jewish community would be consulted in deciding the use of the building. The synagogue in Essen is regarded as the most beautiful and dignified in Europe. It bears witness to the yearnings for closeness with God that lie in the hearts of men. . . . And now this building is to house an exhibition of the German economic miracle?"[37]

Members of Essen's Jewish community were not the only ones disturbed by the city's decision. Essen's local clergy and its branch of the Association for Christian-Jewish Cooperation opposed the plans in letters, in newspaper articles, and even in an appeal to Chancellor Konrad Adenauer. Essen's bishop noted that there were "substantial reasons against a commercial use of the old synagogue." The city responded that "the current plans for the old synagogue represent a dignified use of the building."[38] Most protests focused on the "profane" use of a religious building. Several citizens wrote in to the local newspapers, wondering if such a similarly "absurd" idea would be proposed for "Essen's Münsterkirche or Cologne's Cathedral," while others cautioned against taking the Communist "East as an example" by turning houses of worship into museums. But few opposed the synagogue's transformation into an exhibition of industrial products in light of its history as a site of Nazi persecution, except for one vague mention that it would be better for it to be used as a monument to the "victims of the 1,000-year Reich."[39]

This criticism, although it never threatened the city's proposal, was taken seriously. Hundhausen enlisted the support of West Germany's Jewish leaders to end the discussion. He first received support, albeit tepid, from Julius Dreifuss, president of the State Association of the Jewish Communities in North Rhine–Westphalia, who wrote in a private letter that the exhibition would not "provoke any offense."[40] As criticism of the project continued in the local press, Hundhausen turned to Karl Marx, editor of West Germany's most powerful Jewish newspaper, the *Allgemeine Wochenzeitung der Juden in Deutschland*, to write an article in favor of the project. "I am convinced," Hundhausen anticipated, "that public approval will be given in this article."[41] In March 1961, Marx expressed his thanks to the city of Essen for turning the synagogue into a "living cultural center of our century."[42] Marx delivered his support as promised, even with rhetorical flourish, but perhaps he and other Jewish leaders were relieved for at least something to be done with the building. It is also possible that either Hundhausen knew Marx or higher state officials called upon Marx for a favor. Whatever the reason, Marx's intervention ended public debate about the project.

On November 24, 1961, the newly renovated synagogue opened its doors as the House of Industrial Design. The renovation had cost the city 2 million marks. "Anyone who saw the interior of the old synagogue before will hardly recognize it now," a local journalist observed.[43] The interior had been altered completely, and the grand opening capped the building's transformation with an odd negotiation between past and present. The state cultural minister of North Rhine–Westphalia, Werner Schütz, cautioned Hundhausen in advance that the ceremony had to be "carried out in the right manner" and must be an "hour of reconciliation with our Jewish co-citizens."[44] In his own speech, Schütz touched on the controversy. He noted that "perhaps it would have been a good solution" to turn the synagogue into a "powerful monument . . . of the terrible things in the past" but suggested that the current exhibition somehow would do that. His logic was that visitors would pass by the sarcophagus monument before entering the building, reminding them of past "events."[45] How could an exhibition of dishwashers, stoves, and irons represent the Holocaust in even the obliquest way? But no one asked

The front of Essen's synagogue transformed into the House of Industrial Design in 1961. (Essen Stadtbildstelle)

such questions because by now criticism of the project had faded. Press coverage of the exhibition overlooked the building's history, and visitors warmly praised the exhibition. "The synagogue has been used very well," one visitor gushed; "the city of Essen could not have done any better."[46] It was as if nothing had happened—the synagogue was just reused like any other space in the city. And indeed it was now integrated into Essen's identity as the shopping city. While separated spatially from the emerging shopping district by a highway and excluded from the nearby, historically reconstructed Castle Square, the synagogue was now tied to the city's identity as a bastion of consumerism and industrial ingenuity. Conveniently, the synagogue was even close to the shopping district so that Germans could go buy what they saw on display.

The interior of Essen's synagogue as the House of Industrial Design in 1978. (Essen Stadtbildstelle)

This transformation of Essen's synagogue might seem peculiar, but it un-covers how one local community responded to the deeply anxious past of the Holocaust. In contrast to the GDR and PPR, the West German state de-veloped an official policy of restitution and German-Jewish cooperation, but this shift rarely made its way out of the offices of Bonn to reach local society and politics during the 1950s. The protests that emerged in Essen ignored the issue at stake as the synagogue remained damaged, trees and grass grow-ing out from its charred cupola, pieces of stone falling off its façade onto the nearby street—why no one was around in the first place to take care of the building. Rather, most Esseners went along with the synagogue's transforma-tion with little outrage because the synagogue no longer stood as an empty, discomforting space of violence and persecution. Turning the synagogue into the House of Industrial Design managed the anxiety of the abject past by burying the building's history under display cases of capitalist wonder.

Indeed, the synagogue did not really exist anymore. An unaware traveler to Essen searching for "synagogue" on any basic city map, not knowing to look for "House of Industrial Design," would have been unable to find the building.[47]

Returning Wrocław to "Our Fatherland"

Like Essen, Breslau became a major city in the German empire by the end of the nineteenth century. It benefited from the industrial output of Upper Silesia and became the most important center east of Berlin for manufacturing, banking, and commerce. The city, with its shifting history since the early Middle Ages under the rule of Bohemia, the Kingdom of Poland, Austria, Prussia, Germany, and today Poland, was made up mainly of German-speaking residents by the early twentieth century. In 1740, Prussia seized Breslau from Habsburg control, and it remained part of a German-speaking state until 1945. The Protestant faith dominated the city since the Reformation, but Catholics became a sizeable minority over the nineteenth century, while the Jewish community was the third largest in Germany, with 23,000 members in 1920 (about 4 percent of Breslau's total population). In the late nineteenth century, relations between Jews and Germans were cordial thanks to the tolerant policies of city officials. Breslau's municipal government, a left-liberal coalition that depended on Jewish support in local elections, relaxed the exclusionary practices of social clubs, bestowed the city's highest civic award to Jews, and increased access to higher education. Breslau's Jewish community became acculturated into German society by the turn of the century and built a strong tradition of Jewish life in the city.[48] By the 1930s, Breslau had two main synagogues, seven other houses of worship, a Jewish hospital, and the Jewish Theological Seminary. Founded in 1854, the seminary was Breslau's most famous Jewish institution, training rabbis who came to occupy positions in the United States, Europe, and the Middle East.

As in Essen and Berlin, Breslau's Jewish community expressed its integration into German society through architecture. The Stork Synagogue located on Wall Street in the old town was the first architecturally notable synagogue to mark Breslau's urban landscape. Designed by Carl F. Langhans, son of the architect of Berlin's Brandenburg Gate, the synagogue was constructed in neoclassical style, so that from the outside it barely resembled a religious building. The design reflected the importance of the Enlightenment for Breslau's Jewish population and the growing acculturation even among those of the Orthodox tradition who used the synagogue.[49] Built in 1827–29, the Stork Synagogue was eclipsed forty years later by the monumental New Synagogue located on Schweidnitzer Street. In 1838, the reform rabbi Abraham Geiger, who had a tense relationship with the Orthodox community, set out to establish Breslau as a center of Reform Judaism by encouraging the founding of the Jewish Theological Seminary and the construction of the New Synagogue. Although he later left for Frankfurt am Main in 1863 before the synagogue was erected, he influenced the building's general design.

The Jewish community accepted plans by the well-known Jewish architect Edwin Oppler, who created a massive, cathedral-looking synagogue just near the center of the city's old town. Oppler designed the building in Romanesque, a style that, in his words, "certainly can be considered purely German."[50] Responding to the oriental, Moorish style of Berlin's New Synagogue, which was completed in 1866, he wanted to place Judaism on equal footing with the other confessions in Germany by adopting a "German" architectural style. Just as Körner had intended in Essen, Oppler wanted his building at once to dominate the surrounding landscape and fit into it. But whereas Körner succeeded in creating such a building in the eyes of his contemporaries, Oppler failed in the eyes of his. The enormous, Romanesque synagogue stood out among the Gothic and baroque styles of Breslau's old town. As one critic put it, the synagogue appeared "exotic in the local architectural character of Breslau."[51]

In the end, the tolerance of municipal leaders toward the Jewish minority that allowed such projects to go forward proved fragile. As Breslau's liberal, middle-class governing coalition collapsed in the 1920s, Breslau became a bastion of Nazi support. On November 9, 1938, the Nazis set the New Synagogue on fire and burned it to the ground. "The SS precluded the firefighters in Breslau from saving the synagogue," a Jewish observer wrote in his diary. "Only the nearby buildings and trees were doused. . . . The synagogue itself was burned down with firebombs."[52] The city's other main synagogue on Wall Street survived *Kristallnacht*, given its close proximity to nearby buildings, making it the central Jewish religious building to last into the postwar period. But the vast majority of Breslau Jews, deported to Sobibor, Bełżec, and Auschwitz in 1942–43, did not survive. By 1945, Breslau's Jewish population had a mere thirty survivors.[53]

This number, though, soon greatly increased in the shifting context of the immediate postwar years when Breslau became Wrocław. In 1945, the Great Powers reduced Poland's size by 20 percent because Stalin wanted to keep his wartime spoils in the east. In return, Poland gained a 300-mile-long Baltic coastline and land up to the Oder-Neisse line, which was more economically developed than the territory Poland lost to the U.S.S.R. With a few pen strokes at Tehran and Potsdam, Poland lost the cultural centers of Lwów and Wilno, while gaining the now Polish cities of Wrocław and Gdańsk. The Great Powers also agreed to the "transfer" of about 3.5 million Germans from Silesia, Pomerania, and eastern Prussia followed by the "resettlement" of about 3.5 million Poles from central and eastern Poland. Seeking political legitimacy in a country where Communism had historically been weak, the provisional Polish Communist government carried out the expulsions and supported the idea of an ethnically homogeneous nation-state.[54] The regime embarked on a massive campaign to Polonize the western territories, mythologizing tenth-century Piast Poland, whose political boundaries roughly followed those of the postwar state, as a unified, stable Polish community tied ethnically and geographically to the present. The Communist Party urged Poles to return "home" to the "recovered territories" of the west, where they would find material riches left behind by the expelled German population. As one Communist poster grandly promised: "Historic justice has been done. The power of the Third Reich lies in ruins. The lands, once robbed by Crusades, Bismarck, and Hitler, have returned to the motherland. In panic, the invader has fled across the Oder, leaving behind villages and towns, manor houses, sown fields, developed ponds and gardens."[55]

The Communist leadership encouraged incoming Jews to resettle in Silesia, even though the regime continued to be ambivalent about the long-term presence of the Jewish minority in Poland. Some Jews eagerly responded to such calls and absorbed the state's nationalist rhetoric. Jakub Egit, chair of the Lower Silesian Jewish Committee, suggested that the choice of this area was simple. "Thanks to the liberation of this land by the Red Army . . . seven thousand Polish Jews were saved here who expressed their will to rebuild their new lives precisely on this land. In this way, they wanted to satisfy their lust for revenge and at the same time to receive at least partial compensation for incurred losses."[56] Jewish Communists and Bundists also presented the recovered territories as a viable option to the Zionist alternative of leaving Poland. But most Jews who settled in Lower Silesia were motivated not by politics, nationalism, or revenge; they were looking for a safe place where they could work and live. Many Jewish settlers survived the Holocaust in the Soviet Union and returned to Poland to find their families murdered, their homes stolen, and their country destroyed. Lower Silesia appeared attractive because it was largely free of the antisemitic violence that erupted in central and eastern Poland in 1945–46. Western Poland was in such a state of flux with Germans moving out and Poles moving in that the return of Jews did not provoke the tension that it did in other parts of Poland. At its height, the Jewish population in Lower Silesia reached 82,305 in July 1946, and the possibility of Jewish life reemerging in Poland seemed high.[57]

But the postwar antisemitic violence, even though it never reached western Poland, proved to be too much for most Jews. "The Jews in Poland became panic stricken," wrote a U.S. military rabbi after visiting Poland. "If this could happen in Kielce, they asked, was Jewish life safe anywhere in Poland?"[58] By 1950, only 30,000 Jews decided to stay in Lower Silesia. The number only decreased with each passing year. By 1960, 7,000 to 8,000 Jews lived in the region. The Jewish community in Wrocław mirrored these broader trends. Wrocław became the largest city of Jews in Lower Silesia with about 16,057 in 1946, but its Jewish population dropped to 12,240 just two years later and then declined over the 1950s. In 1963, about 2,000 Jews lived in the city, and after 1968, only a handful remained.[59] In many ways, Wrocław reflects the postwar trajectory of Jewish life in Poland, with an initial surge of energy and hope only to be dashed by the physical and linguistic violence of 1945–46 and 1967–68.

In the immediate postwar years, Wrocław was hardly an easy place to rebuild one's life whether one was Jewish or not. Sitting on the frontier of Poland's "Wild West," it was a city of migrants, as Poles from across the country moved in and out of this unfamiliar place. The three-month battle for the city destroyed the urban landscape. About 68 percent of Wrocław was ruined, with 21,600 buildings damaged. "Endless ruins, the stink of burning, countless huge flies, the clouded faces of occasionally encountered Germans, and most important, the emptiness of the desolate streets," a transplant from

Lwów recalled when he first arrived.[60] Just three days after fighting ended, authorities from the Polish Communist provisional government moved into the city. The removal of Germans, which had begun with the Nazi evacuation of the city in January 1945, continued in the months before the legally sanctioned "transfer" of the population at the Potsdam conference in August 1945. By 1948–49, Wrocław's demographic revolution had largely come to an end. The German population had been expelled and Poles had replaced them. The new Polish Communist government now faced the difficulty of integrating the so-called repatriates into western Poland and making their hometowns "Polish." In a massive myth-making campaign, the regime portrayed the recovered territories as an area that had always been Polish. Historians, writers, art historians, and archaeologists focused special attention on the medieval period, when the dukes and princes of a distinct political entity known at the time as "Poland" ruled Silesia from 1138 to 1335. The following 600 years of history under Bohemian, Habsburg, Prussian, and German rule received less attention, and when they did, even the minutest trace of "Polishness" was emphasized.[61]

Recasting the past in such nationalistic ways was easy in print, but doing so in the built environment was much more difficult, as historian Gregor Thum has shown in his fascinating book on postwar Wrocław, *Die fremde Stadt: Breslau 1945*.[62] Municipal officials replaced German street names and monuments with Polish ones, but these minor changes were not that difficult to make. The real difficultly came with the city's historic buildings, because hardly any of them could be considered "Polish." What should be done with a city constructed during the Bohemian, Habsburg, and Prussian periods? Should its historic buildings be reconstructed or cleared away for the building of a new "Polish" city? Following the lead of Jan Zachwatowicz in Warsaw, historic preservationists in Wrocław argued for reconstructing the city's historic buildings, especially structures of Gothic style that they claimed reflected the architectural past of Piast Poland. Of course, these buildings could hardly be considered "Polish," just as those built in neoclassical style in the nineteenth century could hardly be considered "German," but societies appropriate buildings more or less as they wish to conform to their interpretations of the past at a particular moment in time.

Indeed, Polish urban planners and historic preservationists argued that stripping Breslau of its Germanness would unearth the older, medieval,

Catholic, and deeply Polish Wrocław. In the ruined landscape, they could recover the city's Polish origins that had been destroyed by the German enemy over the years. "In 1945, we came into Lower Silesia with the false belief that we were entering into the old Polish country where the German oppression had wiped out every trace of Polishness," wrote Stanisław Kulczyński, an academic instrumental in rebuilding university life in the city. "The malicious enemy returned this land to us having earlier destroyed almost all of its civilized achievements. Inadvertently, it dug out from the ruins the old, eternally Polish layers that exude beautiful and noble culture."[63] Just as in Warsaw, so, too, in Wrocław urban planners perceived ruins as precious remnants of the nation that could be re-created. They took their task seriously. Emil Kaliski, a historic preservationist who directed the re-creation of Wrocław's old town, described it as almost sacred: "We feel with full awareness the weight of the task that history has put into our hands, the hands of Polish urban planners; it is a task that aims to return to our fatherland this city that once was perhaps more Polish than Kraków."[64]

This vision of rebuilding Wrocław's historic core was largely carried out, although the actual reconstruction occurred more slowly than in Warsaw. Wrocław was an important city in the key region of the recovered territories, but it still was a medium-sized, outer-lying city in a country where scarce funds went first to the capital. Nevertheless, the reconstruction of its old town was remarkable. Historic reconstruction dominated Wrocław's rebuilding more so than even in Warsaw, becoming the architectural approach for Wrocław's transformation into a Polish city. City officials focused on reconstructing a medieval past that involved rebuilding the city's Gothic churches, market square, and Gothic town hall. Gothic architecture, as one city report stated clearly, had "very serious value for propaganda, urban, and architectural reasons."[65] Although most of these buildings were constructed during the Bohemian and Habsburg periods, historic preservationists argued that they must "reemerge again" because they reflect "the historic foundations of the Piast period and above all reveal unique, native Silesian-Polish architectural forms."[66] Gothic architecture brought the city back to its history under the rule of the Piast dukes of Silesia, while rebuilding churches reinforced the city's Polish identity. While Roman Catholicism had long been a defining aspect of Polish society, it became a salient feature of what it meant to be Polish over the nineteenth century during the age of partitions. The

PZPR utilized these deeply rooted national identities to legitimize its rule, even while it engaged in a long battle with the Catholic Church.[67]

In Wrocław, local preservationists focused on rebuilding the churches on the north side of the Oder River, where the city's history as a bishopric began in 1000 CE. This area, known as the Cathedral Island, also contained the first Piast castle and the city's cathedral. It was here that urban planners and historic preservationists believed the traces of Wrocław's Polish past could most fully be recovered. Archaeologists searched for even the minutest trace of the Piasts, while historic preservationists rebuilt the island's many churches into the 1980s. The most celebrated project came with the rebuilding of the cathedral. In 1946, Marcin Bukowski, one of the leading figures in Wrocław's reconstruction, led the first stage of the building's restoration, which was completed in 1951. The restored cathedral, towering above Wrocław's skyline, displayed the city's recovered Polish past on the grandest scale. In 1965, on the twentieth anniversary of the Polish church in western Poland, Stefan Cardinal Wyszyński proclaimed that Wrocław's cathedral had always been "Polish":

> The church is a preeminent conservator of the past. . . . We decode, beloved ones in the Lord, these stone relicts. In this Cathedral from the year 1000 we know our markers. These stone relicts, wonderful markers of the past, say: We were here! Yes! We were here! And we are back here! We have returned to this patriotic house. We recognized the markers that have remained. We understand them. We understand this language. This is our language! The stones speak to us from the walls. . . . When we see these churches of the Piasts, when we listen to their speech, then we know: this is certainly not German land! Those are our traces, traces of the Piasts! They speak to the Polish people without commentary. We do not need any explanations; we understand their language well.[68]

The Polish Catholic Church and the PZPR often collided, but found themselves in an uneasy dance that included at times warm embraces and coordinated moves. The image of the Catholic Church as an eternal bastion of resistance elides when it supported the regime's position on issues such as Polish claims to the recovered territories. Wyszyński's speech absorbed the nationalist framing of Wrocław's reconstruction crafted by the PZPR. The Communist language about building a "socialist city"—more present in Warsaw and certainly in East Berlin and Potsdam—emerged less often in Wrocław as the party faced the pressing need to legitimize its claim to the city and region on Poland's frontier. The party used national identity to build social cohesiveness in a fragmented city of migrants.[69]

But this use of historic reconstruction for building national identity excluded many historic buildings. A number of Prussian buildings were torn down, although a rigid, unequivocal policy of demolishing "German" structures never emerged. Destruction depended on the building and on the people making the decision. Traces of Polishness could be found almost in any building if historic preservationists wanted to restore it.[70] The same, though, was clearly not the case for Jewish sites, which historic preservationists ignored and neglected almost entirely. In the 1950s and 1960s, Breslau as a center of Jewish life vanished from Wrocław's history. Scholarly and popular works focused on the Middle Ages to highlight the "particular attention to the role of Polish elements in the historical processes of the city."[71] This narrow focus, which rarely dealt with the eighteenth, nineteenth, and twentieth centuries, overlooked the period of the Jewish population's expansion and destruction. The few accounts that covered the modern period under German rule made no mention of the city's Jewish community.[72]

Erasing Jewish Breslau, however, occurred above all in the built environment. As the historic buildings of the old town were rebuilt, the city's Jewish sites were neglected and destroyed. Wrocław's main area where Jews once lived, worked, and worshiped, located between the streets of Krupnicza (Graupenstraße), św. Antoniego (Antonienstraße), Włodkowica (Wallstraße), Złote Koło (Goldeneradegasse), and Podwale (Schweidnitzerstraße), never made it onto the city's historic reconstruction program. The Jewish Theological Seminary on Włodkowica was demolished, while the historic core of the Jewish area, Karl Square and Golden Street, lying southwest of the city's Market Square, lay damaged and neglected for thirty years. Once made up of numerous shops and tenement houses, it was cleared away in the early 1970s with the construction of a four-lane highway. Only five apartment buildings on Złote Koło and a sliver of Karl Square were saved, renamed the Jewish Square in 1947 and a few years later the Ghetto Heroes' Square.[73] The spatial effect of this erasure is clear. This area of the old town is distinct from the

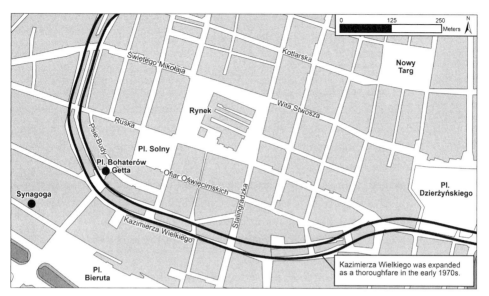

Map of Wrocław showing the Kazimierza Wielkiego thoroughfare. It paved over the historic core of Jewish Breslau, Carl Square, renamed after the war the Ghetto Heroes Square *(Plac Bohaterów Getta)*. (Adapted from *Plan Miasta Wrocławia,* Państwowe Przedsiębiorstw Wydawnictw Kartograficznych, 1957)

carefully rebuilt historic buildings of the nearby Salt and Market Squares, which form the cultural life of the city.

Not far from this area once stood Breslau's most visible Jewish site—the towering New Synagogue. In 1945, it lay in rubble. As historic preservationists began work on the cathedral, city officials cleared away the synagogue's ruins to make room for a parking lot for a nearby police compound. In the 1950s, the surrounding area then became home to Wrocław's most expansive socialist realist housing project. Local architect Roman Tunikowski transformed the area into a central square surrounded by five-story apartment buildings. The housing project of the newly named Tadeusz Kościuszko Square provided a grand entry into the city. Urban planners in Wrocław also attempted to combine the old with the new, although less dramatically so than in Warsaw. What is striking, though, is that urban planners in both cities built large thoroughfares and housing projects precisely in those areas of the city where it did not seem to matter if the ruins of the past were cleared away. No evidence of explicit intention for this exists, but it is common enough to suggest that exclusive, ethnic conceptions of cultural heritage influenced perceptions of urban space when urban planners decided what to restore and destroy.[74]

Indeed, all of Wrocław's Jewish sites gradually decayed over time from disinterest and neglect. In the late 1940s and 1950s, Jewish life in Wrocław existed mainly on Włodkowica Street, where the White Stork Synagogue was located. Both the Religious Congregation of the Jewish Faith in Wrocław and the local, secular branch of the Socio-Cultural Association of Jews used the synagogue and the buildings around it. A vibrant religious and cultural life reemerged in the city right after the war, but the Jewish congregation faced constant problems in securing enough money to maintain its existence. Wrocław city officials paid little attention to the community's needs, forcing Jewish leaders to rely on meager funds from the Religious Association of the Jewish Faith in Warsaw.[75]

With so little support from the city, the Jewish congregation had almost no money to maintain its property. By the early 1960s, the White Stork Synagogue had fallen into deep disrepair from neglect and vandalism. "The synagogue is found to be in such a state that the building is in danger of complete destruction and its current state and appearance create a very unpleasant impression for people attending services," the Jewish congregation wrote in 1963. "The ceiling is falling apart, the majority of the windowpanes are knocked out, and the plaster is coming off the walls. The building is decaying completely." In 1966, city officials even ordered that the Jewish community vacate the building for the "sake of public safety."[76] Jews now had to use a small, fifty-person prayer room in an adjacent building for religious services, hardly large enough for a community of 2,000. In the late 1960s, however, the Department of Religious Affairs in Warsaw seemed to support repairing the synagogue, albeit for curious reasons. It noted that the building was in "too good of condition to tear down," and because it was "not visible from the street its possible repair would not stand out." It also suggested that maintaining the synagogue could be politically useful abroad as "proof of the freedom of religion in the PPR."[77] The last reason hardly surprises, but the second does. Tucked in a courtyard just off a back street, the synagogue would not draw the attention of passersby, but why did such obscurity matter? Why would repairing a synagogue "stand out?" And to whom? Perhaps it would seem conspicuous to a population that the party believed held anti-Jewish biases, or perhaps it would stand out in an urban landscape now deemed Polish.

One can only speculate, but what is intriguing is that someone wrote this phrase down in the first place. Wrocław's rebuilding became an intensely political effort for conceivable reasons. One can understand the regime's intent to legitimize its rule through projects such as rebuilding the cathedral, even if it seems peculiar in a political system where religion was supposed to disappear. But less understandable is why the regime would turn something as minor as repairing a synagogue into a political issue. Discussion about the building did not involve technical, historical, or architectural matters. Historic preservationists and urban planners were not involved at all. One could reasonably claim that in Communist societies virtually everything was political, but different issues became more political at different times. In the mid- to late 1960s, party officials, especially those close to Interior Minister Mieczysław Moczar, embraced the nationalistic language, symbolism, and ideas that had long been the hallmark of National Democracy. The reasoning behind this shift involves a complex of factors that will be examined in the next chapter, but what is important here is that suspicion of Jews became central to this change in Polish Communism, ultimately leading to the anti-Zionist campaign of 1967–68 that forced some 13,000 Jews to flee Poland. While the Communist state had long been wary of supporting Jews in a society where the antisemitic fantasy of Judeo-Communism (*żydokomuna*) held sway, the 1960s marked a shift toward a more intense anti-Jewish stance. It would be too simple to say that antisemitism explains the politicization of Wrocław's synagogue, but opposition to its renovation does reflect how much the growing anxiety about Jews in the mid- to late 1960s permeated discussions about Jewish matters, even ones as seemingly banal as building repairs.

It is hard to imagine, in fact, another explanation for why local and national leaders continued to reject pleas from Jewish leaders to repair the synagogue. In ever more frustrated tones, the main Jewish association in Warsaw "urgently appealed" to the Ministry for Religious Affairs to intervene, while the local Jewish congregation wrote to Wrocław's mayor:

> The Congregation of Jewish Faith in Wrocław is the largest in Poland and the residents of Wrocław are practically deprived of participating

in services because the large and historic synagogue on Włodkowica 9—the only one even in the country—has been closed as of August 30, 1966. . . . The small synagogue on Włodkowica 9 can only house fifty people and thus Polish citizens of the Jewish faith living in Wrocław do not have the possibility of attending Saturday services. . . . The state of things is causing an understandable feeling of dejection among the Jewish residents of Wrocław. . . . In this state of affairs, every reason from a moral, social, and political standpoint exists to justify renovating the only large, historic synagogue with the support and financial assistance of local authorities.[78]

Such appeals fell on deaf ears, and a year later the anti-Zionist campaign decimated Wrocław's Jewish community by forcing most of its members to flee Poland. A handful of Jews stayed in the city, but many joined the thousands who left Poland in the late 1960s. In 1974, the entire province of Wrocław had 331 Jews registered with the Jewish congregation.[79] There were doubtless more people of Jewish origin, but needless to say, Jewish life in Lower Silesia had greatly declined. The synagogue fell into further disrepair, and the city confiscated it from the Jewish congregation in 1974.

Wrocław's two Jewish cemeteries tell similar stories of neglect and destruction. The older one, located on Ślężna Street and dating to the 1850s, became the site of intense fighting during the last days of World War II and was closed after 1945. It fell into a state of severe dilapidation, and in the 1970s city officials demolished the small synagogue located on its grounds. The Jewish congregation managed the city's other Jewish cemetery, located on Lotnicza Street, but it, too, gradually fell into ruin for lack of funds. In 1954, the Socio-Cultural Association of Jews concluded after a recent visit to the cemetery that it was "in a condition of complete neglect." The association also encountered disturbing signs of vandalism: "It was found that countless graves had been dug up with scattered human remains. The graves have been systematically dug up in search of gold teeth and valuables." Warsaw officials responded coolly to this report, saying that Wrocław's Jewish congregation was responsible for the cemetery's upkeep and claiming that a state investigation uncovered no signs of vandalism.[80]

This flippant response reflected the regime's fundamental disregard for Jewish cemeteries. In 1965, Isaac Frenkiel, chair of the Religious Association of the Jewish Faith, concluded that Jewish cemeteries across Poland were "being ploughed up by bulldozers and the bones are being thrown into heaps of trash like carrion."[81] This was happening largely because the state had long ago decided to do nothing to protect them. In 1946–49, Jewish leaders urged state officials to establish a policy of maintaining Jewish cemeteries, but this never happened. Most Jewish cemeteries fell into the hands of the state as "abandoned" property and were rarely protected. In 1964, the minister of public works issued a circular that sanctioned the closing, liquidation, and redevelopment of Jewish cemeteries, which had been occurring on the local level for the past twenty years. It decreed that any Jewish cemetery could be closed and redeveloped if a Jewish congregation had not used it for forty years. This measure incensed Poland's Jewish leaders. One in particular, Rabbi Wawa Morejno from Łódź, sent dozens of letters to Polish officials. He strongly opposed the defilement of Jewish cemeteries and even went so far as to suggest that the Polish regime was vandalizing them just like the Nazis.[82]

State officials were hardly pleased with Morejno's "aggressive tone."[83] But they did for a brief moment consider his concerns. While hostility toward Jews increased over the 1960s, it varied from department to department and from year to year.[84] In the spring of 1965, the Ministry for Public Works drafted a letter to be sent to all regional governments insisting that they treat Jewish cemeteries with more care, noting that "Jewish and Polish representatives living at home and abroad" had voiced concern about their condition. The letter was, however, never sent.[85] A year later, the ministry returned to the issue, likely because of renewed protests from Morejno, Frenkiel, and other Jewish leaders in the summer and fall of 1965. This time it drafted a circular that called for the protection of Jewish cemeteries. Since "Hitler's policies of exterminating the Jewish people" had left hundreds of Jewish cemeteries in Poland unprotected, the circular declared that the state should "assure the orderliness of Jewish cemeteries and keep them in an appropriate condition."[86] This remarkable document was the first time that Warsaw had accepted responsibility for the care of Jewish cemeteries, but it never left the desk on which it was written. Discussion about it suddenly ends after the circular was sent to the Department of Religious Affairs. Perhaps financial and logistical concerns intervened, or perhaps others in the government, possibly in Moczar's increasingly antisemitic Interior Ministry, ended the idea before it went any further. The reason is not apparent from what has been left in the archives, but the regime's policy of neglect, destruction, and liquidation of Jewish cemeteries continued across Poland into the 1980s. The chance to maintain them had been lost.

Building an Antifascist Potsdam

In comparison to Essen and Wrocław, Potsdam had a much smaller Jewish community before the war. In 1925, the community totaled around 600 members. Jewish life centered on the newly built synagogue in Potsdam's old town on Wilhelm Square. Designed in neo-baroque style by J. Otto Kerwien, the synagogue was a small and modestly constructed building, but distinctive for its central location on one of Potsdam's main squares. With Germany's largest Jewish community in nearby Berlin, Potsdam's Jewish community was dwarfed in size and prominence. The same was the case for the city itself. Since the middle of the seventeenth century, Potsdam's identity had been linked to the Hohenzollerns, who selected the town as their second seat of residence next to Berlin. Over the eighteenth century, the city also became an important place for quartering soldiers. These monarchial and military ties became expressed in Potsdam's urban landscape: majestic castles, towering churches, homes, and administrative buildings constructed by Prussia's most famous architects, such as Knobelsdorff and Schinkel, defined its streets.

In April 1945, allied bombs destroyed much of this architectural past. Of 1,656 buildings in the city center, 509 were destroyed, 103 partially damaged, 989 unlivable, and just 55 fully intact. The main ensemble of Potsdam's palace, town hall, and church lay in ruins, while the nearby Wilhelm Square survived no better: only the post office escaped destruction. The synagogue, lightly damaged by the Nazis on *Kristallnacht* given its close proximity to nearby buildings, still existed, but allied bombs damaged its roof and interior. Soviet troops occupied the city, and the reconstruction process soon fell to the local SED, which struggled to reach a consensus about how to rebuild Potsdam. Local SED leaders wanted to build a radically new "socialist" city, but historic preservationists in Berlin fought to save the city's many architectural monuments from postwar destruction.[87] In the 1950s and 1960s, local SED leaders won the most crucial battles, and their approach

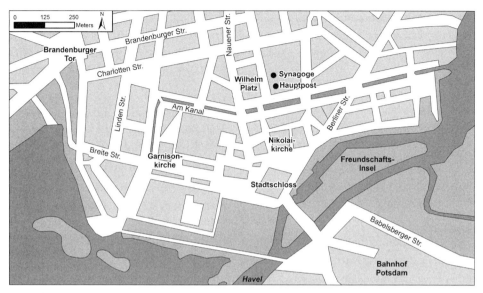

Map of Wilhelm Square in prewar Potsdam. (Adapted from Pharus-Plan Potsdam 1930)

toward urban reconstruction could not have differed more starkly from that of their counterparts in Poland. While the PZPR portrayed itself as the guardian of Poland's national past, the SED treaded more carefully about developing ties with the German past that were too deep in the wake of Nazism. The SED supported historic reconstruction, but not nearly as extensively as the PZPR did.

The GDR, after all, came into existence because of the collapse of a fascist regime and foreign occupation, not because of a Communist revolution. The SED had to navigate carefully through Germany's tortured past to find Communist histories that it could use to justify its existence. It stressed the earlier traditions of the Communist Party of Germany, idolized Communists like Rosa Luxemburg and Karl Liebknecht, and emphasized the proletarian and antifascist origins of German socialism. But while espousing these "progressive" legacies, the party simply dismissed Germany's long history of violence, imperialism, fascism, war, and antisemitism as the products of a failed bourgeois, capitalist system. The SED crafted this selective interpretation of the past in film, literature, art, monuments, historiography, and urban space.[88] The built environment, though, proved especially complicated because it could not easily be molded: plenty of buildings existed that hardly reflected "progressive" strands of German history. Intense debates thus erupted among urban planners and historic preservationists about what to do with the material traces of Germany's past. Depending on who was interpreting what at a particular moment, historic buildings could reflect valuable traces of the past that had to be preserved or fascist, bourgeois ones that had to be cleared away. The SED did not have a clear-cut, stable policy. It demolished many historic buildings, but only after long and contentious discussions about their cultural value and their political importance for building socialism. Consensus was odd, and when it happened, it was telling.

In few other East German cities did conflict over the past emerge more often than in Potsdam. The city's grandiose Prussian buildings and its symbolic ties to the Nazi movement hardly represented a socialist city of workers or an ideal model of antifascism. While the local party newspaper proclaimed that Potsdam's reconstruction was documenting Communism's victory over "reactionary Prussian-German militarism," matters on the ground were more complicated, to say the least.[89] As late as the 1950s, the party was still uncertain about what a "socialist" Potsdam would look like. Just as in East Berlin, urban planners put forward numerous plans, but conflicts among local SED leaders, cultural ministry officials in Berlin, and architectural experts stalled reconstruction for years.

It was not until 1960 that a plan for reconstruction reached some consensus, and even then party officials in Potsdam and Berlin disagreed about how best to implement it into the 1980s. The plan involved wider streets for traffic, more housing, and above all a new "socialist" city center. East German urban planning put great emphasis on the city center, where a large demonstration square, named usually in honor of a Communist hero, served as the ideological and symbolic core of the city.[90] In Potsdam, the SED searched for a local Communist leader to honor, but while the city had an abundance of Prussian kings to offer, it was short on Communist heroes, with one minor exception. In 1912, Potsdam elected Karl Liebknecht to the German parliament, where he emerged as an outspoken opponent of World War I. Five decades later, Liebknecht's political connection to the city became important to party officials who wanted to anchor Potsdam's postwar transformation in a "progressive," socialist tradition; SED officials decided to name

Potsdam's center after him.[91] As the local paper explained, "the old Potsdam was once bound by the ideas of reactionary Prussian-German militarism and the brutalities of fascism and war. . . . [But] today we carry on for ourselves the precious legacy of the antimilitarist Karl Liebknecht."[92] Yet, while Potsdam now had its hero, the SED still had to figure out what to do with the city's many historic buildings that, while damaged, were prominent markers of the urban landscape. By the late 1950s, local party leaders had decided that constructing a socialist Potsdam would have to involve clearing away the past. In 1958, Potsdam's city council declared that "those buildings that were turned into ruins by the terror attack of Anglo-American bombers in April 1945 will be restored only when they are of extraordinary cultural-historical significance, when they do not interfere with all of the demands associated with developing a modern urban traffic system, and when their reconstruction is economically sound."[93]

This decision did not bode well for Potsdam's Prussian buildings, which had long been under attack by some party leaders. In January 1949, Peter Scheib, the SED chairman in Potsdam, published an open letter to the mayor, opposing recent plans to rebuild the war-damaged City Palace, a majestic eighteenth-century Prussian castle that stood in the heart of Potsdam and that was designed by the renowned architect Georg Wenzeslaus von Kno-belsdorff. Scheib opposed its reconstruction because it would be too expensive and would obstruct plans to widen a street, but also because the palace symbolized an ideologically suspect past:

> If today there are still people who know their history, then they ought not to forget that this palace of the Hohenzollerns was built with the sweat and blood of the people of Brandenburg and destroyed through the politics of Prussian militarism. If someone still believes today that our manpower is here to rebuild this broken magnificence of the Ho-henzollerns then he is mistaken. If someone wants to say that we show no sensitivity to historical buildings, then we only need to remember that no one is demanding that the well-preserved Sanssouci be destroyed. But the actions of the Hohenzollerns toward our people were not worthy enough to warrant the rebuilding of a destroyed castle. It was not coincidental that Hitler's henchmen implemented their criminal activities in line with the methods of Frederick II. Even today one

can still see where the politics of the Hohenzollerns led. Thus we are of the view that in light of these actions there is no reason to rebuild these ruins, but rather it is our duty to clear away this rubble of history.[94]

Scheib's position was not popular. In the winter of 1949, a barrage of letters from citizens, politicians, and architectural historians erupted in support of saving the palace. Potsdam's city council declared that "the ruins of the City Palace will be preserved" and used for "a museum and picture gallery or for some other cultural purpose."[95] It appeared as if restoration had triumphed over destruction, and for nearly a decade it had: all of Potsdam's plans included the reconstruction of the City Palace until 1956, when local SED leaders intensified their opposition to its preservation. Reflecting Walter Ulbricht's order to construct cheap, prefabricated apartment complexes, SED leaders argued that the palace's reconstruction would cost too much money and take resources away from building affordable housing.[96] By 1958, the palace's destruction appeared certain. The decision was delayed by continued debate, but in the end the local SED gained the upper hand by securing the support of the Politburo. When the party announced its decision in November 1960, it received intense criticism from citizens, academics, and politicians. East Germany's Institute for Historic Preservation concluded that the palace must be preserved "as the best example of baroque architecture in the German Democratic Republic," but the SED ignored its advice and demolished the building in 1960.[97]

In that same year, the SED moved to destroy another main historic building in Potsdam—its Garrison Church. In 1933, Hitler used this towering, baroque church to open the newly elected parliament of 1933. With some 100,000 spectators lining Potsdam's streets, Hitler and Field Marshal Paul von Hindenburg paraded through the city before giving speeches in the church, where they spoke of deep connections between National Socialism, Imperial Germany, and Prussia. Despite these connections to the Nazi past, the SED for years cared little about the building. In the early 1950s, it even promised that the church would remain intact, and in 1956 the Institute for Historic Preservation placed it under historic preservation.[98] But in 1960 the church came increasingly under attack. In a design competition announced that year, the SED for the first time omitted its reconstruction from the city's rebuilding plans. It appeared as if the Garrison Church would eventually be destroyed, but nearly seven years elapsed before the SED finally tore it down. The order came most likely from Ulbricht, who visited Potsdam that year and told city officials that the church should be removed. Potsdam's city council heeded his orders, writing that "destruction is necessary in order to erase this symbol of Prussian militarism from the memory of local citizens."[99]

What is interesting, though, about the Garrison Church and the City Palace is how late both buildings were torn down. Although in the 1950s the SED put few resources into restoring either one, it did include them in plans for the city's reconstruction. While the party knew that it wanted to build a new Potsdam of wide streets, housing complexes, and demonstration squares, it still had not figured out what to do with Potsdam's architectural past. The turning point came in 1958–60, when the SED decided to construct the "Karl Liebknecht Forum" with its ensemble of a new theater, hotel, demonstration square, and monument to the slain Communist. The former area of the dynamited City Palace would link the city with the nearby working-class district of Babelsberg and form the cornerstone of the socialist Potsdam. This plan took two decades to materialize. The monument to Liebknecht, which was supposed to form the focal point, was not erected until 1983. Still, by 1958–60, the SED had more or less given its verdict on Potsdam's historic buildings in the city center. It decided to restore a few—the Nicholas Church, the town hall, and the royal stable—but the rest would be demolished.

Potsdam's synagogue was one of those buildings ultimately destroyed, but it, too, initially was supposed to be rebuilt. In 1951, commemorating the sixth-year anniversary of Potsdam's destruction, the *Märkische Volksstimme* reported that reconstruction on the synagogue's façade had begun. The three-sentence caption underneath a picture of the synagogue enclosed in scaffolding read: "The façade of the synagogue on Unity Square is being restored. It went up in flames during *Kristallnacht* of 1938. The work of fascist cultural barbarism was only continued by British and American air force squadrons on April 14, 1945."[100] This short report framed the synagogue as part of Potsdam's destruction. The synagogue suffered from the "cultural barbarism" of fascism and war just like any other building in the city. Restoring the synagogue was not for any religious purpose, as city officials clearly knew that the Jewish community no longer existed but rather reinforced the antifascist message of the GDR: the East German state was restoring what the fascists and western allies had destroyed.

This unusual development—repairing a synagogue in a city of no Jews—is not surprising at this early moment in East German history. In the immediate postwar years, it was common to include Jewish persecution in the Communist, antifascist project. Just a month after the war ended, German Communist leaders accepted responsibility for the "consequences" of the Third Reich in an appeal to the German people: "awareness and shame must burn in every German person, for the German people carry a significant part of the shared guilt and shared responsibility for the war and its consequences."[101] Commemorations of *Kristallnacht,* scholarly investigations into the origins of German antisemitism, and discussions about restitution for Jews expanded on the political message of this appeal. But this solidarity with Jews did not last long and indeed was already waning when the report on the reconstruction of Potsdam's synagogue appeared in April 1951. By early 1952, the SED had unleashed its attack against "cosmopolitanism" and purged Jews from the government. Although the campaign ended ten months later during the period of de-Stalinization, it had a lasting impact on the SED's interpretation of the Nazi past. East Germany's antifascist ideology, with its understanding of fascism as a dictatorial and imperialist form of finance capital, now left little room for remembrance of Jewish persecution; German Communists—those who fought against Hitler's regime—were commemorated as the main victims of "fascism."[102]

In the case of Potsdam's synagogue, the difference of a few months mattered greatly. Just before the anticosmopolitan campaign, one could still include Jews in East Germany's antifascist politics. But not afterward: no other mention of the synagogue's rebuilding can be found after the purge, and by 1956 Potsdam's city council moved to tear the building down. City officials began discussions with the Institute for Historic Preservation (IfD) to destroy three structures on the eastern side of Unity Square—two eighteenth-century buildings and the synagogue. Citing Ulbricht's demand to increase the number of apartment buildings, the council proposed using the space for a housing complex. The IfD disagreed because it had just put the two buildings next to the synagogue under historic preservation, which were constructed in neo-Gothic style in 1797–99. The city and the institute argued over these two buildings for the next two years, while caring little about the synagogue because it was never placed on Potsdam's list of his-

toric monuments.[103] Potsdam's chief architect even referred to the synagogue to support his argument for destroying all three buildings, suggesting
that reconstructing the two eighteenth-century buildings "would also mean
that the synagogue . . . would have to be restored as well." Since the building
was "in general of no architectural value," he asked the institute to "clarify"
its position.[104] In 1958, the institute relented and allowed all three buildings
to be demolished. As Potsdam's local party newspaper reported, the decision signaled a clear triumph for the city: "Buildings protected under historic preservation often stand in the way of Potsdam's current building
projects. One only has to think of the façade next to the post office, which
from the beginning was to remain absolutely preserved. . . . [Now] this motto
will be followed: What's valuable will be preserved! What's of no value will
be cleared away!"[105] This article was referring to the two eighteenth-century
buildings, but this decision paved the way for the destruction of the entire
area, including the synagogue.

The city's decision to demolish the synagogue must be placed within the
broader context of Potsdam's reconstruction. By the mid-1950s, constructing apartment complexes had become an important practical and ideological element of East German urban reconstruction: it showed the party's
commitment to economic equality and provided local residents with what
they needed. In Potsdam, one of the central areas targeted for an apartment
complex was Unity Square itself. The plan called for building five-story apartment buildings along the square's eastern side where the synagogue stood. "As
throughout the GDR," the local newspaper cheerfully wrote about the plan,
"we are also starting here in Potsdam to clear away the ruins and to erect in
the spaces of the destruction new, beautiful apartments, stores, and social
buildings."[106] Not everyone, though, greeted the plan with such warm enthusiasm. The project received sharp criticism from experts in East Germany's leading architectural journal, *Deutsche Architektur.* The critique concluded bluntly that the project "perhaps complies with capitalist building
practices, but has nothing in common with socialist urban architecture and
even stands in gross contradiction to it."[107] It suggested that the area be turned
into a park instead, but tellingly never criticized the basic idea of clearing the
area of its past.

Indeed, the silence surrounding the synagogue's destruction is stunning.
No architectural experts, local officials, historic preservationists, or local
residents rushed to save the building. In 1957, Potsdam's local newspaper

published an article protesting the plans to demolish the two buildings next to the synagogue, declaring them "a rare piece of European architectural history."[108] But it said nothing about the synagogue. Even the Institute for Historic Preservation, which also argued for protecting the two Gothic, eighteenth-century buildings, made no effort to preserve the synagogue. In the early postwar years, most preservationists, city officials, and local citizens defined buildings as "historic" in terms of their "age value" and protected structures predating the mid-nineteenth century. In Potsdam, the youngest building on the city's list of historic monuments was a home built in 1838. Unveiled in 1903, the synagogue did not make the list because it was not old enough.[109]

The synagogue's age, however, was not the only reason for the lack of opposition to its destruction. If the synagogue were to stand any chance of being preserved, it would have to be considered a major architectural monument. As the city stated clearly in the year of its destruction: "those buildings that were turned into ruins . . . will be restored only when they are of extraordinary cultural-historical significance."[110] There were, of course, no set definitions for such a subjective quality as a building's cultural importance, but East Germany's historic preservationists continued earlier understandings of cultural heritage that inherently, although not explicitly, excluded Jewish sites. In the 1950s, the staffs of the GDR's historic preservation offices were carried over from earlier years. Historic preservation in Germany had long been a local or regional affair headed by state, city, and provincial conservators. As in Poland, East German preservationists adhered to traditional, long-standing conceptions of national and local heritage. Aside from a new emphasis on "technical monuments" that represented the "activities of work," the canon of historic sites in the GDR rarely deviated from the classical examples of town halls, houses, castles, and even churches. From 1950 to 1955, the GDR supplied 6 million marks to rebuild 336 "culturally important churches."[111] The party used such projects as a way to emphasize the distinctly "German" aspects of the regime. As the director of the IfD put it in 1956, historic preservation "seeks to bring the worker closer to our national tradition by preserving those monuments of our national heritage and thereby arousing love for the homeland *(Heimat).*"[112]

In short, city officials, party leaders, historic preservationists, and ordinary residents ignored the synagogue because it was a Jewish site. The synagogue fell outside narrow, culturally hermetic norms of historic value and never

The former site of Potsdam's synagogue in 2007. (Photo by Michael Meng)

received anything close to the attention that other structures in Potsdam did. Modestly designed by a little-known architect, the synagogue certainly would not have received in the 1950s the kind of interest that the City Palace did, but that it received none in a city of noisy debate about its architectural past is notable. East Germans did not perceive the synagogue as a valuable ruin of the past that had to be preserved; they saw it as worthless rubble that could be pushed aside for building something better.

Selective Historic Preservation

Although historic preservation played different roles in Essen, Potsdam, and Wrocław, a common pattern about Jewish sites emerges from these diverse urban landscapes. Some historic structures attracted interest over others. Potsdam's City Palace, Wrocław's cathedral, and Essen's cathedral received extensive efforts to rebuild them, while Jewish sites never did. Jewish sites did not fit into the building of new urban landscapes and the fashioning of new local urban identities after the war. Multiple reasons explain this exclusion, including architectural style, age value, financial resources, location, and crucially the lack of advocates (buildings become "historic" when people perceive them as important and advocate for their preservation as essential markers of the past that must continue into the future). But the underlying reason is the selective nature of historic preservation. For every building that becomes a historic monument, hundreds of others remain detritus, scraps of the past that might be discovered but likely never will be. Historic preservation is inherently exclusive, but its practitioners make it even more so. Coming mainly from the ranks of the Christian gentry, the intelligentsia, and later the middle class, historic preservationists have long made careful choices about what to preserve, following their own particular cultural tastes and interests. As Jews throughout the nineteenth century moved into new neighborhoods and built grand houses of worship to reflect their emancipation, their older, modest physical spaces—small synagogues and crowded Jewish districts—were razed to make room for modernist urban renewal projects with little protest from preservationists.[113] This disinterest in Jewish sites continued after the war. The material traces of the Jewish "Other" fell outside dominant, narrow definitions of historical and cultural value. As they rebuilt their cities after the war, city officials, urban planners, and historic preservationists demolished and neglected sites of cultural, ethnic, and religious difference. Germans and Poles saw no reason to include the Jewish past in their postwar futures.

Some Jewish leaders, especially in Wrocław with its larger Jewish population, contested this erasure of the Jewish past, but ignoring their pleas was easy, because who cared about a neglected synagogue or Jewish cemetery? Most local residents did not seem to, and Communist officials certainly did not. In Poland and East Germany, both Communist parties embraced anti-cosmopolitan and anti-Zionist politics that at times were clearly prejudicial against Jews. Such overtly anti-Jewish policies rarely surfaced in West Germany, but here, too, the same question applies: Who really cared about Essen's synagogue? City officials turned it into a showcase of consumer products. This decision might not reflect the kind of prejudice against Jews in the Communist East, but it starkly lays bare one local community's ambivalence about Jews a mere fifteen years after a popularly supported political movement made Germany *judenrein*. The destruction of the Essen synagogue, as well as the one in Potsdam, marked the Nazi expulsion of Jews from the city. Both ruined synagogues captured an anxious, abject past that triggered memories of German involvement in the persecution of the Jews, the everyday exclusion that no one could have missed on November 9, 1938 as smoke-filled clouds darkened cities and towns across Germany. After the war, synagogues, such as the ones in Essen and Potsdam, stood quite literally as charred spaces of violence that few Germans wanted to encounter in the 1950s. In this sense, the neglect of the Wrocław synagogue was different. It was not a site that reflected as starkly the breakdown of Polish-Jewish relations during the war that other spaces in Poland such as the Warsaw ghetto did. The city's postwar local population was not the one involved in the synagogue's destruction. The synagogue's neglect, then, reflects more the prejudices of historic preservation and the PZPR's anti-Jewish policies than a local urge to erase a site of traumatic memory, as the cases of Essen and Potsdam do.

In all three cities, though, the memories of these spaces endured even when nothing else did. "Places, places are still there," Toni Morrison writes in *Beloved*. "If a house burns down, it's gone, but the place—the picture of it—stays, and not just in my rememory, but out there, in the world. . . . The picture is still there, and what's more if you go there—you who never was there—if you go there and stand in the place where it was, it will happen again; it will be there for you, waiting for you."[114] Jewish sites in Poland and Germany—destroyed, broken, neglected, and forgotten for years— remained, waiting for someone to go there. Few Poles and Germans ever went there in the 1950s and 1960s, like so many others throughout the world. Few of us care about the cultural markers of people whom we deem, deride, persecute, and expel as "minorities"; we carefully preserve what belongs to "us" while neglecting and destroying what belongs to "them." But this is not always so. In the late 1970s, Poles and Germans started to go there, to Jewish sites. In a dramatic shift, they started to recover the few Jewish sites around them and commemorate those that had been erased from the built environment after the war.

4

Restoring Jewish Ruins

In the mid-1970s, a remarkable and perplexing development in postwar European history began to unfold in divided Germany and Poland. Jewish sites that for over three decades captured little attention now suddenly provoked concern and curiosity. While before Germans and Poles swept Jewish sites away as worthless rubble, they now rushed to protect them as meaningful ruins; while before they erased cultural, ethnic, and religious difference from their urban landscapes, they now wanted it back. This dramatic change emerged first on the local level in small ways: East Berliners cleaning up tombstones at the Jewish cemetery in the district of Weißensee, Varsovians doing the same at their Jewish cemetery on Okopowa Street, Esseners demanding that their synagogue be returned to its prewar interior. As Germans and Poles reflected upon the fact that Jews no longer lived among them, they became concerned about preserving the few material traces of prewar Jewish life left around them. Interest in Jewish sites, though, soon expanded far beyond the local level. By the mid-1980s, Jewish sites were attracting attention from national politicians, tourists, and international Jewish leaders. Some of these people reflected mournfully on the lost past that these spaces embodied, while others sought to restore a sense of "Jewishness" by reconstructing them. In a region of few Jews, a reemergence of Jewish culture and heritage started to take place.

This change happened for a variety of reasons. A simple yet crucial one was the early postwar period of destruction, which turned Jewish sites into rare, valuable fragments of the past. Neglected Jewish sites were the only tangible traces of the prewar Jewish past, and their scarcity excited nostalgia as this past receded ever more away with each crumbling stone. In 1982, the artist Monika Krajewska went across Poland taking photographs of Jewish cemeteries to document the cultural traces of a "former Poland." In 1988, the American writer Richard Kostelanetz made a film about the Jewish cemetery in East Berlin's Weißensee and recounted the story of a former Berlin Jew who described walking into the cemetery as something akin to encountering a "lost civilization that existed in some distant past."[1] The patina of crumbling structures—their decaying stones, fragmented edges, weathered surfaces—attracts and mesmerizes. Ruins reflect the conquering of nature over human artifacts and the saturation of time in space. Time oozes from them and provokes longing for the past—a desire that "wants the time that has flown since then, wants it like old wine or like the evening of a life well-spent," as the German philosopher Ernst Bloch once put it. Nostalgia desires the past, but it is a broken, unfulfilled longing; it provokes affects such as melancholia, mourning, and anxiety but also stimulates curiosity, action, critique, and reflection. Nostalgia is much more complicated than its caricature as just some kitschy, sentimental, reactionary, inauthentic form of memory.[2]

Indeed, the seductive, nostalgic power of ruins has long enamored Europeans at least since the seventeenth century, albeit to varying degrees of intensity as certain periods of time have witnessed stronger interest in ruins than other periods have. Since the 1980s, Europe has been experiencing one of those ruin crazes. In the late 1960s and 1970s, global protest and economic insecurity challenged the modern, optimistic belief in progress. Modernity had not just failed to produce constant improvement, but had caused massive death, inequality, imperialism, and repression in both its capitalist and Communist guises. In the built environment, rows of functional buildings clearly displayed modernity's destructive dialectic and dull aesthetic. Some Europeans responded by preserving the few ruins left around them. These broader critiques of modernity also provoked some writers, artists, intellectuals, and scholars to reconsider how the "historic" had long been defined. The boundaries of historic preservation—long reduced to European, male, bourgeois, white, nationalistic, and Christian conceptions of culture—started to break down over the 1970s and 1980s. Local, grass-roots efforts and civic initiatives broadened and democratized historic preservation in entirely new ways.[3]

Interest in Jewish ruins grew out of these broader social and intellectual trends, but also for specific reasons across national and political borders. In all three countries, growing discussions about the Holocaust and Christian reflections on the history of anti-Jewish hatred stimulated interest in physical traces of the Jewish past. In East Germany and Poland, Jewish sites also became entangled in political conflicts among state officials, opposition members, and international Jewish leaders, while in West Germany, interest in them emerged mainly from local, civic initiatives to explore the Nazi past. Direct political conflict was less intense in West Germany because of that country's more stable political system, whereas in the two Communist societies Jewish sites became yet another issue that divided state and society during the upheaval of the 1980s. These Cold War differences, though, did not produce a clearly divided pattern of memory defined by gradual commemoration of the Holocaust in the democratic West and continued suppression of it in the Communist East. As Poland shows most vividly, memories were hardly static in the Soviet bloc. Poland experienced arguably more searing debates about its complicated relationship with Jews than West Germany did, which discussed the Nazi past numerous times but in ritualistic, vapid ways.[4] The Jewish past became such a touchstone issue in Poland in the wake of the Communist Party's odd response to the student protests of 1968. Communism produced noise, not just more years of silence.

Poland's Verbal Pogrom of 1967–68

"The four of us left—my parents, my sister, and me," Andrzej Karpiński recalled. "About two hundred, maybe three hundred people were at the train station. Friends, colleagues, and the whole family of my mother. My father was crying. . . . We had hand luggage, four large suitcases with our entire life's possessions, an utterly ridiculous thing."[5] Like thousands of others, the Karpińskis gathered at the Gdańsk train station in northern Warsaw on their way out of Poland. They were fleeing a regime that had attacked Jews in the most virulent antisemitic campaign of postwar Europe. Triggered by student protests in the spring of 1968, the PZPR turned on Jews under the euphemistic banner of "anti-Zionism." The campaign had its roots in the tensions of Polish Communist rule. Communism in Poland tended to be less secure than in other Soviet bloc states, especially compared to the GDR, where a better economy, a stronger prewar tradition of Communism, and a remarkably cohesive political leadership produced firmer political stability. Poles were not innately anti-Communist. Many supported Communism, and the regime pursued policies to gain popularity as any state would.[6] Still, Communism in Poland started off in a weaker position because of its perceived antinational connection with Russia; its atheism in a Catholic country; its mythic, antisemitic association with Jews; and memories of the Soviet occupation of eastern Poland during World War II. These factors hardly determined the instability to come; the regime had the chance to gain support in what it believed and offered. But it missed the opportunity, especially with the working class, its most important constituency.[7] The party struggled against restless workers for its entire history, which produced conflict within the party, particularly after the turmoil of 1956, when strikes and protests erupted in the city of Poznań. The party restored Gomułka to power, after expelling him in 1948 for his alleged "nationalist deviation" at the height of Tito's split from Stalin. In 1956, Gomułka briefly gained popular support, but the party soon divided into two factions over the extent of reforming Communism after Soviet leader Nikita Khrushchev declared the end of Stalinism. The Puławska group, named after a Warsaw street where some of its members gathered and lived, tended to be more reform minded in outlook and included some leading Jewish Communists. Its rival, the Natolin group, also named after the part of Warsaw where it met, generally opposed sweeping change, was made up mainly of ethnic Poles, and blamed the errors of Stalinism partly on Jews.[8]

By the early 1960s, another faction had emerged on the scene around the Communist war veteran General Mieczysław Moczar. Appointed interior minister in 1964, Moczar developed a strong base of supporters, known as "Partisans" for their wartime participation in the Communist underground, in the Interior Ministry and in the Union of Fighters for Freedom and Democracy (ZBoWiD). ZBoWiD was the most powerful veteran organization in postwar Poland, with a quarter of a million members. Embracing an ethnically homogeneous idea of the Polish nation, it constructed a cultural memory of the war that focused on Polish victimization and honor. In jockeying for power within the PZPR and believing that Jews threatened Poland, the partisans tarnished their opponents as "Jews" and argued that those pushing for reform were part of a Zionist conspiracy against Poland. The "anti-Zionist" campaign would not have occurred as intensely as it did without Moczar and his allies, who were hostile to even the smallest presence of Jews in postwar Poland.

But it was a series of international and national events that ultimately touched off the fury of hate. Israel's crushing victory in the Six-Day War initiated a flood of anti-Zionist propaganda across the Soviet bloc, but nowhere as intensely as in Poland. Some Poles reacted positively to the Israeli victory against the Soviet-supported Arab states. Gomułka and Moczar were incensed. The Interior Ministry claimed that Polish Jews had orchestrated the response, and Gomułka suggested that those not loyal to Poland should leave. On June 19, 1967, he gave a speech that compared those supporting Israel to a "fifth column." "Israeli aggression against the Arab countries has met with applause in Zionist circles of Jews—Polish citizens," Gomułka said. "We believe that every Polish citizen should only have one fatherland—People's Poland. . . . We do not want a fifth column to arise in our country."[9] Although some Politburo members listening to the speech disliked its strident tone and demanded that the fifth column reference be removed from official versions of it, Gomułka's words sent a clear signal to Moczar's Interior Ministry that the time had come for its long-awaited expulsion of "Zionists."

The campaign began with targeted purges. In 1967, the PZPR banned the American Jewish Joint Distribution Committee from supplying money to the Jewish community and expelled Jews from the armed forces. The campaign then intensified a year later in the midst of opposition to the regime. In March 1968, students at Warsaw University protested the party's decision to ban a performance of Adam Mickiewicz's famous play *Dziady*. The protesters were not looking to overthrow Communism, but to reform and change it from its Stalinist horrors. But the PZPR wanted nothing of their reform and attacked a student rally on March 8 in the hope of quelling the protests. The effort backfired. The unrest spread to other cities for the next two weeks. Gomułka searched for a way to end the student protests, which he feared might extend to workers. He turned to Moczar and his allies, such as Bolesław Piasecki, a wartime fascist turned postwar Communist who established the right-wing, lay Catholic organization PAX, to unleash a verbal attack against the "Zionist" initiators of the protests. A mere three days after the first riots, PAX's newspaper, *Słowo Powszechne,* published an article that explained the student unrest as a "Zionist" conspiracy that had infiltrated the Polish youth and the intelligentsia, making Poles turn away from their "patriotic responsibility for the People's Republic." A purge of state officials soon followed. Roman Zambrowski, a Communist since 1928 and a powerful official in the PPR, was one of the first to be expelled for being a "Zionist." Other Jewish party officials and anyone else labeled a revisionist were forced to resign. By 1970, about 13,000 Jews had left Poland.[10]

Purges and migration lay at the heart of the "anti-Zionist" campaign, but language became the main tool of assault. The year 1968 unleashed an orchestrated pogrom of verbal violence. The PZPR initiated and controlled the campaign, but the hate exploded in frantic, chaotic directions across the state-run print, radio, and television media. The PZPR did not pick up clubs to attack Jews, like so many other rioters did in the history of anti-Jewish violence. They picked up pens and microphones. They attacked Jews from almost every conceivable direction in thousands of press articles.[11] One main line of assault alleged that international Jewish organizations were carrying out a broad "anti-Polish" campaign focused on the breakdown of Polish-Jewish relations during the Holocaust. Based on prejudices against Jews as cosmopolitan, international, conspiratorial, and anti-Polish, this attack claimed that "international Zionism" aimed to smear "Poland's good name" by alleging Polish responsibility for the Holocaust. West German and Israeli agents were "slinging responsibility for the murder of 6 million Jews onto the Polish nation." As another article put it, the "anti-Polish smear campaign of world Zionism" focuses on "the alleged 'crazed' antisemitism in our country and the cooperation of Poles in the extermination of Jews during World War II." A 200-page diatribe, *Israel and the Federal Republic of Germany,* described a vast Zionist "slander campaign" that denied Poland's "generous" rescue of Jews and depicted Poles as the "main helpers of the Nazis in the extermination of the Jews."[12]

This deep, imagined fear that Jews were tarnishing Poland's image had been growing over the 1960s and was triggered partly by increased discussion about the Holocaust across parts of the world, including in Poland, where the Jewish Historical Institute in Warsaw became a leading center in the Soviet bloc for research on the Nazi murder of European Jews.[13] In 1966, the party launched a media campaign against Jerzy Kosinski's recently published book *The Painted Bird,* denouncing the novel about childhood survival in wartime Eastern Europe as anti-Polish. The party also monitored commemorative events on the Holocaust outside Poland, interpreting them as a direct challenge to Polish victimization because of their emphasis on Jewish suffering and their alleged portrayal of Poles as Nazi collaborators. In 1963, in advance of the twentieth anniversary of the Warsaw ghetto uprising, the party expressed concern that "a large exhibition on the issue of Jewish martyrology" was being planned in West Germany with the aim of celebrating the "memory of the victims."[14] Commemorations of the uprising reflected growing interest in the genocide of European Jewry in the United States, Israel, and Europe, interest that had existed in the 1950s but became increasingly more public in the 1960s. This emerging cultural memory of the Holocaust naturally included discussion of Poland, not least because the Warsaw ghetto was a highly remembered event, recalled in performances, monuments, commemorations, and books around the world. It is likely that some commemorations and press coverage portrayed Poles negatively, but to what degree is unknown because little research has been done on anti-Polish prejudice during the 1960s. Some commentators, though, treaded carefully. In 1968, a *New York Times* editorial observed that "not all Poles were passive, of course, nor were all Jews heroes. There were numbers of non-Jewish Poles who lost their lives or risked them to help the doomed thousands in the ghetto. There were even a few Jews who betrayed their own people. But these were the exceptions—on both sides."[15] But nuance mattered little to a party fighting a self-imagined enemy, which allegedly was set out to diminish Polish victimization and imply Polish collaboration with the Nazis.

This fantasy of a Zionist smear campaign reached its height during the summer of 1967, when conflict erupted within the party over a newly published article on the "Nazi concentration camps" in the state's encyclopedia. Reflecting the work of Polish and international scholarship over the past two decades, the article differentiated between "concentration" and "death" camps, explaining that "99 percent" of the death camp victims were Jews.[16] Just several weeks after the Six-Day War, high-ranking party officials closely associated with Moczar pounced on this distinction and argued that it downplayed Polish suffering. As historian Anat Plocker has shown based on extensive archival research, party officials saw the entry as much more than just some technical mistake: it stemmed from a Zionist campaign out to ignore Poland's suffering during the war.[17]

In response, the party diminished Jewish victimization during its commemorations of the Warsaw ghetto uprising, portraying Jewish persecution as one part of the broader suffering of Poles during the war. In a meeting with the World Jewish Congress in 1963, a Polish official admitted openly that the "Zionist aspect" became "entangled" in the decision "against giving the Commemoration of the Warsaw Ghetto Revolt an exclusively Jewish character."[18] Jewish leaders in Poland challenged this marginalization of Jewish suffering. In a meeting with party officials about the twentieth anniversary of the ghetto uprising, the board of the Socio-Cultural Association of Jews indicated that "certain shortcomings and errors" resulted in "inappropriate repercussions." The board regretted the "diminishing" of the "specificity of the Jewish martyrology during the Nazi occupation and attempts to equalize it with the general Nazi politics of extermination." "We believe," the board continued, "that by clearly exposing the full truth about the total extermination of the Jews in the context of the Nazi campaign to destroy [other] nations we can show the deepest viciousness of German fascism."[19] But these protests had little effect. In the leading speech of the twenty-fifth anniversary in 1968 of the Warsaw ghetto uprising, Kazimierz Rusinek, ZBoWiD's general secretary and a leading critic of the encyclopedia article, claimed: "A mistake is being made by those who think and write today that Nazi ideology called for the extermination only of the Jews. Nazism sought the total extermination of Poles, Russians, Jews, and Greeks, the total destruction of France, Italy, and Czechoslovakia, and the total subjugation of the Scandinavians and the English."[20] While Rusinek never denied the Nazi murder of European Jewry, he erased its specificity to reinforce Polish suffering and honor. Poland was at war, and Jews had seized its memory. The party fought back by emphasizing the common fate of both groups and suggesting that Poles had always rescued Jews.[21]

This assault against Jewish memories of the war might seem like a predictable effect of a propaganda machine that went after anything associated with Jews, but it reflected deeper anxieties about the past. The 1968 anti-Zionist campaign turned precisely on the kind of discursive and symbolic politics that shape cultural memories. The perceived challenge that growing international attention to Jewish suffering and alleged discussions of Polish collaboration posed to Polish memory mattered deeply. This international affront had to be confronted seriously because no less than Poland's honor and identity was at stake. Moczar's partisans, who opposed the Nazis during the war, doubtlessly knew much about the everyday ways that Poles became involved in the Nazi persecution of the Jews. Some of Moczar's partisans might have been involved themselves. They deeply feared the Holocaust because it challenged the heroic interpretation of the war that they had been fashioning for the past two decades.[22] They were paranoid about the abject past. They responded by expelling its mnemonic traces during a verbally violent pogrom that pushed some 13,000 Jews out of Poland.

Debating the "Jewish Problem" after 1968

But their actions had deep consequences for Communist Poland. The events of 1968 became a major turning point in Polish postwar history. Many of the country's intellectuals realized that Communism could no longer have a human face, and opposition to the regime grew among students, intellectuals, and workers as the Polish economy weakened in the mid-1970s. The "anti-Zionist" campaign also awakened among Poland's intelligentsia and segments of its population the "Jewish problem," or *problem żydowski.* The campaign shattered the postwar normality of Jews as gone from Poland. Few Jews lived in the country anymore, but their absence provoked reflection like never before in the wake of 1967–68. By the early 1980s, Poland was experiencing its most intense discussion about Polish-Jewish relations since 1945. Many of those involved came from the opposition and wanted to confront the "Jewish problem" as a way to imagine a better, more humane, post-1968 Poland.[23]

Indeed, the first impulses to discuss Polish-Jewish relations emerged among a small group of lay Catholic intellectuals. The lay Catholic intelligentsia formed a distinct milieu in Poland. Centered in Kraków and Warsaw, intellectuals such as Jerzy Turowicz, Stanisław Stomma, Antoni Gołubiew, Zbigniew Herbert, Tadeusz Mazowiecki, Bohdan Cywiński, and Jerzy Zawieyski developed some of the most important forums for open dialogue in Communist Poland. They gathered at the Catholic Intellectual Clubs (KIK) and wrote in the lay Catholic publications *Tygodnik Powszechny, Znak,* and *Więź.* In 1956, a small group of them entered the Sejm, or Polish parliament, as a tiny political faction known as the Znak group, which was created during the period of de-Stalinization. In the 1950s and 1960s, Znak embraced some of the state's ideological priorities, forming a semi-independent voice within the Communist system. These intellectuals were more or less "progressive," with differences naturally from individual to individual. They welcomed the reforms of the Second Vatican Council, appeared more liberal than the Polish Catholic hierarchy, and embraced a more inclusive Polish identity. But they leaned more conservatively on other issues such as gender and sexual equality. With only a few women among their ranks, they continued the prewar tradition of the salon as a male-dominated space of intellectual exchange and rarely challenged heterosexual norms. Most also came from the upper echelons of prewar Polish society, representing the surviving remnant of Poland's nobility that had long dominated the intelligentsia but was now fading in importance after the murderous policies of the Nazis and the efforts of the Communist regime to build a new intellectual elite from the working class and peasantry.

An important core of the group—Turowicz, Stomma, Gołubiew, and Herbert—came from the *kresy,* Poland's eastern borderlands, which the Soviet Union took after 1945. This area, made up of different ethnic, religious, and political groups, was more diverse than the rest of Poland, but its multiethnicity was mythologized after the war. Gołubiew claimed that those who lived in the *kresy* were more likely to identify with the "state" than with the "nation," while Herbert wrote that "Poland without Jews, without Ukrainians, without Armenians, as it was in Lwów . . . stopped being Poland."[24] Few mentioned that the *kresy* witnessed some of the bloodiest attacks against Jews and Ukrainians. Still, some clearly valued multiethnicity, and that was important—however mythologized—because it shaped how they generally thought about Poland's minorities. In 1945, Jerzy Turowicz, editor of *Tygodnik Powszechny,* rejected tying "Catholicism with ideological positions such as totalitarianism, extreme nationalism, and racial antisemitism." In another essay, he criticized exclusively linking Polishness with Catholicism because it could perpetuate "a certain element of intolerance or discrimination."[25] Turowicz crafted his words carefully here, but he clearly was rejecting Roman Dmowski's belief that any attempt to "dissociate Catholicism from Polishness and to separate the nation from its religion and the Church is to destroy the very essence of the nation."[26]

Turowicz, though, was not just wrestling with ghosts. He had a rival in postwar Poland in the form of PAX, the lay Catholic organization that forged close ties with the Communist state and embraced Dmowski's anti-semitism. PAX took over Turowicz's newspaper from 1953 to 1956 at the height of the state's repression of the Catholic Church during Stalinization. The organization came into existence in 1947 thanks to Bolesław Piasecki, an eclectic figure who began his political career before the war as the leader of a small fascist group and ended it in support of Communism. Captured for battling the Soviets in eastern Poland, he convinced his captors that he could help the fledgling regime gain support from Catholics and right-wing radicals. He established PAX to bridge Marxism and Catholicism, to unify believers and nonbelievers under the banner of God, nation, and socialism. Two ideas dominated Piasecki's shifting biography—the *Polak-Katolik* and antisemitism. Piasecki fervently embraced Dmowski's idea that Poland should be made up only of Poles, and he hated Jews.[27]

The worldviews of PAX and Znak collided in 1968. Piasecki became an anti-Zionist propagator with articles in his newspaper, *Słowo Powszechne*, which launched the campaign's opening salvo. Meanwhile, Znak, represented in parliament by six members, initially moved in a different direction. In June 1967, Znak reacted to Poland's response to the Six-Day War by drafting a parliamentary interpellation that criticized the government's position of siding with the Arab states without recognizing Israel's right to exist. The draft implied that Israel deserved special consideration, especially from Poland, "where Jews lived together with us under the same roof for centuries and where in 1939–1945 together we suffered persecution."[28] But this statement was never submitted. Perhaps Znak thought that it would be too risky with news coming from Moscow that the Soviet bloc had officially condemned Israel and would end diplomatic relations with it. The Znak group, however, did not buckle under pressure a year later in response to the PZPR's suppression of the student protests. It drafted another interpellation and this time submitted it. The statement demanded to know: "What does the government intend to do to offer a substantial answer to the burning questions of the youth, which are also nagging questions for a broad section of public opinion, concerning the democratic rights of citizens and the cultural politics of the government?"[29] These were bold words written by a group that had much to lose and almost nothing to gain by expressing them. The student protestors were hardly part of the lay Catholic intellectual milieu. Most identified with the secular left and wanted little to do with Catholicism.

Znak defended them at a dire moment, but its intervention only went so far. It said nothing about the anti-Zionist campaign. This silence was understandable at first. The Znak interpellation appeared on the same day that Piasecki's newspaper published the campaign's opening attack. Although Moczar's anti-Jewish position would have been clear to anyone, no one could possibly have imagined the virulence of hate that was to come. But Znak's silence was not excusable a month later. By now the anti-Zionist campaign had reached its peak, and even Znak was being attacked for its "Zionist" leanings. "Today the [Znak] group departs even further from the interests of Poland," intoned Zenon Kliszko, a member of the Politburo. "It stands on the side of the Zionist and revisionist elements who have inspired and organized this entire provocation."[30]

The Znak group said nothing about these absurd charges. It debated long and hard about how to react. In early April, the Sejm was set to discuss its interpellation, and Znak had to deliver a response. Three days before the session, the group met at the apartment of Jerzy Zawieyski, a prominent writer and Znak member who would deliver the parliamentary reply. Zawieyski read his remarks with great tension and energy, even collapsing in tears at the end.[31] Although he focused on defending the writers under attack, he touched upon the anti-Zionist campaign. Everyone in the room approved his statement except Janusz Zabłocki, who suggested removing the part on the state's anti-Zionism. Zabłocki had been growing closer to Moczar's camp over the past several months and considered creating his own Catholic group to foster closer church-state ties. He soon left Znak, but not before removing the anti-Zionist section of Zawieyski's speech. Why Zawieyski relented is unknown. Perhaps he hoped to ameliorate the growing rift in Znak, or perhaps he did not want to offend Gomułka, whom he clearly admired. "I see him as a dramatic figure with a sense of responsibility not only for the Party, but for the Polish nation," he said on the floor of the Sejm.[32] As a member of the State Council from 1957 to 1968, Zawieyski still, naively and tragically, wanted to believe that the PZPR wanted to reform Communism. He left the Sejm utterly defeated and committed suicide in 1969.

In the end, then, the Znak group voiced no opposition to the anti-Zionist campaign, and two of its members even reinforced the state's linguistic framing of Jews as inherently anti-Polish. At the end of the parliamentary session, Konstanty Łubieński defended Znak as a proud patriotic guardian against Jewish smear tactics. "Like all Poles, we condemn the campaign carried out abroad accusing Poles of participation in the extermination of the Jews," he remarked. The other member was Zabłocki, who explained a month later that he opposed including any reference to the anti-Zionist campaign because neither he nor anyone else cared enough "about an issue that is not our issue." He went on to say that the state should not be led by people "whose solidarity with another fatherland puts them above solidarity with Poland."[33]

Znak's conflicted involvement in 1968 shaped interest in Polish-Jewish relations in the 1970s and 1980s. Interest in the Jewish past, which began just a few years after 1968, stemmed in part from shame that Znak and other Catholics kept so silent. A desire to discuss the "Jewish problem" involved reflecting on Catholicism's long history of anti-Jewish bias but also its most recent failings. Moreover, Znak's role in 1968 brought Poland's religious and secular intellectuals into dialogue with one another. Although both intellectual groups crossed paths before in publications such as *Tygodnik Powszechny* and *Znak,* they tended to keep to themselves throughout the 1950s and 1960s. In the wake of 1968, both circles realized that the regime had targeted them for the common values they shared. Two towering intellectuals, the Catholic writer Bohdan Cywiński and the leftist secular dissident Adam Michnik, sealed the alliance. In 1971, Cywiński published his landmark book *Genealogies of the Indomitable,* which urged the lay Catholic intelligentsia to join with the secular left in fighting for the common values of dialogue, tolerance, and pluralism. Four years later, Michnik came from the other side and attempted to convince the secular left to embrace progressive Catholics such as Cywiński, Turowicz, and Mazowiecki. In *The Church and the Left,* he argued that when it counted most, the Znak group had the courage to defend the secular left. Michnik's book stands as one of the most important intellectual texts of the Polish opposition. It advocated for creating a strong, engaged civil society. This alternative politics, like the New Left on the Iron Curtain's western side, located power in civil society rather than the state. It wanted to empower citizens through open, democratic dialogue and create a pluralistic polity, even if it did not always achieve that goal (few of Poland's opposition leaders, Michnik included, counted themselves as feminists, for example).[34]

A component of this alternative politics involved reflecting on what it meant to be Polish. This rethinking of identity brought the religious and secular intelligentsia into extended discussions about Poland's fraught history with Jews, Germans, and Ukrainians. In *The Church and the Left*, Michnik suggested learning about Poland's "not always glorious past" while embracing its "pluralism, its variety."[35] In 1981, the prominent intellectual Jan Józef Lipski, founder of the opposition group Workers' Defense Committee (KOR), published an essay about Polish nationalism with the searing title "Two Fatherlands—Two Patriotisms: Remarks on the National Megalomania and Xenophobia of Poles." Widely circulated in the clandestine press, the article called for a patriotism that followed the humanistic values of Christianity with its basic creed to "love our fellow man." Lipski criticized Poland's hatred toward Germans, Russians, Czechs, and Ukrainians, but his prose became impassioned when it came to antisemitism. Broadly covering the Middle Ages to 1968, Lipski analyzed with deep regret the history of anti-Jewish hatred in Poland.[36]

Such critical sentiments registered all the more powerfully after the hate of 1968. "For me and my generation—people born after the end of the war—the Jewish problem did not exist," wrote the essayist and Warsaw University Professor Marcin Król. "The Jewish problem, the problem of Polish-Jewish relations, was forced upon us and it was because of March 1968 that I decided to participate in the work on the Jewish cemetery in Warsaw a few years after the March events."[37] Król points to a generation born after the war that had no lived experience of Jews and was young during the period of Stalinization. He rightly stresses that this generation became interested in the Jewish past more eagerly than its parents had, but young people were not the only ones. Some of the leading figures in rediscovering the Jewish past were born in the interwar years or earlier, such as Jerzy Turowicz, Jerzy Woronczak, Jerzy Tomaszewski, and Jan Jagielski.

What seems more salient, then, is that 1968 shattered the social acceptance that Jewish life in Poland had ended and threw into stark question exclusive, nationalistic forms of Polish identity. The absence of Poland's large Jewish community had become assimilated into everyday life; it had become so normal, so banal, that it rarely received much thought. That is not to say that Poles never discussed the "Jewish problem" before 1967–68, but rather that the anti-Zionist campaign made the absence of Jews much more present to Poles who now sought out alternative interpretations of Jews from the regime's portrayal of them as treacherous, anti-Polish Zionists and who sought out different forms of identifying themselves as Poles from the one offered by a state that had expelled some 13,000 Jews. In 1971, members of the Catholic Intellectual Club in Warsaw organized the first annual "Week of Jewish Culture." The members of the club hoped the initiative would provide a better "understanding of a rich and yet poorly known culture" that "lived among us for centuries" but whose "gigantic tragedy in the last war we witnessed."[38] The event offered lectures on topics such as Jewish religious practices, National Democracy, the Kielce pogrom, and Christian-Jewish relations. By paying attention to "forgotten or distorted issues," it contributed to building a "new, rich, and diverse society." Through the "Week of Jewish Culture," the club members hoped to "defend" a cultural heritage from being "cut off from our own history" and from being excluded by a "homogeneous and bland conception of the nation."[39]

At the same time that Poles began to work through the verbal hate and ethnic nationalism of 1968, some Polish Jews started to rediscover their Jewish roots. These Polish Jews, who understood as little about Judaism as their Catholic friends did, rarely thought about their Jewishness until 1968. "In the first dozen or so years of my life," explained Stanisław Krajewski, "I knew absolutely nothing about my Jewish background." A leading voice of "Poles trying to be Jewish," Krajewski pointed to 1968 as the "turning point" in his rediscovery.[40] In 1979, he and others became involved in the Jewish Flying University that was created in the spirit of the nineteenth-century underground "Flying University" of partitioned Poland. Held usually in private apartments and involving as many as 100 people, it sponsored lectures on Jewish history, culture, and religion for both Jews and non-Jews.

A deep sense of loss shaped much of this interest in Jewishness among both Jews and non-Jews. In the 1980s, the journalist and dissident Małgorzata Niezabitowska spent five years traveling across Poland with her husband to document the "remnants" of Jewish life: abandoned Jewish cemeteries and desolate prayer houses, along with the country's "last Jews" who occasionally filled them. On the editorial staff of *Tygodnik Solidarność* and a contributor to *Tygodnik Powszechny*, Niezabitowska published her discoveries in *Remnants: The Last Jews of Poland*. The book contains probing conversations between the non-Jewish Niezabitowska and her Jewish interviewees, which return to the common theme of absence. Speaking with the esteemed historian Szymon Datner, Niezabitowska confesses that, despite years of talking with people, reading books, and looking at old photographs, she still cannot "imagine the world of the Polish Jews that existed on this land such a short time ago. It seems as distant as the ancient Etruscans do from the present-day inhabitants of Rome." Datner describes the "world" of Polish Jewry to her, but he speaks in the past tense. "The world of the Polish Jews was extraordinarily varied, rich, and colorful," he says.[41] This longing for the past rested on simplistic, sentimental, and essentialized imaginations of Jews as different, unique, and strange, yet seemingly authentic, wholesome, and beautiful. As Niezabitowska probes her subjects, her husband follows behind her to snap photographs of Jews and their dilapidated, desolate surroundings. Jews become a reified subject to be discovered, displayed, catalogued, and preserved. They become objects of curiosity and study, intriguing artifacts of the past that could be put into a museum or examined in a series of essays. Indeed, Niezabitowska displayed the contents of her book in an exhibition in Warsaw and reproduced excerpts of it in the premier depository of exotica and discovery, *National Geographic.*[42]

There were, however, a few attempts to engage more critically with Polish-Jewish relations. In November 1980, an underground bulletin published in Wrocław devoted an entire issue to "Jews and Poles" and confessed in its introduction that Jews are a "problem for us." There is the "problem of our conscience, burdened by the excesses of antisemitism before the war, the ghetto benches in universities. There is the problem of the indifference of parts of society to the extermination [of the Jews]."[43] The underground journals *Krytyka, Aneks,* and *Arka* examined the "conscience" of the past, probing topics such as the exclusivity of Polish nationalism, the history of antisemitism, and the issue of Judeo-Communism.[44] These discussions continued in a series of international conferences about Polish-Jewish relations throughout the 1980s held in the United States, Britain, and Israel.

Closer to home, Jan Józef Lipski gave a long speech on the "Jewish question" at a conference on 1968 held in 1981 at the University of Warsaw and attended by several thousand people. It was, though, a deeply confused speech, one that uncovered the anxiety that often surfaced when discussing Polish-Jewish relations. Lipski remained hesitant to probe the history of antisemitism in Polish society. He spoke defensively, especially about what he believed were unfair accusations from the West spread by Jews. "What is written about the Polish nation in the West is sometimes really unjust. . . . I am hurt when I sometimes read about a 'nation of blackmailers.'"[45] Taking his own family's assistance to Jews as reflective of the national whole, he asked: "What are we being hit in the face for today?" "Anti-Polonism is not any morally better than antisemitism or anti-Ukrainianism," he concluded in another speech. Such defensive posturing precluded Lipski from thinking about Poland's relationship to the Holocaust except in equivocating terms. "Did we all do as much as was possible, or too little, or nothing at a time when dying people and our own moral norms called for more than the possible?"[46] In some ways, Lipski even embraced the regime's castigation of Polish collaboration in the Holocaust as subversive and unpatriotic. Although he claimed to distance himself from such "propaganda," he claimed that "Jewish circles" in the West had made "irresponsible accusations" about Poland's "complicity" in the Holocaust. Lipski received criticism for this. In 1987, Jan Gross, who fled Poland in 1968 for the United States, urged him to recognize that Poles provided little assistance to Jews because they accepted the Nazi anti-Jewish policies of ghettoization.[47]

Lipski, however, was not alone in his defensive views. In 1985, when the PZPR showed selections of Claude Lanzmann's film *Shoah,* an eruption of criticism against this "Western" intervention into Polish-Jewish relations exploded onto the pages of Poland's official, Catholic, and underground press. Lanzmann's landmark film is not directly about Poland. Interviews with survivors form its cinematic core, but some of the film's most jarring scenes come from an intentionally portrayed dark, drab, poor, and antisemitic Poland. The film provoked defensive comments about its "anti-Polish" agenda. The state television station received 149 letters largely critical of it.[48] Most intellectuals responded in kind. Jerzy Turowicz could barely restrain his anger, calling the film "definitely partial and tendentious." "It is quite a reflection," he wrote, "of the common, simplistic, and unfair stereotype in the West about the issue of Poles and Jews; it is in a word—anti-Polish." These words received strong criticism from some international followers of the Polish scene. The British historian Timothy Garton Ash wanted Turowicz, a Catholic intellectual of "distinction, integrity, and longstanding opposition to antisemitism," to think more critically about the role that the church played in disseminating anti-Jewish prejudices.[49] Ash, like Gross, wanted his colleague to consider the active ways Poles became involved in the Holocaust.

In the end, these outside interventions provoked little discussion in Poland. Gross's time would come thirteen years later with the publication of *Neighbors*. For the time being, it was an inside voice that started to move in the direction that Lipski, Turowicz, and indeed many Poles resisted. In 1987, the literary critic Jan Błoński published in *Tygodnik Powszechny* his now famous essay "The Poor Poles Look at the Ghetto." Czesław Miłosz's poem "A Poor Christian Looks at the Ghetto" served as Błoński's starting point. Writing in 1943, as smoke still billowed from Muranów, Miłosz imagined himself buried alive among the Warsaw ghetto's charred ruins and dead bodies as an apparently Jewish "guardian mole" bores through the rubble, making his way ever closer to the suffocated, fearful poet. Błoński takes the fear that permeates Miłosz's poem to reflect on the inability of Poles to confront the Holocaust. The fear that paralyzes the poet has paralyzed Polish society. Imagining a conversation between a traveling Pole and a "Westerner," Błoński works through the anxiety and pain that he has felt when the question "Why are Poles anti-Semites?" is inevitably asked. Defensive responses follow ever more frustrated tones that only seek to deny this harmful "accusation." The Polish-Jewish past comes up as a problem to be refuted because, Błoński concludes, Poles remain deeply afraid of their guilt. The Jewish mole has never stopped burrowing into the Polish "subconscious." The only way to work through this anxiety is to accept Miłosz's claim that "yes, we are guilty." Błoński frames Polish guilt as passively sharing responsibility for a crime without actually taking part in it. He, too, cannot characterize Poles as active participants in genocide, even when pressed by "voices claiming just that" from Jews in the West. He concludes instead that had Poles been more "humane" to Jews before the Holocaust, genocide perhaps "would not have met with the indifference and moral turpitude of the society in whose full view it took place."[50]

Błoński's bold yet cautious intervention sparked intense debate. Some 200 people published responses to his essay. Supporters agreed that Poles needed to think about their dark pasts as a way to embrace a more open idea of Polish identity. The journalist Ewa Berberyusz wrote that Polish society "found it easier to turn its back on what was happening," while Jerzy Turowicz went much further than he did two years earlier and confessed that the Catholic

Church "propagated" antisemitism. Błoński's opponents would have none of this unpatriotic talk, which they interpreted as an assault on Polish victimization and honor. Władysław Siła-Nowicki, an important Solidarity lawyer, could have easily been mistaken for a PZPR spokesman. He framed the problem exactly as the party had since the mid-1960s, claiming that Błoński's article reflected the "quintessence" of a "virulent anti-Polish propaganda campaign conducted endlessly for dozens of years by the enemies of . . . the Polish nation." Kazimierz Kąkol, a state official who played a major role in the "anti-Zionist" campaign, placed Błoński's essay firmly within broader, Western attempts to defame the Polish nation.[51] Just as in 1968, so twenty years later: the Jewish mole caused such fear and anxiety that the only response for some was defensive, hysterical refutation.

As these debates about Polish-Jewish relations raged in the underground and Catholic press, the PZPR started to shift its own thinking about the "Jewish problem." The party acted largely for political reasons as its rule became unstable after 1968. In late 1970, Gomułka was forced out of office for the second and final time. In the midst of a weakening Polish economy, he made the costly mistake of raising food prices with no advance warning just weeks before Christmas. Strikes erupted in the shipyards on the Baltic coast, and workers set the party headquarters in Gdańsk on fire. Gomułka responded harshly: 41 people were killed, 1,000 injured, and 3,200 arrested. Soviet leader Brezhnev grew alarmed, and Gomułka quickly stepped down. Edward Gierek, a Communist since 1931 and a member of the Politburo since 1959, replaced him as first secretary in December 1970. Gierek tried to stabilize the regime by modernizing the Polish economy through increased consumption, improvements in agriculture, and opening up to Western markets. Gierek also attempted to improve Poland's image abroad. He liked to portray himself as a pragmatic, worldly leader, drawing on his personal biography as a young miner in France and Belgium and meeting often with leaders from the United States, France, West Germany, and Austria. Much of this outreach was by necessity; billions of dollars in foreign loans were propping up the Polish economy.

As part of Gierek's international outreach, the regime slowly shifted its approach toward the Jewish minority. But it also had to do so. The party's "Jewish problem" did not just suddenly disappear with the departure of 13,000 Jews. In a paradox that doubtless no one in Moczar's Interior Ministry could have foreseen, the party's "Jewish problem" only continued after 1968, albeit now it was not an imagined one in the minds of Communist leaders but a real one with actual consequences for the Polish state. Just as 1968 made Poles and Jews more aware of the Jewish past, it did the same among Jews outside Poland, especially in the United States and Israel. While Jews abroad certainly thought of Poland before 1968, the anti-Zionist campaign made it front and center. This growing international interest in Poland initially came from leaders of Jewish organizations and Orthodox religious communities who became deeply concerned about the state of Jewish life in the country. Since so few Jews now lived in Poland, Jewish leaders became interested mainly in symbolic issues such as the poor condition of Jewish sites and the lack of attention to Jewish suffering at Auschwitz. In three years, from 1976 to 1979, Jewish leaders and Polish state officials met nine times in discussions that lasted several days about the preservation of Jewish sites, the return of confiscated Jewish property, and the need to remember the genocide of the Jews. These meetings involved prominent Jewish leaders, such as Elie Wiesel, Nahum Goldmann, and Yitzhak Arad, as well as representatives from the World Jewish Congress, the American Federation of Polish Jews, the Federation of Polish Jews in Israel, and groups of American and Israeli rabbis. Many of these Jewish leaders either had survived the Holocaust in Poland or were born there, making their interest in preserving the material traces of Jewish life and ensuring the memory of the Holocaust deeply personal.[52]

The PZPR initially interpreted their interest in Poland through the ideational frames of 1967–68. Although Gierek enacted important economic and foreign policy changes, he and his top officials had participated in the anti-Zionist campaign. Kazimierz Kąkol, Gierek's point man in the 1970s for Jewish issues as head of the Office of Religious Affairs, was in fact one of the mouthpieces of 1968. In the 1970s, Kąkol and others described interest from Jewish leaders as the "Jewish problem," a phrase stamped on hundreds of pages coming from the Central Committee, the Foreign Ministry, and the Interior Ministry. This flood of paper claimed that "national-Zionist circles" threatened Poland through their control of "the powerful mass media" in the West. This conspiratorial attack used every "pretext" to carry out an "anti-Polish campaign" by making "slanderous claims about 'traditional Polish antisemitism'" and "to burden our nation with the guilt and joint responsibility for the Nazi extermination of the Jews and the destruction of Jewish culture." The party took this "campaign" seriously, arguing that because "Jewish organizations have such an enormous influence" in "Western countries," the campaign was having a "negative effect on the political and economic interests of our country."[53]

The PZPR's anxiety about Jews had barely subsided. But this time the party reacted to it differently. If in the spring of 1968 the PZPR solved its self-imposed "Jewish problem" by forcing Jews to leave Poland, it now came to believe that the best way to handle its new, post-1968 "Jewish problem" was to bring them virtually back into the country. In notes on a meeting concerning "the matter of counteracting attacks against Poland by international Jewish circles," the party suggested creating "appearances of a Jewish authenticity" in Poland by preserving Jewish sites and emphasizing the specificity of the Holocaust at death camps such as Auschwitz.[54] Kazimierz Kąkol took the lead on this new approach. In 1978, he insisted that the "complex of Jewish matters" carried "great weight" and could be either of "great harm or of a good deal of benefit" to the party. "It cannot be taken care of in the old style, temporarily without a broader political perspective."[55] After meeting with a group of American rabbis in 1976, he sent a memo to each municipal government in Poland, indicating that the state "maintains in principle" that "all existing Jewish cemeteries shall be preserved." Doubtlessly aware that the state was not going to put any money behind this, he added that "in practice" this meant ending the long-standing policy of liquidating cemeteries and putting them to other uses.[56]

Warsaw, Poland's most visible city and the one most often visited by international Jewish leaders after Auschwitz, became the centerpiece of this emerging strategy. Although much of what was left of Jewish Warsaw after the Nazi occupation vanished over the 1950s, a few Jewish sites remained in the capital. Warsaw had two Jewish cemeteries, a synagogue, a Jewish historical institute, and a state-run Jewish theater. These Jewish spaces, especially the synagogue and the cemeteries, had fallen into pitiful shape after years of neglect. In a city of ninety registered Jewish community members, their ruined condition dramatically captured the collapse of Jewish life in Poland after the Holocaust and 1968, which Jewish leaders and international journalists duly noted. In 1973, James Feron, a *New York Times* foreign correspondent, published a long article on Warsaw. He declared that "Poland is

perhaps witnessing a final chapter of the thousand-year-old history of Polish Jewry." Warsaw's abandoned Jewish spaces provided the most arresting
evidence for his conclusion. "We were circling the Nożyk Synagogue . . .
looking for an open door. The century-old building is the last synagogue
still standing in Warsaw, and it looks ready for the wrecker's hammer."
Feron moved on to Warsaw's main Jewish cemetery on Okopowa—the
"largest and possibly busiest surviving Jewish site for Warsaw Jews." That
Feron described a resting place of the dead as more lively than a synagogue
is deliberate irony, but he leaves it at that and returns to his theme of pur-
poseful destruction: "One whole section in the most remote corner has been
systematically looted, evidently some years ago. A rumor persists that Polish
authorities will build a road through the cemetery, or turn it into a park."[57]
Feron's piece reinforces stereotypical images of Poland as gray, drab, cold,
lifeless, and antisemitic that probably surprised few American readers, only
confirming their assumptions of the Jewish graveyard of Communist Eastern Europe.

But Feron's article, while based on Cold War prejudices of the antisemitic,
dictatorial East, described the results of postwar neglect and destruction. It
underscored just how difficult it was going to be for the party to re-create
a "Jewish authenticity" in a capital of crumbling Jewish sites. Plans to build a
road through the cemetery were not rumors. At a meeting when the idea
was first discussed in 1956, the Socio-Cultural Association of Jews in Poland opposed the plan because it would involve exhuming around 5,400
graves. The city's chief engineer urged Jewish leaders to think of its "civic
approach" to the "needs" of Warsaw residents.[58] As years passed, the city continued to press Jewish leaders on the issue, but they refused to relent, arguing that the "cemetery is a symbol of the great tragedy of Polish Jewry" and
destroying any part of it would "provoke outrage among Jews in Poland and
throughout the entire world."[59] City officials eventually shelved the project
in the 1970s, realizing that building a road through a Jewish cemetery in its
capital city would be politically unwise, to say the least.

The PZPR also faced a similar difficulty with the Nożyk Synagogue. The
building had been closed since 1968 and symbolized the ravages of the party's approach toward Jews. Kąkol understood the symbolic potency of this
ruined space and urged that the state renovate it. He saw the synagogue as a
public relations coup that the state could exploit with its increasing number

Warsaw's Nożyk Synagogue in 1975 after three decades of neglect. (© Phyllis Myers)

of visitors. Yet Kąkol was the lone voice supporting the synagogue's restoration for years. In 1979, Poland's prime minister responded to his request for 8 million złoty by suggesting that "rich Jewish organizations in the West" could pay for the expenses. Kąkol replied that this was a small sum compared to the financial claims that "international Jewish circles" could make for confiscated Jewish communal property.[60] As few seemed persuaded, Kąkol grew worried about the international repercussions of the synagogue's dilapidated condition and appealed directly to Gierek for intervention:

> For many years, the Office for Religious Affairs has pointed out that the rebuilding of the Warsaw synagogue would be an important showpiece politically for Poland. . . . It was expected that it would be rebuilt as quickly as possible. Unfortunately, the reconstruction work is being carried out very sluggishly. Intervention from this office over the past years has led to no visible results. . . . Meanwhile, each day that its rebuilding is delayed causes negative political consequences. Tourists

from the West, and among them a large number of aggressive representatives from Jewish circles, visit the synagogue as a general rule. Its pitiful appearance is causing undesirable commentaries and political repercussions for our country.[61]

Kąkol's plea had no immediate effect. Another three years passed until finally in the summer of 1982 the PZPR approved the synagogue's reconstruction.

The timing was pivotal. In April 1983, Poland was to host an international commemoration of the Warsaw Ghetto Uprising's fortieth anniversary. Numerous tourists, Jewish leaders, and journalists were going to be in the capital. The last thing the state wanted was more bad press; it had plenty of that over the past two years. As the Polish economy faltered and opposition grew in the wake of 1968, resistance to Communism increased dramatically in the late 1970s and then grew stronger when Pope John Paul II, newly selected from his former position as archbishop of Kraków, returned to his native Poland in 1979. The pope was greeted by crowds in the hundreds of thousands, and his visit gave spiritual and emotional momentum to the opposition movement. A year after the pope's visit, workers organized strike committees in response to the party's increase in the price of meat served in factory cafeterias and created a national trade union called Solidarity, which rapidly morphed into a broad and diverse opposition movement of 9 million Poles. The Communist leadership was shocked, but above all in turmoil over what was turning into something much more than just any normal labor protest. Moscow became worried and threatened invasion. In the fall of 1981, the PZPR acted forcefully and put General Wojciech Jaruzelski in charge. Jaruzelski quickly declared martial law. The state detained Solidarity leaders and cynically used antisemitic attacks in the media to try to weaken the movement's appeal. As news outlets across the world reported these events, Jaruzelski's regime desperately searched to improve its image in any way possible. When the issue of Warsaw's synagogue crossed his desk, Jaruzelski probably lunged for a pen to sign it. He ordered the building's reconstruction because its "devastated condition" was souring "relations with influential Jewish circles in the world."[62] Jaruzelski demanded that the project be completed in a short ten months, just before the state's massive fortieth anniversary of the Warsaw Ghetto Uprising. At the synagogue's reopening on April 18, 1983, the new director of the Department of Religious Affairs,

Adam Łopatka, presented the state's actions as a heroic attempt to rescue "Jewish monuments" from "Nazi barbarism."[63]

The party hoped that such a public gesture might mollify Jewish concerns, but it had the opposite effect. Interest in Poland from abroad only continued. In 1983, Sigmund Nissenbaum, a Warsaw Jew who survived the Holocaust and settled in Constance on the German-Swiss border, returned to his hometown for the ghetto uprising commemoration to find his city's Jewish sites in shambles. He was saddened by the condition of the Jewish cemetery in his childhood district of Praga, where many of his relatives were buried. The Nazis had destroyed many of its gravestones, and after the war about 5,000 had been piled together by a tractor. Parts of the cemetery were used for pasture in the 1950s. Nissenbaum established a foundation to take care of the cemetery and other Jewish sites in Poland. Officially recognized by the state in 1985, the Nissenbaum Family Foundation restored tombstones and erected a new gate for the cemetery. The PZPR welcomed its work, not least because of the hard currency it brought into Poland, but it also worried that the foundation might gain too much influence over a sensitive topic.[64]

The greatest threat, though, to the state's authority ultimately came not from abroad but from within Poland. Segments of the opposition resisted the party's sudden embrace of the Jewish past, especially in 1983 and 1988, when the PZPR staged two massive commemorations of the Warsaw Ghetto Uprising. The opposition boycotted both of them and organized its own events. In years past, members of the Catholic Intellectual Club and the Jewish Flying University had been organizing small, unofficial commemorations at the Warsaw ghetto memorial, but the one in 1983 was larger and more directly political. Marek Edelman, the uprising's only surviving leader living in Poland, rejected the state's invitation to attend its ceremony in a highly public letter. Edelman refused to participate in a ceremony when "words and gestures are completely falsified."[65] The clandestine ceremony took place on April 17 and gathered about a thousand people. This clearly worried the secret police, which noted that the "majority of Polish society" viewed the state-sponsored ceremony "with little interest as an event for foreign Jews."[66] The police prevented Edelman from leaving his home and stopped Solidarity leader Lech Wałęsa on his way to Warsaw. Dozens of police cars lined the streets of Muranów on the day of the unofficial ceremony.

Participants placed flowers at the base of Rapoport's monument and gave several speeches. The event lasted about an hour before the police dispersed the crowd. "To many of the demonstrators, the jackbooted policemen, with their long gray-blue belted overcoats, caps, and submachine guns, recalled the stark photographs of similarly dressed Nazi soldiers here 40 years ago," the *New York Times* wrote.[67] The PZPR probably could not have imagined a more damaging indictment. Opposition leaders probably could not have imagined a better one. They, too, were acting for political reasons and to gain international attention: the banners, protests, and unofficial ceremonies were all part of the carnival of revolution that was unfolding in Poland as Communism weakened.[68]

But some opposition members clearly also became interested in the Jewish past as part of their imagination of a better Poland in the wake of the regime's attack against Jews in 1967–68. In 1988, the state celebrated the forty-fifth anniversary of the ghetto uprising in another massive international event that brought it and the opposition into competition once again. The unofficial ceremony was initiated mainly by Jacek Kuroń. Born in 1934 in Lwów (now Lviv) into a family with strong ties to the Polish Socialist Party, Kuroń followed the trajectory of other European intellectuals who moved away from their fervent embrace of Communism. He joined the Polish Communist youth organization at the age of fifteen, but in 1965 criticized the regime for straying from the principles of Marxism and then severed all ties with Communism after 1968. Kuroń cared deeply about Poland's relationship with its minorities, working tirelessly toward reconciliation with Jews and Ukrainians in particular. As an eight-year-old boy, he witnessed the suicide of a fourteen-year-old Jewish girl for whom his father provided shelter and false identity papers. Her death made a deep impression on him, as did his trips through the Lwów ghetto on the streetcar en route to the swimming pool, where he saw "people lying in the street dying of thirst" while he later chewed on "large, juicy cherries."[69] In April 1988, Kuroń handed over to Western journalists an appeal that a number of opposition members and intellectuals had signed regarding the upcoming anniversary of the ghetto uprising. It expressed profound loss. "For eight centuries the Polish land was a shared land. The fate of Polish Jews is part of Poland's fate, and their faith, language, culture, and tradition were an essential component of its social landscape." The appeal continued with "deep regret" that

Poles did not always "notice this truth." "We express with deep sadness that everything we could and were able to do to save our brothers was too little for what was needed." It ended by calling on Polish society to pay "remembrance to Polish Jews" on April 17 at the unofficial celebration of the ghetto uprising. Kuroń predicted that the event would express "the voice of an independent society," and by the sheer numbers it did.[70] It began at the ghetto memorial with about 2,000 people and grew as the crowd moved through the streets toward the *Umschlagplatz*. Perhaps as many as 10,000 Poles attended the ceremony. Gathered with friends in his apartment that evening, Kuroń triumphantly declared that the "voice of society" had been heard. "The government in Poland never speaks in the name of society."[71]

Perhaps that was true, but what Polish "society" was actually saying was less clear. Some Poles had become interested in the Jewish past as a way to imagine a different Poland, but that did not necessarily involve thinking deeply about the traumatic, dark parts of that history. No later than the following evening did the difficulty of talking about Polish-Jewish relations beyond a few noble sentences again become starkly apparent. Hundreds of people packed into a small church in the Solec district of Warsaw on a warm, spring evening for a panel discussion that lasted well over two hours. When the floor opened for questions, the defensive posturing began as "fifty years of unresolved anger and guilt flooded the room." That description, coming from an American Jewish observer, probably is an exaggeration that speaks to its own kind of unresolved trauma, but still one can imagine that the discussion was emotive like during the Błoński and *Shoah* controversies. Three audience members apparently stood up in defiance. "'People always say the Poles didn't do enough for the Jews; it's not fair! We hear so much about Poles who betrayed Jews; why not talk about the Poles who risked their lives to help Jews?'"[72] Once the crowds dispersed and the banners were put away, the problem of Polish-Jewish relations was as sensitive as ever.

What is more, it is not clear how broadly Polish interest in the Jewish past stretched. Outside the capital, the condition of Jewish sites quickly deteriorated and interest in them declined. Warsaw was exceptional. No other Polish city experienced such intense attention from party, opposition, and Catholic leaders. This was the case not just for Poland's small towns, the vanished *shtetls*, but also for its larger cities, including Wrocław. By the 1970s, Wrocław's Jewish community had declined to a few hundred members after its postwar high of

Wrocław's synagogue after years of neglect. (Fundacja Bente Kahan, Centrum Kultury i Edukacji Żydowskiej we Wrocławiu)

16,057 in 1946. Crumbling Jewish sites were almost all that was left, and by the early 1960s the White Stork Synagogue had fallen into nearly total disrepair. The building's condition had become so poor that local officials had to close it in 1966 for the "sake of public safety."[73] Wrocław's Jewish congregation now had to use a small, fifty-person prayer room in an adjacent building. After many of Wrocław's Jews fled Poland in 1968, the synagogue was largely abandoned, although a few members still appeared to be using it. In 1972, city officials demanded that the Jewish congregation "vacate and leave the illegally occupied establishment" within seven days. The Jewish congregation responded tersely that what it called an "establishment" was the "only synagogue in the city of Wrocław."[74] City officials reacted by legally confiscating the building from the Jewish congregation in 1974.

The city was now officially the building's owner and faced the same problem that Essen did two decades earlier: what now to do with it? In 1970, city officials placed the synagogue on its list of historic monuments as an example of classical architecture, but this did little. The building was neglected for the next twenty years, receiving more attention from teenagers as a local hangout than from city officials as an important historic monument.[75] A number of plans surfaced throughout the 1970s and 1980s: city officials first suggested using the synagogue for storage and then proposed turning it into a library reading room for Wrocław University, drawing up plans for an entirely new interior with space for book storage, a reading room, and a cafe. But these plans were never implemented for lack of funds, and in 1984 the city turned the building over to a local cultural center to do something with it. By the mid-1980s, the city was becoming increasingly anxious about making an "urgent decision" regarding the synagogue.[76] In 1989, it transferred the property yet again, this time to Wrocław's Musical Academy, which planned to use it as a concert hall. As all of these different plans were circulating among city officials, Wrocław's historic preservationists said nothing about them. The archives of the city's conservation department and the local branch of Poland's renowned Workshops for the Conservation of Architectural Monuments do not contain any protests against the synagogue's neglect or against the many plans to alter its interior. This silence is conspicuous in a city that took pride in its extensive historic reconstruction program. By 1989, the synagogue was the only prominent religious site in the old town that had not been extensively restored.

And yet, paradoxically, just as the synagogue continued to be completely ignored, interest in the city's oldest Jewish cemetery started to grow. In the early 1970s, the city planned to level the cemetery, but protests from local architectural historians prevented this from happening. In 1975, the city agreed to place the cemetery on its list of historic monuments, although this was largely perfunctory, and it was indeed thanks to the efforts of one local architectural historian, Maciej Łagiewski, that the Jewish cemetery was eventually restored. A basic interest in the cemetery's architectural history seemed to motivate him. "I am searching for the history of the city," he explained.[77] Although associated with the Wrocław Museum of Architecture, Łagiewski worked with little support from the state and had only a small staff of conservationists. Still, his efforts brought wider attention to the history of Jewish life in Wrocław. Local newspapers started to run a number of articles on the Jewish cemetery, and Łagiewski himself organized an exhibition entitled "Wrocław Jews, 1850–1945" in the town hall in 1989.[78]

This interest in Wrocław's Jewish past also attracted attention in the United States, Israel, Great Britain, and especially West Germany. The Friedrich-Ebert Foundation provided funds for the restoration of the tombstone of the Jewish labor leader Ferdinand Lassalle. In 1989, Johannes Rau, deputy chairman of the Social Democratic Party, led a delegation to Lassalle's grave on the 125th anniversary of his death. German newspapers applauded this effort to preserve one of the "last traces of German culture in the Silesian capital," turning the Jewish cemetery into a "German" space to comment on the postwar defilement of "German" culture after the expulsions. Reporting on a visit to "Breslau," one journalist spoke of his struggle to find any sign of the "German past" until he came upon the Jewish cemetery and "suddenly" he stood before "tombstones with German inscription." He entered a familiar world when Breslau had the "second largest Jewish community" in Germany.[79] Another article spoke of the many years that the cemetery had been left to ruin with "weeds meters high" and "shattered gravestones," implying that its neglect amounted to malevolent destruction of German culture.[80] The Jewish cemetery became a spatial metaphor for postwar German suffering. "With a few exceptions," another article wrote, "the Polish victors bulldozed all German cemeteries as they seized the Oder-Neisse territory after 1945. It did not happen any differently in Breslau—the German-Jewish cemetery is a true exception."[81] In a kind of cultural colonization, Wrocław became Breslau and the Jewish cemetery became German.

But if German tourists became interested in the cemetery as some lost, neglected German space, what motivated Poles to restore it as they ignored the synagogue? That small, relatively inexpensive work could be done on it was certainly one reason, but perhaps Poles saw the cemetery, unlike the synagogue, as a particularly sacred space that deserved proper respect. People invest enormous energy and money into cemeteries, although usually only ones directly connected to their own ancestors and collective groups.[82] Thus the case of Wrocław's Jewish cemetery uncovers something quite unusual: people recovering a space that had long been neglected and excluded from their collective concerns and identities. What exactly this resignification of Jewish space meant more broadly was not clear. The well-known Polish journalist Ewa Berberyusz described a scene in front of Wrocław's Jewish cemetery as a large crowd of people of "various professions and ages" waited to enter its grounds. "Why are they going?" After all, for decades "no

one was interested in this place." She concluded with a hint of skepticism—
"a herd instinct, a transformed consciousness, a new relationship toward
Jews?"[83] Berberyusz was probably right to leave the question open, but this
interest did signal the beginnings of something distinct, the stirrings of interest in cultural difference—a nostalgic embrace of Poland's multiethnic
past—that only intensified after the collapse of Communism in Wrocław
and across Poland. To be sure, this nostalgia often rested on mythic imaginations of cultural symbiosis and harmony that overlooked the traumas of
the past, but at times it also provoked searing discussions about Polish history and identity. These debates were intense, emotive, and divisive because
nothing less than the meaning of being Polish was at stake. Discussing the
Jewish past triggered hysterical refutation among some and profound attempts among others to rethink Polishness in the wake of the largest antisemitic campaign of postwar Europe.

East Germany's "Jewish Problem"

As in Poland, East Germany's interest in the Jewish past unfolded in the
midst of great political and social change. In 1971, Erich Honecker replaced
Ulbricht as first secretary a year after Gomułka stepped down from his post.
Ulbricht's departure was less dramatic than that of his Polish counterpart.
East Germany was generally more stable and had a stronger economy thanks
to free trade agreements with West Germany, although it slowed considerably in the 1970s with the rising costs of foreign imports. Political unrest
and opposition started to grow as the economy faltered. The SED did not
suffer a massive blow to its legitimacy like the PZPR did in 1968, but over
the years East Germans became impatient with the party's inability to deliver consumer goods, its demonization of countries like Israel, and its deg-
radation of the environment. Even seemingly banal issues—like the poor
condition of Jewish sites—became rallying points for activism against the
regime. As political opposition increased and the economy worsened, the
party looked to strengthen relations with the United States and shifted its
approach toward Jews as one way to improve its image abroad.[84]

Just as in Poland, though, interest in the Jewish past in East Germany initially emerged far outside official Communist offices, on the grass-roots level,
among Christian groups that grew tired of the party's incessant attacks

against "Zionists." While the GDR never unleashed anything close to Poland's anti-Zionist campaign, it could hardly be called a friend of Israel. In June 1967, just after the Six-Day War ended, Ulbricht remarked that just as "Polish, Dutch, and Hungarian citizens, women, children, elderly, and men were murdered under the Hitler regime," so, too, now were "thousands of Arabs, men, women, and children" being killed. A month later, the *Berliner Zeitung* published a cartoon of Defense Minister Moshe Dayan gripping Jerusalem and Gaza as Hitler stands nearby, saying, "Keep it going, Colleague Dayan."[85] Similar attacks continued throughout the 1970s, culminating in 1975 when the GDR supported the UN resolution that characterized Zionism as a form of racism. This resolution triggered a strong response from Protestant leaders, who until now had kept silent about the state's anti-Zionism. In a public statement, the leaders of the Federation of Protestant Churches in the GDR condemned the resolution and said that as "Germans in the past we denied the right to the existence of the Jewish people to a terrifying degree."[86] This statement sparked local interest in Christian-Jewish relations across the GDR. Local pastors and church youth groups sponsored lectures on Jewish topics and organized preservation efforts at Jewish cemeteries. In 1978, on the fortieth anniversary of *Kristallnacht,* East German churches hosted discussions about the Nazi persecution of the Jews. "We call to the attention of the churches the fortieth anniversary of *Kristallnacht* and remember it with shame," the Conference of the Protestant Leadership wrote. "An enormous guilt lies on our people. . . . In light of the failure and manifest guilt of Christianity, today everything must be done to spread knowledge about historic and contemporary Jewry."[87]

Local efforts to restore Jewish sites became one of the main ways to increase understanding about the Jewish past. Starting in the late 1970s, Christian youth organizations such as the Mission for Symbolic Atonement (*Aktion Sühnezeichen*) organized preservation efforts across the GDR. In 1978, the group gathered for the fortieth anniversary of *Kristallnacht* to walk along a "track of silent remembrance" that ended in front of the ruins of the Oranienburger Street synagogue.[88] In 1986, a number of young Christians worked at the Orthodox Jewish cemetery in the district of Mitte. One member wrote poignantly about the experience. Walking through East Berlin in search of the few "traces" of Jewish life left in the city, he made "painful discoveries" about its past. "I know that the people who lived and worked in these buildings were expelled and killed by Germans," he explained. "The immense and abstract number of 6 million murdered Jews became some-what more comprehensible to me in this concrete area."[89]

Just as Christians began contemplating the Nazi past, a small number of East Germans started to discover their Jewish roots. In 1986, Irene Runge, who moved to the GDR from New York City when she was seven, developed a secular Jewish club in East Berlin. Runge had earned a doctorate from Humboldt University and continued to believe in the GDR's "antifascist tradition" into the late 1980s.[90] She established "For Ourselves" for secular Jews like herself who had little interest in the official Jewish community and who were turned off by its strict Orthodox definition of membership. She came to the idea after a trip to New York, when she experienced the "fervor" of American Jewish life beyond synagogue.[91] The group reached about 250 members before the collapse of Communism, larger than East Berlin's official Jewish community.

The SED carefully monitored these activities, but it, too, had changed in some ways. In the late 1970s, the party loosened its strict Marxist-Leninist interpretation of the past. Although the SED had long grounded the East German state in German history, it now broadened what it officially recognized as "progressive" elements of the past. The Jewish communities in East Berlin, Leipzig, and Dresden received state support to develop an array of cultural programs from lectures on Jewish literature to concerts featuring synagogue music. A popular biography of Moses Mendelssohn appeared in 1979, and the state supported the first exhibition on Jewish history during the fortieth anniversary of *Kristallnacht.* The SED also started to discuss more openly the Holocaust. Television programs such as *While the Syna-gogues Burned, Don't Sleep at Home,* and *Concerned: Factory Action* ex-plored Jewish persecution and resistance.[92] While many of these changes took place in the GDR's waning years, they reflect more than simply desper-ate, cynical efforts by a collapsing regime.

But these broader shifts in SED policy had mixed results on the local built environment. In Potsdam, SED officials appeared particularly resistant to demands from residents to preserve the city's Jewish sites, never seeming to grasp the increasingly philosemitic approach coming from East Berlin. Potsdam's Jewish cemetery—the only major Jewish site left in the city—was in terrible condition by the 1970s. In 1949, the city had agreed to maintain the cemetery, but then did nothing with it for the next three decades. By the late 1970s, the cemetery's neglect started attracting attention from local residents. In 1978, Theodor Goldstein, a Jewish resident of Potsdam who survived the Holocaust, complained to city officials about the cemetery's "unsatisfactory" condition. On a recent trip to the cemetery with his youth group, a local Christian pastor reported that a number of tombstones had been vandalized.[93] In 1983, a local resident explained that a woman told her that the city had prohibited citizens from visiting the cemetery given its "disorderly condition." She bluntly let city officials know how much this surprised her:

> The reasoning behind such a prohibition is not at all satisfactory since everyone knows that today there are no Jewish citizens who can see to the regular upkeep of this cemetery because of the Nazis' complete an-nihilation of the Jewish people. But still this place should be left open to the people as a place of remembrance for this brutal genocide. The fact that state institutions have prohibited visitations to it can easily be as-sociated with antisemitic tendencies.[94]

The city responded that "the woman . . . certainly received the wrong infor-mation. The cemetery is not in a condition in which it cannot be seen."[95] In the end, a handful of local residents had to take it upon themselves to pre-serve the cemetery. Goldstein led the effort, a fact not lost on one Potsdam resident. "It is a disgrace for the city of Potsdam that the only living Jew in Potsdam, who is seventy-eight years old, must see to the maintenance of the cemetery," he wrote. "There are overturned tombstones. . . . Rain comes through the mortuary's roof. As a citizen of the GDR, [I think] it is shame-ful that the state has not given more support to the cemetery."[96]

Some local residents were also disturbed by how city officials dealt with Potsdam's other Jewish site—the former space of the synagogue. On No-vember 9, 1978, city officials gathered in front of where the synagogue once stood—now an apartment building—to dedicate a plaque in remembrance of *Kristallnacht* that read: "Here stood the synagogue of Potsdam's Jewish Community. During the nights of November 9 and 10, 1938, this synagogue was plundered and destroyed by the fascists." The citizens assembled there probably were unaware that the "fascists" were not the only ones who had torn it down, that in fact the war and a wrecking ball in 1958 had also caused the synagogue's destruction. City officials left that part of the story out. They also seemed uncertain about using the plaque for commemorative purposes. In 1982, a group of citizens gathered in front of the former synagogue on the anniversary of *Kristallnacht*. The city apparently disapproved of their actions. In a three-page letter to Potsdam's mayor, a local citizen described how authorities prevented residents from placing flowers in front of the plaque. Three separate bouquets were removed, and when pressed to explain who might be doing this, a police officer on the scene explained that it was "most likely done by order."[97]

But such disputes over Jewish sites were even more common in East Berlin. By the late 1970s, a similar kind of "Jewish problem" had emerged in the GDR's capital as it had in Poland's. East Berlin's Jewish community had dwindled to a few hundred members and its Jewish sites were crumbling away. "It's our bad luck," the GDR's minister for religious affairs admitted candidly to an American Jewish magazine.[98] Indeed, hundreds of tombstones had fallen over at the Jewish cemetery on Schönhauser Avenue in the district of Prenzlauer Berg, while the city's most visible site, the New Synagogue on Oranienburger Street, still stood in its bombed-out form. In the mid-1970s, state officials became increasingly concerned about these sites. One memo noted that something had to be done with the ruins of the Oranienburger Street synagogue, suggesting that they be torn down to make room for nearby "important, economic operations" or be restored to house a Jewish museum with "international monetary support." Another memo stressed the urgency of doing something given the number of "international Jewish tourists" coming to East Berlin.[99]

But the SED did not heed its own advice until the mid-1980s, when several highly public controversies about Jewish sites forced it to act. The first erupted in 1986, when city officials resurrected an old plan to build a highway over part of the Jewish cemetery in the district of Weißensee. A storm of protest ensued from Jewish leaders, ordinary citizens, and West German journalists. The dissident Bärbel Bohley collected 130 signatures opposing the plan. "It is irresponsible," the protest letter read, "to destroy this piece of cultural history that is not only a part of the history of Jews but also of our history."[100] Newspapers in West Berlin covered the issue, which especially angered the SED because now it would "get played up through the

imperialistic media as 'desecrating a cemetery.'"[101] Johannes Hildebrandt, a
local pastor and organizer of the working group "Christians and Jews,"
worked tirelessly behind the scenes to convince state officials to abandon the
project, while Heinz Galinski, West Berlin's main Jewish leader, did the
same in personal letters to Honecker. In the end, the stream of protest
proved too much. In October 1986, Honecker canceled plans for the road.[102]

Honecker reacted similarly to another controversy about a Jewish cemetery that erupted around the same time. In 1980, East Berlin's Jewish community warned city officials about the Jewish cemetery of Berlin's former
Orthodox community Adass Israel, which over the years had been turned
into a dump. But city officials did not listen and turned the property over to
the Ministry of State Security, which planned to build an administrative
building on part of it. In 1984, the Jewish community warned again that this
was not a good idea, not least of all because Jewish tourists were visiting the
cemetery in ever greater numbers. The city responded by drafting an order
for the cemetery to be preserved, but it came too late. The cemetery's condition had already attracted attention from journalists and citizens abroad.[103]
One letter in particular—from the West Berlin Jew Mario Offenberg—caused
enormous trouble for the state. A descendant of an Adass Israel family, Offenberg grew up in Israel and came to West Berlin to complete his dissertation at the Free University. He visited the cemetery and was shocked at what
he saw. In July 1985, he sent an impassioned letter to Klaus Gysi, the GDR's
minister of religious affairs. "How could this have happened? Why was this
continued destruction never brought to anyone's attention? Why was it
never prevented and stopped? Why was no one prosecuted for it? How could
this have gone so far?" He wondered how a Jewish cemetery could be treated
with such "efficient destruction and methodical desecration" right here "in
Berlin, the capital of the GDR, thirty and some years after the collapse of
fascism and its murderous antisemitism." Offenberg noted sardonically that
the cemetery "survived the dark night of fascism almost undamaged."[104]
These attacks initially provoked defensive responses from the SED. Offenberg's actions were attempts from "imperial circles from the FRG, the USA,
and Israel" to challenge the "basic, antifascist position of our state," wrote
the director of the Central Committee's Department for Church Affairs.[105]
Honecker, who seemed to understand the sensitivity of the matter, responded
more calmly when the matter reached his desk. Offenberg had written directly

to him after waiting three months without any response from Gysi. Honecker wrote back in ten days and assured that the cemetery would be restored. He delivered as promised. Less than six months later, Offenberg, Honecker, Gysi, surviving members of Adass Israel, and Jewish community members from both Germanys were standing together to reopen the restored cemetery.[106]

Honecker's swift response to this controversy marked the key turning point in the history of Jewish sites in East Berlin. By the late 1980s, the SED decided to restore a select number of them in the midst of shifting Cold War realities. Both local and international pressure forced the SED to act. The party wanted to improve its blemished image abroad and gain control over a controversial topic, which it knew segments of East German society had become interested in exploring. This shift reached its height in 1988 when Honecker announced that the GDR would restore the New Synagogue and turn it into a Jewish museum. The selection of this building could not have been more ironic. Although the synagogue survived *Kristallnacht* with only minor damage, it sustained severe destruction during the war. For forty years, East German officials struggled to figure out what to do with it. In 1961, 1965, 1975, and 1981, the Jewish community urged party officials to turn the synagogue into a Jewish museum. A local resident, Salomea Genin, made a similar recommendation, suggesting that the synagogue could become a space to foster a secular Jewish identity in the GDR.[107] All five requests were rejected. Thus a Jewish site that had been rejected for rebuilding as late as 1981 had now suddenly become a building of immense symbolic meaning, so much so that the party was even brought to rhetorical flourishes: "during the years that the so-called final solution to the Jewish question was prepared, this building became throughout Berlin and Europe a symbol of Jewish life, of Jewish solidarity, but also of the brutality of the Nazi annihilation of the Jews."[108] The synagogue was to be a monument to the Holocaust and a Jewish museum that would showcase the GDR's new approach to the Jewish minority. In 1987, Klaus Gysi even framed the project as a symbolic gesture of accepting limited responsibility for Nazi crimes, which East Germany had steadfastly resisted over the past forty years. Meeting with the World Jewish Congress in Geneva, he remarked that "we are Germans and thus we naturally are responsible for what was done in the name of Germans, even if those who did it were our fiercest opponents."[109] Coming from someone

Ceremonial groundbreaking of the New Synagogue's restoration. Peter Kirchner, chairman of East Berlin's Jewish community, is far left; Erich Honecker is to the right of East Berlin mayor Erhard Krack, who is speaking, and to the right of him is Siegmund Rotstein, president of the Association of Jewish Communities in the GDR. (Bundesarchiv Bild 183–1988–1110–032)

who was persecuted as a Communist and a Jew, Gysi's statement reinforced the political message of East German antifascism, while subtly acknowledging the GDR's historical responsibility for the Holocaust as a German state.

In 1988, the synagogue's groundbreaking coincided with the GDR's elaborate celebration of the fiftieth anniversary of *Kristallnacht*. What the Warsaw Ghetto Uprising anniversary was for the PZPR, the *Kristallnacht* anniversary was for the SED. The state hosted numerous events from lectures on German-Jewish history to a Politburo viewing of "Nathan the Wise." Some 140 events in over sixty cities took place across the GDR. As in Poland, dissidents and church leaders organized their own anniversary events. Churches held services; led commemorative events at Jewish cemeteries; hosted exhibitions, seminars, and lectures; and published their own pamphlets.[110] The Stasi, the East German secret police, watched for any hints of political protest. Some church groups connected Jewish persecution with their own plight under the Communist dictatorship, and a leaflet distributed at a silent protest in Leipzig co-opted the anniversary for its own political purposes: "If we accept the memory of the pogrom for ourselves, we must exercise our responsibility as human beings; the responsibility for human freedom in our country; the responsibility for peace, justice, and safeguarding the environment."[111] In general, though, East Germans simply seemed unimpressed with the state's sudden embrace of the Jewish past. The Stasi concluded that many East Germans believed that the party was restoring Jewish sites for "political propaganda."[112] Others just seemed disinterested in the entire affair. At a church gathering of 440 people in Karl Marx City, one pastor claimed that the East German population appeared more interested in obtaining car replacement parts than learning about the "murder of an entire people and the extermination of a culture."[113]

What is more, a series of anti-Jewish attacks erupted across the GDR in the months leading up to the anniversary. In May 1988, the Jewish community of Thüringen received a frightening phone call. A male voice asked: "Who is there?—Who is there?—Jews—Are there still any? Are they still here? Forgot about you. The ovens are still warm. They are calling for you."[114] A number of Jewish sites were also vandalized. The Stasi removed three swastikas that had been smeared on a plaque at the Jewish cemetery in Fürstenwalde, and tombstones were damaged at Potsdam's Jewish cemetery. The worst attack, however, occurred in East Berlin. In February 1988, five teenagers jumped over the wall of the Jewish cemetery on Schönhauser Avenue in the district of Prenzlauer Berg and destroyed about a hundred tombstones. The police quickly arrested the boys and the state prosecuted the case with a panicked, zealous urgency in fear that it might receive press coverage just before its commemorative events. It staged a public trial to demonstrate the GDR's resolve to eliminate right-wing extremism. The defendants received harsh sentences ranging from six months to two years, but were later released in 1990.[115]

As the SED sought to mitigate these incidents, it confronted one final issue that it clearly wanted resolved before the November celebration. In 1988, the question of returning Jewish property arose once again in the wake of the controversy over the Weißensee Jewish cemetery. Honecker proposed to Gysi that the issue be resolved once and for all by simply giving the strip of land back to the Jewish community. This suggestion raised the complicated question of Jewish property. In a candid, three-page letter to Honecker, Gysi portrayed the political repercussions of the state's confiscation of Jewish property over the past four decades, saying that it was now on the verge of becoming a "small sitting time bomb." Gysi pointed out that the GDR's control of property seized by the Nazis implied that it had become "de facto the legal successor to the old fascist Reich" and that refusing to return Jewish property was prejudicial, given that "all churches and religious communities in the GDR and in Berlin . . . have fully received their property." He suggested returning those holdings the Jewish community was currently using, the five out of some eighty pieces the community had been given the right to use in the 1950s. Returning all property, he noted, would be "impossible from a practical standpoint." Honecker agreed with Gysi, and on February 25, 1988 the GDR prepared to return five pieces of property to the Jewish community.[116] In the GDR's waning hours, its highest officials confronted the costs of their party's earlier policies. What motivated Gysi and Honecker is not entirely clear. As a Communist of Jewish decent, Gysi had little interest in the Jewish community, but expressed concern about some Jewish issues. It is possible that he and perhaps Honecker shared some sense of responsibility for preserving Jewish sites and returning confiscated property. But their main concern was to protect the GDR's image at a shifting, Cold War moment.

Rediscovering Jewish Sites in West Germany

In contrast to the governments in East Germany and Poland, the West German federal state never faced the "Jewish problem" of abandoned and crumbling Jewish sites in the 1980s. Part of the reason lies simply in the swift rebuilding of West German cities after the war. The shattered spaces of Jewish life vanished from the urban landscape, one of the consequences of West Germany's rapid economic recovery. As the state-run economies of East Germany and Poland failed to take off, urban reconstruction stretched on for decades there and left numerous historic buildings standing into the 1980s. The Soviet bloc offered a landscape of Jewish ruins that Jewish leaders, citizens, church leaders, dissidents, and party leaders could contest. Moreover, West Germany actively preserved some Jewish sites. In the 1950s, the federal government largely dealt with its "Jewish problem" after long negotiations with the Jewish Restitution Successor Organization (JRSO), which wanted to find a proper way to deal with Jewish communal property. For most Jewish sites—schools, hospitals, community centers, and synagogues— the JRSO left it up to local and state officials to decide what to do with them. But the JRSO needed a more structured approach for Jewish cemeteries, which had to be maintained under Jewish religious law. In 1951, the JRSO and the Central Council of Jews in Germany turned to the federal Interior Ministry to see if it would maintain the some 2,000 Jewish cemeteries in West Germany. The Interior Ministry seemed to understand the issue, which it had been thinking about after a surge of attacks against Jewish cemeteries in the late 1940s.[117] Still, it took years for the federal government to reach an agreement with the JRSO as the various bureaucracies fought over funding. As no resolution appeared in sight by the mid-1950s, the Interior Ministry brought the issue to a cabinet meeting of Adenauer's government. Explaining that protecting Jewish cemeteries was a "pressing issue" for Jewish leaders in Germany and abroad, it advocated strongly for passing the measure.[118] In August 1956, the cabinet agreed and announced the plan in its annual good wishes to the Jewish community on Rosh Hashanah. In a letter to Central Council president George van Dam, West Germany's interior minister announced that the state had agreed to accept responsibility for the maintenance of Jewish cemeteries "in order to secure equality and freedom for our Jewish co-citizens."[119]

This decision did not mean, though, that the issue of Jewish sites simply vanished. On the contrary, it reemerged in the 1980s as conflicts over neglected and altered Jewish sites erupted across the Federal Republic. The difference was that in West Germany, with a few exceptions, these efforts typically stayed confined to the local level, attracting less attention from national politicians and international Jewish leaders. Local politicians participated in these efforts, but the role of the state was minimal in West Germany. In a democratic society sure of its international standing among Jewish leaders after three decades of restitution, these local efforts neither threatened the state's power nor posed any serious challenges to its foreign policy. But their sheer multiplicity stands out. In the 1980s, West Germans encountered Jewish sites in cities, towns, and villages across their country: the synagogue in Kippenheim was renovated and turned into a Jewish museum after serving as storage for agricultural products for three decades; a citizens' coalition fought to preserve the archaeological remnants of Frankfurt's Jewish

community; a controversy erupted as a new mall was built on part of the
Jewish cemetery in Hamburg; the synagogue in Rendsburg was turned into
a Jewish museum after functioning as a fish smokehouse since 1939. And
the list could go on much longer. These attempts sparked intense discussion
among citizens, politicians, historic preservationists, local Jewish leaders,
and urban planners, and did not always come to the resolution that local
activists in support of them wanted. The City of Frankfurt preserved only
traces of its Jewish past and displayed them in the cellar of a service center
constructed on top of the former Jewish district.[120]

What is important, though, is the urge to mark, contest, and discuss the
absence of Jewish life that these spaces reflected. Why did this impulse
emerge in West Germany in the 1980s? In Poland, interest in Jewish sites
stemmed from a mix of political contestation, international attention, and
searing debates about Polish-Jewish relations, while in the GDR it came
mostly from the state as a result of both external and internal pressure put
on it. The West German case mirrors more closely the Polish one in that
highly public discussions about the Holocaust stimulated local interest in
Jewish sites. Of course, significant differences between the two cases exist.
In Poland, 1968 was central to the surge of interest in Jewish-gentile relations, whereas in the Federal Republic it was of less singular importance,
despite common perceptions and arguments to the contrary. The events of
1968 have reached mythic proportions in Germany. Historians, journalists,
politicians, and ordinary citizens often celebrate 1968 as Germany's cathartic moment of liberalization and democratization, a heroic watershed of
students protesting the oppressive silence and conservative politics of their
parents. Jürgen Habermas has described 1968 as an attempt to counteract
"the collective avoidance of German responsibility for National Socialism
and its horrors," and political scientist Claus Leggewie has suggested that it
signaled the "antifascist reestablishment of the Federal Republic of Germany."[121] While students certainly challenged the postwar refrain that ordinary Germans knew nothing about Nazi crimes, they rarely reflected deeply
on the Holocaust. They raised the "Nazi past," but their understanding of it
only tangentially related to Hitler's genocidal horrors in Eastern Europe.[122]

Indeed, when the Holocaust made it onto their minds in the 1960s, it was
not the way they remembered years later. Some students and leftists dis-
tanced themselves from "the great atonement market" of West German

philosemitism and embraced anti-Jewish prejudices.[123] Israel's swift victory in the Six-Day War triggered anti-Jewish sentiment in West Germany. The most extreme, radical form erupted on November 9, 1969, when a left-wing militant group placed a bomb in the West Berlin Jewish community center on Fasanen Street to disrupt a planned commemoration of *Kristallnacht*. Although the bomb never went off, the perpetrators got their loud and angry message across. The police found a letter left in the building. "Every memorial in West Berlin and the FRG," it said, "suppresses the fact that the *Kristallnacht* of 1938 is being repeated today by Zionists in the occupied territories, in the refugee camps, and in the Israeli prisons. . . . The Jews who were expelled by fascism have themselves become fascists."[124] This particular incident is admittedly an extreme example, but anti-Jewish sentiments pervaded parts of the New Left more than its members at the time and years later wanted to acknowledge.

And yet, that said, the image and memory of the 1960s as years of radical democracy and protest shaped public, political discussions about the Nazi genocide of European Jewry, especially among politicians of the Social Democratic Party and the Greens, a left-leaning party made up mainly of environmental activists, who over the 1970s and 1980s increasingly became outspoken proponents of reflecting on the Holocaust as a constituent part of Germany's democratic renewal.[125] By the 1980s, the broad, vague impulse of 1968 to confront the "Nazi past" had inspired some West Germans to discuss the persecution of the Jews. This is not to say that segments of West German society had not reflected on the Holocaust earlier. They certainly did, even as early as the 1950s, especially the churches, which provided important forums for discussions about German-Jewish relations and trips to Auschwitz. Since 1967, hundreds of West Germans have traveled to Poland to learn about the Holocaust through the youth organization Mission for Symbolic Atonement.[126] But what was different in the 1980s was that the Holocaust became a central issue for West Germany's increasingly left-leaning political, intellectual, and cultural elite. It had become an important part of West German cultural memory. By the early 1980s, leftist and left-liberal intellectuals made significant inroads in West Germany's museums, universities, schools, and media after thirteen years of Social Democratic rule under the leadership of Chancellors Willy Brandt and Helmut Schmidt. These intellectuals, educators, writers, and politicians tended to espouse, with different shades of intensity, the ideas of Jürgen Habermas, who argued for embracing the Holocaust as a central part of being German. They sought to reform the political culture of the Federal Republic, fight for human rights, and reflect on the German past.[127]

Their insistence on the importance of memory provoked strong resistance from conservative politicians and intellectuals, who refused to make the Holocaust a central part of German identity. In 1982–83, when the Christian Democrat Helmut Kohl became chancellor, conservatives sought to repeal what they saw as an excessive attack on German identity by the left. Their fears emerged precisely at the moment when what it meant to be "German" seemed especially precarious in the midst of demographic changes in West Germany. Since the 1960s, the country had been recruiting "guest workers" to maintain its "economic miracle" with cheap labor. Most came from Turkey and were supposed to leave once they finished working but did not. By the early 1980s, West Germany had about 5 million foreign workers. West Germans struggled to deal with this new reality. Germany has historically been a country of emigration, with nearly 5 million Germans moving to the United States across the nineteenth century. Christian Democrats denied that West Germany had become an "immigrant nation," especially one made up of non-Christian Turks. Conservatives also opposed attempts to change Germany's citizenship law of 1913, which defined citizenship in terms of blood rather than birth. The Nazi past became, then, a touchstone issue for the release of broader anxieties about Germanness. The last thing conservatives were going to tolerate was a handful of once radical, now middle-aged "68ers" telling them that they should embrace a postnational identity around the memory of the Holocaust. Of course, some of the most vocal proponents of such ideas, not least of all Habermas, who was born in 1929, were not 1968ers at all, but nuance mattered little since the perception of 1968 as a disturbing cultural revolution injected verve and urgency to the "spiritual-moral change" that Kohl promised.[128]

What followed was a series of intense political debates between the right and the left: over Kohl and Ronald Reagan's visit to the Bitburg cemetery where SS soldiers were buried; over historian Ernst Nolte's plea for a "normalized" Nazi past; and over the construction of history museums in Bonn and West Berlin. Much has been written about these debates, so what is important here is the general outcome that they helped to engender. These debates ultimately produced a "culture of contrition" among West Germany's political, intellectual, and cultural elite.[129] The Holocaust as a central element of German identity became embraced more than the conservative attempt to treat it as a normal, comparable past. A kind of political correctness took hold by the late 1980s that stressed public remembrance and contrition.

This attention to the Holocaust captivated mostly politicians, intellectuals, writers, and artists, but the media played a crucial role in popularizing it. In the 1980s, the television channel ZDF showed numerous productions about the Nazi persecution of the Jews. These films mostly involved survivor stories that elided German responsibility, but the sheer number of programs alone did much to widen interest in the Holocaust. The print media contributed its part, and not just through highbrow, intellectual weeklies such as *Die Zeit* but also through tabloids like *Bild,* which published terse, blunt editorials about the Nazi murder of the Jews. Axel Springer's populist and tawdry paper—issues are rarely complete without some form of female nudity—would hardly seem like the venue for spreading a leftist culture of contrition. But German-Jewish reconciliation has long been one of the political foundations of Springer's media empire. By the late 1980s, then, key parts of West German society and politics had started to embrace the Holocaust as a central part of German identity.[130]

But with this interest came a number of paradoxes that erupted with particular clarity on the local level. In Essen, the city's main Jewish site, its towering stone synagogue, housed until 1978 an exhibition on the consumer products of the West German economic miracle. In 1961, the city unveiled the exhibition after nearly fifteen years of attempting to resolve its "synagogue problem." City officials had found a solution, but it hardly ended discussion about the building. At the unveiling of the exhibition itself, the cultural minister of North Rhine–Westphalia, Werner Schütz, realized as he spoke that perhaps he had agreed to an idea that did not seem entirely right. He suggested that "perhaps it would have been a good solution if in the future the [synagogue] had been devoted only to the purpose of remembrance, as a powerful monument and eloquent accuser of the terrible things in the past."[131]

This unease with the synagogue's transformation continued long after the exhibition was unveiled, as journalists, Christian leaders, politicians, and historians pushed city officials to change the building's use. In the 1960s, local newspapers and the Essen branch of the Association of the Victims of the Nazi Regime, commonly known by its German abbreviation VVN, pressed city officials to build a monument for the "victims" of Nazism. In 1964, the *Neue Ruhr Zeitung* demanded that the city "finally" erect a "dignified monument for all victims of war and terror."[132] It invited five individuals from the city government, the Jewish community, and the Protestant church to comment on the proposal. All supported the basic idea, but none suggested whose victimization the memorial should commemorate. Only the Christian Democratic mayor narrowed the category slightly to those who suffered during the war "and in particular those for whom it was a deadly crime to have another opinion or to be Jewish." The chairman of the Jewish community responded that "our victims" had their own memorial, but he welcomed a "communal monument for the terror and death of the past."[133]

These broader discussions about building a monument stimulated interest in Essen's synagogue. In 1966, a principal of a local high school published a short piece in the *Westdeutsche Allgemeine Zeitung* calling for the construction of a contemporary history museum.[134] The suggestion sparked numerous letters to the editor, fifteen of which the newspaper reprinted. Several proposed putting the museum in the synagogue because, as one explained, the building "itself is through its own history a part of the evidence" of the period. Another wrote that a museum would be a "better, more suitable use" of the building than its currently "crude" purpose. "The city settled on this solution," it continued, "for monetary reasons, but it should only be a temporary solution."[135] A letter co-written by Ernst Schmidt, an active VVN and German Communist Party member who would later install a new exhibition in the synagogue, strongly advanced this idea. Calling the exhibition "crude" was to "put it very mildly," he exclaimed. He added that a museum in the synagogue would allow "our city leaders to make up for their own failures and crudities in dealing with the past." The local Jewish community had no reservations about the plan, suggesting that it, too, was still uncomfortable with the display of industrial, consumer products in the synagogue. "It is difficult," it wrote, "to find a suitable purpose for this building that was erected as a house of worship."[136]

In 1967, Schmidt proposed at the VVN's annual meeting to construct a museum in the synagogue. The museum would address ten themes, including the Nazi seizure of power, the persecution of the Jews, resistance, occupied Europe, Stalingrad, and postwar peace. The focus stretched broadly with Jewish victimization merely one part of a larger narrative about Nazi persecution and Communist resistance. As Schmidt explained, "thousands of social democrats, communists, trade unionists, Catholics, Protestants, and Jews starved, were convicted by special courts, were put under the guillotine, were beaten to death in the concentration camps, were gassed or shot while fleeing."[137] The VVN, dominated by Communists with ties to East Germany, embraced an antifascist interpretation of the past that emphasized political persecution. The organization had branches throughout West Germany and was the main association of its kind in the GDR, but it was particularly strong in places like Essen, with its historical ties to worker radicalism and Communism. In 1973, Schmidt and the local VVN put some of these ideas into practice. They organized the first exhibition on the Third Reich in Essen in a bookstore named after the famous German Communist Karl Liebknecht, who was murdered just after World War I. The local press paid little attention to the exhibition, but a sizeable crowd of people attended it. One was a brilliant student from the University of Bochum. Detlev Peukert, who would publish his first book three years later on worker opposition to Nazism in the Ruhr, rapidly became one of his generation's most imaginative historians before his sudden death in 1990 at the age of thirty-nine. A member of the German Communist Party before switching to the Social Democratic Party, Peukert had much in common with Schmidt. Schmidt was no rising star, but he completed his PhD in history at the University of Bremen on the workers' movement in the Ruhr. Peukert grew close to Schmidt, visiting his home often, as they forged an intergenerational friendship to increase knowledge about the history of Nazi Germany.

Schmidt and Peukert worked together on an exhibition on the Third Reich that they hoped would be housed in the synagogue. The period 1978–79 proved to be fateful years for their plans. In 1978, West Germans commemorated *Kristallnacht* like never before, during its fortieth anniversary.[138] In Essen, the anniversary triggered interest in the synagogue's destruction and postwar transformation. Writing in the *Westdeutsche Allgemeine Zeitung,* a Social Democratic state representative criticized the wording on the plaque placed before the synagogue in 1949. He derided the phrase "Jews had to lose their lives," calling it a "harmful belittlement of the most evil, outrageous actions of German history." In late September, the *Neue Ruhr Zeitung* reported that local SPD leaders supported the idea of transforming the synagogue into a museum for contemporary history.[139] This was the first indication of official support for changing the exhibition. The idea gained traction, pushed by a sense of outrage with the city's postwar use of the building. As one local citizen put it, "Give due reverence back to the synagogue! This form of restitution is perhaps Essen's moral duty. What a blasphemy it was after the war to debase this old architectural monument of Essen into an exhibition room of industrial products, washing machines, and schnapps glasses."[140] Local church leaders added to the growing chorus of criticism. In November 1978, the local chapter of the Organization for Christian-Jewish Cooperation founded the "Old Synagogue" working group to develop plans for turning the building into a memorial for "all victims of violence."[141] Finally, on the actual day of the fortieth anniversary of *Kristallnacht,* a memorial took place inside the synagogue. The glass cases filled with consumer goods were temporarily pushed aside as the group gathered in the building to recall its destruction forty years earlier. The surrounding "profanation" of the space made a deep impression on Essen's mayor, who spontaneously uttered: "We must make a drastic change here!"[142]

The mayor followed up on his words. A month later, Schmidt, Peukert, and city officials gathered to discuss an exhibition on resistance in the Third Reich, and the synagogue surfaced as the most desirable location. Peukert drafted a preliminary sketch of the exhibition's layout, which he divided into four parts: the Nazi seizure of power, the Third Reich, World War II, and 1945.[143] But plans came to a halting stop on January 18, 1979. At 3:30 in the afternoon, Schmidt, at work, received a call from Peukert. "You can forget the synagogue as the exhibition space," he exclaimed, "It is on fire!"[144] Schmidt ran up the stairs, where he had a view of the downtown. He watched as smoke puffed out from the building. Coming just two months after the *Kristallnacht* anniversary, one can easily imagine what he and others were thinking. This time, though, a burning cigarette ignited the fire, not barrels of gasoline. The fire did finally free the way for a new use of the building, quite literally so, as the entire exhibition was destroyed. In January 1980, Essen's city council accepted the plan to turn the synagogue into a museum on resistance and persecution during the Third Reich. This decision represented a clear triumph for Schmidt, Peukert, and the VVN. The exhibition

Unveiling the exhibition "Resistance and Persecution" in Essen, Detlev Peukert motions to people in attendance on November 9, 1980. (Essen Stadtbildstelle)

was unveiled ten months later, on November 9, 1980. Called "Resistance and Persecution in Essen, 1933–1945," it followed the conceptual design that Peukert had laid out in 1978–79. The exhibition focused on the "rise, meaning, and effects of the Nazi regime."[145] Mirroring Peukert's own scholarly interest in resistance, it was intended to reveal how Germany reached 1933 and what local Esseners did to oppose the regime once it was established. In telling this story, the exhibition gave attention to violence and persecution, but here, too, the focus was broad, grouping together as victims "Jews, ordinary opponents, the old parties, resistance fighters, war prisoners, and foreign workers."[146]

Indeed, the synagogue now represented the suffering, persecution, and resistance of the German population as a whole. "The synagogue is a memorial for all victims of violence," one local newspaper put it.[147] This formulation oddly placed Jews on the same level as Germans who were supposedly resisting rather than perpetrating Nazi crimes. It elided German involvement in the everyday persecution of Jews over twelve years of Nazi rule, which Esseners clearly were still uncomfortable in confronting. The Holocaust permeated the stones of Essen's synagogue. Few other spaces laid bare more starkly the involvement of Esseners in expelling Jews from their city. The exhibition took this feared past and made it soothing for its local audience. The pamphlet for the exhibition began by describing a photo of the synagogue. It was not the photo snapped in 1938, capturing a crowd of Esseners gawking at the burning building, but rather was an image taken just after the war that showed the synagogue in a city full of "rubble and ash." According to the pamphlet, this picture reflected "destruction in a material, moral, and physical sense" and the plight of the "few who were prepared to offer resistance." The use of this photo, placed in the synagogue where the Torah ark once stood, drew on the powerful image of the bombed-out German city to recall the suffering of Germans.[148]

On November 9, 1980, about 800 Esseners gathered in a synagogue renovated for the second time. In 1961, the unveiling took place two weeks after the anniversary of *Kristallnacht*. Perhaps the organizers thought that opening a display of industrial products on the very anniversary of the building's desecration might suggest uncomfortable parallels. But in 1980, city officials seemed confident that their display matched the anniversary's solemnity. They had gotten it right this time. Just as in 1961, Essen's mayor stood up to speak about the building. Horst Katzor of the Social Democrats touched on the "terrible times," "guilt," "murder," and "undesirable crimes" that the building symbolized before moving to a perhaps intonated "but," a sound and word that his audience's ears probably registered with fulfilled anticipation. "But this building in the middle of the city is also a symbol of courage, bravery, inner greatness, human dignity, steadfastness, sturdy belief, unique sacrifice—examples for us and future generations." The "old synagogue belongs" to all Germans who suffered and resisted Nazism. "The people, who in this city did not succumb to the madness of Nazism, and who still believed in life after barbarism, even though the stranglehold of barbarism took to the air, are our hope. The old synagogue belongs to them."[149] It was a stunning interpretation of the synagogue's meaning. On the very anniversary of its violent destruction, the mayor crafted a narrative of recovery and hope about a victimized German population that had made it through tough times, tragedy, and barbarism to build the peaceful, democratic society of today.

In West Berlin, encounters with Jewish spaces unfolded differently. Berlin never had a definably Jewish area of town or a centralized Jewish site like Essen or other West German cities did. The city's more diffuse urban landscape meant that West Berliners rediscovered their city's Jewish past in their local districts and neighborhoods. Since almost all of West Berlin's synagogues had been erased from the urban landscape, these efforts focused mainly on demarcating what was no longer present, working through the absence of Jewish life by publishing local histories, sponsoring museum exhibitions, writing guidebooks, and erecting monuments.[150] This interest emerged just as local history was becoming popular in West Berlin. In the early 1980s, the city became home to a number of local history workshops that sought to produce narratives different from those of professional historians. These organizations embraced "everyday history," with its emphasis on experience, as opposed to the grand, structural narratives of social history dominant at the time. Using less traditional types of historical sources such as oral history, they focused on understanding one's own local world, or as the saying went, to "excavate where you stand" *(Grabe wo du stehst)*. In 1981 and 1983, the Berlin History Workshop and the Active Museum of Fascism and Resistance were founded. Both supported local, everyday approaches to Berlin's past with a particular interest in gender history, the Nazi period, and German-Jewish relations.

In West Berlin, history workshops emerged in each of the city's districts. One of the most active ones was established in the affluent, middle-class district of Schöneberg. In 1983, this neighborhood group organized an exhibition on the Nazi period about "Life in Schöneberg-Friedenau." Intended to engage the "failures of the official historiography," the exhibition looked at the past from "below" to reconstruct a "piece of everyday life in Nazi Berlin."[151] While preparing the exhibition, the organizers discovered that a sizeable Jewish population had once lived in the district, especially around the area of the Bavarian Square. They began searching for material about Jewish life in Schöneberg and presented their research five years later in an open-air exhibition. These two exhibitions spurred further interest in the district's Jewish past. In the late 1980s, Schöneberg's local history museum initiated a major research project on the Nazi persecution of Jews. Carried out almost entirely by volunteers who sifted through Nazi documents an hour or so before going to work, the year-long project unearthed a plethora of material about the everyday persecution of Jews in Schöneberg. The richest source base came from the Nazi regional financial office, which held hundreds of documents about the confiscation of Jewish property. This collection revealed that nearly 6,000 Jews had been deported from the district. This high number shocked ordinary residents and local politicians. Calls to commemorate the persecution of the district's Jewish population immediately followed. The Schöneberg branch of the SPD submitted a city council resolution to build a monument around the Bavarian Square to remember "the 6,000 Jewish victims." It argued that residents of the district should know "where the people that the Nazis deported to the concentration and death camps lived."[152] The city approved the idea and established the Working Group for a Memorial at the Bavarian Square, a civic organization charged to carry out a competition for the memorial and to assemble material about Jewish life in the district.

Part of this sudden interest in the district's Jewish past came from sentimental nostalgia for a rich, cultural life that had been lost. In 1933, about 16,000 Jews lived in Schöneberg. Most of them came from the middle class and had integrated into German society. In the prewar and postwar imaginary of "Jewish Berlin," Schöneberg, along with the districts of Wilmersdorf, Tiergarten, and Grunewald, formed the "aristocratic, assimilated" west as opposed to the "proletarian, unassimilated" east found along the streets of the Barn Quarter, or *Scheunenviertel,* where the city's Eastern European Jewish population tended to live.[153] By the 1980s, some local residents mourned the loss of this seemingly rich world of acculturated German Jewry. In the words of the local SPD paper, "just as in Eastern Europe the Jewish culture of the 'shtetl' was completely destroyed, so too here in Germany Jewish life in many regions disappeared without a trace. . . . Jewish culture once formed a fundamental part of Berlin's urban culture." But today, alas, no one remembers this past, that Schöneberg was once the "Jewish Switzerland" with "intellectuals," "professionals," and prominent figures such as Einstein walking its streets. Schöneberg's Jewish population seemingly reflected the best elements of German-Jewish relations.

But it also represented their violent breakdown—a fact that the project interpreted with remarkable directness. Just a few sentences after the ones quoted above came a sharp, bitter turn to past violence and present apathy: "Today, those of us who in our beautiful, old 'Berlin apartments' enjoy the blessings of Wilhelmian architectural design often do not know that these apartments and houses were the setting for indescribable tragedy."[154] Local SPD party members and leaders wanted to make sure that such forgetting would no longer happen. They organized an effort to place posters on all the houses where deported Jews had lived in remembrance of the fiftieth anniversary of *Kristallnacht*. On November 9, 1988, over seventy houses had temporary, cardboard plaques on them with the names, ages, and deportation dates of Jews. This act had a lasting impact on the design of the monument that was eventually erected around the Bavarian Square. In 1989, the district government hosted an open-air exhibit of designs and collected ideas from local residents. More than half who submitted ideas favored a decentralized design much like the cardboard campaign. At a panel discussion sponsored by the Berlin History Workshop, the organizers agreed that it would not be "a solitary monument," but one made up of individual "stumbling blocks" that provide concrete, localized experiences of Jewish suffering.[155]

The idea was to situate and localize the past as a seemingly ordinary part of the built environment, dramatizing the fact that the gradual, step-by-step persecution of the Jews unfolded as a "normal" process of everyday life accepted and absorbed by German society. As the description for the competition put it: "In the normality of the past, these events crept in and could be seen and experienced by anyone alert on a daily basis. The crimes of exclusion and mass murder began before everyone's eyes and were implemented through the participation, cognizance, and acquiescence of many."[156] The artists who designed the memorial, Renata Stih and Frieder Schnock, articulated this normalized prejudice through a set of signs posted throughout the Bavarian Square. The signs included on one side a Nazi anti-Jewish law and on the other a seemingly innocuous, ordinary image. For example, a sign with an image of musical notes read: "Jews are excluded from choral groups, August 16, 1933." If one follows the posts, the ever-increasing persecution of the Jews becomes clear. Located on otherwise everyday streets in quiet, suburban Berlin, the signs are at once jarring and normal parts of the urban landscape, precisely their point. As the district mayor put it, the "really terrifying" aspect of the numerous Nazi laws is that the "majority of the German population accepted" them.[157]

By articulating the normality of Nazi persecution and hate, the memorial could not have differed more from the exhibition installed in the Essen synagogue. Politically engaged citizens on the left organized both projects, but with different interpretations of the Nazi past in mind. While the Essen synagogue was appropriated to reflect German persecution and resistance, the Schöneberg memorial inscribed into the built environment the everyday persecution of Jews by German society. Given its postwar history as a stronghold of leftist and alternative politics, West Berlin perhaps not surprisingly reflected a local embrace of broader intellectual, political, and cultural attempts in the 1980s to make Holocaust memory a central part of German identity. Essen, with its strong ties to the labor movement, socialism, and Communism, reflected the lingering presence of an older, antifascist interpretation of Nazism among the left that emphasized German victimization and resistance.

The Presence of Absence

In 2005, Michael Berenbaum, long involved in Holocaust memorialization in the United States, commented that Warsaw residents are encountering the "presence of the absent." "Jews lived among them for 1,000 years, and the city has remnants of the presence of Jews, but now they have to grapple with the fact that they are absent," he explained.[158] In fact, Poles and Germans have been encountering Jewish absence since the 1980s in traces located on their everyday streets. While Jewish sites likely only captured the interest of a small segment of society, that they did at all is striking. Violence has torn communities apart across the globe, and few people have expressed interest in confronting the shattered spaces of their persecuted minority populations with the kind of intensity and emotional passion that Germans and Poles have. In 1979, Jerzy Ficowski, a wartime resistance fighter, Communist dissident, poet, and scholar of Roma and Jewish culture, wrote sardonically about the erased memories of postwar Muranów:

Muranów rises tall
on layers of dying
its foundation on bone
its cellars in crevices

emptied of screams
Be that as it may, it is what it is
There is the peace of tidied up groans
the black afterglow of a fire gone dead
mighty stands Muranów
on the burial of memory
most letters reach their addressee
Be that as it may, it is what it is
And I, like it, have been reconstructed
on a surface of ash
beneath stars of shattered glass
Be that as it may, it is what it is
I would like only to keep silent
but keeping silent I lie
I would like only to walk
but by walking I trample.[159]

Some Germans and Poles felt deeply ashamed, even guilty, that for so long no one cared if a Jewish cemetery was vandalized, or if a synagogue displayed industrial products. They could no longer lie. They could no longer trample.

But why now in the 1980s? Why not earlier? Some Poles and Germans became interested in Jewish sites now simply because they reflected something different along their dull postwar streets. By the 1980s, Jewish sites had become old and rare after decades of destruction and neglect. "Artifacts of initially transient and diminishing value that fall into the limbo of rubbish are often later resurrected as highly valuable relics," David Lowenthal writes.[160] With their jagged edges and time-soaked stones, Jewish sites evoked curiosity and concern; they became valuable relics of the past that had to be saved from extinction. Initiatives to preserve, restore, and commemorate thrive on a mix of intrigue and anxiety about a past that appears to be slipping ever more away from the future. Furthermore, some Germans and Poles longed for a multiethnic past that they believed Jewish sites reflected. Their nostalgia for Jews was often sentimental, and it often marginalized the Holocaust by taking refuge in a prewar past imagined to be free of tension, hatred, and violence. But at times it was also deeply introspective and bitingly sharp. As Ficowski's poem so brilliantly captured, Jewish sites—with their shattered histories of destruction, neglect, and erasure over the past forty years—provoked some Germans and Poles to think critically about themselves and their pasts.

Most of all, though, Polish and German interest in Jewish sites grew out of specific local, national, and political contexts. In Poland and East Germany, the anti-Jewish policies of both Communist parties became untenable in the midst of shifting Cold War realities. As the SED and PZPR sought to improve their images abroad, Jewish sites attracted attention from tourists, Jewish leaders, and journalists. In response, both parties restored a few sites in their capitals and staged commemorations of the Holocaust. Segments of the growing opposition saw the party's shift as nothing more than crass, hypocritical attempts to curry favor with international Jewish leaders. Because some of them had been working on preserving Jewish sites for years, they knew well the regime's long-standing policy of neglect and destruction. Jewish spaces became another issue that divided state and society, although not as much as dissidents would have always liked to believe. In Poland, parts of the opposition movement and the lay Catholic intelligentsia reinforced the framing of the "Jewish problem" consolidated by the Communist Party in its verbal hate campaign of 1967–68. Opposition members also displayed their embrace of Jewishness for political gain and transnational consumption; they could be at times just as politically motivated as Communist leaders.

But such direct tension between state and society certainly existed less often in the Federal Republic. Because West Germany had long established good relations with international Jewish leaders over decades of restitution, Jewish sites never became a transnational problem that involved international, national, and local leaders. Instead, conflict over Jewish sites was limited to the local level. In Essen, politically engaged citizens pressed city officials to change the use of the synagogue for over a decade, while in West Berlin organizers of the Schöneberg memorial sought to create a historical narrative different from the one fashioned by professional historians and conservative politicians. In both cities, left-leaning, politically active citizens aimed to bring attention to their understanding of the Third Reich, which they believed had been forgotten. They criticized West Germany's supposed "amnesia," which they claimed stemmed from incomplete democratization under the conservative rule of the Christian Democratic Party

(CDU) for the first twenty years of the republic. Segments of the left were nervous with the Christian Democrats now back in power, and with conservatives determined to "normalize" the Nazi past, deflect questions about West Germany's immigrant population, and implement a broad "spiritual-moral change." The actors in Essen and West Berlin were not cast in the drama of revolution, although a few might have dreamt of such roles, but they were just as powerfully engaged in creating change as were their counterparts in the East.

5

Reconstructing the Jewish Past

In 1997, Marcin Kacprzak, a young Pole living in the small town of Płock close to Warsaw, wrote a letter to the Polish-Jewish magazine *Midrasz* about his attraction to absent Jews. "For a long time now I have felt an indescribable connection to the Jews who existed and who are no more. . . . Each time I passed the old Jewish cemetery or the old Jewish district I felt something . . . I am not sure what to call it exactly—nostalgia, curiosity, fascination?" He went on to write that perhaps it was "curiosity in a different culture, so mysterious." In the 1990s, the American writer Ruth Ellen Gruber began documenting her travels through the "vestiges of a vanished civilization." "Standing alone on the crest of a small hill, the synagogue, probably dating to the 18th century, is a massive structure that seems to have battled hard against its own destruction," she wrote in the *New York Times* about a discovery in the Polish village of Rymanów.[1] Jewish sites had evoked curiosity as early as the late 1970s, but since 1989 they have attracted an ever-growing audience from local residents to global travelers. If searching for the Jewish past started out as a local affair, it has become much broader, with tens of thousands of tourists from the United States, Israel, Canada, and the United Kingdom traveling to Poland and increasingly Germany in search of the Jewish past. Although Jewish sites are still anchored in local and national contexts, they have become transnational over the past twenty years.

The German word *Spurensuche*, "search for traces," captures well this impulse to search both far and near for Jewish ruins. As the "traces" of the word indicates, actual, concrete sites are important: Kacprzak senses a connection to Jews as he passes by his local Jewish cemetery, while Gruber travels across Europe in search of synagogues and cemeteries to write about and photograph. Physical spaces seem particularly real to them. They can be

The synagogue in Działoszyce in 2007. Although a number of Jewish sites have been restored since the 1980s, Jewish ruins still mark the landscape, especially in Poland. (Photo by Robert Cohn)

touched, experienced, discovered, and photographed, and they are the last, tangible traces of a fading past. Like any ruins, Jewish sites evoke curiosity, melancholia, nostalgia, and mourning. They provoke efforts to locate, recover, and restore: Germans, Poles, and Jews have rebuilt prewar Jewish sites and constructed new Jewish spaces, especially museums, that display artifacts of the past. Many Jewish ruins still exist, especially in Poland, but they are fast becoming themselves artifacts of a bygone era.

Indeed, restoration, preservation, and commemoration have become so common that now some commentators have suggested that Europe has turned into a continent of virtual, reconstructed Jewish spaces without any "real" Jews. Tourism and memory have produced kitschy Jewish Disneylands of Klezmer music, restaurants, museums, and anything else that can be marketed as "Jewish." Cultural commodification has diluted a once pure culture, leaving behind just inauthentic, restored traces of memory.[2] It is true that restoration disrupts the temporal process of decay and smoothes over exactly what made ruins interesting in the first place, those neglected, raged, crumbling edges that frighten and seduce. Most rebuilt ruins cease to be ruins unless shards of the past are explicitly incorporated into their new surfaces. But does restoration make them somehow "unreal" and "inauthentic?" What is "really" Jewish and what is not in a world of multiple meanings of Jewishness? In contemporary Kraków, for example, anthropologist Erica Lehrer suggests that Poles involved in the creation of the city's Jewish quarter are not quite as non-Jewish as they might seem at first look. She reads their identification with Jewishness as a form of critique that disrupts precisely the stable cultural, religious, and ethnic assumptions that underpin notions of cultural authenticity. As scholars Barbara Kirshenblatt-Gimblett and Jonathan Karp have put it, Jewishness must be analyzed "as contingent and contextual rather than definitive and presumptive."[3]

Perhaps, then, the concept of authenticity should just be discarded. But the problem is that the affective quality of authenticity—the desire for "realness" and "uniqueness"—remains central to our contemporary world. German thinker Walter Benjamin once defined authenticity as the "aura," or the sense of distance and authority with which we endow works of art.[4] Although he believed that modern technological reproduction would free art from this uniqueness, the opposite has occurred in our globalizing, capitalist world. The desire for temporal distance and perceived uniqueness has only increased in the midst of anxieties about inauthenticity with the rapid expansion of technological reproduction and consumption.[5] In the built environment, people have become attracted to vernacular sites as if in these spaces they can intuitively, as James Young writes, "sense the invisible aura of past events."[6] A good part of the contemporary obsession with Jewish sites reflects such a desire for a rooted sense of authenticity, which involves constructions and reifications of Jewishness, but does not produce some seemingly fake culture. Rather, Germans, Poles, and Jews imbue these spaces with new meanings and uses. For some, Jewish sites symbolize the Holocaust; for others, they appear as authentic spaces of cosmopolitanism, multiethnicity, and pluralism; for still others, they serve as houses of worship and cultural centers. Jewish sites are now more than ever mediated through a complex web of meanings, interpretations, and uses. This diversification stems from the transnational appeal of the Jewish past, but also from the substantial expansion of Jewish religious life that has been taking place in Germany and Poland since 1989. Some commentators have portrayed Jewish communal life as more authentic than the supposed kitschy obsession with Jewish culture, but here, too, such arguments are simplistic and overlook the complex ways that past, present, and future overlap in the built environment.

Reemerging Jewish Communities after 1989

Since the collapse of Communism, Poland and Germany have been experiencing a reemergence of Jewish communal life. This has happened in both countries, but especially in reunited Germany, which has become home to one of the largest and until recently fastest-growing Jewish communities in Europe thanks to tens of thousands of Russian Jewish immigrants. The migration started during the waning hours of the East German regime, when the new government of Lothar de Maizière opened its borders to Jews from the Soviet Union. What began as a trickle became a flood after German unification. Germany's historically liberal refugee laws—quite different from its strict naturalization laws—allowed Jews to enter the country with the legal rights of immigrants for about fifteen years. The German parliament tightened restrictions on foreign immigration in 1993 and overhauled the system in 2005. Now the number of foreigners entering the country has decreased. In 2007, a mere 2,502 Jews came to Germany, down sharply from a high of 19,437 in 1997. Still, in total some 200,000 Jews from the former Soviet Union have come to Germany since 1989. These predominantly Russian-speaking Jews have increased Germany's Jewish religious community by 250 percent. In 2005, the Central Council of Jews reported a total of 105,733 registered Jewish community members, with the largest community located in Berlin. This migration of Russian Jews reflects what has long been occurring throughout Germany's postwar history—Germany has become an immigrant country. It has 7.1 million foreigners, or 8.7 percent of the population.[7]

Although the Jewish community has welcomed this influx of Jews, the transition has not been easy. Despite being the founder of Reform Judaism, Germany's Jews today are largely Orthodox. The local community maintains the Halakhic law and is answerable to the Central Council, a central, organizing body formed in 1950 with the idea that the small Jewish community needed to form a unified community. The Russian Jewish population has complicated this postwar balance. A number of them either know little about Judaism or do not meet the conservative, religious criteria for membership in the community. Russian immigrants who consider themselves Jewish because the Soviet state marked them as such might or might not be halakhically Jewish. If they do not have Jewish mothers, they cannot become full, religious members of the community. This has naturally caused resentment, frustration, and anger among Russian Jews. Many have also arrived in need of jobs, housing, education, and welfare support. Although many Russian Jews are well educated, they have struggled to find suitable work, with doctors, engineers, teachers, and intellectuals settling for jobs outside their fields. Their needs have overwhelmed the local communities, the Central Council, and the state. Finally, there is the issue of "integration," the catchword of late not only for German society as a whole as it wrestles with what it means to be an immigrant nation but also for the Jewish community. Just as demands have grown for Germany's Turkish immigrant population to acculturate into German society, so, too, have parallel assumptions surfaced about Russian Jews among the still predominantly German-speaking leadership of the Jewish community and the Central Council. The assumption is that Russian Jews should integrate into the religious life of the community by learning German and becoming versed in Jewish practice. The problem is that such "integration" assumes a German cultural and religious superiority that some Russian Jews resent. Many have little attachment to German culture and little desire to practice religious Judaism, especially Orthodoxy. The result has been fissure in the once seemingly unified community.[8]

Perhaps no other Jewish community in Germany reflects this fragmentation more acutely than the one in Berlin. The new German capital has become home to the country's largest Jewish community of 11,000 members and eight synagogues. Although Berlin's fractious and at times chaotic community dominates Jewish life in the capital, it is no longer the sole representative of Berlin Jews as it once was during the Cold War. A number of Jewish organizations have emerged since 1989 that offer different spaces for Jews. There are secular, cultural ones, such as the Jewish museum in Kreuzberg or Centrum Judaicum in Mitte, as well as smaller, religious groups such as Adass Israel, Chabad Lubavitch, and the World Union of Progressive Judaism. The

Jewish Cultural Club, founded by Irene Runge in East Berlin in the late 1980s, offers secular lectures and discussions about Judaism. Bet Deborah provides space for feminists, while Yachad does the same for gays and lesbians. Several American Jewish institutions have also established offices in Berlin. The American Jewish Committee, founded in 1906, opened an office on Potsdamer Platz in 1998, while the Ronald Lauder Foundation, created in the mid-1980s by the son of the cosmetics magnate Estée Lauder, operates a Jewish learning center in the Rykestrasse synagogue in Prenzlauer Berg. The Internet has also provided limitless space for diversification. Cyberspace has become a central forum for Jews in Berlin to create many varied communities through chat groups and information portals.[9]

Such diversity of Jewish life is less visible across the German border. Poland has witnessed a dramatic revival of Jewish life after 1989, but on a smaller scale. No steady stream of Jewish immigrants pours into Poland, but the country now has about 10,000 Jews, which is up from about 2,000 to 3,000 in the late 1980s. These new Jews are Polish citizens who fall into two main groups: 1968ers who discovered their Jewishness during the anti-Zionist campaign, and 1989ers who have become Jewish for a variety of reasons. These young Poles form the bulk of Poland's expanding Jewish community. Some become Jewish for religious reasons; some in search of an imagined cosmopolitanism, believing that Jewishness represents a pluralistic, open, tolerant, and progressive form of Polishness; and others because they see Jewishness as something different, interesting, and cool. As the 1968er Stanisław Krajewski put it: "You know, young people try various alternative, minority ways of life, also religion. So for Jews it may be Judaism, just because it's such an alternative, minority religion."[10]

Several international institutions have been central to this rediscovery of Jewish roots. The Lauder foundation established an office in Warsaw in 1992 and has played a vital role in Poland's revival of Jewish life through its educational programs, youth retreats, and funding of projects such as the Polish-Jewish magazine *Midrasz*. The foundation subsidizes the Religious Union of Mosaic Faith, which is headed by the American rabbi Michael Schudrich. As political scientist Claire A. Rosenson discovered, young Polish Jews credit the Lauder foundation and Schudrich for strengthening Jewish life in Poland, but seem ambivalent about whether Orthodoxy makes sense for their contemporary lives.[11] Just as in Germany, Orthodoxy dominates official

Jewish life in Poland, with few other established Jewish alternatives. But this is now changing as Jewish life in Poland is becoming more diverse. Since 1999, a Reform community has existed in Warsaw led by Rabbi Burt Schuman of New York, and Kraków has become a dynamic space for Jews and non-Jews with its many Jewish organizations, groups, and activities.

The experience of Polish Jews is deeply shaped by their interactions with non-Jewish Poles, whose attitudes about them matter greatly in a country of few other ethnic and religious minorities. Although immigrant workers are now moving into Poland, especially from Vietnam, Jews remain the country's most prominent ethnic "other." Poles tend to frame Jews as either a complicated problem to discuss or an exotic fascination to experience (there is also the far-right, antisemitic demonization of Jews as perniciously anti-Polish that has gained strength since 2001). Since 1989, discussions about Polish-Jewish relations have sparked enormous controversy. In 1998, ultra-nationalist Polish Catholics placed hundreds of crosses at Auschwitz, which ignited intense debate about Polish and Jewish interpretations of the war, while two years later Jan Gross, a professor at Princeton University who left Poland in 1968, published his landmark study about Polish involvement in the murder of Jews in the village of Jedwabne. In the spring of 2008, a flurry of reactions about another intervention from Gross flooded Poland's media, this time about the murder of Jews in Kielce after the war. As these controversies about the past have unfolded, some Poles have become fascinated with almost anything associated with "Jews." This involves an almost insatiable desire for Jewish studies programs, festivals, Isaac Bashevis Singer, Klezmer music, wooden carvings, and the like. Although this interest probably engages only a small part of the total population, it often reinforces the dominant mental framing of Jews as different and strange, as exotic objects of wonder to view or complicated problems to discuss. Finally, the issue of returning Jewish property has complicated Polish-Jewish relations. In 1997, the Polish government passed a law for the return of Jewish communal property. The process has dragged on for more than a decade, and what exactly restitution will mean in the end for the preservation of Jewish sites is uncertain. The Jewish community now faces the delicate and complex task of deciding what to do with Jewish sites that have been returned to it (the Foundation for the Preservation of Jewish Heritage in Poland was established to assist in this task).[12]

Traveling to a Vanished World

As Jewish life has been reemerging in Germany and Poland, the material traces of the prewar past have attracted international attention like never before. This interest in Jewish heritage sites, coming mostly from Americans and Israelis, takes on a variety of forms. In 1979, Zvi Kestenbaum, a rabbi and Holocaust survivor living in Brooklyn, New York, helped establish the United States Commission for the Preservation of America's Heritage Abroad. Kestenbaum had long been involved in pushing local governments in Eastern Europe to preserve Jewish cemeteries. Under a law signed by President Reagan in 1987, the commission received federal funding in 1990 to preserve "those cemeteries, monuments, and historic buildings" in danger of destruction.[13] The commission has supported preservation work and published extensive surveys of Jewish sites, prepared by leading experts, such as Eleonora Bergman, Samuel Gruber, and Jan Jagielski, but its main goal has been to get European countries to sign formal agreements with the United States to ensure the protection of Jewish sites. Since 1992, it has signed twenty-three such agreements, including ones with Germany and Poland. The establishment of this little-known though striking body—a federal commission that largely preserves the cultural heritage of a single ethnic group in places as distant as Turkey—came at a particular moment in time. In the 1970s and 1980s, American and Israeli Jews started to trace their family roots back to Europe. In 1977, Dan Rottenberg published the first handbook on Jewish genealogy, *Finding Our Fathers,* while the genealogical periodicals *Toledot* (1977) and *Avotaynu* (1985) appeared around the same time. This turn to roots stemmed partly from curiosity, but also for other reasons. As Zionism has steadily lost its appeal among a minority of Jews in the United States and Israel, some have turned to the vanished Jewish "world" of Europe in search of new Jewish identities. Europe has become a space to celebrate Jewish life in diaspora, long derided by the Zionist call for immigration to Israel. This "quest" for Europe's Jewish past has taken on many forms.[14] It has entailed something as simple as walking up to the attic to look through boxes of memorabilia, or as involved as traveling to Europe to visit Jewish sites. Jewish tourism to Europe began in the 1960s during the postwar boom in leisure travel, but it has exploded over the past twenty years, mirroring broader trends in the growth of heritage tourism across the world.[15] It has expanded so much that now Jewish travel comes with its own stock patterns and stories. It often involves experiencing the space where Jewish history has ended. Germany, Poland, and indeed much of Europe appear as the graveyards of Jewish life. Nothing more than crumbling Jewish spaces exist there—"traces, echoes, and a few monuments," Eva Hoffmann announces at the start of *Shtetl*.[16] This is, of course, not the case for all Jewish tourists. Some Jews recognize the growth of Jewish life since 1989, or travel to Europe to explore their family heritage, not just to commemorate the Holocaust. The perceptions and motivations depend on who is traveling, but still the image of Europe as the vanished Jewish world has become a dominant trope, especially when authors, journalists, and writers discuss Poland and Eastern Europe.

While statistics are hard to come by, Jewish tourists visit Poland more than they do Germany because many American and Israeli Jews trace family roots back to Poland. Berlin is the main exception, but Poland has particular appeal and evokes a complex of feelings that Germany does not. Poland is at once imagined as the familiar, welcoming place, where the rich, pure, and authentic culture of the *shtetl* blossomed, and remembered as the graveyard where this glorious heritage came to a tragic burial. Jews have long imagined Poland and Eastern Europe in these conflicted ways since 1945. In the early postwar decades, connections to the old world appeared in memorial books, photographic displays, festivals, and theatrical performances, such as *Polish Jews: A Pictorial Record* (1947), *The Earth Is the Lord's* (1949), *Life Is with the People* (1952), and, of course, *Fiddler on the Roof* (1964).[17] Since the collapse of Communism, though, tourism and travelogues have become the central vectors of Jewish cultural memories of Eastern Europe as tens of thousands of Jews have poured into the region. Coming likely from affluent, middle-class backgrounds (they have to afford the trip), they perceive "Eastern Europe" as the foil to their own liberal, bourgeois sensibilities. Eastern Europe appears as drab, corrupt, backward, digressive, poor, and intolerant. This image of the "east" stretches back to the Enlightenment, but became solidified during the Cold War and has persisted after the collapse of Communism with a commensurate shift from anti-Communism to anti-Polish sentiment. Jewish tourists often tell the same anxiety-ridden stories of neglect and destruction complete, as one traveler put it, with the "stock scenes" of the "successful or disappointed hunt for the family house and graves—the forlornly untended Jewish cemetery—the old synagogue turned into a pizzeria or discotheque."[18] If Poles make it into these stories, they often appear as simple-minded, threatening peasants. Walking through an abandoned, overgrown Jewish cemetery in Majdan, one Jewish traveler became anxious when he saw two Poles nearby: "I knew too well what had happened to Jews in these forests. I grabbed my guide, walked to the far end of the cemetery before they could spot us and left."[19]

Jewish travel to Europe has become a kind of "secular ritual."[20] Jews travel less for pleasure and more out of obligation to encounter the Holocaust and perform their identity as Jews. Indeed, the state of Israel and March of the Living host annual, pilgrim-like trips to Auschwitz. In 1988, the Israeli Ministry of Education organized its first youth trip to Poland with the expressed aim of developing "stronger links to the history of Israel" and preparing future citizens "to guard the future of the nation and the state."[21] The March of the Living, established by Israeli and North American Jewish educators in the late 1980s, is shaped by a similar Zionist message and has brought thousands of Jews from across the world to march from Auschwitz to Birkenau on Holocaust Memorial Day. Although these youth voyages have recently tried to broaden their focus, they are still centered on the death camps and reinforce negative impressions of Poland that probably many participants had before they left. The trip concludes with flying from Poland to Israel. As one student from Hollywood, Florida, put it, the students travel "from hell to heaven, from despair to joy." Another, from Boca Raton, summed up Poland simply: "We couldn't find anything good there."[22]

Jewish tourism is, though, hardly monolithic. Holocaust memory clearly dominates and shapes it, but an ambivalent nostalgia—an unresolved, uneasy sentiment of loss and fantasy for home—compels Jews to travel to Europe. This longing remains deeply discomforting; it is often entangled with traumatic memories of violent displacement. Writing about his return to Czernowitz, Israeli writer Aharon Appelfeld speaks at once of "fresh breezes of summer" and deep "sorrow." "Czernowitz expelled its Jews, and so did Vienna, Prague, Budapest, and Lemberg. Now these cities live without Jews, and their few descendants, scattered through the world, carry memory like a wonderful gift and a relentless curse."[23] This curse—what the poet Paul Celan called "black milk"—nourishes and nauseates, repels and attracts, seduces and disgusts. Such conflicting emotions naturally nurture negative impressions, but Jewish tourism involves more than just a performative, ritualistic act of group identity formation. Some Jewish travelers reject the ideological impulses of trips such as the March of the Living and contest negative assumptions about Jewish life in Europe. In 2009, for example, the American Jewish performing artist Maya Escobar created an exhibition called *Berlin's Eruv*, which she displayed on the Internet. Berlin does not have an eruv, a space marked in public that allows observant Jews to carry items such as keys on the Sabbath, which Jewish religious law otherwise prohibits, but Escobar created a "metaphorical eruv" through interviews with Jews about the spaces they inhabit in Berlin, documenting a Jewish community "frequently overshadowed by the city's prominent monuments and memorials commemorating Jewish life (death)." As she explains on her website, "*Berlin's Eruv* is a conceptual project that addresses the assumed nonpresence of Jews in Germany."[24]

Jewish Sites in "Cosmopolitan" Capitals

As Jewish tourism has expanded greatly since 1989, Germans and Poles have only intensified their interest in the Jewish past. This fascination stems largely from the perception of Jewish culture as uniquely rich, authentic, and cosmopolitan, and perhaps not surprisingly has become manifested above all in urban space. For Jews have long been linked to the city. Their cosmopolitanism comes from their association with urban life for good or bad depending on who is doing the interpreting. In the late nineteenth century, the antisemitic press portrayed Jews as city dwellers with innumerable, undesirable characteristics: the rootless cosmopolitan who has no ties to the nation; the city-dwelling banker who causes economic misfortune; the urban criminal who brings prostitution, pornography, and incest. In an industrializing, changing world, Europeans scorned Jews for the social, cultural, and economic anxieties of modernity that they allegedly symbolized. But some perceived Jewish cosmopolitanism as desirable. In 1925, the Austrian journalist and Jewish convert to Christianity Hugo Bettauer published his novel *The City without Jews*, which imagined what life would be like in Vienna with no Jews. This odd, sardonic work became a bestseller, was made into a film, and inspired Artur Landsberger to write his own version for Berlin. The book, the movie, and its Berlin copy portrayed impoverished life without Jews. All three accounts end with Jews returning just in time to prevent the collapse of cultural and economic life.[25] These books, when read today, seem eerily close to the actual removal of Jews fifteen years later with the exception that there was, of course, no happy ending. The impoverishment was now more than real. In 1956, the scholar Harry Zohn, in an essay titled "The City without Jews," described the "provincialism of daily life, the brutalization of taste, the reduction of cosmopolitanism" in contemporary Vienna. In 1979, German author Bernt Engelmann lamented the cultural loss of Jews over 400 pages, while in 1984 Czech writer Milan Kundera made Jews out to be the "principal cosmopolitan" in his recovery of the tolerant, multiethnic myth of "Central Europe."[26] A similar kind of impulse has emerged since 1989. In contemporary Europe, the presence of Jews, or more precisely Jewish heritage, has become code for what one desires rather than dislikes. Restored or newly created Jewish sites signify cosmopolitanism in a postfascist and post-Communist world.

This cosmopolitan framing of the Jewish past has become most pronounced in Berlin, which is home to not only the largest, most diverse Jewish population in Germany but also the most visible explosion of interest in what is perceived to be Jewish. Contemporary Berlin is perhaps ideal for such a rediscovery. Edgy, young, energetic, and the current European darling of papers like the *New York Times,* Berlin has exploded onto the post-1989 imagination as a hip, cool, tolerant, free-flowing, almost-everything-goes kind of city where one can drink, smoke, dance, and sex the night away. With a budget deficit in the billions of euros and a weak economy from the city's forty-year division, Berlin is poor and stagnant, but revels in its image as a cosmopolitan, fun loving, tourist-haven city. "Berlin is poor, but sexy," according to its hip and media-friendly mayor, Klaus Wowereit.[27] This image elides the reality on the streets. Berlin has problems with right-wing extremism, and its sizeable Turkish population is separated from most Berliners in the district of Kreuzberg. Still, the image endures in part because it builds on the earlier imagination of West Berlin as the fascinating, edgy place to be right on the Cold War border. Millions of tourists keep coming to the city, with over 17 million in 2007. Most tourists rarely visit the city's districts where its divisions are apparent, and many seem to absorb the image of the "new Berlin." The majority of the 2,164 tourists interviewed by the city's marketing firm described Berlin with such adjectives as "multicultural," "creative," "alternative," "young," "innovative," "vibrant," "historically interesting," and "dynamic."[28]

A central part of this image is Berlin's embrace of its Jewish past, which has increased dramatically since the fall of the Berlin Wall. Today, it is trendy to be Jewish in Berlin. In 1998, the bimonthly magazine *Zitty* took stock of this hype in a six-page article. Such an essay's appearance in *Zitty*—a popular events magazine that along with its competitor, *Tip,* serves as a kind of cultural arbiter in the city—alone speaks to the popularity that "what counts as Jewish" has in the city. The front cover of the issue carried a cubic, psychedelic-looking Star of David with the headline on the bottom right corner, "Trendy Judaism: The Hype about the Star of David." The article began with the evidence: the Jewish restaurants, stores, organizations, and cultural clubs; the menus that cannot leave out the bagels; the countless city tours of "Jewish Berlin"; the nightly Klezmer music. The article, though, resisted reveling in this cosmopolitanism as many Berliners and tourists do and attempted to confront its dilemmas in a series of interviews with Jewish academics, artists, writers, and community members. Most Berlin Jews were skeptical of this hype and viewed it as a form of cultural domination that exoticizes Jews. The Jewish writer and gadfly Henryk Broder mockingly observed that "the good souls were not there when the train with my mother was rolling out; such enthusiasm was much more guarded then." Julius Hans Schoeps, professor of Jewish history at Potsdam University, argued that "positive" evaluations of Jews reflected inversions of negative stereotypes that can easily slip into hatred. The co-founder of the Jewish artistic group Meshulash, Gabriel Heimler, went so far as to call this "domination of Jewishness with socially suited clichés a 'cultural Shoah.'" Such comments are extreme to say the least. One Jewish community member noted more insightfully that it can be "stressful to be a Jew here" because Germans view Jews as different and exotic, people to be studied, experienced, preserved, discovered, and identified.[29]

This rediscovery of "Jewish Berlin" largely involves encountering Jewish traces in the urban landscape, especially in one area of town—the so-called Barn Quarter, or more commonly known by its German name, the *Scheunenviertel.* Located in the middle of the city and once part of East Berlin, the Scheunenviertel has become a trendy place in the city with a number of bars, restaurants, cafes, and art galleries. The city has poured 1.5 billion euros into carefully restoring the surrounding neighborhood, which had fallen into disrepair during the GDR.[30] In the late 1980s, the East German state planned to tear down most of the dilapidated buildings, but a grassroots protest campaign precluded their destruction. In the past decade, the area has been gentrified and has become a central area of the "New Berlin." Its carefully restored buildings serve as a spatial marker of democracy's progressive triumph, a public display of the new Berlin rescuing this quaint, historic neighborhood from the urban disaster of Communist urban planning.

Central to this rescue effort is reclaiming the area's Jewish past. The Scheunenviertel has become Berlin's Jewish district, a cultural construct that only partially reflects the area's history. In the late nineteenth century, Eastern European Jews fleeing from the pogroms of 1881 and 1905 settled in the tenement houses of Berlin Mitte. By 1925, about 30,000 Jews lived in this part of town, making up 10 percent of the population. Mostly Orthodox and relatively poor, they stood out from the city's acculturated, middle-class Jewish community, but did not form an isolated community.[31] Berlin never had one single, densely populated Jewish neighborhood like Warsaw; its population lived in all parts of the city by 1900. Still, Berliners imagined the Scheunenviertel as the city's "Jewish district" in large part because of the Eastern European Jews who lived there. By the 1920s, the area was constructed as a quaint *shtetl* within the metropolis, drawing on long-standing orientalist perceptions of Eastern European Jews. "Suddenly, in the middle of Berlin I was in surroundings like Lviv," the Jewish actor Alexander Granach recalled about his time there in the 1920s. "Jews walk about dressed like those in Galicia, Romania, and Russia."[32] This mental mapping of "Jews" with the "east" stretches back to the Enlightenment when Eastern European Jews were seen as dirty and backward, yet also authentic and beautiful. In 1822, Heinrich Heine captured this mix of repulsion and attraction perhaps best when he wrote after visiting Poland, "In spite of the barbarous fur cap which covers his head, and the still more barbarous notions which fill it, I esteem the Polish Jew."[33] This ambivalent reaction to the Eastern European Jew reached a climax in World War I, when many German soldiers encountered Jews in Poland. In the early interwar years, exotic Eastern European Jews emerged in a number of literary and pictorial representations. They became "authentic" traces of Jewishness in a modern, assimilating world.[34]

But in the late 1920s and 1930s, this strangeness was more often derided than celebrated. In Berlin, antisemitic novelists and writers created the Scheunenviertel as the city's "ghetto."[35] The area, home to pimps, bars, and prostitutes, seemed like the ideal space to make racist connections between criminality, moral degeneration, urbanization, and Jews.

The contemporary construction of the Scheunenviertel rests on similarly essentialized notions of Jews as exotic, as Eastern European, as Orthodox, as Hasidic that have almost nothing to do with the history of Berlin's Jewish community. The Eastern European Jew represents the authentic albeit now vanished world of the dirty, backward, yet beautiful and romantic *shtetl*.[36] Tourism has played a major role in perpetuating these myths. In one week alone, at least ten city tours walk the streets of Jewish Berlin, and they often orient the traveler to the Scheunenviertel.[37] The journey begins in Mitte, passing through the renovated apartment buildings of the Scheunenviertel and the grounds of the former Jewish cemetery on Grosse Hamburger Street and ending at the New Synagogue on Oranienburger Street, where one can buy items in shops with Jewish ritual objects in their windows or dine in restaurants called Makom. Tourists become involved in this drama as much as the German storekeepers, guides, and writers who stage it. In 1992–93, the traveling American installation artist Shimon Attie showcased a slide projection of prewar images of "Jewish street life in Berlin" on the buildings of "Berlin's former Jewish quarter, the Scheunenviertel." Although obviously more so than the work of any normal tourist, his re-creation of this seemingly authentic, now lost "world of the Jewish working class" reflects the intertwined mental mapping of the faraway traveler and the local guide, engaged as they are in a process of creation and experience that affects both the identity of place and the actual, material treatment of space.[38]

Some have argued that this interest in the Scheunenviertel has produced a "Jewish Disneyland." The Berlin Jewish publicist Iris Weiss, who herself once led tours in the city including one called "Jewish Disneyland—The Marketing of Jewishness," sees a number of problems with this re-created "Jewishness" in the area around Oranienburger Street. Her complaint mirrors the main concern expressed by other Jews in Berlin that the "fictitious" is becoming "real." "The themes of Jewish Disneyland are romanticism, exoticization, folklorization, and historicization of everything Jewish. As a result, that which is really Jewish becomes (or is made) invisible."[39] This virtual Jewish world, she claims, rarely reflects on the Holocaust and ignores the "real" Jewish life in the city. These remarks hold some truth. Locals and tourists mark Jews for their difference and strangeness, although now for their celebrated cosmopolitanism. They come to the Scheunenviertel to experience a different "world" from what they find in other areas of Berlin such as the Brandenburg Gate, Unter den Linden, and Potsdamer Platz. Weiss also marshals some compelling evidence. The American singer Gayle Tufts, who lives in Berlin, remarked glibly, "The fact that right here in Berlin's former Jewish quarter one can get bagels, a typical Jewish bread that you find everywhere in New York, well, that's almost a sign of healing."[40] Still, Weiss's observations suffer from contradictions. She assumes that a definable, real "Jewishness" exists, reducing it to an identifiable element—religion—in a city of multiple meanings of Jewishness. She does exactly what she critiques by assuming a reified, singular understanding of Jewishness.

What is more, Weiss overlooks the multiple meanings of "Jewish Berlin," made up of spaces in which different temporal layers intermingle and collide. For example, the Lauder foundation, with financial support from the Skoblo family, opened a Yeshiva in the synagogue on Brunnen Street in Berlin Mitte. Built in 1910 and used as office space during the GDR, it was neglected for nearly twenty years after 1989 until the Skoblo family bought the property and restored it to house a center for Torah learning for boys. Other examples abound, but the one that most reflects this intermingling of past, present, and future is the building that has become the symbol of "Jewish Berlin," more photographed and celebrated than any other—the New Synagogue on Oranienburger Street. In 1988, Erich Honecker promised to rebuild this bombed-out building to house the newly created "Centrum Judaicum," which was to be a cultural center, archive, museum, and Holocaust memorial. The fall of the Berlin Wall intervened, but the synagogue's rebuilding continued throughout the 1990s. The building's exterior was returned to its original, prewar design with its majestic golden cupola, but the interior of the building was not restored.[41] The exterior reinforces the image of the new Berlin defining itself from its fascist and Communist pasts. The beautifully restored façade symbolizes the democratic embrace of Jewishness after decades of pernicious suppression under Communism, forgetting the early postwar years when West Berlin demolished numerous synagogues, a period much different from the present when live television, 3,000 guests, and massive security lavished the unveiling of the New Synagogue in 1996.[42] When one walks by the carefully restored exterior, the building indeed seems to reflect a reconstructed staging of the Jewish past in the urban landscape, little more than a physical and mental façade of "Jewish Berlin." But when one walks inside, such a reading proves superficial. An exhibition narrates the history of Berlin's Jewish community and focuses on the building's violent destruction, brought into sharp relief by the large glass wall that looks out onto an empty space where the 3,200-seat prayer hall once stood until East German officials cleared away its ruins in 1956. The building stands mainly as a memorial to the past, but it has also become a space for the city's Jewish community. The synagogue's small prayer room is one of the only two liberal houses of worship officially recognized by the community where men and women can participate equally. The New Synagogue stands at once as a monument, a cultural center, and a house of worship, a multilayered space for tourists, politicians, scholars, locals, and practicing Jews.

Such multiple meanings surface, however, less often outside Berlin when one moves to the Polish capital. Warsaw has neither Berlin's sizeable Jewish community nor its millions of tourists. The only other city in Poland that matches, if not exceeds, Berlin's "hype about the Star of David" is Kraków, which has become a major tourist destination. But Kraków is an exceptional case in Poland, and in Europe for that matter (Prague is probably the only other city that rivals it). The local and international interest that has produced "Jewish Kazimierz" exists in no other Polish city. Part of the reason is that Kraków's Jewish sites escaped destruction during the war. Although neglected throughout the postwar years, they survived and today provide an "authentic" setting for Jewish restaurants, museums, and shops. In contrast, Jewish sites in many other Polish cities were heavily damaged during the war and were later torn down after 1945. In Warsaw, the Nazis leveled the Jewish district of Muranów, and the PZPR used the area to build a sprawling, socialist realist housing complex. Jewish Warsaw disappeared almost entirely.

But a few fragments of it survived, and today Poles are reclaiming them—indeed, at times, with actual hands and a shovel. In July 2002, the historic preservationist Janusz Sujecki teamed up with the researcher Anna Przybyszewska of the Lauder foundation to see if they could uncover traces of the synagogue in Praga on the Vistula's right bank. Built in 1840 and demolished in 1961 to make room for a playground, it was Warsaw's oldest synagogue. Sujecki and Przybyszewska found fragments of the building's foundation, and like the lost traces of an ancient, exotic past that grace the pages of *National Geographic,* their discovery made it into the popular historic preservation magazine *Spotkania z Zabytkami.* Since then, plans have surfaced to rebuild the synagogue. The Warsaw Jewish community has opposed the idea. "The destruction of the synagogue was barbaric, but it already happened," its vice-chairman remarked. "Plans to rebuild it after so many years later are simply unrealistic. For what? For whom?"[43] The idea, however, shows few signs of going away at the moment. If the estimated 5 million złoty can be raised, a new synagogue might be built in Warsaw.

Similarly, the sole surviving tenement houses of Muranów on Próżna Street have become important Jewish ruins worthy of preservation. This small side street in the heart of Warsaw runs into Grzybowski Square, a central part of prewar Jewish life and today the location of the city's main synagogue. The city's Yiddish theater and a few Jewish shops round out the area, while the surrounding streets reflect the past utopias of Communist urban planning. The area became home to Warsaw's most celebrated, socialist realist building project, Stalin's gift to Poland—the Palace of Culture and Art that today is the focal point of Warsaw's skyline. The rediscovery of this area began in the late 1980s, when a group of architects, historic preservationists, and historians fought to put the tenement houses on Próżna Street on the city's list of historic monuments. In March 1987, city officials relented after a bombardment of petitions from the Jewish Historical Institute, the Warsaw branch of the Society for Historic Preservation, the Socio-Cultural Association of Jews, and the Group of Cultural Conservators.[44]

But plans to save the neglected buildings emerged only years later. In 1997–98, the Lauder foundation purchased the tenement houses on Próżna Street with the intention of "reconstructing the appearance of the street from the time when the majority of its residents were Jews."[45] The street was to have a kosher restaurant, Jewish bookstore, bakery, and shop, but would not be exactly "as it was before the war." Instead, the "material setting" of the street would be returned.[46] When asked by a journalist if this would not produce a "Jewish Disneyland," the director of the project replied that Próżna would be an "authentic" Jewish space: "Próżna will be a living part of Warsaw, as well as of Jewish Warsaw."[47] The project was estimated to cost about $10 million, but work on it never began and the buildings fell deeper into disrepair with each passing year. In 2004, the Lauder foundation dropped the project and sold the buildings to an Austrian developer, who is planning to use them to build a luxury hotel. Plans for restoring this "Jewish" street now seem unlikely.

This decision, though, has not been popular. The Warsaw section of *Gazeta Wyborcza,* Poland's largest and most influential newspaper, has included sharp commentaries about plans to build a luxury hotel on Próżna. "The talk is no longer about kosher restaurants and Jewish stores. Today what matters is economic calculations," one article read.[48] Another decried the street's "sad and lifeless" appearance, which has not changed since 1989 despite numerous promises.[49] In 2008, the Jewish Historical Institute hosted a roundtable discussion to "save" Próżna from the grip of "commercial investments" that threaten to "kill the climate of this Jewish nook." It called for "restoring" this fragment of "former Jewish Warsaw" as a place that at once will serve as a tourist destination and an area for recovering the "multiculturalism" and "diversity" that Warsaw "lost after the war." The organizers admit that they do not want the street to become an "open-air ethnographic museum," but their proposal assumes that a fixed, definable Jewishness exists that can be restored and displayed as "authentic and real."[50]

Since 2004, the "Jewishness" of Próżna Street has also resurfaced in the annual "Singer's Warsaw" Jewish festival. Inspired by the Jewish festival in Kraków, this one started out as a celebration of the hundredth anniversary of Isaac Bashevis Singer's birth. Singer grew up in Warsaw before leaving for the United States in 1935. The festival has grown since 2004 into an annual event, with the entire street of Próżna turning into an imagined Jewish world. The street takes on its "prewar appearance" as "Singer returns to Próżna."[51] Just as in Berlin, where the staging of the Jewish past takes place in the Scheunenviertel, so, too, does it unfold in Warsaw within a physical space that seems authentically Jewish, as if the festival's musicians, artists, and shopkeepers seem more real along Próżna than they would elsewhere in the city. The festival reflects a restorative nostalgia for "Jewish Warsaw" and glosses over the tensions of prewar Polish-Jewish relations when few Poles would have looked so favorably upon Muranów's dirty, cramped tenement houses. It reflects an urge to discover something authentic and old, to experience one of the few streets left in Warsaw that still has "prewar buildings" in an urban landscape of drab Communist buildings and glossy capitalist skyscrapers.[52] The festival on Próżna also provides a bit of cosmopolitanism to one of the world's most ethnically homogeneous capitals.

There are, however, a few exceptions that scratch below the festival's simplistic recovery of the Jewish past. In 2006, a group of artists installed several exhibitions about Jews and the Holocaust in the building on Próżna no. 9. Once part of the Warsaw ghetto, the building today sits in a catastrophic state with rain coming through its roof. This is the structure that the Austrian developer has slated to turn into a luxury hotel, but for a brief moment it served as a testament to the destruction of Polish Jewry. One artist narrated the death of her family in the Warsaw ghetto through a display of toys in an aquarium, while another showed an Israeli film of elderly Jews singing Polish songs. A review of the exhibition published in *Gazeta Wyborcza* applauded these efforts to move beyond the "sentimental-folk climate" and the "fiction" of "playing back" the past in the festival just outside the building. "The artistic exhibition in Próżna no. 7/9 is something different," the journalist wrote; "no orchestral beats, no singing cantors, no Jewish cuisine, no folk paper cut-outs. Here nobody believes it is possible to go back to the past."[53] Moreover, interest in the Jewish past has multiplied over the past several years in Warsaw, and new venues are quickly eclipsing the centrality of Próżna. A new festival organized by the Jewish community that is about the "present, not history" debuted in 2010; the project "Muranów Station" describes in depth the prewar, wartime, and postwar history of Warsaw's Jewish district; and Café Chłodna 25 has hosted numerous lectures, exhibitions, and readings about the city's Jewish past, among, of course, many others as befitting a place that clearly aspires to become the hottest scene for Warsaw's artists and intellectuals. Located right near the bridge that linked the two parts of the ghetto on a surviving fragment of the prewar, cobblestoned street, the café appears deeply aware of its location—the first picture posted on its blog was of the ghetto bridge. In 2010, the café organized, along with the Jewish community and other cultural groups in the city, a two-day event on Jewish culture with concerts, exhibitions, lectures, discussions, and films.[54]

But the newest and by far most ambitious venue of Jewishness in Warsaw is the Museum of the History of Polish Jews currently being built. In a transnational effort that has involved funding and organization from Germany,

Israel, the United States, the United Kingdom, Sweden, and the Netherlands, the idea to build the museum came from Jerzy Halberstadt and
Grażyna Pawlak, who worked at the Jewish Historical Institute in the 1980s
before going on to the United Holocaust Memorial Museum and the Lauder
foundation. In 1996, they formed a committee to plan the museum with Je-
shajahu Weinberg, a Warsaw native and major initiator of the United States
Holocaust Memorial Museum. The planning for the Museum of the History
of Polish Jews in Warsaw, as for any project of its size, has moved slowly, but
it has generally received positive responses in Poland. In 1997, the Warsaw
city council donated about 145,000 square feet of land for the museum, and
the Polish government has committed $26 million toward the costs of con-
struction (the rest has come from donations, including 5 million euros from
the German government). The jury selected eleven designs by some of the
world's most renowned architects, including Daniel Libeskind and Peter
Eisenman. Libeskind, himself of Polish-Jewish background, was believed to
be the favorite, but the winning prize went to the Finnish architects Rainer
Mahlamäki and Ilmari Lahdelma, with their compact design of glass dra-
matized by a large tear that cuts through the building, reflecting the "complicated and tragic" historical journey of Jews in Poland.[55] On June 26, 2007,
the groundbreaking of the museum took place with dignitaries from around
the world. The Polish president, Lech Kaczyński, emphasized the importance
of the museum in offering a "tremendous opportunity to overcome a mutual
lack of understanding," while the chief rabbi of Tel Aviv, Yisrael Meir Lau,
said that the museum will ensure that no one "forget[s] the Jews of this land."[56]
The museum is scheduled to open in 2012.

Located on the former site of the ghetto just in front of Rapoport's monument, the museum rests on a plot of land steeped in layers of time—the
center of prewar Jewish life, the site of mass murder, and the space of the
socialist future. Although the Communist rebuilding of Muranów tried to
erase the district's past, it succeeded only in clearing away its physical markers. It could not suppress its memories. A recent study of middle-aged residents living in Muranów showed a strong awareness of the district's Jewish
history. The Jewish museum will likely only strengthen this connection.[57]
Close to the *Umschlagplatz* and surrounded by socialist realist apartment
buildings, it sits in an area that reflects the absence of Jewish life in the city,
captured by the museum's design: the large tear through the building looks

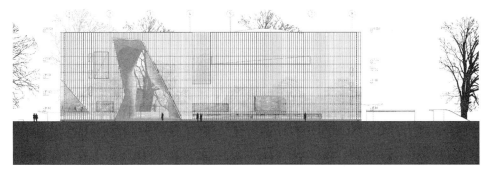

Sketch of Warsaw's Museum of the History of Polish Jews, which is being built on the former site of the ghetto surrounded by Communist-era apartment buildings. (© Studio Lahdelma & Mahlamäki)

out to the ghetto uprising monument. The Holocaust will be an important part of the museum, but it is not intended to be just a "Holocaust museum," as the organizers and Polish press have stressed.[58] The master plan for the exhibition envisions seven galleries that narrate Polish-Jewish history from its earliest beginnings to the present. The gallery on the interwar period that includes a virtual reconstruction of Nalewki Street, Warsaw's commercial center of Jewish life, has attracted particular attention in Polish newspapers. Visitors will be able to travel along the street as it "once was before the war, as described by the writer Isaac Bashevis Singer."[59] A restorative impulse partially animates the project, which strives to "restore the presence of this culture" and become one of the "Jewish symbols of contemporary Warsaw."[60] But the museum also understandably seeks to offer a more complex interpretation of Polish-Jewish relations than the one often held by Jewish tourists, who see the country as frozen in the 1940s, as nothing more than the landscape of the Holocaust.

The purpose of the museum is also a direct response to Europe's other, most celebrated and discussed post-1989 Jewish museum, designed by Warsaw's runner-up—the famed Daniel Libeskind. The idea for the museum, at first an expansion of the Berlin City Museum founded in 1962, emerged in the early 1970s when the West Berlin Jewish community under Heinz Galinski organized an exhibition on the history of Jewish life in the city. The exhibition, entitled "Achievement and Fate: The 300-Year History of the Berlin Jewish Community," focused on the positive contribution of Jewish culture and avoided the Nazi period. The Holocaust was an implicit but nebulous aspect of the exhibition. The goal was to show that "the best times of communal existence and impact can reemerge in contemporary Berlin after a terrible caesura."[61] The positive response to the exhibition encouraged Galinski to push for a permanent one in West Berlin. The Berlin Museum director at the time, Irmgard Wirth, supported the idea and argued that the exhibition should be integrated into the city museum to avoid separating German and Jewish history into two parts. Galinski agreed with this idea, and Wirth submitted a general plan for the exhibition that envisioned sections on the history of Berlin Jewry, Jewish religion, and the cultural accomplishments of the city's Jewish leaders.[62] Wirth described the project as a "reestablishment" of the city's prewar Jewish museum, which the Berlin community opened in 1933 and the Nazis closed down in 1938. The Jewish museum would signify the continuance of Jewish life after Nazism, displaying Jews as a "fixed, integral part of cultural life in West Berlin."[63] The city council approved the plan, but years passed with little action as officials searched for a location. By the mid-1980s, when the East German leadership announced its plans for a Jewish museum in the New Synagogue, the city rushed to find a solution. In 1986, it temporarily installed the Jewish department in the newly restored Martin Gropius building about a mile away from the Berlin Museum. At the opening of the exhibition, West Berlin mayor Eberhard Diepgen of the Christian Democrats noted that it would be "false" to "reduce" German-Jewish history to "terrible times," because that would fail to consider the "long, fruitful history of interaction between Christians and Jews" as well as the "great contribution of Jews to German intellectual life."[64] Recycling the myth of cultural symbiosis, the mayor bracketed off the Nazi period as an exceptional moment in an otherwise harmonious history of German-Jewish relations.

Galinski supported this temporary solution, but adamantly insisted that the city build an annex to the Berlin Museum to integrate the Jewish section with the city museum, reflecting his continued belief in showcasing Jewish history as part of Berlin's history.[65] An integrated museum itself was to reflect the integration of Jews in Berlin society. Galinski eventually got his way. In November 1988, at the height of East Germany's fiftieth anniversary of *Kristallnacht,* the city agreed to expand the Berlin Museum by building an annex for the Jewish department and launched a major architectural competition. The competition materials emphasized that the annex should be integrated into the current building to dramatize "Jewish history as a definite component of Berlin."[66] The museum was still envisioned to be about the cultural, economic, and religious development of German-Jewish history, although by the late 1980s a stronger emphasis on the Holocaust started to emerge in discussions about the exhibition's contents.[67] But these ideas were vaguely formulated, and exactly how to narrate Jews as an integrated part of the city's history after the Holocaust was unclear. In contrast to Warsaw, where the concept of the exhibition was developed before the design competition, the architects for the Berlin Jewish Museum had little sense of the exhibition's overarching purpose.

The result was predictable. Libeskind's design conflicted with the idea of the integrated museum. The building reflects the failure of integration. It is an architectural meditation on the Holocaust, with its empty voids, underground axes, Holocaust tower, and Garden of Exile. The museum stands as a ruin that reflects emptiness, what Libeskind calls "built-in absence." "What is not visible is the richness of the former Jewish contribution to Berlin," Libeskind noted in a lecture in 1995. "It cannot be found in artifacts because it has been turned to ash."[68] And yet the exhibition installed in the building after intense discussions over the 1990s strives for a unified narrative of German-Jewish history over two millennia. Just as in Warsaw, the museum is not supposed to be only about the Holocaust. As the American museum director Michael Blumenthal explained, the exhibition displays the "ups and downs" of German-Jewish history.[69] In his speech at the opening of the museum in 2001, German president Johannes Rau put it clearly: "The Berlin Jewish Museum does not want to be and should not be a Holocaust museum.... We must keep alive the memory of this catastrophe. This building, which today we are opening, does that, this exhibition does that. But that must not lead to the wrong conclusion that the Holocaust is the sum of German-Jewish history."[70]

The construction of Jewish museums in Berlin and Warsaw produce similar meanings. In certain ways, both museums intersect with the rediscovery of "Jewish Berlin" and "Jewish Warsaw" along the streets of Oranienburger and Próżna. They hope to move beyond the clichés that these productions reinforce, but at the same time they reflect a similar urge for cosmopolitanism. Both museums make Jews an integral part of German and Polish society. They help produce cosmopolitan capitals as Germans and Poles,

Berlin's Jewish museum appearing as if it were a ruin. Libeskind inscribed "built-in absence" into the structure to represent the trauma of the Holocaust. (© Studio Daniel Libeskind, photographer Manfred Beck)

especially on the left, take plurality and cosmopolitanism to be crucial components of Germanness and Polishness after a century of war, genocide, ethnic strife, and expulsions. The stakes are different in Berlin and Warsaw. Centered in the district of Kreuzberg, Berlin's most concentrated area of Turks, the Jewish museum's narrative of acculturation, destroyed by unchecked prejudice, implies contemporary meanings about its immigrant population. By displaying the cultural achievements of Germany's "Jewish co-citizens" (*jüdische Mitbürger*), the museum emphasizes the demand of assimilation. If they integrate, Germany's minorities might reach the improved demarcation of being "foreign co-citizens" from their current status as "foreigners" (*ausländische Mitbürger* over *Ausländer*).

Warsaw has different contemporary implications. While in the process of becoming more ethnically diverse, Warsaw is still largely Berlin's opposite— almost entirely ethnically homogeneous thanks to the policies of an earlier Berlin. But Warsaw's museum offers a powerful symbol of Poland embracing its rich, Jewish heritage as it returns to "Europe." The new Poland—democratic, tolerant, cosmopolitan—showcases its "normality" by recovering the Jewish past. Both museums become cosmopolitan symbols of tolerance and successful remembrance. Recalling the Jewish past confirms the righteousness of liberal democratic values and celebrates their triumph over fascism and Communism. For most of the twentieth century, Jews appeared as quintessential cosmopolitans for which they were more likely to be derided than celebrated. Philosemitism is not just the inverse of antisemitism, but it does often essentialize and appropriate. Jews become an object of display and serve as markers of successful change from the past. This is not a German and Polish peculiarity—witness the Smithsonian National Museum of the American Indian and the Smithsonian National Museum of African American History and Culture, to take just two American examples. It is a peculiarity of both the allure and the fragility of cosmopolitanism itself, an idea that celebrates human difference as much as it creates it.

Jewish Spaces in Wrocław, Essen, and Potsdam

This cosmopolitan embrace of Jewishness can also be found outside the capitals of Warsaw and Berlin. Beginning in the 1980s, local citizens in Wrocław became interested in moving beyond their city's postwar image as a bastion of Polish culture by exploring its German and Jewish pasts. This rediscovery of Breslau's memory increased after the fall of Communism when Wrocław became stylized as the "multicultural metropolis," the eternally fluctuating border town rich in its variety and diversity. As the city's official website boasts to prospective visitors: "Wrocław is an excellent example of a multicultural metropolis situated at the interface of ethnically diverse areas."[71] The website even offers the postwar expulsions as evidence of the city's diverse history, suggesting that "multiculturalism again left a very deep impression on the city's character after the Second World War, when the city's German population was largely replaced by people arriving from various regions of Poland, including those resettled from the eastern provinces of Poland taken over by the Soviet Union."[72] Such imaginative constructions of the multicultural metropolis do not come, though, just from a few marketing experts in the city's tourist office. Since 1989, writers, journalists, and historians have rushed to rediscover the city's shifting, multiethnic past.[73] The most prominent example is Norman Davies, whom Poles admire probably more than any other historian for his hagiographic narratives, including one on Wrocław published in 2003. Davies interprets Wrocław as a "microcosm" of diversity, multiplicity, and cosmopolitanism. He plays with the city's at least fifty recorded names—Vratislavia, Wrotizla, Vretslav, Presslaw, Breslau, Wrocław—in a grandiose and solipsistic account. He crafts a past different from the twentieth century's harsh realities when the city's prewar Jewish population was murdered, its former German residents were expelled, its current inhabitants were resettled there, and its postwar Jewish population was expelled. The provincialism of the book conflicts with the invented cosmopolitanism of the subject, reinforced all the more by Davies's seemingly innocuous subtitle—"a portrait of a central European city." The concept of "Central Europe," long constructed by Czech, Polish, Hungarian, and Slovak writers, is "Eastern Europe's" foil: sophisticated, urban, tolerant, diverse, cosmopolitan, multiethnic, multilingual.[74]

And Jewish. "Jewishness" has become a defining code for Central Europe. In Wrocław, the White Stork Synagogue has become an important space of the "multicultural metropolis." Its celebrated status marks a dramatic shift from the building's appropriation in the late 1980s and early 1990s. Just before the collapse of Communism, city officials continued to search for a suitable use for the crumbling structure. The last solution proposed before 1989 was to transform the synagogue into a performance hall for the Wrocław Musical Academy, but a lack of funds prevented this from happening. Shortly after the collapse of Communism, the new Wrocław Jewish community, under the leadership of Jerzy Kichler, expressed interest in renovating the synagogue. In 1993, it secured funds from the Foundation for Polish-German Cooperation, but the music academy owned the building and did not want to return it to the Jewish community. In 1992, it sold the synagogue just as the community had made it clear that it wanted it back. The new owner, a local developer, seemed equally intractable. In 1993–94, Kichler and other Jewish community members attempted to negotiate with him, but he kept demanding a higher price every time they met. The Jewish community turned to the city and the citizens of Wrocław for help. In a public letter in 1995, it wrote with frustration that it had to fight for its own property: "The authorities of the German Reich pursued the extermination of the Jewish population in Wrocław. After the war, Polish authorities robbed the Jewish community of all of its property and to this day this injustice has not been redressed."[75]

On April 21, 1995, the Council of Ministers in Warsaw intervened and returned the synagogue to the Jewish community after a long, extended series of negotiations. The council based its decision on a 1971 law that allowed religious organizations in the "recovered territories" to reclaim their property (Poland passed an official restitution law for Jewish communal property two years later in 1997). This decision cleared the way for the building's renovation after thirty-five years of neglect. "I feel sick when I look through the window," Kichler remarked to a local newspaper.[76] In 1996, the building's reconstruction began, and finally, in 2010, it was finished. As the synagogue has slowly been brought back to life, it has become a celebrated space in the multicultural metropolis, a site to experience and discover the city's Jewish past among both Jews and non-Jews. In 1996, a local musical director established the Choir of the White Stork Synagogue. The group has been performing concerts in the synagogue and elsewhere in Poland for over a decade now. Although developed in consultation with Kichler, the choir is made up mainly of non-Jews who sing in Hebrew and Yiddish. It has played an instrumental part in the city's annual "Festival of Jewish Culture."[77] Taking place mainly in the synagogue, the Wrocław version is less kitschy than its Warsaw counterpart on Próżna Street. It involves mainly lectures, film showings, theatrical performances, book readings, and Klezmer concerts.

Kichler and the local Jewish community are also more directly involved in these events than is the case in Warsaw. While many of the locals attending the events are non-Jewish, this is not simply a "Jewish revival minus the Jews."[78] Wrocław has the second largest Jewish community in Poland after Warsaw, with around 1,000 members. The Jewish community has made

Wrocław's synagogue being restored in 2006. (Photo by Michael Meng)

reaching out to non-Jews an important priority. In 2005, it established the Wrocław Center for Jewish Culture and Education and appointed as head the Jewish-Norwegian performing artist Bente Kahan, who established a foundation in her name. The Kahan foundation organizes Klezmer concerts, theatrical performances, and educational activities and is carrying out the final stages of the synagogue's transformation, which will eventually house a museum on the history of Jews in Wrocław. The museum will preserve "the rich heritage of the city's decimated Jewish community."[79] Because the building also serves as a place of religious worship, it is unclear exactly how this interplay between past and present will be negotiated in one space.

This revival of Jewish culture in the city has been welcomed and celebrated. In 2006, Bente Kahan received the Wrocław Mayor's Prize, while the local edition of *Gazeta Wyborcza* has published numerous articles on Jewish life in the city. Two coffee table–style books on the history of Jews in Wrocław appeared in 1994 and 2000.[80] The presence of Jewish culture fits into the city's image as a "multicultural metropolis" that Kichler, Kahan, and others have absorbed. Kahan writes about a "vital Jewish heart in the middle of Europe," while Kichler helped establish the "District of Four Religions" that celebrates the presence of the Jewish, Catholic, Protestant, and Orthodox faiths in the area surrounding the synagogue. At the opening of the renovated building in May 2010, Wrocław mayor Rafał Dutkiewicz spoke of "returning to our city once and for all its Jewish heart. Wrocław's Jewish heritage is part of the identity and culture of every resident in the city."[81] These cultural constructions of cosmopolitanism not only overlook the city's violent, destructive history but also rest on exaggerated interpretations of the present. The synagogue took over fifteen years to complete in a city of beautifully restored buildings. The contrast becomes clear when one walks just a few blocks away from the lively, tourist-centered old town to the street where the synagogue stands next to the Jewish community's dilapidated building. Wrocławians currently embrace the city's German and Austrian pasts more enthusiastically than they do its Jewish heritage.[82]

In fact, the only open Jewish cemetery in the city remains in deep disrepair. Lacking funds to maintain it, the Jewish community depends on others for help. A group of American students from Albion and Alma Colleges have been coming to Wrocław since 1999 to restore the cemetery. After visiting Prague, Berlin, Kraków, and Auschwitz, the group makes its way to the border city of Wrocław, but there they do not find the richly textured multiculturalism that the city promises. Coming likely from middle-class backgrounds with little knowledge of Poland beyond a few clichés, they spend their time in the "jungle" of the Jewish cemetery helping out a community too "old and poor to cook for themselves," let alone "perform hard labor."[83] If there is a revival of Jewish life in the city, it seems to have escaped them altogether. This view of the present is as naïve as is the one of the multicultural metropolis, but it shows the continued neglect of some Jewish sites even as others are restored. It also points to a clear tension between past and present. The transnational attraction to the Jewish past mixes awkwardly with the ongoing rebuilding of Jewish life. In this case, American tourists overlook it, while the Kahan foundation hopes to integrate a heritage museum in the same building in which Jews gather to worship.

This uneasy relationship between past and present is even starker in Essen, which has seen yet another shift in the synagogue's postwar history since the House of Industrial Design exhibition was removed in 1979–80. In 1979, Ernst Schmidt and Detlev Peukert convinced city officials to change the exhibition after a fire broke out in the building. The newly installed exhibition, "Resistance and Persecution in the Third Reich," explored the suffering and resistance of Germans with little attention to the Nazi persecution of the Jews. Yet this appropriation of the synagogue did not last long. As the Jewish past and the Holocaust became the subject of intense discussion throughout the Federal Republic in the 1980s, segments of Essen's population wanted to change the building's function to express more explicitly its Jewishness. In the early 1980s, a local committee on the synagogue discussed proposals to restore the synagogue's interior to its original prewar design, which had been heavily damaged in *Kristallnacht* and then completely altered in 1960. Local Protestant church leaders were especially pushing for restoration.[84] They were joined by former Jewish residents of Essen who returned to the city in the early 1980s only to find that the synagogue's interior had been transformed into a functional exhibition space. Moreover, local Jewish community members and regional Jewish leaders voiced discomfort with the exhibition that Peukert had designed, arguing that it ignored the history of the very community that once worshiped in the building. The chairman of Essen's Jewish community suggested that a permanent exhibition on Jews in Essen was "paramount," and Abraham Hochwald, chief rabbi of North Rhine–Westphalia, urged city officials to include a "clearer explanation of the Jewish fate" in the current exhibition because the "overwhelming number of victims were Jews."[85] As criticism of the exhibition mounted, Essen's mayor called a high-level meeting with Jewish leaders in the fall of 1986. He announced that the city would restore the building's interior to its original form and revise the current exhibition to emphasize the Nazi persecution of the Jews.[86]

This meeting produced the most significant change in the synagogue's postwar history since its adaptation into a museum of industrial products. After two years of meticulous reconstruction work that cost state and federal governments 12 million marks, the synagogue was returned to its basic prewar interior. It was not a complete replica; it was intentionally restored not to obscure "the irreparable damage the building suffered" since 1938.[87]

Prewar interior of Essen's synagogue. (Essen Stadtbildstelle)

But the synagogue now looked more like it did in 1913 than it ever had since 1945. City officials also installed a new exhibition in the building that focused on Jewish life in Essen. The exhibition, called the "Stations of Jewish Life: From Emancipation to the Present," was placed in the synagogue's newly restored main hall, while Peukert's original exhibition on resistance and persecution stayed the same with the exception that it was moved to the balcony, its importance and visibility clearly reduced.

These changes provoked mixed reactions. The local press celebrated the restoration of this "masterwork" by the Essen architect Edmund Körner. The building's architectural splendor still continued to amaze, perhaps all the more so in the 1980s when Essen's urban landscape had little to offer other than rows of modernist department stores, towering skyscrapers, and wide boulevards.[88] But few articles explored why the synagogue needed to be restored in the first place. The building's destruction, especially during

Interior of Essen's synagogue after restoration in 1986–88. (Essen Stadtbildstelle)

the postwar period, rarely surfaced as important. One newspaper article included photos of the building from 1913, 1938, and 1945, billing them as "three pictures that exemplify German history."[89] A photo from 1961 with the building's interior turned into an industrial museum did not make it. Another article began by saying that "after 1945 much was destroyed," but went into little detail about exactly what.[90] Esseners could talk about the building's destruction during the barbaric Nazi dictatorship, but not during the civilized West German democracy. The installation of the new exhibition triggered even more ambivalent responses. City officials found themselves in an awkward position. As one noted frankly, the synagogue belongs to "Jews" but since 1945 it had been taken over by "non-Jews."[91] The exhibition had to be reworked to satisfy the growing concerns of Jewish leaders, while not dismissing altogether the work of non-Jews such as Schmidt and Peukert. Someone was bound to be offended. It turned out to be Schmidt who dismissed the new exhibition. "There must not be two exhibitions," he exclaimed. "Two exhibitions will mean that one will be valued over the other."[92] But this was a battle Schmidt had already lost. On November 5, 1988, the synagogue reopened its doors to a restored interior and new exhibition on Jewish life. It marked the building's third post-1945 transformation. Just as in 1961 and 1981, so, too, now a large crowd gathered for the ceremony to hear speeches about the synagogue's importance. Mayor Peter Reuschenbach said that the building counteracted "any attempts to smooth over our history," while Johannes Rau, the minister-president of North Rhine–Westphalia and future German president, urged Esseners to act "against forgetting and silence."[93] The synagogue, long incorporated into Essen's identity of postwar consumption and briefly turned into a symbol of German resistance and victimization, now appeared as a Jewish space that never should be forgotten.

Indeed, the synagogue has now just undergone yet another change—its fourth—that marks even more clearly its Jewishness. In February 2008, Essen's city council approved a 7.4 million euro plan to transform the building into a "House of Jewish Culture."[94] A building whose "Jewish character for too long was 'deformed, concealed, or ignored'" no longer aims to be a memorial that "reduces Jews only to the role of the victim" but is to be an "open house, a meeting point for lively exchange." As the Israeli-born director Edna Brocke put it, the new exhibition moves beyond the "See, I told you so pedagogy" of focusing on reminding Germans of Nazi crimes. The Peukert-Schmidt exhibition moved out of the building, while the sarcophagus memorial outside the building's front door that the city erected in 1949 to the "Jews who had to lose their life" was taken down. The exhibition on the "Stations of Jewish Life" has become part of a larger cultural space for exchange between Jews and non-Jews. The newly designed space was grandly unveiled in July 2010 just in time for Essen's debut as the regional hub of the 2010 "European Capital of Culture." Just as in 1961, 1981, and 1988, Essen's mayor spoke of the synagogue's importance in front of a large crowd gathered in the building. He connected the restored synagogue to its original unveiling in 1913, saying that "today is once again a good day for this building and for our city."[95]

This new cultural center promises, as one local journalist wrote, to be spoken of in the "same breath with the Jewish museum in Berlin."[96] Essen might dream of being put alongside Berlin as a leading intellectual and cultural center in Germany, but this sleepy shopping city will never get there. Even if it did, the comparison would not be apt, because this latest shift in the synagogue's purpose could not be more different from developments in Berlin, where the Holocaust deeply marks the urban landscape with its Jewish museum and most recently its sprawling Holocaust memorial right near the Brandenburg Gate.[97] The Essen case suggests the emergence of a shifting relationship to the Holocaust as Germany's Jewish community has expanded. Essen's Orthodox community has close to a thousand members. Although the "House of Jewish Culture" is secular, it reflects the desire among some Jews and Germans to contextualize the Holocaust at a moment when the Jewish community is more secure, confident, and stable than it has ever been since 1945. It reflects a certain discomfort with the ritualistic, redemptive German emphasis on the Holocaust.

A similar tendency is, in fact, emerging in Potsdam, where Jewish life has also grown since 1989. This once Prussian military town, now self-proclaimed "European-influenced city," draws a large number of tourists to visit its palaces just outside the city center but continues to be dwarfed by nearby Berlin. Its downtown, dominated by drab East German apartment buildings except for the historically preserved Dutch Quarter, hardly fits the city's billing that Potsdam is "without a doubt one of Germany's most beautiful cities."[98] Potsdam also suffers from problems with right-wing extremism. In 2006, a German citizen originally from Ethiopia was nearly beaten to death at a Potsdam bus stop. Occurring just as Germany was about to invite millions of tourists for the World Cup, the incident attracted prolonged coverage in the national media about the threat of right-wing violence. This explosion of anxiety came just as minorities within and outside Germany were making lists of "No-Go Areas" that foreigners should avoid.

Potsdam is certainly not a no-go area, but that it triggers such associations has only made the revival of Jewish life there all the more important, even if it is often overlooked with Berlin's booming Jewish life and hype only a commuter rail ride away. There is indeed little hype in Potsdam, but there is a notable presence of Jewish life that is all the more astonishing because a Jewish community has not existed in the city since the late 1930s. Today, the Orthodox community has about 400 Jews, mainly from the former Soviet Union.[99] Its prayer house lies in the center of town, and just around the corner sits the Moses Mendelssohn Center for European Jewish Studies. Founded in 1992 and directed by the outspoken Julius Hans Schoeps, son of a famous German-Jewish family, the center focuses on academic scholarship, but its many public lectures, conferences, and cultural activities make it an important part of Jewish life in Potsdam. Its quarterly newsletter, *Dialog,* aims to stimulate broader conversations about Jewish culture, religion, and history.[100] Each year Potsdam also hosts with Berlin a Jewish film festival. Founded in 1995, the festival welcomes Jewish artists from around the world to both cities to display their work.

But the most symbolic development is the plan to construct a new synagogue in Potsdam. The building of new synagogues has long carried importance in postwar Germany. Synagogues are highly visible, spatial markers of Jewish presence and reflect the notion that "who builds a house stays."[101] The fact that Jews wish to live in Germany still stirs discussion and reflection even as the country has become home to a new Jewish diaspora. In 2006, for example, Munich unveiled a 57 million euro Jewish center with a synagogue, museum, and kindergarten that replaced the city's main synagogue destroyed in 1938. Although the new building could not be erected on the same plot of land on which the old one had been, the new building was constructed only a few blocks away and given the same name. Unveiled on the anniversary of *Kristallnacht* by the German president with hundreds of onlookers and 1,500 police officers, this new presence of Jews in Hitler's "capital of the movement" served as a powerful symbol of renewal after the Holocaust. Potsdam's new synagogue has received much less attention, but its Jewish community faces similar questions: Is the new synagogue to replace the old one? Where should it be located? In what kind of style should it be constructed? How should the building negotiate the past and present, memory and communal life?

Discussions about these questions have been going on with various degrees of intensity since the mid-1990s. In particular, the Jewish community and the city have struggled to figure out where the building should be located. Several different locations have emerged. In 1995, the city agreed to give the community an abandoned church in nearby Babelsberg, but the Jewish community disliked the idea of being located outside Potsdam.[102] The old synagogue was, after all, located right in the heart of the city. As the Babelsberg location lost appeal, plans to construct a replica of the old synagogue gained traction. Since 1990, a local, grass-roots organization, the Working Group for the Construction of Potsdam's Historic Downtown, had been urging city officials to rebuild the synagogue as part of restoring the old, Wilhelmian square of which it was the architectural focal point. The local Jewish community welcomed the idea, and Potsdam's city council officially approved the plan in January 1998. But no sooner had these plans been accepted than the idea became "precarious" and "a complex problem."[103] The synagogue's re-creation would have involved tearing down an apartment building and relocating its residents. The idea quickly seemed impractical and seemed more like a nostalgic urge to reconstruct "old" Potsdam than an attempt to meet the needs of the current Jewish community. As Julius Schoeps put it, Potsdam has a "new Jewish community—it should build a synagogue in a different location."[104] Plans for the synagogue stalled and no viable alternative surfaced for years, as the Jewish community insisted that it would not pay for a new plot of land.[105] In late 2004, the city offered to sell for one euro a spot on Palace Street where the community currently resides in an old, drab East German apartment building. The current plan is to tear down the building and erect a synagogue, library, and community center. In 2005, the Jewish Community of Potsdam founded the Building Organization of the Potsdam Synagogue to raise private donations and hold an architectural competition.

But plans for the synagogue have moved slowly and frustration has mounted. "We have four hundred community members," one member explained, "but our prayer room is only seventy square meters large; we have to fight for seats at gatherings with the shortage of space."[106] Standing in front of the old synagogue on the anniversary of *Kristallnacht,* another community member remarked: "Without a synagogue in Potsdam it is difficult to get my children excited about our religion."[107] The main problem has been money, as private and public funds have been slow in coming, but recently the project has finally been moving forward, albeit with one final twist. In April 2009, the synagogue's building organization held an architectural competition and selected a design by the Berlin architect Jost Haberland. With a simple, unadorned façade, the design has provoked sharp criticism, especially from the Israeli musician and Potsdam resident Ud Joffe, who has led the charge against a building he claims does not appear "Jewish" and is not focused enough on religion. He thinks the synagogue will become a "Russian cultural center" of secular Jews. The conflict has escalated. In March 2010, Joffe interrupted a meeting about the building's latest design with a fifteen-foot banner that read "Potsdam isn't building a synagogue," while in May 2010 the police barred him from entering a meeting of the synagogue's building organization. Joffe has the support of Potsdam's longtime rabbi, Nachum Pressmann, who suddenly broke with the Potsdam Jewish community to form a "traditional" community in June 2010 with Joffe.[108] The synagogue, though, appears to be going forward and will likely be completed by 2012 with state funds.

Redemptive Cosmopolitanism

"No other buildings exist in Germany that are inaugurated with greater expenditure, larger ceremonial events, and more intense public response and media coverage than synagogues and other 'Jewish' buildings," the architectural critic Manuel Herz observes.[109] Although writing about Germany, he could have written something similar about Jewish buildings in Poland. The opening of the Warsaw Jewish museum will probably come close to being the event for Poland that the Berlin Jewish museum was for Germany. As highly symbolic spaces, Jewish sites engender multiple meanings depending on who is encountering them. For many Jewish tourists, Jewish sites reinforce identities of victimization and persecution. To be sure, some Jews have expressed unease with Holocaust tourism and have critiqued what they see as American and Israeli political uses of Jewish suffering. Writing about Holocaust travel to Poland, the Israeli writer and politician Avraham Burg praises his son for not "joining the trend," as "he, like me, does not want to base his Israeli, Jewish, and universal identity on the worst trauma in human experience."[110] Still, linking Jewishness in Germany and Poland with the past is likely to continue, despite the expansion of Jewish communal life since 1989.

It will continue because non-Jewish Germans and Poles also reduce Jewishness to the past. Their recovery of Jewish heritage stems from different motives and produces different meanings; there is one, though, that I would like to highlight by way of concluding, a common fragment from the diverse, shifting landscape of the contemporary moment that stands out as salient to German and Polish interest in the Jewish past. Generational changes, Holocaust memory, nostalgia, tourism—all of these have much to explain, but above all Germans and Poles have become attracted to Jewish culture because it signifies something that they desire. Some want tolerance, multiethnicity, plurality, and cultural difference, or at least they want prominent displays of it. Some want cosmopolitanism, to put a single word on it, some sixty years after the war when the diversity of the interwar years can only be reconstructed through memory. Wanting cosmopolitanism is perhaps not a bad thing, but locating it in restoration and commemoration—literally in physical spaces and metaphorically in the commemorated presence of the past that rebuilt sites signify—poses certain problems. In making Jews present again in highly visible, symbolic spaces, Germans and Poles seek closure with the past and re-create a multiethnic present from the ruins of multiethnicity. Restoring Jewish culture in the built environment produces a comforting, redemptive sense of renewal that deflects critical reflection on the past and ignores the complex realities of the present. In public, political discourse, some Germans and Poles turn Jewish spaces into signifiers of what I call redemptive cosmopolitanism, a performative embrace of the Jewish past that celebrates the liberal, democratic nation-state rather than thinking critically about its past and present failures.[111]

In Germany, cosmopolitanism comes from the left and celebrates pluralism, democracy, pacifism, the rights of minorities, and "Europe." It strives to move beyond the ethnic nation-state, arguing that citizens are part of a democratic, constitutional state rather than a specifically German community. The most well-known proponent of liberal cosmopolitanism is the philosopher Jürgen Habermas, who has envisioned a postnational, constitutional patriotism with supra allegiances to Europe.[112] In Poland, cosmopolitanism also draws support from the left and espouses similar notions of tolerance, pluralism, and civic citizenship. But if Germany locates its supra identity in contemporary Europe, Poland finds it in the mythologized multicultural past of the Polish-Lithuanian Commonwealth. Poland's version also intersects more deeply with religion, as progressive Catholics continue to confront the ethnic and religious exclusivity of the "Polish-Catholic." As politician and writer Tadeusz Mazowiecki put it, Poles need to embrace "open Polishness with open Catholicism."[113] This cosmopolitan embrace remains, however, more contested in Poland, where two competing ideas of the nation—one more civic-secular and the other more ethnic-religious— have collided since the collapse of Communism. The ethnic vision, espoused by the right, derides cosmopolitanism as a foreign "Jewish" import that threatens to destroy Poland's ties with Catholicism. Leftist writers, intellectuals, and politicians respond to these attacks, but the right has the edge at the moment in Poland.[114]

Still, in both countries, some Poles and Germans celebrate Jewish sites as public spaces of cosmopolitanism based on mythic understandings of the pre-Holocaust past as a harmonious period of cultural tolerance. In 2005, the Polish president Aleksander Kwaśniewski remarked at length about what the Jewish museum would showcase: "The Jewish community, which has lived here for eight hundred years, found in Poland a climate of freedom and tolerance. Many generations of Polish Jews had made a splendid spiritual, cultural, and economic contribution here and made an enormous contribution to our joint history, while also drawing on Polish influences and experiences."[115] Similarly, Germany's commissioner for cultural affairs argued that the Berlin Jewish museum showed how German culture "has always been, and today, under changed conditions, continues to be the result of cross-pollination and synthesis between diverse cultures and influences."[116]

The restoration of Jewish sites displays tolerance and cosmopolitanism for all to see as Germans and Poles ceremoniously bring Jews back into their societies: Jews become "co-citizens" and "co-stewards of this land" *(Mitbürger, współobywatele, współgospodarze)*. In Wrocław, the mayor spoke of recovering the city's "Jewish heart" during the opening of the restored White Stork Synagogue, while Essen's mayor framed the newly unveiled "House of Jewish Culture" as a "central indicator of openness, humanity, and tolerance."[117] In 2003, Maciej Kozłowski, who had just finished serving as Poland's ambassador to Israel, argued that "above all Poland and Poles need the Museum of the History of Polish Jews" because it will "reclaim an important part of our own, genuine, not distorted, history"—the "multiethnic Poland of the Jagiellonian dynasty."[118] And in 2001, speaking in Washington, DC, the German foreign minister Joschka Fischer noted that the loss of Jews has made German "culture poorer ever since," a cultural void "painfully visible—especially where I live, in the old Jewish quarter of Berlin, the town of Moses Mendelssohn, who lies buried in the old Jewish cemetery not far from my apartment." Moving away from this lost past, Fischer turned to Germany's "second chance" in the contemporary moment: "Only when our Jewish fellow-citizens can live in freedom and security in Germany, will Hitler's terrible antisemitism finally be defeated."[119]

Fischer stated it clearly—Jews serve as yardsticks of national recovery that one can measure through monuments, speeches, memorials, and the building of new synagogues. Restoring Jewish culture purifies Germans and Poles of past sins. Jewish spaces become signifiers of successful rehabilitation and respectful remembrance, markers of progress that exhibit the arrival of tolerant democratic societies in the new Europe. This cosmopolitan performance manages the anxiety of the Holocaust through remembrance and symbolic gestures of tolerance: celebrating the Jewish past smoothes over discomforting, anxious histories. Rather than lingering mournfully on past violence, redemptive cosmopolitanism offers closure from it.[120]

In two countries on a dark continent that has seen genocide, war, expulsions, and ethnic hatred, redemptive cosmopolitanism has appeal, to put it modestly, especially in Germany as the main source of Europe's violent half century and the country where the leftist belief in redemption through "enlightened knowledge" has deep roots stretching back to the early years of the Social Democratic Party.[121] The allure of redemptive cosmopolitanism is perhaps not altogether troubling, given its alternative, and embracing the Jewish past can stimulate self-critical, historically conscious thinking, as I will suggest in my concluding remarks, but redemptive cosmopolitanism—to highlight one final contradiction—remains deeply selective.[122] Some Germans and Poles might now tolerate Jews, but rarely other minorities. The social, cultural, and legal position of immigrants who have come to their countries through postcolonial, labor, and asylum migration is precarious. This is especially true for Germany, but Poland has a growing immigrant population as well. As a columnist in Wrocław noted, Poles have no problem with cosmopolitanism when it comes to restoring Jewish or German buildings, but teaching Islam in a city with a growing immigrant population is "something different—an attack on us, the Polish school system, our national identity."[123] Even more difficult would be accepting gays and lesbians in Polish society. As Poland and Germany struggle with how open they really want to be, the embrace of the Jewish "co-citizen," the display of restored Jewish sites, and the building of Jewish museums provide numbing doses of solipsistic tolerance. Redemptive cosmopolitanism rejoices in the strength of liberal-democratic institutions in the new Europe free of fascism and Communism; it produces a kind of provincialism that harnesses a singular past for democracy's celebrated, cathartic, and finalized arrival. It requires little—few painful reflections about the catastrophic collapse of democracy in the past, few serious moments of thinking about its limits in the present. And that is precisely its appeal.

Conclusion

When the Nazi regime finally collapsed in 1945, Europeans confronted what they did or did not do to their Jewish neighbors. The thousands of Europeans who rescued Jews were tragically few in most parts of the continent. Genocide happens when people make and allow it to happen. It requires perpetrators and compliant populations. Germans were, of course, most complicit, but they had plenty of collaborators in Italy, France, Hungary, Romania, Bulgaria, Slovakia, and Croatia. The situation differed in the Nazi-occupied states of Eastern Europe. There the lines between what counted as "resistance" and "collaboration" appeared at times less distinct with daily survival so starkly at stake. Most ordinary people were probably trying to survive rather than thinking about acting with heroic strength or catastrophic fragility. This proved especially true for Poland, Ukraine, and Belarus, the bloodlands of twentieth-century European totalitarianism.[1] But in these areas, too, the murder of Jews involved the participation of many people and unfolded before the indifferent eyes of many more. There was less official collaboration in these parts, but plenty of collusion in Nazi crimes among the local population. This tragic history of violence became after 1945 an anxious, abject past, which Europeans have been wrestling with for decades.

Indeed, in their cities, towns, and villages, Europeans have been confronting the spatial markers of expulsion and genocide. Encountering Jewish sites has not been easy for anyone on the continent. As European societies recovered from the war, the bonding memories of ethnic national identity left little space for recalling Jewish suffering and complicity; memories of victimization and resistance proved much more popular and comfortable to recall.[2] There has been no easy way to handle the legacies of the Holocaust, no clear model of postwar repair on either side of the Iron Curtain. "Every occupied country in Europe developed its own 'Vichy Syndrome,'" the historian Tony Judt writes.[3] But, while true, the anxiety of the abject past has been more palpable for some Europeans than for others. Germans and Poles have encountered the effects of the Holocaust—those hundreds of shattered Jewish spaces—in intense, complicated ways like few other Europeans over the past sixty years. The result has been a distinctive postwar history.

This history began just after the war, when Poles and Germans faced the problem of what to do with confiscated Jewish property. Jewish leaders made it clear what should happen: Jewish property should be returned without question. Government officials responded differently depending on which side of the Iron Curtain they were on. In East Germany and Poland, state authorities refused to return Jewish property, despite numerous pleas from Jewish leaders that they do so. As the SED purged its country of "cosmopolitanism" and the PZPR feared helping Jews with stereotypes of Judeo-Communism popular among segments of Polish society, both parties abandoned Jews on a number of issues with property being no exception. This turn of events would not necessarily have been predictable to a reasonable observer in 1945. Since the late nineteenth century, socialists and Communists fought to expand democratic rights to include oppressed groups such as Jews. That is partly why some Jews became attracted to leftist movements in the first place. Anti-Jewish prejudices certainly permeated segments of the left before the war, but not nearly like they did after 1945. Stalin's own personal paranoia about Jews explains part of this change, but Communists knew that fighting for Jews gained them little in societies where hatred of Jews had become a normalized part of everyday life in the years before and during the war. Jews had become a political liability after 1945 in societies that clearly disliked them. As the SED and PZPR sought to legitimize their rule, they abandoned and attacked Jews. Anti-Jewish policies became a tool to secure political power in the Communist East in the wake of the Holocaust. In contrast, support for Jews became a requirement for power in the democratic West. The American occupiers made that clear from the beginning, arguing that combating antisemitism and supporting Jews would be essential to democratization. Some powerful German politicians believed the same, but the occupiers were the main ones pushing for restitution. Few German intellectuals, church leaders, writers, journalists, and ordinary citizens strongly supported it. Restitution fell far short of becoming an accepted part of West German politics and society in the early postwar years. In this sense, the divergence of the West German case from its Communist neighbors appears less stark. No social norm called for the return of Jewish property in any of these three states. Few Germans and Poles wanted to give up the spoils of genocide on either side of the Iron Curtain.

An even smaller number wanted to preserve the physical traces of Jewish life just after the war. Germans and Poles saw Jewish sites as simply worthless rubble that could be cleared away or ignored. Essen's synagogue, once an integral part of the built environment, was long excluded from Essen's transformation into the "shopping city." City officials abandoned the synagogue for fifteen years until turning it into the House of Industrial Design, making it a peculiar space to showcase the city's new postwar identity as a hub of capitalist consumption. In Wrocław, Jewish leaders struggled to secure even the slightest amount of support for their properties in a city of massive historic reconstruction. As historic preservationists rushed to restore the city's "Polish" past, they neglected its synagogue and Jewish cemeteries. Further pleas from Jewish leaders went unanswered as the Polish regime became increasingly suspicious of the Jewish minority by the mid-1960s. Unlike in Wrocław, no Jewish community reemerged in Potsdam. Its synagogue remained damaged for thirteen years until city officials tore it down in 1958. As local party leaders sought to construct a new, socialist Potsdam, they built in its place an apartment complex. Historic preservationists did not oppose this decision even as they fought for the protection of other historic sites in the city; their cultural biases excluded Jewish sites as artifacts of the past worthy of preserving and restoring.

Jewish sites also rarely fit into the postwar reconstruction of divided Berlin and Warsaw. In the wake of immense destruction, Warsaw symbolized Poland's redemption and survival after Nazism. In an eclectic blend of old and new, urban planners combined modernism, socialist realism, and historic reconstruction into rebuilding Poland's martyr city. As historic preservationists rebuilt the old town, urban planners searched for spaces to display the socialist future. Muranów became one of those areas when it was turned into a massive housing complex. Such grandiose plans did not shape divided Berlin's reconstruction. With the main exception of the competing Cold War projects of the Stalin Avenue and the Hansa Quarter, both Berlins implemented a practical form of urban modernism that involved few symbolic architectural projects; rows of plain, functional housing complexes lined the streets of both cities. But by the early 1960s, city officials had demolished nearly all of Berlin's synagogues to make room for new buildings. Only a few traces of the Jewish past were left, almost all located in East Berlin, where reconstruction was slower with the weaker East German economy and the chaos of GDR urban planning.

In five diverse urban landscapes, Jewish sites were transformed, neglected, and demolished for the building of something better. These parallel histories, shaped by different local, national, and political contexts, defined the early postwar period. Guided by urban modernism and socialist realism, urban planners had little interest in keeping much of anything historic just after the war, and seemingly banal factors such as location, age value, and architectural style influenced what few structures they did restore. Most Jewish sites were also closed and vacant, with some exceptions such as the synagogue in Wrocław, which the local Jewish congregation used until the late 1960s when the state confiscated it. In many cases, then, city officials probably saw Jewish sites as nothing more than empty, abandoned buildings that could be bulldozed like any other. Still, the wartime destruction of Polish and German cities presented urban planners with an unprecedented opportunity to restructure the city as they wished. Urban renewal promised a better future by reshaping the city and clearing "blight," which across the globe has so often meant demolishing minority and poor neighborhoods. Dominant economic, cultural, ethnic, racial, and gender norms have long shaped how cities are constructed.[4] In Warsaw, urban planners paved over the ghetto ruins for the building of the socialist future, while in Essen city officials turned the synagogue into a consumerist space to celebrate West Germany's transformation into a thriving capitalist country. As Germans and Poles looked to the capitalist and socialist future, they only restored a select number of historic sites, and these almost always tended to be buildings of the "German" and "Polish" past. The ethnic homogeneity of divided Germany and Poland deeply shaped the postwar urban landscape in both democratic and Communist societies. In the 1950s and 1960s, Germans and Poles were still uneasy about ethnic, cultural, and religious difference as they expunged unwanted spatial traces of a long-stigmatized and long-persecuted minority.

In war-torn societies longing for normality, Germans and Poles were also averse to encountering the traumas of the past. They wanted a "normal" life after such immense devastation, and building their postwar lives involved, among other things, clearing away markers of unsettling memories.[5] Poles and Germans paved over, forgot, and transformed Jewish sites not necessarily out of malice, but out of a deep sense of anxiety about the Holocaust. In the two Germanys, Jewish sites symbolized the assault on the German-Jewish community like few other spaces. To keep these shattered symbols around would involve encountering symbols of violence, complicity, and indifference. In the early postwar years, most Germans simply did not want to confront their role in the social, civic, economic, and physical death of Jews. They crafted instead myths about widespread victimization, ignorance, and resistance. Poles also recalled their moments of suffering and resistance, but these were hardly myths. Poland had Europe's largest resistance movement against Hitler and suffered from the brutality of Nazi imperialism like few other countries. The Nazis killed 5 million of its citizens. Yet Poles rarely recalled the suffering of their Jewish neighbors, and often perceived the genocide of European Jewry as a threat to their own memories of victimization and resistance. The Holocaust was not "their" suffering, and it opened up the darker, less heroic parts of Polish history. Few other spaces in Poland triggered these intertwined anxieties more forcefully than the Warsaw ghetto, an area that reflected the Nazi persecution of the Jews and the collapse of Polish empathy on a catastrophic scale. Poles buried the ghetto's traumatic ruins both literally and metaphorically: the new Muranów, sanitized of its past, was integrated into the banality of postwar life like any other space in the city.

Not everyone, however, submitted to this postwar normality of erasure and neglect. Jewish leaders contested the destruction of Jewish sites, if often to little effect. In Wrocław and West Berlin, the two cities with the largest Jewish communities in the 1950s and 1960s, Jewish leaders generally had little influence on how city officials handled Jewish sites. But this was not always so. In East Berlin, the Jewish community precluded the city from destroying the façade of the New Synagogue, while in Warsaw the Central Committee of Jews in Poland constructed what has become one of the most important Holocaust memorials in the world—the Warsaw ghetto monument—which marked the history of the ghetto on the urban landscape no matter what was built there. The postwar history of Jewish sites is thus not just one of Germans and Poles encountering Jewish ruins. It is a triangular history of Germans, Poles, and Jews, even if the balance of power was clearly asymmetrical, especially during the early postwar years.

Indeed, for things to change, Poles and Germans had to rethink their perceptions of Jewish sites and, more broadly, of Jews. This started to happen in the 1970s. In one of the more remarkable shifts in postwar European history, Germans and Poles went from seeing Jewish sites as worthless rubble to perceiving them as evocative ruins that had to be preserved. This transformation came about in large part simply as younger generations of Poles and Germans grew up in societies with much less intense hostility toward Jews, but it also emerged for specific reasons across local, national, and political borders that had little to do with generational changes. In East Germany and Poland, Jewish sites became national and international issues, as the two Communist parties experienced growing pressure from abroad and at home to rethink their earlier anti-Jewish policies. Just as the SED and PZPR were looking to improve their images abroad, tourists, international Jewish leaders, and foreign journalists became concerned about the poor condition of Jewish sites in their countries. Growing international interest turned Jewish space into a major issue that both Communist parties had to mitigate. Both parties decided to restore a few sites in their capital cities and hold events commemorating the Holocaust, but this only made the problem worse. International attention grew stronger, and segments of society dismissed their sudden embrace of Jews as insincere. Jewish sites became yet another issue that separated state and society, especially in Poland in the wake of the "anti-Zionist" campaign. Such direct political conflict was less apparent in West Germany, where Jewish sites never became an international problem because of the country's long-standing philosemitic policy formulated at the dawn of the Cold War. Instead, they remained a locally contested issue. As the Holocaust became widely discussed in the 1980s, historians, religious leaders, politicians, and ordinary citizens, typically on the left, challenged the early postwar erasure and neglect of Jewish sites. These civic initiatives did not provoke anxiety among national leaders, who had little to fear about West Germany's relationship with the United States and Israel.

In all three states, though, Poles and Germans shared a common purpose in wanting to contest dominant memories and explore a long-neglected past. Some Poles and Germans challenged themselves and were challenged by others to reflect upon their relationship with Jews. Jewish sites provoked discussions about the place of cultural, ethnic, and religious difference in the postwar nation-state, and triggered searing reflections on the very histories of violence, destruction, neglect, and erasure that they symbolized. The 1980s were pivotal years in West Germany, Poland, and East Germany as Poles and Germans struggled, disagreed, and wrestled with what kind of memory—what kind of identity more deeply—they wanted some forty years after the war. Of course, not all Poles and Germans were motivated by such weighty, introspective questions. Some simply became attracted to Jewish sites out of curiosity; others out of fascination for an exotic past; still others out of longings for an imagined multicultural world so seemingly different from their ethnically homogeneous present. These nostalgic impulses emerged from the ashes of genocide when Jews were now largely gone and no longer a real political, social, and cultural "problem." Longing can, after all, only "survive in a long-distance relationship" as the desired object remains something sought after, yet never grasped.[6]

Finally, interest in preserving Jewish ruins emerged at a particular moment when international curiosity in divided Germany and Poland increased dramatically. Jews and non-Jews from other parts of the world had long expressed interest in these countries, but not to the degree that they did in the 1980s. Tourists, religious leaders, journalists, writers, and photographers traveled to Germany and Poland in search of the Jewish past like never before. Travel was strongest to Poland (and continues to be), but it also played an important role in the two Germanys. In short, interest in Jewish sites became over the 1980s transnational. Jewish sites attracted local, national, and international attention from a wide variety of people who imbued them with diverse meanings.

This multiplying, multidirectional interest stimulated restoration efforts from the smallest village to the metropolis, and only increased after the collapse of Communism. Since 1989, tens of thousands of American and Israeli tourists have been traveling to Germany and Poland. The end of Communism obviously allowed for this tourism to expand by opening the borders, but it alone explains neither the surge in interest from abroad nor the seemingly endless projects to restore and memorialize that define the present moment. The events of 1989 are often viewed as a major historical caesura, a revolution on the order of the French Revolution in 1789 that precipitated momentous change. Such an observation is generally true for Europe, but it often dismisses the Communist period as just some frozen, totalitarian moment when almost nothing changed. "Polish and Jewish relations were in the freezer," Michael Schudrich, Poland's chief rabbi, remarked. "The fall of Communism was the single most positive event for these relations in 50 years."[7] I have suggested otherwise by uncovering the multiple, changing encounters with the Jewish past in East Germany and Poland.[8] The 1980s set the foundation for the transnational interest in the Jewish past that has unfolded since the collapse of Communism. The local helped enable the transnational: the rediscovery and preservation of Jewish sites in the 1980s provided some of the cultural spaces for tourists, architects, museum directors, and tour guides to discover in the 1990s.

What has noticeably changed since 1989—beyond the multiplicity—is the sheer diversity of encounters with Jewish sites. People from various backgrounds interpret Jewish sites differently, but they often become attracted to them for similar reasons—a consciousness of the Holocaust; longings for "authenticity" and "cosmopolitanism" in a globalizing world; quests for new ways of thinking about themselves as Poles, Germans, and Jews; and yearnings for a lost prewar past. Americans, Israelis, Germans, and Poles—Jews and non-Jews—encounter Jewish spaces in conflicting and different ways, but also at times in synergy with each other. Moreover, many layers of time now overlap in Jewish sites. As Jewish life has grown in Poland and Germany, some synagogues have become houses of worship and cultural centers. The past still saturates these sites, but in more complex ways than ever before. In one space—Essen's synagogue, Warsaw's Muranów—Europe's fraught, varied histories of acculturation, genocide, war, democracy, and Communism intermingle and collide. To encounter Jewish sites today is to encounter Europe's twentieth century.

What, though, are we to make of this transformation from wholesale erasure of the Jewish past to almost frenetic commemoration? What does all this memory mean for German, Polish, and Jewish relations at the start of a new century? I would like to turn briefly to one final example as a way to approach these questions—two films produced for PBS's *Frontline* by the Polish-Jewish survivor and American citizen Marian Marzynski in which Jewish space and the Holocaust dominate. *Shtetl*, produced in 1996, follows an American Jew, Nathan Kaplan, as he travels to his parents' hometown in Brańsk about sixty miles east of Warsaw. As the two men walk through the streets of this impoverished small town, they search for the traces of Jewish life. Their tour guide is the non-Jewish Pole Zbyszek Romaniuk, who has made it his life's work to rediscover Brańsk's Jewish past, including digging up and restoring Jewish tombstones buried throughout the village. This is, though, no ordinary heritage trip. Marzynski sets out to explore the role Poles played in persecuting Jews during the Holocaust. His task takes him to the United States and Israel, where an intense scene unfolds with a group of Israeli high school students who have just returned from Poland. The students attack Romaniuk, who becomes angered by their accusations of Polish complicity and their ignorance of Nazi-occupied Poland. Like many outside Eastern Europe, the students know little about the wider context of Nazi policies that killed millions of Poles, Ukrainians, Belorussians, Soviet POWs, and Roma while targeting for complete destruction European Jews.

Marzynski's other film, *A Jew among the Germans* (2005), is shorter and less intense. Marzynski seems detached as he moves through Berlin, although his opening line that he has entered the "land of my enemy" gives the film predictable tension. One of the more interesting scenes takes place just outside the Berlin Jewish Museum as Marzynski and his American friend, Thomas Mehrel, debate with a curator the importance of the Holocaust. The German explains that the museum is not supposed to be only about genocide, but Marzynski and his friend do not listen to him and repeat that the Holocaust must be central to the museum. Marzynski even oddly implies that the Libeskind building does not provide enough spaces to "contemplate Jewish death."[9] These two films offer at times absorbing moments, but they can be tedious, even frustrating. The cultural superiority of Americans and of Jewish life outside Europe is assumed from the beginning. Romaniuk (and Poland) endures this insolence the most: the stark imagery of the impoverished, crumbling Brańsk versus the affluent, groomed Atlanta suburb, the peasant with dirt-ingrained hands versus the American crisply typing on a word processor. In both films, Marzynski never speaks to any Jews living in Germany and Poland. Both countries are just Jewish graveyards, this after the expansion of Jewish communal life since 1989. Marzynski even throws in for good measure that it is a "well-known secret" that Russian Jews have "fabricated their Jewish origin" to come to Germany.[10]

Marzynski has some valid points. A number of Poles and Germans remain ambivalent about the Holocaust and recall more frequently their own victimization. They also embrace exclusive notions of identity that stigmatize Jews, Turks, Afro-Germans, and other "minorities" (especially, in Poland, homosexuals). Prejudice most certainly exists in both countries and has even motivated some to vandalize Jewish sites.[11] But Marzynski's viewpoint has limitations. Marzynski dismisses why a German would spend his free time curating a Jewish museum, or why a Pole would go around his small town digging up buried Jewish tombstones. He seemingly would agree with the explanation provided by the *Boston Globe* that Romaniuk's actions are simply "mysterious."[12] Marzynski, who understandably has tragic memories of both places but who nevertheless seems overcome by a hermeneutics of suspicion, overlooks several deeper questions about Polish and German interest in the Jewish past.[13] What does this attraction to Jewishness involve? What are both its problems and possibilities?

In many ways, this interest in Jewishness reflects, I have argued, a distinct form of managing a deeply discomforting past. While in the early postwar years Germans and Poles dealt with the anxiety of the Holocaust by expelling its memory, they now control it by recalling it in official, public life. While earlier Germans and Poles expelled ethnic, cultural, and religious differences from their postwar cities, now they seek to restore and exhibit them. This mode of memory—what I have called redemptive cosmopolitanism—underpins broader celebrations of democracy's triumph over fascism and Communism. Public recollection and commemorative cosmopolitanism signify revived multiethnicity in the new Europe, which has triumphantly overcome the traumas and divisions of the twentieth century.

Redemptive cosmopolitanism has three distinct features. First, it is publically articulated and performed. In bringing Jews back—at least symbolically—into national society, Germans and Poles display tolerance and diversity for all to see through massive, highly visible projects in the built environment. Second, this symbolic reincorporation of the Jewish past into the present holds out the promise of national redemption. Restoring "Jewishness" heals and renews. It cleanses the nation of its sins through its existence: nostalgia, memory, celebration, and restoration mark the emergence of a new tolerant nation proudly aware of its past. And finally third, this memory culture is often passive, and sometimes exclusive. Redemptive cosmopolitanism provides periodically administered amounts of soothing, intoxicating cosmopolitanism, but engenders few painful reflections about the collapse of democracy in the past and few moments of critical thinking about its limits in the present.

The dilemmas of redemptive cosmopolitanism are strongest in Germany. As Germans remain anxious about how inclusive they want to be, some celebrate Jewishness rather than confront what it means to live in a complex, immigrant nation. The lavish attention paid to new synagogues—the hundreds of police, spectators, and politicians—never happens for mosques. But redemptive cosmopolitanism is more than just selective; it is also at times exclusive. Some Germans believe today that they have fully purged themselves and the German nation of racism, prejudice, xenophobia, and anti-semitism by accepting democracy and by "mastering" a dark past like practically no one else in the world. Remembering has become a way to assert Germany's transformation into a tolerant, democratic polity. Yet this celebration of Germany's democratization and memorialization blinds some Germans from recognizing new forms of racism, prejudice, and bigotry that have emerged around them.

In August 2010, for example, Thilo Sarrazin, a Social Democratic politician and at the time board member of Germany's Federal Bank, published a widely discussed book titled *Germany Does Away with Itself: How We Are Putting Our Country at Risk*. In the book's fourth paragraph, Sarrazin announces that "people are different—namely more or less intellectually gifted, lazier or more industrious, more or less morally built—and that is not changed no matter how much education and equal opportunities exist."[14] He claims that intelligence is 50 to 80 percent hereditary, and suggests that some groups of people, Jews above all, are genetically more intelligent than others. Recycling the myth of German-Jewish symbiosis, Sarrazin venerates "German Jews" as model minorities, portraying them as the opposite of Germany's new ethnic minorities. In his mind, Germany's Turks, Arabs, and Africans come from less educated backgrounds, have generally failed to integrate into German society, and have provided little to the country's economy. Sarrazin suggests that Germany is rapidly becoming "dumber" as the fertility rate of superior non-immigrant Germans decreases and the birthrate of less intelligent immigrants increases. Citing Charles Darwin and Francis Galton, he concludes: "The pattern of generative behavior in Germany since the middle of the 1960s is not only not a Darwinian natural selective breeding in the sense of the 'survival of the fittest,' but a culturally conditioned, man-made negative selection since the sole renewable resource Germany has, namely its intelligence, in relative and absolute terms is becoming depleted at a fast pace."[15]

What is most surprising about these words—beyond that a prominent politician wrote them in the first place—is that they found support in Germany. While Sarrazin had to resign from his position at the Federal Bank because of his pseudoscientific, biological reasoning, his book sold over 1 million copies, turning him into "a hero of the people."[16] In reaction to this popular response, a number of mainstream politicians and commentators defended some of Sarrazin's claims, especially his argument that integration has failed because of opposition to it from inflexible immigrants and feeble multiculturalists. As in many other parts of Europe, attacking immigration and multiculturalism has become respectable in Germany.[17] Indeed, few critics, commentators, and politicians forcefully challenged Sarrazin's core anti-immigrant message partly because they were uncomfortable discussing the new forms of prejudice that exist in Germany.[18] To do so would call into question Germany's successful postwar transformation into a tolerant society aware of its past.

Sarrazin's ideas, though, did outrage some German intellectuals, and perhaps none more so than Jürgen Habermas, who has worked his entire career to build a liberal, democratic, and tolerant Germany mindful of its history. Habermas has long hoped that awareness of the Holocaust would create a critical, post-national German identity.[19] Memory would challenge Germans to oppose ethnically exclusive imaginations of the nation. But that has not happened for a growing number of Germans, and some Sarrazin supporters even invoked Germany's "Judeo-Christian" heritage to articulate a narrow ethnic, cultural, and religious understanding of Germanness.[20] Writing in the *New York Times*, Habermas could barely contain his anger about this most recent turn in Germany's politics of memory. "With an arrogant appropriation of Judaism—and an incredible disregard for the fate the Jews suffered in Germany," he wrote, "the apologists of the leitkultur [national guiding culture] now appeal to the 'Judeo-Christian tradition,' which distinguishes 'us' from the foreigners."[21]

Unlike Germany, Poland is not an immigrant country at the moment. Ethnic minorities constitute less than 2 percent of the Polish population, and most come from nearby countries such as Ukraine (although this is beginning to change with increased labor migration, especially from Vietnam). Still, like any nation-state in the world, Poland faces questions about cultural, ethnic, religious, and sexual difference. Although the post-Communist left has dominated Polish politics since 1989, the right has gained strength since 2001, when the nationalist League of Polish Families gained 7.9 percent of the vote in parliamentary elections. From May 2006 to August 2007, the league was part of the Polish government with its leader, Roman Giertych, heading the education department. The party attacked Jews, feminists, and homosexuals through media outlets such as the right-wing Catholic station Radio Maryja. As a way to blunt the antisemitism and homophobia of his party, Giertych made public gestures of tolerance such as visiting Jedwabne to commemorate the murder of the town's Jews in the Holocaust.

The dilemmas of redemptive cosmopolitanism are thus quite apparent and troublesome, but are there any openings for them to be overcome, for locating a different kind of cosmopolitanism in recovered heritage and memory? I think and hope that there are. Polish and German interest in the Jewish past can also point to a more reflective cosmopolitanism—an openness to difference that is rooted in a consciousness of the past but that thinks critically and actively about the present. To think positively about cosmopolitanism admittedly carries risk. The idea has other problems beyond its redemptive tendencies.[22] Cosmopolitanism has had a long and contradictory career. First coined by the Cynics and later developed by the Stoics, it became popular during the Enlightenment, when the German philosopher Immanuel Kant articulated a cosmopolitan vision of nonviolence. But Kant's idea of "perpetual peace" did not lead to much peace and even helped justify European imperialism. As Paul Gilroy put it, Kant's "worldly vision" became "imperialistic particularism dressed up in seductive universal garb."[23] Nevertheless, a number of thinkers have recently been reconceptualizing cosmopolitanism as a way to grapple with one of the central paradoxes of our world: even as we become more entangled with each other, our national, religious, sexual, ethnic, cultural, and religious identities have only strengthened. These identities remain important and do not appear to be going away. Thinking about how to live together in a world of difference has thus become a serious political and philosophical issue. "Every nation has its others, within and without," the political theorist Seyla Benhabib writes.[24] What are the rights of others? Do we have obligations to strangers? How are we to live in our diverse local, national, and global worlds? These questions elicit no single answers from cosmopolitan theorists; speaking in uniformity is not very cosmopolitan, after all. Cosmopolitans disagree about the role of the state, the individual, the community, the particular, the universal, but they come together in reflecting on worlds beyond their own (the cosmos) in order to rethink their own worlds (the polis).

Like the Enlightenment philosophers before them, some contemporary philosophers have kept with the global concept of universal norms. In *For Love of Country,* Martha Nussbaum defines a cosmopolitan as "the person whose allegiance is to the worldwide community of human beings."[25] Other thinkers, though, have posited a less universal form of cosmopolitanism, one that is inflected in particular contexts but still recognizes the importance of common obligations. The philosopher Kwame Anthony Appiah has envisioned a cosmopolitan patriotism. While rooted in our particular identities, this cosmopolitanism recognizes the "idea that we have obligations to others that stretch beyond those to whom we are related by the ties of kith and kin" but does not expect or desire "that every person or every society should converge on a single mode of life."[26] This cosmopolitanism differs from the caricature of the rootless world citizen. In Appiah's view, cosmopolitans can stay rooted in their national, religious, ethnic, and cultural contexts if they so choose. An openness and concern about those who are different are the crucial features. Indeed, in *Precarious Life,* Judith Butler reflects on the global effects of the United States' violent response to 9/11 and stakes out a nonviolent ethics based on the idea of human vulnerability, a sense of interdependence that demands respect for the lives of others. Butler asks why it is easy to grieve the lost lives of Americans, Christians, and Israelis and hard to mourn those of Iraqis, Muslims, and Palestinians. Similarly, in *Cosmopolitical Claims,* the literary critic B. Venkat Mani locates cosmopolitanism in the novels of Turkish-German writers who interrogate their local, national, ethnic, and cultural affiliations. His cosmopolitanism emerges in the crossing, displacing, and unsettling of identities, in critiques of rigid conceptions of nation, community, and ethnicity.[27]

Pulling together Appiah's insight about the local inflections of cosmopolitanism with Butler and Mani's urge for critical self-reflection and interrogation, I see possibilities for cosmopolitical claims in the contemporary interest in the Jewish past. Embracing Jewishness in Germany and Poland can motivate self-reflexive, historically conscious thinking that disrupts rigid ways of categorizing human difference and that actively challenges exclusive, hermetic ideas and practices in the present.[28] Of course, I am aware of the overarching dilemma here. Our own identities are entangled in perceptions of others whom we typically identify as different, as having ethnic, religious, cultural, or sexual affiliations distinct from "ours." This construction of difference rests on stereotypes, including when we see difference as something we desire, wish to identify with, even want to imitate. This attraction to difference, this desire to cross-identify with the Other—playing Indian, for example, in postwar America—essentializes, commodifies, and dominates the native for one's own psychic fantasies.[29] But as problematic as this is, it can in rare moments provoke self-reflection and historic consciousness. The German museum curator and the Polish restorer of Jewish tombstones do not just embrace difference; they challenge normative, rigid notions of belonging and identification. They unsettle the boundaries of Germanness, Polishness, and Jewishness by crossing them.[30]

Or, to return to the built environment: the small town of Płock outside Warsaw has only a few traces of the Jewish minority left. In 1951, the town's Great Synagogue was demolished, while its oldest Jewish cemetery was cleared away; a school now sits on the cemetery's former grounds. A small synagogue still exists, in crumbling condition, but an organization emerged in 2007 to convert it into a Jewish museum. In 1997, a young Pole named Marcin Kacprzak described passing by these empty Jewish spaces. "A few buildings, a cemetery overgrown with grass," he wrote. "That is it. There is nobody to remember. That is why I try to cultivate the memory. . . . It is very hurtful to see antisemitism among the people."[31] Such words and actions could be read as just further examples of narcissistic sentimentalism, cultural appropriation, or redemptive cosmopolitanism. But what if some Poles and Germans are just trying to rethink what it means to be German and Polish through their recovery of the Jewish past? What if they are just trying to make small efforts to reconcile with Jews? In reflecting on this possibility, I am struck by the willingness of some Poles and Germans—even if they make up a small minority in the end—to encounter difference and think about its traumatic eradication sixty years ago. I come at this as an American who has seen little of the same in my own country. To me, some Germans and Poles are imagining more self-critical identities. Contemporary interest in the Jewish past involves more than just commodification, instrumentalization, appropriation, and domination. Jewish ruins—the New Synagogue in Berlin with its vacuous sanctuary of pebbles, or the district of Muranów with its buried rubble that eludes forgetting—stand as modernity's empty shells. Jewish ruins can provoke mourning for what has been lost and be an impulse for building stronger, more introspective democracies.

Indeed, some Jews and non-Jews use Jewish spaces for conversation and discussion, a central component of cosmopolitanism for Appiah. In Essen, the synagogue's director, Edna Brocke, envisions the new House of Jewish Culture becoming a place to "interact with one another in an unselfconscious and unencumbered way."[32] In Warsaw, the Jewish museum aims to be a place of dialogue. Its educational division sponsors programs for Polish and Israeli students and workshops such as the "My Muranów" project that encourages Polish students to discover Warsaw's former Jewish district. In Wrocław, the White Stork Synagogue has become a vibrant meeting space for Jews and non-Jews. Developments such as these have led the writer Diana Pinto to conclude that Poland is at the "heart of Europe's cultural renewal" and that Germany presents a unique opportunity for Jews and non-Jews to interact in "Jewish space."[33] The cosmopolitan possibility of this engagement lies in provoking Germans, Poles, and Jews to reflect upon the past to think critically about their own present and future.

And ultimately these efforts challenge all of us to do the same—to interrogate our own provincialism, whether American, German, Jewish, Polish, or other. For the cosmopolitan possibility involves precisely thinking beyond the singularly defined evil of Nazism. As the German-Jewish political thinker Hannah Arendt put it, "the greatest danger of recognizing totalitarianism as the curse of the century would be an obsession with it to the extent of becoming blind to the numerous small and not so small evils with which the road to hell is paved."[34] The potential of cosmopolitan remembrance lies not in some universal, normative memory recalled with the promise of becoming "part of the foundation of a global civic society."[35] It lies not in attempts to brandish cosmopolitanism to redeem the liberal, democratic present from the Nazi past for the "pleasure of savoring one's sensitiveness" in lofty phrases about "never again" that since 1945 have echoed so vacuously as genocide has erupted and new forms of prejudice have taken hold.[36] In the public realm of cultural memory, the possibility of embracing a violent past exists in those moments of unsettling our own provincialism, of triggering multiple and varied cosmopolitical challenges about the collapse of human compassion in our own local and global worlds, past and present.

Notes

Abbreviations

AAN	Archiwum Akt Nowych
AAS	Archiv "Alte Synagoge"
ACJ	Archiv Centrum Judaicum
AGTS	Archiv zur Geschichte von Tempelhof/Schöneberg
AHR	*American Historical Review*
AJDC	Archive American Jewish Joint Distribution Committee, New York or Jerusalem
AMKZ	Archiwum Miejskiego Konserwatora Zabytków we Wrocławiu
APW	Archiwum Państwowe m. st. Warszawy
APWr	Archiwum Państwowe we Wrocławiu
BA (SAPMO)	Bundesarchiv-Berlin, Abteilung DDR and Stiftung Archiv der Parteien und Massenorganisationen der DDR
BAK	Bundesarchiv-Koblenz, Abteilung BRD
BLHA	Brandenburgisches Landeshauptarchiv
BOS	Biuro Odbudowy Stolicy
BROV	Bundesamt zur Regelung offener Vermögensfragen
BStU	Bundesbeauftragte für die Unterlagen des Staatssicherheitsdienstes der ehemaligen Deutschen Demokratischen Republik
CDU	Christlich Demokratische Union Deutschlands
CEH	*Central European History*
CKŻP	Centralny Komitet Żydów Polskich
CZA	Central Zionist Archive
DA	*Deutsche Architektur*
DT	*Der Tagesspiegel*
EEPS	*East European Politics and Societies*
ESA	Essen Stadtarchiv
EZA	Evangelisches Zentralarchiv

FODZ	Fundacja Ochrony Dziedzictwa Żydowskiego
FRG	Federal Republic of Germany
GDR	German Democratic Republic
GW	*Gazeta Wyborcza*
HGS	*Holocaust and Genocide Studies*
IfD	Institut für Denkmalpflege
IFiS	Instytut Filozofii i Socjologii
IPN	Instytut Pamięci Narodowej
JDC	American Jewish Joint Distribution Committee
JMH	*Journal of Modern History*
JRSO	Jewish Restitution Successor Organization
JSS	*Jewish Social Studies*
JTC	Jewish Trust Corporation
KIK	Klub Inteligencji Katolickiej
LAB	Landesarchiv Berlin
LBA	Leo Baeck Archive
LBIYB	*Leo Baeck Institute Year Book*
MA	*Märkische Allgemeine*
MAP	Ministerstwo Administracji Publicznej
MfS	Ministerium für Staatssicherheit
MV	*Märkische Volksstimme*
NA-College Park	National Archives, College Park
NRZ	*Neue Ruhr Zeitung*
NYRB	*New York Review of Books*
NYT	*New York Times*
OMGUS	Office of Military Government of the United States
ONR	National Radical Camp
PAN	Polska Akademia Nauk
PNN	*Potsdamer Neueste Nachrichten*
PPR	Polish People's Republic
PSA	Potsdamer Stadtarchiv
PWN	Państwowe Wydawnictwo Naukowe
PZPR	Polska Zjednoczona Partia Robotnicza
RAES	Ruhrlandmuseum, Archiv Ernst Schmidt
ROBDZ	Regionalny Ośrodek Badań i Dokumentacji Zabytków we Wrocławiu
SED	Sozialistische Einheitspartei Deutschlands
SMA	Soviet Military Administration
SPD	Sozialdemokratische Partei Deutschlands
SR	*Slavic Review*
TL	*Trybuna Ludu*
TP	*Tygodnik Powszechny*

TSKŻ   Towarzystwo Społeczno-Kulturalne Żydów w Polsce
UdW   Urząd do Spraw Wyznań
USHMM   United States Holocaust Memorial Museum
VVN   Vereinigung der Verfolgten des Naziregimes
WAZ   *Westdeutsche Allgemeine Zeitung*
WW   *Wieczór Wrocławia*
YIVO   YIVO Institute for Jewish Research
YVA   Yad Vashem Archive
YVS   *Yad Vashem Studies*
ZA   Zentralarchiv zur Erforschung der Juden in Deutschland
ZBoWiD Związek Bojowników o Wolność i Demokrację
ŻIH   Żydowski Instytut Historyczny
ZRWM   Związek Religijny Wyznania Mojżeszowego
ŻW   *Życie Warszawy*

Introduction

1. George Axelsson, "Proud Berlin Now a Mass of Ruins," *NYT,* February 11, 1945. Numbers from Hartwig Beseler and Niels Gutschow, *Kriegsschicksale deutscher Architektur: Verluste—Schäden—Wiederaufbau,* vol. 1 (Neumünster, Germany: Karl Wachholtz Verlag, 1988), 135; dusty Berlin from Paul Steege, *Black Market, Cold War: Everyday Life in Berlin, 1946–1949* (New York: Cambridge University Press, 2009), 29.

2. Galdwin Hill, "Breakdown of Economy Poland's First Concern," *NYT,* October 28, 1945; "Eisenhower Is Acclaimed by Throngs in Warsaw," *NYT,* September 22, 1945.

3. Robert Bevan, *The Destruction of Memory: Architecture at War* (London: Reaktion, 2006); Ben Kiernan, *Blood and Soil: A World History of Genocide and Extermination from Sparta to Darfur* (New Haven, CT: Yale University Press, 2007); Norman Naimark, *Fires of Hatred: Ethnic Cleansing in Twentieth-Century Europe* (Cambridge, MA: Harvard University Press, 2001), 193–95.

4. Yitskhok Varshavski, "Yede Yidishe Gas in Varshe—Geven a Shtot Far Zikh," *Forverts,* July 2, 1944; quoted in Jan Jagielski, *Jewish Sites in Warsaw* (Warsaw: City of Warsaw, 2002), 14–15.

5. Gabriela Zalewska, *Ludność żydowska w Warszawie w okresie międzywojennym* (Warsaw: PWN, 1996), 63; AAN, MAP, 786, CKŻP list of Jews, June 15, 1945. The postwar numbers are especially difficult to calculate. See Alina Skibińska, "Powroty ocalałych," in *Prowincja noc: Życie i zagłada Żydów w dystrykcie warszawskim,* ed. Barbara Engelking, Jacek Leociak, and Dariusz Libionka (Warsaw: IFiS PAN, 2007), 582.

6. "Łapię łączność z gruntem," *GW,* April 17, 2003.

7. Lee I. Levine, *The Ancient Synagogue: The First Thousand Years* (New Haven, CT: Yale University Press, 2005), 126; Michael M. Laskier, *North African Jewry in*

the Twentieth Century: The Jews of Morocco, Tunisia, and Algeria (New York: New York University Press, 1994), 336.

8. I want to stress "main" here because Germany and Poland witnessed the reconstruction of Jewish life after the Holocaust. Michael Brenner, *After the Holocaust: Rebuilding Jewish Lives in Postwar Germany,* trans. Barbara Harshav (Princeton, NJ: Princeton University Press, 1997); Jay Geller, *Jews in Post-Holocaust Germany* (New York: Cambridge University Press, 2005); Ruth Gay, *Safe among the Germans: The Liberated Jews after World War II* (New Haven, CT: Yale University Press, 2002); Bożena Szaynok, *Ludność żydowska na Dolnym Śląsku 1945–1950* (Wrocław: Wydawnictwo Uniwersytetu Wrocławskiego, 2000).

9. Agata Tuszyńska, *Lost Landscapes: In Search of Isaac Bashevis Singer and the Jews of Poland,* trans. Madeline G. Levine (New York: William Morrow and Company, 1998), 3, 8, and 5.

10. Ernest Landau, "Zweckentfremdete heilige Stätten," *Allgemeine Wochenzeitung der Juden in Deutschland,* March 2, 1951.

11. AJDC, New York, JDC Geneva to New York, August 20, 1963.

12. A. M. Rosenthal, "Forgive Them Not, for They Knew What They Did," *NYT,* October 24, 1965.

13. Frank Biess, *Homecomings: Returning POWs and the Legacy of Defeat on Postwar Germany* (Princeton, NJ: Princeton University Press, 2006); Barbara Engelking, *Holocaust and Memory: The Experience of the Holocaust and Its Consequences,* trans. Emma Harris (New York: Leicester University Press, 2001); Norbert Frei, *Adenauer's Germany and the Nazi Past: The Politics of Amnesty and Integration,* trans. Joel Golb (New York: Columbia University Press, 2002); Norbert Frei, *1945 und wir: Das Dritte Reich im Bewusstsein der Deutschen* (Munich: Deutscher Taschenbuch Verlag, 2005); Saul Friedländer, *Memory, History, and the Extermination of the Jews of Europe* (Bloomington: Indiana University Press, 1993); Neil Gregor, *Haunted City: Nuremberg and the Nazi Past* (New Haven, CT: Yale University Press, 2008); Jonathan Huener, *Auschwitz, Poland, and the Politics of Commemoration, 1945–1979* (Athens: Ohio University Press, 2003); Wulf Kansteiner, *In Pursuit of German Memory: History, Television, and Politics after Auschwitz* (Athens: Ohio University Press, 2006); Kaja Kaźmierska, *Doświadczenia wojenne Polaków a kształtowanie tożsamości etnicznej: Analiza narracji kresowych* (Warsaw: IFiS PAN, 1999); Herbert Marcuse, *The Legacies of Dachau: The Uses and Abuses of a Concentration Camp, 1933–2001* (New York: Cambridge University Press, 2001); Robert G. Moeller, *War Stories: The Search for a Usable Past in the Federal Republic of Germany* (Berkeley: University of California Press, 2001); Michael C. Steinlauf, *Bondage to the Dead: Poland and the Memory of the Holocaust* (Syracuse, NY: Syracuse University Press, 1997); Harald Welzer, Sabine Moller, and Karoline Tschuggnall, *"Opa war kein Nazi:" Nationalsozialismus und Holocaust im Familiengedächtnis* (Frankfurt am Main: Fischer, 2002); Iwona Irwin-Zarecka, *Neutralizing Memory: The Jew in Contemporary Poland* (New

Brunswick, NJ: Transaction, 1989); Geneviève Zubrzycki, *The Crosses of Auschwitz: Nationalism and Religion in Post-Communist Poland* (Chicago: University of Chicago Press, 2006).

14. "Bilder aus der Vergangenheit: Ein Besuch auf dem alten Berliner jüdischen Friedhof in der Schönhauser Allee," *Jüdische Illustrierte* 7, no. 3 (1957): 2.

15. Diana Pinto, "The Third Pillar? Toward a European Jewish Identity," *Golem: Europäisch-jüdisches Magazin* 1 (1999): 37–38.

16. Gordon Cohn, "Traces of a Vanished World," *Avotaynu* 14, no. 4 (1998): 61.

17. Susan Crane, *Collecting and Historical Consciousness in Early Nineteenth-Century Germany* (Ithaca, NY: Cornell University Press, 2000); Peter Fritzsche, *Stranded in the Present: Modern Time and the Melancholy of History* (Cambridge, MA: Harvard University Press, 2004); Rudy Koshar, *Germany's Transient Pasts: Preservation and National Memory in the Twentieth Century* (Chapel Hill: University of North Carolina Press, 1998); Julia Hell and Andreas Schönle, eds., *Ruins of Modernity* (Durham, NC: Duke University Press, 2010); David Lowenthal, *The Past Is a Foreign Country* (New York: Cambridge University Press, 1985); Georg Simmel, "The Ruin," in *Georg Simmel, 1858–1918: A Collection of Essays,* ed. Kurt H. Wolff (Columbus: Ohio State University Press, 1959), 259–66; Alois Riegl, "The Modern Cult of Monuments: Its Character and Its Origin," trans. and ed. Kurt W. Forster and Diane Ghirardo, *Oppositions* 25 (Fall 1982): 21–51; Nick Yablon, *Untimely Ruins: An Archaeology of American Urban Modernity, 1819–1919* (Chicago: University of Chicago Press, 2009).

18. Hasia R. Diner, *Lower East Side Memories: A Jewish Place in America* (Princeton, NJ: Princeton University Press, 2002).

19. Building on the work of George Steinmetz and John Connelly, I am comparing not "independent" cases, but ones linked analytically and empirically around a shared issue (in my case, the common problem of Jewish sites after the Holocaust). George Steinmetz, *The Devil's Handwriting: Precoloniality and the German Colonial State in Qingdao, Samoa, and Southwest Africa* (Chicago: University of Chicago Press, 2007); John Connelly, *Captive University: The Sovietization of East German, Czech, and Polish Higher Education, 1945–1956* (Chapel Hill: University of North Carolina Press, 1999).

20. I say "transnational" not because it is popular these days, but for several reasons. Semantically, I use it as an umbrella term that captures the multiple layers of analysis that I examine—the local, national, regional, international, and political (by "political" I mean the different political cultures of democracy and Communism). Transnational involves thinking below, across, and within the nation. Furthermore, my study uses "transnational" as both an empirical descriptor and an analytical perspective: (1) it explores a historical issue that existed across national and political borders after 1945; (2) it analyzes transnational encounters with Jewish sites (i.e., local, national, regional, international, and political encounters); (3) it uncovers historical links, connections, processes, and patterns

across different cities; and (4) it makes comparative readings of similarities and differences. In terms of the fourth reason, I disagree with the recent dismissal of comparative history by some transnational historians. Influenced by modernization and Marxist theories, comparative history has problematically created national and regional "peculiarities," but that does not mean its basic practice of thinking about similarities and differences should be discarded. See "AHR Conversation: On Transnational History," *AHR* 111, no. 5 (2006): 1440–64; Thomas Bender, *Rethinking American History in a Global Age* (Berkeley: University of California Press, 2002); Deborah Cohen and Maura O'Connor, eds., *Comparison and History: Europe in Cross-National Perspective* (New York: Routledge, 2004); Jürgen Osterhammel, *Geschichtswissenschaft jenseits des Nationalstaats: Studien zu Beziehungsgeschichte und Zivilisationsvergleich* (Göttingen: Vandenhoeck & Ruprecht, 2001); Kiran Klaus Patel, "Überlegungen zu einer transnationalen Geschichte," *Zeitschrift für Geschichtswissenschaft* 52, no. 7 (2004): 626–45; Philipp Ther, "Beyond the Nation: The Relational Basis of a Comparative History of Germany and Europe," *CEH* 36, no. 1 (2003): 45–73.

21. Julia Brauch, Anna Lipphardt, and Alexandra Nocke, eds., *Jewish Topographies: Visions of Space, Traditions of Place* (Burlington, VT: Ashgate, 2008); Jens Hoppe, *Jüdische Geschichte und Kultur in Museen: Zur nichtjüdischen Museologie des Jüdischen in Deutschland* (New York: Waxmann, 2002); Jürgen Lillteicher, *Raub, Recht und Restitution: Die Rückerstattung jüdischen Eigentums in der frühen Bundesrepublik* (Göttingen: Wallstein, 2007); Monika Murzyn, *Kazimierz: Środkowoeuropejskie doświadczenie rewitalizacji* (Kraków: Międzynarodowe Centrum Kultury, 2006); Sabine Offe, *Ausstellungen, Einstellungen, Entstellungen: Jüdische Museen in Deutschland und Österreich* (Berlin: Philo, 2000); Katrin Pieper, *Die Musealisierung des Holocaust: Das Jüdische Museum Berlin und das U.S. Holocaust Memorial Museum in Washington D.C.* (Cologne: Böhlau, 2006); Jan Philipp Spannuth, *Rückerstattung Ost: Der Umgang der DDR mit dem "arisierten" Eigentum der Juden und die Rückerstattung im wiedervereinigten Deutschland* (Essen: Klartext, 2007); Kazimierz Urban, *Cmentarze żydowskie, synagogi i domy modlitwy w Polsce w latach 1944–1966* (Kraków: Nomos, 2006).

22. Omer Bartov, *Erased: Vanishing Traces of Jewish Galicia in Present-Day Ukraine* (Princeton, NJ: Princeton University Press, 2007); Svetlana Boym, *The Future of Nostalgia* (New York: Basic Books, 2002); Ruth Ellen Gruber, *Virtually Jewish: Reinventing Jewish Culture in Europe* (Berkeley: University of California Press, 2002); Marianne Hirsch and Leo Spitzer, *Ghosts of Home: The Afterlife of Czernowitz in Jewish Memory* (Berkeley: University of California Press, 2010); Michel Laguerre, *Global Neighborhoods: Jewish Quarters in Paris, London, and Berlin* (Albany: State University of New York Press, 2008).

23. The historiography on postwar Jewish history is focused mainly on the early postwar years with the exceptions of work on Poland in 1967–68 and Germany after 1989. For the German cases, see Michael Meng, "After the Holocaust:

The History of Jewish Life in West Germany," *Contemporary European History* 14, no. 3 (2005): 403–13; Peter Monteath, "The German Democratic Republic and the Jews," *German History* 22, no. 3 (2004): 448–68. Such historiographical essays do not exist for Poland; some recent works include Natalia Aleksiun, *Dokąd dalej? Ruch syjonistyczny w Polsce, 1944–1950* (Warsaw: Trio, 2002); Grzegorz Berendt, ed., *Społeczność żydowska w PRL przed kampanią antysemicką lat 1967–1968 i po niej* (Warsaw: IPN, 2009); Grzegorz Berendt, *Życie żydowskie w Polsce w latach 1950–1956: Z dziejów Towarzystwa Społeczno-Kulturalnego Żydów w Polsce* (Gdańsk: Wydawnictwo Uniwersytetu Gdańskiego, 2006); Anna Cichopek, *Pogrom Żydów w Krakowie* (Warsaw: ŻIH, 2000); August Grabski, Maciej Pisarski, and Albert Stankowski, *Studia z dziejów i kultury Żydów w Polsce po 1945 roku* (Warsaw: Trio, 1997); Jan Gross, *Fear: Antisemitism in Poland after Auschwitz* (New York: Random House, 2006); Krystyna Kersten, *Polacy, Żydzi, komunizm: Anatomia półprawd 1939–1968* (Warsaw: Niezależna Oficyna Wydawnicza, 1992); Szaynok, *Ludność*. On the built environment and nostalgia, see Boym, *The Future of Nostalgia*; Koshar, *Germany's Transient Pasts;* Gavriel Rosenfeld, *Munich and Memory: Architecture, Memory, and the Legacy of the Nazi Past* (Berkeley: University of California Press, 2000); Gregor Thum, *Die fremde Stadt: Breslau 1945* (Berlin: Siedler, 2003). The literature on cosmopolitanism is enormous; a good place to begin is David Inglis and Gerard Delanty, *Cosmopolitanism,* 4 vols. (New York: Routledge, 2010).

24. Important exceptions are Lynn Rapaport, *Jews in Germany after the Holocaust: Memory, Identity, and Jewish-German Relations* (New York: Cambridge University Press, 1997); Daniel Levy and Natan Sznaider, *The Holocaust and Memory in the Global Age,* trans. Assenka Oksiloff (Philadelphia: Temple University Press, 2006).

25. Alon Confino, "Telling about Germany: Narratives of Memory and Culture," *JMH* 76, no. 2 (2004): 389–416; Alon Confino, "Collective Memory and Cultural History: Problems of Method," *AHR* 102, no. 5 (1997): 1386–1403; Alon Confino and Peter Fritzsche, eds., *The Work of Memory: New Directions in the Study of German Society and Culture* (Urbana: University of Illinois, 2002), 1–21; Kansteiner, *Pursuit,* 316–33. Exceptions from sociologists and historians include Kaźmierska, *Doświadczenia;* Marcuse, *Legacies;* Moeller, *War Stories;* Lutz Niethammer, ed., *"Die Jahre weiß man nicht, wo man die heute hinsetzen soll": Faschismuserfahrungen im Ruhrgebiet* (Bonn: Dietz, 1983); Welzer, Moller, and Tschugnall, *"Opa."* Finally, the analytical dichotomy of suppression and recall has produced grand narratives about Holocaust memory. The periodization is well known: the Holocaust was suppressed (1940s–1950s), was gradually recalled (1960s–1980s), and now has been confronted with general frequency (1990s–2000s). A recent challenge to this periodization is Hasia R. Diner, *We Remember with Reverence and Love: American Jews and the Myth of Silence after the Holocaust, 1945–1962* (New York: New York University Press, 2008).

26. Sarah Farmer, *Martyred Village: Commemorating the 1944 Massacre at Oradour-sur-Glane* (Berkeley: University of California Press, 1999); Gregor, *Haunted City*; Koshar, *Germany's Transient Pasts;* Marcuse, *Legacies;* Rosenfeld, *Munich;* James Young, *The Texture of Memory: Holocaust Memorials and Meaning* (New Haven, CT: Yale University Press, 1994). My approach to memory draws on the works of Paul Ricoeur, Jan Assmann, Aleida Assmann, and Jeffrey Olick. Ricoeur, recovering Aristotle, defines memory as "of the past" and emphasizes how it is interpreted in time. This hermeneutical understanding shapes my overarching approach: I analyze interpretative encounters with the Jewish past at different present moments since 1945. These interpretations remain embedded in cultural meanings, identities, and narratives. The Assmanns have proposed the concepts of communicative and cultural memory as a way to theorize more explicitly the social and cultural layers of memory that Halbwachs, Nietzsche, and Warburg began investigating before them. I am interested mainly in cultural memory—encounters and interpretations of the past articulated in public that are linked to broader cultural identities. Jeffrey Olick has distinguished between mnemonic products (stories, rituals, monuments, etc.) and mnemonic practices (recall, representation, commemoration, celebration, regret, renunciation, disavowal, denial). I examine mainly the practices of cultural memory, namely, how Germans, Poles, and Jews have encountered and interpreted Jewish sites. That is, I examine the process of memory—the question of *how* rather than of *what*; or, as Ricoeur puts it, in memory (*la mémoire*) as effectuation versus memories (*les souvenirs*) as effects. Finally, while I speak of Germans, Poles, and Jews, I do not conceive of them as inherently stable, cohesive ethnic groups with intrinsically competing cultural memories (here I am influenced by Brubaker, Cooper, and Rothberg). Paul Ricoeur, *Memory, History, Forgetting,* trans. Kathleen Blamey and David Pellauer (Chicago: University of Chicago Press, 2004); Aleida Assmann, *Der lange Schatten der Vergangenheit: Erinnerungskultur und Geschichtspolitik* (Munich: Beck, 2006); Jan Assmann, *Religion and Cultural Memory,* trans. Rodney Livingstone (Stanford, CA: Stanford University Press, 2006); Jeffrey Olick, "From Collective Memory to the Sociology of Mnemonic Practices and Products," in *Cultural Memory Studies: An International and Interdisciplinary Handbook,* ed. Astrid Erll and Ansgar Nünning (New York: Walter de Gruyter, 2008), 151–62; Rogers Brubaker and Frederick Cooper, "Beyond Identity," *Theory and Society* 29, no. 1 (2000): 1–47; Michael Rothberg, *Multidirectional Memory: Remembering the Holocaust in the Age of Decolonization* (Stanford, CA: Stanford University Press, 2009).

27. Here I am indebted to Reinhart Koselleck, *Zeitschichten: Studien zur Historik* (Frankfurt am Main: Suhrkamp, 2000).

28. Larry Wolff, *Inventing Eastern Europe: The Map of Civilization on the Mind of the Enlightenment* (Stanford, CA: Stanford University Press, 1994). Wolff's argument has recently been criticized for placing the formation of "Eastern Europe"

too early, but I think it is still valid for showing the origins of the idea. See Bernhard Struck, *Nicht West—nicht Ost: Frankreich und Polen in der Wahrnehmung deutscher Reisender zwischen 1750 und 1850* (Göttingen: Wallstein, 2006); Ezequiel Adamovsky, "Euro-Orientalism and the Making of the Concept of Eastern Europe in France, 1810–1880," *JMH* 77, no. 3 (2005): 591–628.

29. Tony Judt, *Postwar: A History of Europe since 1945* (New York: Penguin, 2005), 806.

30. Quotes from Omer Bartov, "Eastern Europe as the Site of Genocide," *JMH* 80, no. 3 (2008): 577, 593. See also Bartov, *Erased*.

31. Ulrike Jureit, "Opferidentifikation und Erlösungshoffnung: Beobachtungen im erinnerungspolitischen Rampenlicht," in *Gefühlte Opfer: Illusionen der Vergangenheitsbewältigung*, Ulrike Jureit and Christian Schneider (Stuttgart: Klett-Cotta, 2010), 19–103; A. Dirk Moses, *German Intellectuals and the Nazi Past* (New York: Cambridge University Press, 2007).

32. Here I am partially engaging with Jeffrey Herf's excellent book, *Divided Memory: The Nazi Past in the Two Germanys* (Cambridge, MA: Harvard University Press, 1997). Concentrating on the 1940s and 1950s, Herf sensibly argues that the political systems of democracy and Communism produced a divided memory of the Nazi past. I agree with him in the realm of high politics during these years. But taking a broader temporal view and looking at urban space, I show that this "divided memory" was not always so clearly divided on the local level of cities, where Cold War politics did not penetrate as deeply and forcefully.

33. For Germany, see Roger Chickering, *We Men Who Feel Most German: A Cultural Study of the Pan-German League* (Boston: Allen & Unwin, 1984); Geoff Eley, *Reshaping the German Right: Radical Nationalism and Political Change after Bismarck* (New Haven, CT: Yale University Press, 1980); Pieter M. Judson, *Guardians of the Nation: Activists on the Language Frontiers of Imperial Austria* (Cambridge, MA: Harvard University Press, 2006); Jeremy King, *Budweisers into Czechs and Germans: A Local History of Bohemian Politics, 1848–1948* (Princeton, NJ: Princeton University Press, 2002); Helmut Walser Smith, *The Continuities of German History: Nation, Religion, and Race across the Long Nineteenth Century* (New York: Cambridge University Press, 2008); Brian E. Vick, *Defining Germany: The 1848 Frankfurt Parliamentarians and National Identity* (Cambridge, MA: Harvard University Press, 2002). For Poland, see Patrice M. Dabrowski, *Commemorations and the Shaping of Modern Poland* (Bloomington: Indiana University Press, 2004); Keely Stauter-Halsted, *The Nation in the Village: The Genesis of Peasant National Identity in Austrian Poland, 1848–1914* (Ithaca, NY: Cornell University Press, 2001); Brian Porter, *When Nationalism Began to Hate: Imagining Modern Politics in Nineteenth-Century Poland* (New York: Oxford University Press, 2000); Brian Porter, *Faith and Fatherland: Catholicism, Modernity, and Poland* (New York: Oxford University Press, 2011); Timothy Snyder, *The Reconstruction of Nations: Poland, Ukraine, Lithuania, Belarus, 1569–1999* (New Haven, CT: Yale

University Press, 2003); Andrzej Walicki, *Philosophy and Romantic Nationalism: The Case of Poland* (Notre Dame, IN: University of Notre Dame Press, 1982).

34. I am drawing on Jan Gross, David Engel, and Helmut Walser Smith, who have stressed the importance of continuities in understanding the Holocaust and the early postwar years. I agree with David Engel that we need a broader historical framework than just the war years. A longer history of how the twisted road of nationalism became hateful in both the German and Polish cases would be ideal here if space were no issue. Gross, *Fear;* David Engel, "On Continuity and Discontinuity in Polish-Jewish Relations: Observations on *Fear,*" *EEPS* 21, no. 3 (2007): 534–48; Smith, *Continuities.*

35. William W. Hagen, "Before the 'Final Solution': Toward a Comparative Analysis of Political Anti-Semitism in Interwar Germany and Poland," *JMH* 68, no. 2 (1996): 351–81; Ezra Mendelsohn, *The Jews of East Central Europe between the World Wars* (Bloomington: Indiana University Press, 1983).

36. Saul Friedländer, *Nazi Germany and the Jews: The Years of Persecution, 1933–1939* (New York: HarperCollins, 1997).

37. Carolyn J. Dean, *The Fragility of Empathy after the Holocaust* (Ithaca, NY: Cornell University Press, 2005), 101.

38. Marion Kaplan, *Between Dignity and Despair: Jewish Life in Nazi Germany* (New York: Oxford University Press, 1998), 5. See also Avraham Barkai, *Vom Boykott zur "Entjudung": Der wirtschaftliche Existenzkampf der Juden im Dritten Reich* (Frankfurt am Main: Fischer, 1988); Frank Bajohr, *"Arisierung" in Hamburg: Die Verdrängung der jüdischen Unternehmer 1933–1945* (Hamburg: Christians, 1997). On popular opinion in Nazi Germany, see David Bankier, *The Germans and the Final Solution: Public Opinion under Nazism* (Cambridge: Blackwell, 1992); Robert Gellately, *Backing Hitler: Consent and Coercion in Nazi Germany* (New York: Oxford University Press, 2001); Ian Kershaw, *Popular Opinion and Political Dissent in the Third Reich, Bavaria 1933–45* (New York: Oxford University Press, 1983); Peter Longerich, *"Davon haben wir nichts gewusst!" Die Deutschen und die Judenverfolgung 1933–1945* (Munich: Siedler, 2006). On the local level, see Frank Bajohr, "The 'Folk Community' and the Persecution of the Jews: German Society under National Socialist Dictatorship, 1933–1945," *HGS* 20, no. 2 (2006): 183–206; Wolf Gruner, "The German Council of Municipalities (Deutscher Gemeindetag) and the Coordination of Anti-Jewish Local Politics in the Nazi State," *HGS* 13, no. 2 (1999): 171–99; Wolf Gruner, "Die NS-Judenverfolgung und die Kommunen: Zur wechselseitigen Dynamisierung von zentraler und lokaler Politik 1933–1941," *Vierteljahrshefte für Zeitgeschichte* 48, no. 1 (2000): 75–126; Michael Wildt, *Volksgemeinschaft als Selbstermächtigung: Gewalt gegen Juden in der deutschen Provinz 1919 bis 1939* (Hamburg: Hamburger Edition, 2007).

39. Juliusz Bardach, Bogusław Leśnodorski, and Michał Pietrzak, eds., *Historia ustroju i prawa polskiego* (Warsaw: PWN, 1993), 469–70.

40. Eva Plach, *The Clash of Moral Nations: Cultural Politics in Piłsudski's Poland, 1926–1935* (Athens: Ohio University Press, 2006).

41. Quoted in Antony Polonsky, *Politics in Independent Poland, 1921–1939* (Oxford: Clarendon, 1972), 172.

42. The periodization of interwar anti-Jewish violence into four waves is from Joanna Beata Michlic, *Poland's Threatening Other: The Image of the Jew from 1880 to the Present* (Lincoln: University of Nebraska Press, 2006), 111–13. See also Anna Landau-Czajka, *W jednym stali domu: Koncepcje rozwiązania kwestii żydowskiej w publicystyce polskiej lat 1933–1939* (Warsaw: PAN, 1998); Anna Landau-Czajka, "Żydzi w oczach prasy katolickiej okresu II Rzeczypospolitej," *Przegląd Polonijny* 18, no. 4 (1992): 97–113; William W. Hagen, "The Moral Economy of Popular Violence: The Pogrom in Lwów, November 1918," in *Antisemitism and Its Opponents in Modern Poland,* ed. Robert Blobaum (Ithaca, NY: Cornell University Press, 2005), 124–47; Hagen, "Before the 'Final Solution'"; Dariusz Libionka, "Obcy, wrodzy, niebezpieczni: Obraz Żydów i kwestii żydowskiej w prasie inteligencji katolickiej lat trzydziestych w Polsce," *Kwartalnik Historii Żydów* no. 3 (2002): 318–38; Mendelsohn, *Jews of East Central Europe;* Włodzimierz Mich, *Obcy w polskim domu: Nacjonalistyczne koncepcje rozwiązania problemu mniejszości narodowych 1918–1939* (Lublin: Wydawnictwo Uniwersytetu Marii Curie-Skłodowskiej, 1994); Ronald Modras, *The Catholic Church and Antisemitism: Poland 1933–1939* (Chur, Switzerland: Harwood Academic Publishers, 1994); Monika Natkowska, *Numerus clausus, getto ławkowe, numerus nullus, "paragraf aryjski": Antysemityzm na Uniwersytecie Warszawskim 1931–1939* (Warsaw: ŻIH, 1999); Waldemar Paruch, *Od konsolidacji państwowej do konsolidacji narodowej: Mniejszości narodowe w myśli politycznej obozu piłsudczykowskiego, 1926–1939* (Lublin: Wydawnictwo Uniwersytetu Marii Curie-Skłodowskiej, 1997); Brian Porter, "Antisemitism and the Search for a Catholic Identity," in *Antisemitism and Its Opponents,* ed. Blobaum, 103–23; Porter, *Faith and Fatherland*; Szymon Rudnicki, *Obóz Narodowo-Radykalny: Geneza i działalność* (Warsaw: Czytelnik, 1985); Szymon Rudnicki, "Anti-Jewish Legislation in Interwar Poland," in *Antisemitism and Its Opponents,* ed. Blobaum, 148–70; Jolanta Żyndul, *Zajścia antyżydowskie w Polsce w latach 1935–1937* (Warsaw: Fundacja im. Kazimierza Kelles-Krauza, 1994).

43. Jochen Böhler, *Auftakt zum Vernichtungskrieg: Die Wehrmacht in Polen 1939* (Frankfurt am Main: Fischer, 2006); Elizabeth Harvey, *Women and the Nazi East: Agents and Witnesses of Germanization* (New Haven, CT: Yale University Press, 2003); Czesław Madajczyk, *Polityka III Rzeszy w okupowanej Polsce* (Warsaw: PWN, 1970); Alexander B. Rossino, *Hitler Strikes Poland: Blitzkrieg, Ideology, and Atrocity* (Lawrence: University Press of Kansas, 2003); Phillip T. Rutherford, *Prelude to the Final Solution: The Nazi Program for Deporting Ethnic Poles, 1939–1941* (Lawrence: University Press of Kansas, 2007); Timothy Snyder, *Bloodlands: Europe between Hitler and Stalin* (New York: Basic Books, 2010). On Ukraine and Belarus,

see Karel C. Berkhoff, *Harvest of Despair: Life and Death under Nazi Rule* (Cambridge, MA: Harvard University Press, 2004); Christian Gerlach, *Kalkulierte Morde: Die deutsche Wirtschafts- und Vernichtungspolitik in Weissrussland 1941 bis 1944* (Hamburg: Hamburger Edition, 1999); Wendy Lower, *Nazi Empire Building and the Holocaust in Ukraine* (Chapel Hill: University of North Carolina Press, 2005); Dieter Pohl, *Die Herrschaft der Wehrmacht: Deutsche Militärbesatzung und einheimische Bevölkerung in der Sowjetunion 1941–1944* (Munich: Oldenbourg, 2008).

44. Czesław Łuczak, "Szanse i trudności bilansu demograficznego Polski w latach 1939–1945," *Dzieje Najnowsze* 26, no. 2 (1994): 9–14.

45. Gunnar S. Paulsson, *Secret City: The Hidden Jews of Warsaw, 1940–1945* (New Haven, CT: Yale University Press, 2002). On rescue, see also Jan Grabowski, *Rescue for Money: Paid Helpers in Poland, 1939–1945* (Jerusalem: Yad Vashem, 2008); Nechama Tec, *When Light Pierced the Darkness: Christian Rescue of Jews in Nazi Occupied Poland* (New York: Oxford University Press, 1986).

46. Quoted in Michlic, *Poland's Threatening Other,* 190. See Jan Grabowski, *"Ja tego Żyda znam!" Szantażowanie Żydów w Warszawie, 1939–1943* (Warsaw: IFiS PAN, 2004); Barbara Engelking-Boni, *"Szanowny panie Gistapo": Donosy do władz niemieckich w Warszawie i okolicach w latach 1940–1941* (Warsaw: IFiS PAN, 2003); Jan T. Gross, "A Tangled Web: Confronting Stereotypes Concerning Relations between Poles, Germans, Jews, and Communists," in *The Politics of Retribution in Europe: World War II and Its Aftermath,* ed. István Deák, Jan T. Gross, and Tony Judt (Princeton, NJ: Princeton University Press, 2000), 74–130.

47. Paweł Machcewicz and Krzysztof Persak, eds., *Wokół Jedwabnego* (Warsaw: IPN, 2002); John Connelly, "Poles and Jews in the Second World War: The Revisions of Jan T. Gross," *Contemporary European History* 11, no. 4 (2002): 641–58; Antony Polonsky and Joanna B. Michlic, eds., *The Neighbors Respond: The Controversy of the Jedwabne Massacre in Poland* (Princeton, NJ: Princeton University Press, 2004); Marci Shore, "Conversing with Ghosts: Jedwabne, Żydokomuna, Totalitarianism," *Kritika: Explorations in Russian and Eurasian History* 6, no. 2 (2005): 345–75; Andrzej Żbikowski, *U genezy Jedwabnego: Żydzi na Kresach Północno-Wschodnich II Rzeczypospolitej* (Warsaw: ŻIH, 2006).

48. Jan T. Gross, *Revolution from Abroad: The Soviet Conquest of Poland's Western Ukraine and Western Belorussia* (Princeton, NJ: Princeton University Press, 1988).

49. Żbikowski, *U genezy Jedwabnego;* Gross, "Tangled Web"; Ben-Cion Pinchuk, *Shtetl Jews under Soviet Rule: Eastern Poland on the Eve of the Holocaust* (Cambridge: Blackwell, 1991).

50. Andrzej Żbikowski, "Pogromy i mordy ludności żydowskiej w Łomżyńskiem i na Białostocczyźnie latem 1941 roku w świetle relacji ocalałych Żydów i dokumentów sądowych," in Machcewicz and Persak, *Wokół,* 159–271; Gross, *Fear,* chapter 6; Agnieszka Pufelska, *Die "Judäo-Kommune": Ein Feindbild in Polen:*

Das polnische Selbstverständnis im Schatten des Antisemitismus, 1939–1948 (Paderborn: Schöningh, 2007); Joanna B. Michlic, "The Soviet Occupation of Poland, 1939–41, and the Stereotype of the Anti-Polish and Pro-Soviet Jew," *JSS* 13, no. 3 (2007): 135–76.

51. David Engel, *In the Shadow of Auschwitz: The Polish Government-in-Exile and the Jews, 1939–1945* (Chapel Hill: University of North Carolina Press, 1987); David Engel, *Facing a Holocaust: The Polish Government-in-Exile and the Jews, 1943–1945* (Chapel Hill: University of North Carolina Press, 1993).

52. Engelking-Boni, *"Szanowny panie Gistapo";* Barbara Engelking, Jacek Leociak, and Dariusz Libionka, eds., *Prowincja Noc: Życie i zagłada Żydów w dystrykcie warszawskim* (Warsaw: IFiS PAN, 2007); Grabowski, *Ja tego Żyda znam;* Jan Gross, *Golden Harvest* (New York: Oxford University Press, 2012); Alina Skibińska and Jakub Petelewicz, "The Participation of Poles in Crimes against Jews in the Świętokrzyskie Region," *YVS* 35, no. 1 (2007): 5–48; Andrzej Żbikowski, ed., *Polacy i Żydzi pod okupacją niemiecką 1939–1945: Studia i Materiały* (Warsaw: IPN, 2006), chapters 4–10. See also the essays forthcoming in *EEPS* edited by Jan Gross stemming from a conference on the Holocaust in Poland that he organized with Jan Grabowski at Princeton University in October 2010.

53. Michał Głowiński, *The Black Seasons,* trans. Marci Shore (Evanston, IL: Northwestern University Press, 2005), 93–96.

54. Klaus-Peter Friedrich, "Collaboration in a 'Land without a Quisling': Patterns of Cooperation with the Nazi German Occupation Regime in Poland during World War II," *SR* 64, no. 4 (2005): 711–46; John Connelly, "Why the Poles Collaborated So Little—and Why That Is No Reason for Nationalist Hubris," *SR* 64, no. 4 (2005): 771–81.

55. Omer Bartov, *Hitler's Army: Soldiers, Nazis, and War in the Third Reich* (New York: Oxford University Press, 1991); Christopher Browning, *Ordinary Men: Reserve Police Battalion 101 and the Final Solution in Poland* (New York: HarperCollins, 1992); Suzanne Brown-Fleming, *The Holocaust and Catholic Conscience: Cardinal Aloisius Muench and the Guilt Question in Germany* (Notre Dame, IN: University of Notre Dame Press, 2006); Eckart Conze, et al., *Das Amt und die Vergangenheit: Deutsche Diplomaten im Dritten Reich und in der Bundesrepublik* (Munich: Karl Blessing Verlag, 2010); Peter Hayes, *Industry and Ideology: IG Farben in the Nazi Era* (New York: Cambridge University Press, 1987); Thomas Kühne, *Kameradschaft: Die Soldaten des nationalsozialistischen Krieges und das 20. Jahrhundert* (Göttingen: Vandenhoeck & Ruprecht, 2006); Michael Phayer, *The Catholic Church and the Holocaust, 1930–1965* (Bloomington: Indiana University Press, 2000); Harald Welzer, *Täter: Wie aus ganz normalen Menschen Massenmörder werden* (Frankfurt am Main: Fischer, 2005).

56. Jeffrey Herf, *The Jewish Enemy: Nazi Propaganda during World War II and the Holocaust* (Cambridge, MA: Belknap Press of Harvard University Press, 2006).

57. Henry Friedlander, *The Origins of Nazi Genocide: From Euthanasia to the Final Solution* (Chapel Hill: University of North Carolina Press, 1995); Kershaw, *Popular Opinion;* Nathan Stoltzfus, *Resistance of the Heart: Intermarriage and the Rosenstrasse Protest in Nazi Germany* (New York: W. W. Norton, 1996).

58. Quoted in Ben Barkow, Raphael Gross, and Michael Lenarz, eds., *Novemberpogrom 1938: Die Augenzeugenberichte der Wiener Library, London* (Frankfurt am Main: Jüdischer Verlag im Suhrkamp Verlag, 2008), 222. On local involvement and reactions to the pogrom, see Wolfgang Benz, "The November Pogrom of 1938: Participation, Applause, and Disapproval," in *Exclusionary Violence: Antisemitic Riots in Modern German History,* ed. Christhard Hoffmann, Werner Bergmann, and Helmut Walser Smith (Ann Arbor: University of Michigan Press, 2002), 141–59; Alan E. Steinweis, *Kristallnacht 1938* (Cambridge, MA: Belknap Press of Harvard University Press, 2009); Wildt, *Volksgemeinschaft.*

59. Julia Kristeva, *Powers of Horror: An Essay on Abjection,* trans. Leon S. Roudiez (New York: Columbia University Press, 1982), 2. In finding Kristeva's psychoanalytic concept useful to social analysis, I am drawing on Iris Marion Young, "Abjection and Oppression: Dynamics of Unconscious Racism, Sexism, and Homophobia," in *Crises of Continental Philosophy,* ed. Arleen B. Dallery and Charles E. Scott (Albany: State University of New York Press, 1990), 201–13; Matthew P. Fitzpatrick, "The Pre-History of the Holocaust? The *Sonderweg* and *Historikerstreit* Debates and the Abject Colonial Past," *CEH* 41, no. 3 (2008): 477–503.

60. Eric Santner, *Stranded Objects: Mourning, Memory, and Film in Postwar Germany* (Ithaca, NY: Cornell University Press, 1990).

61. For a summary of this messianic nationalism and its permutations from the nineteenth century to the present, see Zubrzycki, *Crosses of Auschwitz,* chapters 1–2.

62. Tadeusz Borowski, *This Way for the Gas, Ladies and Gentlemen,* trans. Barbara Vedder (New York: Penguin, 1967), 178.

63. "Bonded memory" from J. Assmann, *Religion;* "threatening Other" from Michlic, *Poland's Threatening Other.*

64. See Marcuse, *Legacies.* On the social meanings and power of West German narratives of victimization, see Gregor, *Haunted City.*

1. Confronting the Spoils of Genocide

1. CZA, C3/1676, report on restitution, November 15, 1946 (emphasis in the original). On early Jewish discussions about restitution, see Constantin Goschler, *Schuld und Schulden: Die Politik der Wiedergutmachung für NS-Verfolgte seit 1945* (Göttingen: Wallstein, 2005), 40–46.

2. Siegfried Moses, *Die jüdischen Nachkriegsforderungen* (Tel Aviv: Irgun olej merkas Europa, 1944); Nehemiah Robinson, *Indemnification and Reparations: Jewish Aspects* (New York: Institute of Jewish Affairs of the American Jewish Congress and World Jewish Congress, 1944).

3. AAN, MAP, 786, CKŻP to premier, June 6, 1946.

4. Martin Dean, Constantin Goschler, and Philipp Ther, eds., *Robbery and Restitution: The Conflict over Jewish Property in Europe* (New York: Berghahn Books, 2007); Anna Cichopek-Gajraj, "Jews, Poles, and Slovaks: A Story of Encounters, 1944–48" (PhD diss., University of Michigan, 2008), chapter 4; Maud S. Mandel, *In the Aftermath of Genocide: Armenians and Jews in Twentieth-Century France* (Durham, NC: Duke University Press, 2003), 64–76. On the confiscation of Jewish property across Europe, see Martin Dean, *Robbing the Jews: The Confiscation of Jewish Property in the Holocaust, 1933–1945* (New York: Cambridge University Press, 2008).

5. McCloy quoted in Ayaka Takei, "The Jewish People as the Heir: The Jewish Successor Organizations (JRSO, JTC French Branch) and the Postwar Jewish Communities in Germany" (PhD diss., Waseda University, 2002), 216. See Jay Howard Geller, *Jews in Post-Holocaust Germany, 1945–1953* (New York: Cambridge University Press, 2005), 17–52; Anthony Kauders, *Democratization and the Jews: Munich, 1945–1965* (Lincoln: University of Nebraska Press, 2004), 63–73.

6. Constantin Goschler, *Wiedergutmachung: Westdeutschland und die Verfolgten des Nationalsozialismus, 1945–1954* (Munich: Oldenbourg, 1992), 60–62.

7. Draft in BA (SAPMO), DQ 2/3321. On the broader picture, see Norman M. Naimark, *The Russians in Germany: A History of the Soviet Zone of Occupation, 1945–1949* (Cambridge, MA: Harvard University Press, 1995).

8. Jürgen Lillteicher, *Raub, Recht und Restitution: Die Rückerstattung jüdischen Eigentums in der frühen Bundesrepublik* (Göttingen: Wallstein, 2007), 53–61 and 68–76.

9. Military Government Law 59, November 10, 1947, in *Amtsblatt der Militärregierung Deutschland—Amerikanisches Kontrollgebiet,* Ausgabe G, 1. See Goschler, *Wiedergutmachung,* 106–26.

10. Jeffrey Herf, *Divided Memory: The Nazi Past in the Two Germanys* (Cambridge, MA: Harvard University Press, 1997), 267–333; Geller, *Jews in Post-Holocaust Germany,* 123–59 and 219–56.

11. On these issues more broadly, see Ayaka Takei, "The 'Gemeinde Problem:' The Jewish Restitution Successor Organization and the Postwar Jewish Communities in Germany, 1947–1954," *HGS* 16, no. 2 (2002): 266–88.

12. CZA, S35/196, minutes of Budget Advisory Committee, December 20, 1948.

13. Ibid., Nussbaum to JRSO, January 14, 1949.

14. AJDC-Jerusalem, Geneva IV, 9/1a, file 2, Haber to Kagan, December 18, 1952.

15. Ibid., van Dam to Ferencz, August 20, 1953.

16. H. G. van Dam, "Das Erbe des deutschen Judentums," *Allgemeine Wochenzeitung der Juden in Deutschland,* May 8, 1952.

17. AJDC-Jerusalem, Geneva IV, 9/1a, file 2, Ferencz to van Dam, May 16, 1952.

18. Ibid., Marx to Ferencz, June 4, 1952. On Jewish life in West Germany, see Michael Brenner, *After the Holocaust: Rebuilding Jewish Lives in Postwar Germany,* trans. Barbara Harshav (Princeton, NJ: Princeton University Press, 1997); Ruth

Gay, *Safe among the Germans: Liberated Jews after World War II* (New Haven, CT: Yale University Press, 2002); Jael Geis, *Übrig sein—Leben "danach": Juden deutscher Herkunft in der britischen und amerikanischen Zone Deutschlands 1945–1949* (Berlin: Philo, 2000); Geller, *Jews in Post-Holocaust Germany;* Atina Grossmann, *Jews, Germans, and Allies: Close Encounters in Occupied Germany* (Princeton, NJ: Princeton University Press, 2007); Anthony Kauders, *Unmögliche Heimat: Eine deutsch-jüdische Geschichte der Bundesrepublik* (Munich: Deutsche Verlags-Anstalt, 2007); Irmela von der Lühe, Axel Schildt, and Stefanie Schüler-Springorum, eds., *"Auch in Deutschland waren wir nicht wirklich zu Hause": Jüdische Remigration nach 1945* (Göttingen: Wallstein, 2008); Anke Quast, *Nach der Befreiung: Jüdische Gemeinden in Niedersachsen seit 1945* (Göttingen: Wallstein, 2001); Lynn Rapaport, *Jews in Germany after the Holocaust: Memory, Identity, and Jewish-German Relations* (New York: Cambridge University Press, 1997); Susanne Schönborn, ed., *Zwischen Erinnerung und Neubeginn: Zur deutsch-jüdischen Geschichte nach 1945* (Munich: Meidenbauer, 2006); Donate Strathmann, *Auswandern oder hierbleiben? Jüdisches Leben in Düsseldorf und Nordrhein, 1945–1960* (Essen: Klartext, 2003); Jürgen Zieher, *Im Schatten von Antisemitismus und Wiedergutmachung: Kommunen und jüdische Gemeinden in Dortmund, Düsseldorf und Köln 1945–1960* (Berlin: Metropol, 2005).

19. CZA, L47/31/1, CORA, case no. 1237, October 29, 1954.

20. LAB, B Rep. 025–11, Unterlagen zu den IRSO-Globalverträgen, "12 Punkte zur Rückerstattung 1933–1945 angeblich entzogener jüdischer Vermögenswerte."

21. Ibid.

22. NA-College Park, RG 466/250/84/23/1, report no. 21, May 24, 1950.

23. *Die Restitution* no. 11, February 1951; *Die Restitution* no. 1, April 1950.

24. Goschler, *Wiedergutmachung,* 172–80.

25. LAB, B Rep. 002, 4866, vol. 2, minutes of meeting, June 26, 1950; LAB, B Rep. 002, 4866, vol. 1, notes on meeting, October 15, 1952.

26. AJDC-Jerusalem, Geneva IV, 9/1b, file 2, Ferencz to Kagan, October 5, 1953; AJDC-Jerusalem, Geneva IV, 9/1c, file 1, report, January 26, 1955; AJDC-Jerusalem, Geneva IV, 9/1b, file 5, Ferencz to Kagan, July 3, 1955.

27. AJDC-Jerusalem, Geneva IV, 9/1b, file 3, statement of income and expenditures, December 31, 1959; AJDC-Jerusalem, Geneva IV, 9/1b, file 1, Jacobson to Beckelman, September 10, 1954.

28. AJDC-Jerusalem, Geneva IV, 9/1b, file 2, Ferencz to Kagan, October 3, 1953.

29. AJDC-Jerusalem, Geneva IV, 9/1b, file 1, Harber to Jordan, September 30, 1953.

30. Ibid., Ferencz to Kagan, January 18, 1954.

31. Ibid., Schreiber to JRSO, April 8, 1954.

32. Ibid., Kagan to JRSO, May 10, 1954.

33. Adenauer's remark reported in ibid., Ferencz to Kagan, April 17, 1954. Report on Adenauer's meeting in ibid., Ferencz to Lowenthal, July 29, 1954.

34. AJDC-Jerusalem, Geneva IV, 9/1b, file 5, Ferencz to Kagan, May 11, 1955.

35. Ibid., Ferencz to Kagan, July 2, 1955.

36. Walter Schwarz, "Die Wiedergutmachung nationalsozialistischen Unrechts durch die Bundesrepublik Deutschland: Ein Überblick," in *Wiedergutmachung in der Bundesrepublik Deutschland,* ed. Ludolf Herbst and Constantin Goschler (Munich: Oldenbourg, 1989), 54. On the complications and experiences of restitution in practice, see Norbert Frei, José Brunner, and Constantin Goschler, eds., *Die Praxis der Wiedergutmachung: Geschichte, Erfahrung und Wirkung in Deutschland und Israel* (Göttingen: Wallstein, 2009); Lillteicher, *Raub, Recht und Restitution.*

37. Lillteicher, *Raub, Recht und Restitution,* 137. On narratives of victimization, see Frank Biess, *Homecomings: Returning POWs and the Legacy of Defeat on Postwar Germany* (Princeton, NJ: Princeton University Press, 2006); Neil Gregor, *Haunted City: Nuremberg and the Nazi Past* (New Haven, CT: Yale University Press, 2008); Wulf Kansteiner, *In Pursuit of German Memory: History, Television, and Politics after Auschwitz* (Athens: Ohio University Press, 2006); Herbert Marcuse, *The Legacies of Dachau: The Uses and Abuses of a Concentration Camp, 1933–2001* (New York: Cambridge University Press, 2001); Robert G. Moeller, *War Stories: The Search for a Usable Past in the Federal Republic of Germany* (Berkeley: University of California Press, 2001).

38. ACJ, 5B1, nr. 28, Meyer to Finance Ministry, September 30, 1950.

39. Thomas Schüler, "Das Wiedergutmachungsgesetz vom 14. September 1945 in Thüringen," *Jahrbuch für Antisemitismusforschung* 2 (1993): 118–38; Jan Philipp Spannuth, *Rückerstattung Ost: Der Umgang der DDR mit dem "arisierten" Eigentum der Juden und die Rückerstattung im wiedervereinigten Deutschland* (Essen: Klartext, 2007), 83–84.

40. Draft in *Schriftenreihe des Bundesamtes zur Regelung offener Vermögensfragen,* vol. 7 (Berlin: Bundesamt zur Regelung offener Vermögensfragen, 1994), 9-24.

41. BA (SAPMO), DY 30 IV 2/2.027/31, Merker to Zuckermann, January 13, 1948.

42. Ibid., memo, March 21, 1948; Gesetz über die Betreuung der Verfolgten des Naziregimes und die Vorbereitung für die Wiedergutmachung, articles 28 and 29.

43. Karin Hartewig, *Zurückgekehrt: Die Geschichte der jüdischen Kommunisten in der DDR* (Cologne: Böhlau, 2000), 300–12; Herf, *Divided Memory,* chapters 4–5.

44. BLHA, Rep. 203, nr. 1830, SMA order nr. 82, April 29, 1948.

45. Angelika Timm, *Hammer, Zirkel, Davidstern: Das gestörte Verhältnis der DDR zu Zionismus und Staat Israel* (Bonn: Bouvier, 1997), 70–80.

46. BLHA, Rep. 203, nr. 1828, Meyer to Brandenburg's president, July 21, 1949; Brandenburg to SMA, August 1, 1949.

47. See the exchanges in ACJ, 5B1, nr. 107.

48. LAB, C Rep. 100–01, nr. 49, debate proceedings, December 4, 1947.

49. LAB, C Rep. 100–05, nr. 812, city council decision, February 26, 1948.

50. LAB, C Rep. 001, nr. 145, debates from June 10, 1948 to November 11, 1948.

51. *Schriftenreihe*, vol. 7, 205; BA (SAPMO), DO 4, nr. 1337, Jewish Community to Central Committee of the SED, November 5, 1959.

52. Letters in LAB, C Rep. 104, nr. 382, C Rep. 105, nr. 6912, and BA (SAPMO), DY 30 IV/2/14, nr. 249.

53. LAB, C Rep. 104, nr. 6912, City Finance Department to Jewish Community, June 5, 1951; LAB, C Rep. 104, nr. 382, Finance Department, September 1951.

54. Herf, *Divided Memory,* chapter 5; Catherine Epstein, *The Last Revolutionaries: German Communists and Their Century* (Cambridge, MA: Harvard University Press, 2003), 130–57.

55. Shulamit Volkov, "Antisemitism as a Cultural Code: Reflections on the History and Historiography of Antisemitism in Imperial Germany," *LBIYB* 23 (1978): 25–46.

56. "Lehren aus dem Prozess gegen das Verschwörerzentrum Slansky," *Dokumente der Sozialistischen Einheitspartei Deutschlands,* vol. 4 (Berlin: Dietz, 1954), 202, 204, 206, and 207.

57. Robert Levy, *Ana Pauker: The Rise and Fall of a Jewish Communist* (Berkeley: University of California Press, 2001), chapter 8; Audrey Kichelewski, "Imagining the 'Jews' in Stalinist Poland: Nationalists or Cosmopolites?," *European Review of History* 17, no. 3 (2010): 505–22.

58. Gavin I. Langmuir, *History, Religion, and Antisemitism* (Berkeley: University of California Press, 1990), 275–305.

59. LAB, C Rep. 101, nr. 1816, Office of Church Affairs to Ebert, April 21, 1953; LAB, C Rep. 104, nr. 382, Ebert to Finance Department, June 5, 1953.

60. *Schriftenreihe,* vol. 7, 205–7 and 227–29, memo, May 1956, and city decision, March 11, 1958. On the debate, see *Schriftenreihe,* vol. 7, 201–26, and Spannuth, *Rückerstattung,* 141–44.

61. Quoted in Spannuth, *Rückerstattung,* 141.

62. BA (SAPMO), DY 30 IV 2/2.027/31, memo, March 21, 1948.

63. Quoted in Hartewig, *Zurückgekehrt,* 275.

64. Dean, *Robbing the Jews,* 173–396.

65. *Raporty Ludwiga Fischera, gubernatora Dystryktu Warszawskiego 1939–1944* (Warsaw: Książka i Wiedza, 1987), 108; Jan Grabowski, "Polscy zarządcy powierniczy majątku żydowskiego: Zarys problematyki," *Zagłada Żydów* 1 (2005): 255–56.

66. Zygmunt Klukowski, *Dziennik z lat okupacji Zamojszczyzny 1939–1945* (Lublin: Lubelska Spółdzielnia Wydawnicza, 1958), 255.

67. Paweł Machcewicz and Krzysztof Persak, eds., *Wokół Jedwabnego,* vol. 1 (Warsaw: IPN, 2002), 40.

68. Marcin Zaremba, "Gorączka szabru," *Zagłada Żydów* 5 (2009): 193–220.

69. *Zarys działalności CKŻP w Polsce za okres od 1 stycznia do 30 czerwca 1946* (Warsaw: CKŻP, 1946); Albert Stankowski, "Nowe spojrzenie na statystyki dotyczące emigracji Żydów z Polski po 1944 roku," in *Studia z historii Żydów w Polsce po 1945 r.,* ed. Grzegorz Berendt, August Grabski, and Albert Stankowski (Warsaw: ŻIH, 2000), 103–51; Józef Adelson, "W Polsce zwanej ludową," in *Najnowsze dzieje Żydów w Polsce w zarysie (do 1950 roku),* ed. Jerzy Tomaszewski (Warsaw: PWN, 1993), 389–400.

70. The exact numbers are not known. See Jan Gross, *Fear: Antisemitism in Poland after Auschwitz* (New York: Random House, 2006), 35; David Engel, "Patterns of Anti-Jewish Violence in Poland, 1944–1946," *YVS* 26 (1998): 43–85.

71. David Engel, "On Continuity and Discontinuity in Polish-Jewish Relations: Observations on *Fear,*" *EEPS* 21, no. 3 (2007): 540–41.

72. Ibid., 544 (emphasis in original). See Anna Cichopek, *Pogrom Żydów w Krakowie: 11 sierpnia 1945* (Warsaw: ŻIH, 2000); Engel, "Patterns"; Gross, *Fear;* Bożena Szaynok, *Pogrom Żydów w Kielcach 4 lipca 1946* (Warsaw: Bellona, 1992); Joshua D. Zimmerman, ed., *Contested Memories: Poles and Jews during the Holocaust and Its Aftermath* (New Brunswick, NJ: Rutgers University Press, 2003).

73. Gross, *Fear;* Engel, "Patterns."

74. Joanna Michlic, "The Holocaust and Its Aftermath as Perceived in Poland: Voices of Polish Intellectuals, 1945–1947," in *The Jews Are Coming Back: The Return of the Jews to Their Countries of Origin after WWII,* ed. David Bankier (New York: Berghahn, 2005), 206–30.

75. Daniel Blatman, "The Encounter between Jews and Poles in Lublin District after Liberation, 1944–1945," *EEPS* 20, no. 4 (2006): 598–621.

76. Andrzej Paczkowski, *Zdobycie władzy 1945–1947* (Warsaw: Wydawnictwa Szkolne i Pedagogiczne, 1993); Andrzej Friszke, *Opozycja polityczna w PRL 1945–1980* (London: Aneks, 1994); Krystyna Kersten, *Między wyzwoleniem a zniewoleniem: Polska 1944–1956* (London: Aneks, 1993).

77. "Z historii Rady Pomocy Żydom w Polsce," *Dziennik Ludowy,* September 9, 1945, 3.

78. Zuzanna Ginczanka (pseudonym for Zuzanna Polina Gincburg), untitled but often known as *"Non omnis moriar"* (probably 1942), trans. Bożena Shallcross. I kindly thank Professor Shallcross and Indiana University Press for granting me permission to publish her translation. Bożena Shallcross, *The Holocaust Object in Polish and Polish-Jewish Culture* (Bloomington: Indiana University Press, 2011), 37–8.

79. "Ustawa z dnia 6 maja 1945 r. o majątkach opuszczonych i porzuconych," *Dziennik Ustaw Rzeczypospolitej Polskiej* no. 17, 1945. This law was preceded by "Dekret z dnia 2 marca 1945 r. o majątkach opuszczonych i porzuconych," *Dziennik Ustaw Rzeczypospolitej Polskiej* no. 9 (1945).

80. "Dekret z dnia 8 marca 1946 r. o majątkach opuszczonych i poniemieckich," *Dziennik Ustaw Rzeczypospolitej Polskiej* no. 13 (1946).

81. Cichopek-Gajraj, "Jews, Poles, and Slovaks," 169–84. On extending the deadline, see USHMM, RG-67.006M, WJC, Series B, box 25, folder 12, Robinson to Winiewicz, September 8, 1947; Robinson to Winiewicz, December 7, 1948.

82. Maciej Pisarski, "Emigracja Żydów z Polski w latach 1945–1951," in Berendt, Grabski, and Stankowski, *Studia z historii Żydów,* 39.

83. Some Polish-Jewish leaders attempted to push for a successor organization. AAN, MAP 786, CKŻP to premier, June 6, 1946; Szymon Rogoziński, "Drażliwa kwestia," *Opinia,* July 25, 1946; political proclamation of the Jewish Democratic Party, January 1947, republished in August Grabski, *Działalność komunistów wśród Żydów w Polsce (1944–1949)* (Warsaw: ŻIH, 2004), 199.

84. AJDC-Jerusalem, 45/54, file 779, memo on individual claims, April 4, 1948.

85. "Referat I sekretarza KC PPR wygłoszony na rozszerzonym plenum KC," in *Polska Partia Robotnicza: Dokumenty programowe 1942–1948* (Warsaw: Książka i Wiedza, 1984), 283.

86. USHMM, RG 15.089, reel 1, MAP circular, February 2, 1945.

87. AAN, MAP 786, KO-ŻZR to Presidium of the Council of Ministers, October 9, 1946.

88. USHMM, RG-15.089, reel 1, CKŻP to JDC, January 27, 1948.

89. AAN, MAP 788, MAP to Main Liquidation Office, August 3, 1946.

90. USHMM, RG 15.089, reel 1, MAP circular, February 2, 1945.

91. Article 13 of the May 6, 1945 law. The revised law on abandoned and former German property published on March 8, 1946 included the same provision (Article 12, paragraph 2).

92. AAN, MAP 1099, Białystok to MAP, November 11, 1945.

93. For the numbers, see Stankowski, "Nowe spojrzenie."

94. Dozens of requests in AAN, MAP, B-2612 and B-2613.

95. AAN, UdW, 132/273, registry of synagogues, December 12, 1979.

96. USHMM, RG 68.045, reel 50, "Brief Information about Restitution Problems in Poland," undated but before 1948; USHMM, RG 15.089, reel 1, CKŻP to JDC, January 27, 1948.

97. AAN, UdW, 26/476, Kraków Jewish Congregation (KJC) to Attorney General, July 30, 1957.

98. Ibid; AAN, UdW, 26/476, KJC to Ministry for Public Utilities and Housing, August 13, 1956; AAN, UdW, 26/476, KJC to Premier, August 19, 1957.

99. Ibid., July 1957 letter.

100. AAN, UdW, 26/476, UdW to KJC, April 1958 (draft copy).

101. AAN, UdW, 131/512, Kraków Provincial Government to District Liquidation Office, September 22, 1947; AAN, UdW, 131/512, certificate from Kraków Provincial Government, July 26, 1946.

102. AAN, UdW, 131/512, Supreme Court Decision, October 15, 1960.

103. AAN, UdW, 131/512, UdW to Kraków Department of Religious Affairs (KDRA), April 24, 1963.

104. AAN, UdW, 131/512, UdW to KDRA, October 22, 1962; UdW to KDRA, April 24, 1963. For earlier letters expressing a similar line of reasoning, see AAN, UdW, 131/512, UdW to Finance Ministry, July 31, 1958; AAN, UdW, 131/78, UdW to Justice Ministry, February 21, 1959.

105. *Jewish Life in Poland* no. 12 (1950): 2, copy located in USHMM, RG-67.006M, WJC, Series B, box 11, folder 1; Lucjan Blit, *The Anti-Jewish Campaign in Present-day Poland: Facts, Documents, Press Reports* (London: Institute of Jewish Affairs, 1968), 6. See Padraic Kenney, "Whose Nation, Whose State? Working-Class Nationalism and Antisemitism in Poland, 1945–1947," *POLIN: Studies in Polish Jewry* 13 (2000): 224–35; Audrey Kichelewski, "A Community under Pressure: Jews in Poland, 1957–1967," *POLIN: Studies in Polish Jewry* 21 (2008): 159–86; Paweł Machcewicz, *Polski rok 1956* (Warsaw: Mówią Wieki, 1993); Joanna Beata Michlic, *Poland's Threatening Other: The Image of the Jew from 1880 to the Present* (Lincoln: University of Nebraska Press, 2006), 196–261; Bożena Szaynok, *Z historią i Moskwą w tle. Polska a Izrael 1944–1968* (Warsaw: IPN, 2007); Marcin Zaremba, *Komunizm, legitymizacja, nacjonalizm: Nacjonalistyczna legitymizacja władzy komunistycznej w Polsce* (Warsaw: Trio, 2001).

106. Gross, *Fear,* 243.

107. Mario Keßler, *Die SED und die Juden—zwischen Repression und Toleranz* (Berlin: Akademie Verlag, 1995), 32–46; Michlic, "Holocaust and Its Aftermath."

108. Herf, *Divided Memory,* 267–333.

2. Clearing Jewish Rubble

1. Quoted in Jan Jagielski, *Jewish Sites in Warsaw* (Warsaw: City of Warsaw, 2002), 14–15.

2. Erica Burgauer, *Zwischen Erinnerung und Verdrängung—Juden in Deutschland nach 1945* (Hamburg: Rowohlt Verlag, 1993); Harry Maòr, "Über den Wiederaufbau der jüdischen Gemeinden in Deutschland seit 1945" (PhD diss., Universität Mainz, 1961); Kazimierz Urban, *Mniejszości religijne w Polsce 1945–1991: Zarys statystyczny* (Kraków: NOMOS, 1994). For the GDR and PPR, see also Grzegorz Berendt, *Życie żydowskie w Polsce w latach 1950–1956: Z dziejów Towarzystwa Społeczno-Kulturalnego Żydów w Polsce* (Gdańsk: Wydawnictwo Uniwersytetu Gdańskiego, 2006); Karin Hartewig, *Zurückgekehrt: Die Geschichte der jüdischen Kommunisten in der DDR* (Cologne: Böhlau, 2000); Joanna Nalewajko-Kulikov, *Obywatel Jidyszlandu: Rzecz o żydowskich komunistach w Polsce* (Warsaw: Instytut Historii PAN, 2009); Jaff Schatz, *The Generation: The Rise and Fall of the Jewish Communists in Poland* (Berkeley: University of California Press, 1991); Marci Shore, *Caviar and Ashes: A Warsaw Generation's Life and Death in Marxism, 1918–1968* (New Haven, CT: Yale University Press, 2006).

3. EZA, 103/27, Heinrich Grüber appeal, October 12, 1956.

4. Eric Mumford, *The CIAM Discourse on Urbanism, 1928–1960* (Cambridge, MA: MIT Press, 2000).

5. Hans Scharoun, "Vortrag anläßlich der Ausstellung 'Berlin plant—erster Bericht' gehalten am 5.9.1946," in *Hans Scharoun: Bauten, Entwürfe, Texte,* ed. Peter Pfankuch (Berlin: Akademie der Künste, 1933), 158.

6. On the similarities of socialist realism and urban modernism, see Katherine Anne Lebow, "Nowa Huta, 1949–1957: Stalinism and the Transformation of Everyday Life in Poland's 'First Socialist City'" (PhD diss., Columbia University, 2002), 52; Karl D. Qualls, *From Ruins to Reconstruction: Urban Identity in Soviet Sevastopol after World War II* (Ithaca, NY: Cornell University Press), 49–55.

7. Edward D. Wynot, Jr., *Warsaw Between the World Wars: Profile of the Capital City in a Developing Land, 1918–1939* (Boulder, CO: East European Monographs, 1983), chapter 5.

8. Robert Fishman, *Urban Utopias in the Twentieth Century* (New York: Basic Books, 1977), 12.

9. Cathleen M. Giustino, *Tearing Down Prague's Jewish Town: Ghetto Clearance and the Legacy of Middle-Class Ethnic Politics* (Boulder, CO: East European Monograph Series, 2003); David Ira Snyder, "The Jewish Question and the Modern Metropolis: Urban Renewal in Prague and Warsaw, 1885–1950" (PhD diss., Princeton University, 2006); Howard Gillette, *Between Justice and Beauty: Race, Planning, and the Failure of Urban Planning in Washington, DC* (Baltimore, MD: Johns Hopkins University Press, 1995); David Schuyler, *A City Transformed: Redevelopment, Race, and Suburbanization in Lancaster, Pennsylvania, 1940–1980* (University Park: Pennsylvania State University Press, 2002).

10. Juan Goytisolo, *Landscapes of War: From Sarajevo to Chechnya,* trans. Peter Bush (San Francisco: City Lights, 2000), 185; wreckage piling skyward is Walter Benjamin's powerful image in "Theses on the Philosophy of History," in *Illuminations,* ed. Hannah Arendt, trans. Harry Zohn (New York: Schocken, 2007), 257–58.

11. Few scholars have analyzed the erasure of Jewish communal sites in postwar Berlin and Warsaw. Peter Reichel has a short section on Berlin, while David Ira Snyder has two chapters on Warsaw. Snyder's work bears some similarity to mine, but he interprets the ghetto's rebuilding as an intrinsic outcome of urban modernism and renewal. I agree with some of his arguments, but I also read Muranów's transformation as a response to the anxiety of the abject past for which discussion of Bohdan Lachert is important (Snyder does not mention Lachert). See Peter Reichel, *Politik mit der Erinnerung: Gedächtnisorte im Streit um die nationalsozialistische Vergangenheit* (Munich: Carl Hanser Verlag, 1995), 202–11; Snyder, "Jewish Question."

12. Harold Hammer-Schenk, *Synagogen in Deutschland: Geschichte einer Baugattung im 19. und 20. Jahrhundert* (Hamburg: Christians, 1981); Carol Herselle Krinsky, *Synagogues of Europe: Architecture, History, Meaning* (Cambridge, MA: MIT Press, 1985); Saskia Coenen Snyder, "Acculturation and Particularism in the Modern City: Synagogue Building and Jewish Identity in Northern Europe" (PhD diss., University of Michigan, 2008).

13. Steven M. Lowenstein, "Jewish Residential Concentration in Post-Emancipation Germany," *LBIYB* 28 (1983): 491.

14. On demography and settlement, see Eleonora Bergman, "The 'Northern District' in Warsaw: A City within a City?," in *Reclaiming Memory: Urban Regeneration in the Historic Jewish Quarters of Central European Cities,* ed. Monika Murzyn-Kupisz and Jacek Purchla (Kraków: International Cultural Centre, 2009), 287–99; Artur Eisenbach, "The Jewish Population in Warsaw at the End of the Nineteenth Century," in *The Jews in Warsaw: A History,* ed. Władysław Bartoszewski and Antony Polonsky (Cambridge: Blackwell, 1991); Barbara Engelking and Jacek Leociak, *The Warsaw Ghetto: A Guide to the Perished City,* trans. Emma Harris (New Haven, CT: Yale University Press, 2009), 1–24; Peter J. Martyn, "The Undefined Town within a Town: A History of Jewish Settlement in the Western Districts of Warsaw," in *Jews,* ed. Bartoszewski and Polonsky, 55–83; Gabriela Zalewska, *Ludność żydowska w Warszawie w okresie międzywojennym* (Warsaw: PWN, 1996). On Polish-Jewish emancipation, see Artur Eisenbach, *The Emancipation of Jews in Poland, 1780–1870,* trans. Janina Dorosz (Cambridge: Blackwell, 1991); Theodore R. Weeks, *From Assimilation to Antisemitism: The "Jewish Question" in Poland, 1850–1914* (DeKalb: Northern Illinois University Press, 2006).

15. On Muranów, see Stephen D. Corrsin, *Warsaw before the First World War: Poles and Jews in the Third City of the Russian Empire, 1880–1914* (Boulder, CO: East European Monographs, 1989); Engelking and Leociak, *Warsaw Ghetto,* 13–24; Bernard Mark, "Literarysze Trybune i Tłomackie 13," *Księga wspomnień 1919–1939* (Warsaw: Czytelnik, 1960); Bernard Singer, *Moje Nalewki* (Warsaw: Czytelnik, 1959).

16. Eleonora Bergman, *"Nie masz bóżnicy powszechnej": Synagogi i domy modlitwy w Warszawie od końca XVIII do początku XXI wieku* (Warsaw: Wydawnictwo DiG, 2007). For an excellent overview of Warsaw's architectural history, including the Bank Square project, see Snyder, "Jewish Question," 304–23.

17. Gershon David Hundert, *Jews in Poland-Lithuania in the Eighteenth Century: A Genealogy of Modernity* (Berkeley: University of California Press, 2004); Weeks, *Assimilation to Antisemitism.*

18. Singer, *Nalewki,* 7.

19. Małgorzata Berezowska, "Obraz demograficzny Warszawy czasu wojny i okupacji," in *Straty Warszawy 1939–1945: Raport* (Warsaw: Urząd Miasta Stołecznego Warszawy, 2005), 283–307. On the Warsaw Uprising, see Włodzimierz Borodziej, *The Warsaw Uprising of 1944,* trans. Barbara Harshav (Madison: University of Wisconsin Press, 2006); Miron Białoszewski, *A Memoir of the Warsaw Uprising,* trans. Madeline Levine (Evanston, IL: Northwestern University Press, 1991); Norman Davies, *Rising '44: The Battle for Warsaw* (New York: Penguin, 2005); Barbara Engelking and Dariusz Libionka, *Żydzi w powstańczej Warszawie* (Warsaw: Centrum Badań nad Zagładą Żydów IFiS PAN, 2009).

20. Krystyna Czarnecka, Grażyna Kurpiewska, Joanna Szapiro-Nowakowska, "Straty w nieruchomościach," in *Straty Warszawy, 373*; Wojciech Fałkowski,

"O mieście, które miało zginąć: Prace nad opisaniem i oszacowaniem strat Warszawy i jej mieszkańców," in *Straty Warszawy,* 12.

21. *Warsaw Accuses* (Washington, DC: Library of the Polish Embassy, 1946), 12 and 37.

22. Adam Miłobędzki, "Polish Architecture in the Period 1918–1939," *Rassegna* 18, no. 65 (1996): 6–13; Jadwiga Roguska, "The Radical Avant-Garde and Modernism in Polish Interwar Architecture," *Rassegna* 18, no. 65 (1996): 14–37.

23. Janusz Zarzycki, "Ewolucja planu urbanistycznego Warszawy w latach 1945–1949," *Warszawa Stolica Polski Ludowej,* vol. 11 (Warsaw: PWN, 1972), 69–112; Stanisław Dziewulski, Adam Kotorbiński, and Wacław Ostrowski, "Zadanie odbudowy Warszawy," *Studia Warszawskie,* vol. 11 (Warsaw: PWN, 1972), 294–317. Initial plans drew on Szymon Syrkus and Jan Chmielewski, *Warszawa funkcjonalna: Przyczynek do urbanizacji regjonu Warszawskiego* (Warsaw: Stowarzyszenie Architektów Polskich, 1935).

24. Stanisław Albrecht, *Warsaw Lives Again!,* exhibition pamphlet (n.p., Committee on Exhibition, 1946).

25. Gropius recounted in Helena Syrkus, "Warszawa oskarża—Warszawa żyje," in *Fragmenty stuletniej historii 1899–1999: Relacje, wspomnienia, refleksje,* ed. Tadeusz Barucki (Warsaw: SARP, 2000), 277–78; Lewis Mumford, "Warsaw Lives," in Albrecht, *Warsaw Lives Again*; Ostrowski quoted in *Straty Warszawy,* 659.

26. David Crowley, "Paris or Moscow? Warsaw Architects and the Image of the Modern City in the 1950s," *Kritika: Explorations in Russian and Eurasian History* 9, no. 4 (Fall 2008): 769–98; David Crowley, *Warsaw* (London: Reaktion, 2003).

27. Bolesław Bierut, *Six-Year Plan for the Reconstruction of Warsaw* (Warsaw: Książka i Wiedza, 1951), 125 and 77.

28. The most thorough contemporary articulation of socialist realism in the built environment was Edmund Goldzamt, *Architektura zespołów śródmiejskich i problemy dziedzictwa* (Warsaw: PWN, 1956). See Vladimir Paperny, *Architecture in the Age of Stalin: Culture Two,* trans. John Hill and Roann Barris (New York: Cambridge University Press, 2002). On the Stalinist period more broadly, see Dariusz Jarosz, *Polacy a stalinizm, 1948–1956* (Warsaw: PAN, 2000); Padraic Kenney, *Rebuilding Poland: Workers and Communists, 1945–1950* (Ithaca, NY: Cornell University Press, 1997).

29. Bohdan Rymaszewski, *Klucze ochrony zabytków w Polsce* (Warsaw: Ośrodek Dokumentacji Zabytków, 1992), 56–66.

30. "Piękno Warszawy której już nie ma, a którą wskrzesimy," *Stolica,* November 3, 1946.

31. Ibid.

32. Jan Zachwatowicz, "Program i zasady konserwacji zabytków," *Biuletyn Historii Sztuki i Kultury* 8, no. 1-2 (1946), 48.

33. APW, BOS, file 2062; Jan Zachwatowicz, "Walka o Kulturę," *Kronika Odbudowy Warszawy,* September 1, 1946.

34. Restorative nostalgia from Svetlana Boym, *The Future of Nostalgia* (New York: Basic Books, 2002); Walter Benjamin, "The Work of Art in the Age of Its Technological Reproducibility," in *The Work of Art in the Age of Its Technological Reproducibility and Other Writings on Media,* ed. Michael W. Jennings, Brigid Doherty, and Thomas Y. Levin (Cambridge, MA: Harvard University Press, 2008).

35. Stanisław Ossowski, "Odbudowa stolicy w świetle zagadnień społecznych," in *Dzieła,* vol. 3, ed. Nina Assorodobraj and Stanisław Ossowski (Warsaw: PWN, 1967): 412, 395, 398, and 395.

36. Stanisław Ossowski, "Na tle wydarzeń Kieleckich," *Kuźnica* 38, no. 55 (1946): 5.

37. APW, BOS, 244, list of historic monuments, 1945.

38. "1.5 miliona cegieł w dwa dni: Raźnie pracuje się na Muranowie gdy jest muzyka i bufet," *ŻW,* September 4, 1949; "Z cegieł Muranowa powstanie osiedle: Młodzież zgłasza się do pracy," *ŻW,* September 6, 1949; "Akademicy pracują na Muranowie: 130 cegieł 'wydobycia' na głowę," *ŻW,* October 24, 1949.

39. Vladka Meed, *On Both Sides of the Wall,* trans. Steven Meed (New York: Holocaust Library, 1993), 262; Jacob Pat, *Ashes and Fire,* trans. Leo Steinberg (New York: International Universities Press, 1947), 13.

40. Adolf Berman, "Rocznica wielkiego czynu," *Przełom,* April 19, 1948; "Getto warszawskie," *Głos Ludu,* April 17, 1945. For an excellent analysis, see Marci Shore, "Język, pamięć i rewolucyjna awangarda: Kształtowanie historii powstania w Getcie Warszawskim w latach 1944–1950," *Biuletyn Żydowskiego Instytutu Historycznego* no. 4 (December 1998): 44–61; Marci Shore, "Children of the Revolution: Communism, Zionism, and the Berman Brothers," *JSS* 10, no. 3 (2004): 23–86.

41. "Zarys nowej Warszawy: Referat kierownika BOS inż. Piotrowskiego na VII sesji KRN," *ŻW,* May 23, 1945; APW, *Biuletyn Wewnętrzny BOS* January 31, 1946, 3.

42. Albrecht, *Warsaw Lives Again!,* 12.

43. On the rubble problem, see "Problem gruzu," *Stolica,* May 23, 1948; "Co zrobić z gruzem?," *Stolica,* July 18, 1948. For the first plans, see "Plan odbudowy Warszawy: Muranów," *Skarpa Warszawska* no. 26 (1946): 2; "Muranów—dzielnica mieszkaniowa," *Architektura* 17, no. 1 (1947): 8–11.

44. APW, BOS, 2059, Bohdan Lachert, "Przemówienie wygłoszone na zebraniu pracowników BOS," January 7, 1946. My thanks to Jacek Leociak for pointing this speech out to me.

45. Anna Wiktoria Benesz, "Architekt Bohdan Lachert: Monografia twórczości do roku 1939" (MA thesis, Instytut Historii Sztuki, Uniwersytet Warszawski, 1980).

46. Bohdan Lachert, "Muranów—Dzielnica mieszkaniowa," *Architektura* 19, no. 5 (1949): 129 and 132.

47. ŻIH, CKŻP, 308/217, Lachert report, April 28, 1948; Aniela Daszewska, "...a na Muranowie...," *Wieś* no. 37 (1950), 6. On the monument, see James

Young, *The Texture of Memory: Holocaust Memorials and Meaning* (New Haven, CT: Yale University Press, 1994), 155–84.

48. ŻIH, CKŻP, 308/217, Lachert report, April 28, 1948. For an excellent elaboration of noncompetitive, multidirectional memories to which my remarks here are indebted, see Michael Rothberg, *Multidirectional Memory: Remembering the Holocaust in the Age of Decolonization* (Stanford, CA: Stanford University Press, 2009). A similar multidirectional flow of memory is also evident in the case of early postwar Yugoslavia. See Emil Kerenji, "Jewish Citizens of Socialist Yugoslavia: Politics of Jewish Identity in a Socialist State, 1944–1974" (PhD diss., University of Michigan, 2008), chapter 6.

49. Jerzy Wierzbicki, "Dzielnica mieszkaniowa Muranów (Próba krytyki)," *Architektura* 22, no. 9 (1952): 225, 222, and 224; Bohdan Lachert, "Muranów z doświadczeń 3 lat prac urbanistyczno-architektonicznych," *Miasto* no. 9 (September 1952): 29–32.

50. Klaus-Peter Friedrich, "Kontaminierte Erinnerung: Vom Einfluss der Kriegspropaganda auf das Gedenken an die Warschauer Aufstände von 1943 und 1944," *Zeitschrift für Ostmitteleuropa-Forschung* 55, no. 3 (2006): 395–432; Jacek Leociak, "Zraniona pamięć (Rocznice powstania w getcie warszawskim w prasie polskiej, 1944–1989)," in *Literatura polska wobec Zagłady*, ed. Alina Brodzka-Wald, Dorota Krawczyńska, and Jacek Leociak (Warsaw: ŻIH, 2000), 29–49.

51. "W ósmą rocznicę powstania w getcie," *TL*, April 19, 1951.

52. *ŻW*, September 1, 1949.

53. "Architekci dawnej Warszawy," *Stolica*, August 8, 1948; "Gruba Kaśka i Tłomackie," *Stolica*, August 13, 1961.

54. APW, 253, CKŻP to Office for Conservation, January 31, 1949; response to CKŻP, March 9, 1949; APW, 253, Ministry of Building to Ministry of Culture, March 30, 1951; Janusz Sujecki, "Fundament przetrwał," *Spotkania z Zabytkami* no. 8 (2003): 33.

55. Quoted in Benedikt Goebel, ed., *Der Umbau Alt-Berlins zum modernen Stadtzentrum: Planungs-, Bau- und Besitzgeschichte des historischen Berliner Stadtkerns im 19. und 20. Jahrhundert* (Berlin: Braun, 2003), 272.

56. Thomas Childers, "'Facilis descensus averni est': The Allied Bombing of Germany and the Issue of German Suffering," *CEH* 38, no. 1 (2005): 75–105; Elizabeth Heineman, "The Hour of the Woman: Memories of Germany's 'Crisis Years' and West German National Identity," *AHR* 101, no. 2 (1996): 354–95; Ina Merkel, . . . *und Du, Frau an der Werkbank: Die DDR in den 50er Jahren* (Berlin: Elefanten, 1990), 31–47; Mary Nolan, "Air Wars, Memory Wars: Germans as Victims during the Second World War," *CEH* 38, no. 1 (2005): 7–40.

57. On Cold War Berlin, see Paul Steege, *Black Market, Cold War: Everyday Life in Berlin, 1946–1949* (New York: Cambridge University Press, 2009). On its reconstruction, see Brian Ladd, *Ghosts of Berlin: Confronting German History in the Urban Landscape* (Chicago: University of Chicago Press, 1998).

58. Hans Scharoun, "Vortrag anlässlich der Ausstellung 'Berlin plant—erster Bericht,'" in *Hans Scharoun: Bauten, Entwürfe, Texte* (Berlin: Akademie der Künste, 1974); Walter Moest, *Der Zehlendorfer Plan: Ein Vorschlag zum Wiederaufbau Berlins* (Berlin: Druckhaus Tempelhof, 1946); Frank Werner, *Stadtplanung Berlin: Theorie und Realität* (Berlin: Kiepert, 1976).

59. Walter Ulbricht, *Der Fünfjahrplan und die Perspektiven der Volkswirtschaft: Referat und Schlusswort auf dem III. Parteitag der SED* (Berlin: Dietz, 1950), 49.

60. Quoted in Goebel, *Umbau Alt-Berlins,* 273–74.

61. Werner Durth, Jörn Düwel, and Niels Gutschow, *Ostkreuz-Aufbau: Architektur und Städtebau der DDR,* vol. 2 (Frankfurt am Main: Campus Verlag, 1998).

62. Gerhard Puhlmann, *Die Stalinallee: Nationales Aufbauprogramm, 1952* (Berlin: Verlag der Nation, 1953); *Die Stalinallee—die erste sozialistische Straße der Hauptstadt Deutschlands Berlin* (Berlin: Deutsche Bauakademie, 1952).

63. Quoted in Johann Friedrich Geist and Klaus Klüvers, *Das Berliner Mietshaus 1945–1989* (Munich: Prestel Verlag, 1989), 354.

64. Rolf Schwedler, "Der Wiederaufbau in West-Berlin," in *Die unzerstörbare Stadt: Die raumpolitische Lage und Bedeutung Berlins* (Cologne: Carl Heymanns Verlag, 1953), 189; Jeffrey M. Diefendorf, *In the Wake of War: The Reconstruction of German Cities after World War II* (New York: Oxford University Press, 1993), 54–66.

65. G. Schneevoigt, "10 Jahre Wiederaufbau in Berlin," *Berliner Bauwirtschaft* 11, no. 1 (1960): 8–11; Dieter Hanauske, *Bauen, bauen, bauen . . . ! Die Wohnungspolitik in Berlin (West) 1945–1961* (Berlin: Akademie Verlag, 1995), 366–419.

66. *Die Stadt von morgen: Gegenwartsprobleme für alle* (Berlin: Verlag Gebr. Mann, 1959), 32. See Johanna Hartmann, "'Aber wenn die Frau aus ihren Grenzen tritt, ist es für sie noch viel gefährlicher': Geschlechtermodelle für die Stadt von morgen," in *Die Stadt von morgen: Beiträge zu einer Archäologie des Hansaviertels Berlin,* ed. Annette Maechtel and Kathrin Peters (Cologne: Walther König, 2008), 200–209.

67. Gerhard Jobst, "Ordnung im Städtebau," *Bauwelt* 44, no. 3 (1953): 48.

68. Quoted in Hanauske, *Bauen,* 356.

69. Peter Müller, *Symbolsuche: Die Ost-Berliner Zentrumsplanung zwischen Repräsentation und Agitation* (Berlin: Gebr. Mann Verlag, 2005), 102 and 171.

70. ACJ, 5 A 1, nr. 001, Jewish Community to Soviet Central Command, December 12, 1945.

71. LAB, E Rep. 200–22, nr. 100, Siegmund Weltlinger, "Die Jüdische Gemeinde zu Berlin—ihre Lage und ihre Wünsche," March 20, 1946.

72. AJDC-New York, 45/54, 377, JDC Berlin Quarterly Report, June 1947. On postwar Berlin Jewish life, see Atina Grossmann, *Jews, Germans, and Allies: Close Encounters in Occupied Germany* (Princeton, NJ: Princeton University Press, 2007); Angelika Königseder, *Flucht nach Berlin: Jüdische Displaced Persons, 1945–1948* (Berlin: Metropol, 1998).

73. LAB, B Rep. 002, nr. 4860, Jewish Community to Weltlinger, November 28, 1946.

74. AJDC-New York, 45/54, 376, JDC Berlin to New York, March 9, 1949.

75. BA (SAPMO), DY 30/IV/2.027, nr. 20, report, February 28, 1947. For the U.S. reports, see AJDC-New York, 45/54, no. 303, OMGUS, "The Survival of Anti-semitism," May 16, 1947, and "Prejudice and Antisemitism," May 22, 1948.

76. ACJ, 5 A 1, nr. 0126, Jewish Community to SMA, November 4, 1947.

77. LAB, B Rep. 002, nr. 4866, Weltlinger to SMA, October 25, 1945.

78. LAB, B Rep. 002, nr. 4866, Jewish Community to Weltlinger, July 1, 1946.

79. ACJ, 5 B 1, nr. 0126, Jewish Community to Magistrat, July 23, 1946.

80. ACJ, 5 B 1, nr. 0126, decision of OMGUS, July 26, 1946; LAB, B Rep. 002, nr. 4866, Bd. II, Jewish Community to Weltlinger, May 4, 1948.

81. LAB, C Rep. 101–04, nr. 64, Jewish Community to Magistrat, January 21, 1947. Quote from LAB, C Rep. 101–04, nr. 64, mayor's conversation with Jewish Community, January 31, 1947.

82. LAB, C Rep. 101–04, nr. 64, city council decision, February 16, 1948.

83. ACJ, 5 B 1, nr. 505, Jewish Community request, June 15, 1952; LAB, C Rep. 100–05, nr. 872, Magistrat decision, November 5, 1952.

84. ACJ, 5 B 1, nr. 496, Jewish Community to Magistrat, June 15, 1953; BA (SAPMO), DY 30/ IV 2/14, nr. 249, Jewish Community to Berlin Regional Director of the SED, October 21, 1953.

85. BA (SAPMO), DY 30/IV 2/14, nr. 249, minutes of meeting, December 12, 1955; BA (SAPMO), DY 30/IV 2/14, nr. 249, memo of Berlin Regional Director's Office of the SED, July 6, 1956. See also Lothar Mertens, *Davidstern unter Hammer und Zirkel: Die Jüdischen Gemeinden in der SBZ/DDR und ihre Behandlung durch Partei und Staat, 1945-1990* (Hildesheim: Olms, 1997), 160–64.

86. BA (SAPMO), DY 30/IV 2/14, nr. 249, memo of Berlin Regional Director's Office of the SED, July 6, 1956.

87. "Bilder aus der Vergangenheit: Ein Besuch auf dem alten Berliner jüdischen Friedhof in der Schönhauser Allee," *Jüdische Illustrierte* 7, no. 3 (1957): 2.

88. LAB, C Rep. 131–12, nr. 27, notes on meetings, June 22, 1959 and April 13, 1964.

89. LAB, C Rep. 104, nr. 290, memo of the Institute for Historic Preservation, December 17, 1955; LAB, C Rep. 104, nr. 290, Institute for Historic Preservation to Jewish Community, October 31, 1957; LAB, C Rep. 104, nr. 290, minutes of meeting, January 13, 1965.

90. BA, DO 4/1337, Jewish Community to Minister of Church Affairs, March 7, 1961.

91. LAB, B Rep. 207, nr. 143, police report, April 17, 1953.

92. Ibid., Health Office to Building Inspection, January 14, 1954.

93. Ibid., JRSO to Building Inspection, January 5, 1954.

94. Ibid., Building Inspection to district mayor, April 15, 1954.

95. LAB, B Rep. 002, nr. 9789, Building Inspection to Property Office, February 10, 1955.

96. LAB, B Rep. 207, nr. 143, Reparations Office to Senator for Building, February 22, 1956.

97. LAB, B Rep. 002, nr. 9789, Urban Planning to Property Office, May 15, 1954.

98. LAB, B Rep. 002, nr. 8643, *Drucksachen des Abgeordnetenhauses von Berlin,* June 30, 1956.

99. "Fest der Versöhnung—Tag des Neubeginns!," *Allgemeine Wochenzeitung der Juden in Deutschland,* November 15, 1957.

100. "Begegnung mit Leo Baeck," *Aufbau,* July 13, 1945.

101. Interview by Michael Brenner, *Nach dem Holocaust: Juden in Deutschland, 1945–50* (Munich: Beck, 1995), 148.

102. Text reprinted in Hans-Gerd Sellenthin, *Geschichte der Juden in Berlin und des Gebäudes Fasanenstraße 79/80: Festschrift anläßlich der Einweihung des Jüdischen Gemeindehauses* (Berlin: Jüdische Gemeinde zu Berlin, 1959), 126.

103. "Enlightened knowledge" from Michael Geyer, "The Politics of Memory in Contemporary Germany," in *Radical Evil,* ed. Joan Copjec (New York: Verso, 1996), 170.

104. Ernst Reuter, "RIAS-Ansprache zum 13. Jahrestag der 'Reichskristallnacht' am 9. November 1951," in Ernst Reuter, *Schriften, Reden,* vol. 4 (Berlin: Propyläen, 1972), 474. See Jeffrey Herf, *Divided Memory: The Nazi Past in the Two Germanys* (Cambridge, MA: Harvard University Press, 1997), chapters 7–8; Jay Geller, *Jews in Post-Holocaust Germany* (New York: Cambridge University Press, 2005), chapter 4.

105. Ernst Reuter, "Ansprache auf der Gedenkfeier des Bezirksamtes Neukölln zum 10. Jahrestag der Vernichtung des Warschauer Ghettos am 19. April 1953," in Ernst Reuter, *Schriften, Reden,* vol. 4 (Berlin: Propyläen, 1975), 714–15.

106. Willy Brandt, "Die Judenverfolgungen in Deutschland," January 1, 1938 in *Berliner Ausgabe,* vol. 1 (Bonn: Dietz, 2000), 392–97; Willy Brandt, "Zur Nachkriegspolitik der deutschen Sozialisten," July 1944 in *Berliner Ausgabe,* vol. 2 (Bonn: Dietz, 2000), esp. 188–89.

107. *Berlin: Chronik der Jahre 1957–58: Schriftenreihe zur Berliner Zeitgeschichte,* vol. 8 (Berlin: Heinz Spitzig, 1974), 323–24.

108. Ibid., 323.

109. "Grundstein für jüdisches Gemeindehaus," *DT,* November 11, 1957.

110. LAB, B Rep. 002, nr. 9792, Jewish Community to Amrehn, July 4, 1958.

111. Ibid., Jewish Community to Amrehn, May 15, 1958.

112. LAB, B Rep. 202, nr. 1330, JRSO to Building Inspection, February 22, 1955.

113. LAB, C Rep. 101–04, nr. 28, undated but probably in 1949.

114. Correspondence on the synagogue in LAB, B Rep. 211, nr. 1865.

115. Julia Kristeva, *Powers of Horror: An Essay on Abjection,* trans. Leon S. Roudiez (New York: Columbia University Press, 1982), 4; ŻIH, CKŻP, 308/217, Lachert report, April 28, 1948.

116. Barbara Engelking, *Holocaust and Memory: The Experience of the Holocaust and Its Consequences,* trans. Emma Harris (New York: Leicester University Press, 2001); Jonathan Huener, *Auschwitz, Poland, and the Politics of Commemoration, 1945–1979* (Athens: Ohio University Press, 2003); Michael C. Steinlauf, *Bondage to the Dead: Poland and the Memory of the Holocaust* (Syracuse, NY: Syracuse University Press, 1997).

117. Sarah Farmer, *Martyred Village: Commemorating the 1944 Massacre at Oradour-sur-Glane* (Berkeley: University of California Press, 1999).

118. W. E. B. Du Bois, "The Negro and the Warsaw Ghetto," *Jewish Life* (May 1952): 15. For an opposite interpretation that to me misreads the redemptive memory politics of Warsaw's reconstruction as I have presented them here, see Rothberg, *Multidirectional Memory,* 127.

119. Frank Biess, *Homecomings: Returning POWs and the Legacy of Defeat on Postwar Germany* (Princeton, NJ: Princeton University Press, 2006); Herf, *Divided Memory;* Dagmar Herzog, *Sex after Fascism: Memory and Morality in Twentieth-Century Germany* (Princeton, NJ: Princeton University Press, 2005); Norbert Frei, *1945 und wir: Das Dritte Reich im Bewusstsein der Deutschen* (Munich: Deutscher Taschenbuch Verlag, 2005); Wulf Kansteiner, *In Pursuit of German Memory: History, Television, and Politics after Auschwitz* (Athens: Ohio University Press, 2006); Herbert Marcuse, *The Legacies of Dachau: The Uses and Abuses of a Concentration Camp, 1933–2001* (New York: Cambridge University Press, 2001); Robert G. Moeller, *War Stories: The Search for a Usable Past in the Federal Republic of Germany* (Berkeley: University of California Press, 2001).

120. Germans have long perceived *Kristallnacht* as a central moment in Nazi anti-Jewish policy. Harald Schmid, *Erinnern an den "Tag der Schuld": Das Novemberpogrom von 1938 in der deutschen Geschichtspolitik* (Hamburg: Ergebnisse, 2001); Harald Schmid, *Antifaschismus und Judenverfolgung: Die "Reichskristallnacht" als politischer Gedenktag in der DDR* (Göttingen: V&R Unipress, 2004).

3. Erasing the Jewish Past

1. Hanno Rauterberg, "Ein Land auf Abriss," *Die Zeit,* January 11, 2007.

2. Józef E. Dutkiewicz, "Sentymentalizm, Autentyzm, Automatyzm," *Ochrona Zabytków* 14, nos. 1–2 (1961): 5. On postwar historic preservation, see Sigrid Brandt, *Geschichte der Denkmalpflege in der SBZ/DDR: Dargestellt an Beispielen aus dem sächsischen Raum, 1945–1961* (Berlin: Lukas Verlag, 2003); Brian William Campbell, "Resurrected from the Ruins, Turning to the Past: Historic Preservation in the SBZ/GDR, 1945–1990" (PhD diss., University of Rochester, 2005);

Burkhard Körner, *Zwischen Bewahren und Gestalten: Denkmalpflege nach 1945* (Petersberg: Imhof, 2000); Bohdan Rymaszewski, *Klucze ochrony zabytków w Polsce* (Warsaw: Ośrodek Dokumentacji Zabytków, 1992); Andrzej Tomaszewski, ed., *Ochrona i konserwacja dóbr kultury w Polsce, 1944–1989* (Warsaw: Ministerstwo Kultury i Sztuki, 1996).

3. Jan Zachwatowicz, "Program i zasady konserwacji zabytków," *Biuletyn Historii Sztuki i Kultury* 8, no. 1 (1946): 5.

4. Zbigniew Mazur, *Wokół niemieckiego dziedzictwa kulturowego na Ziemiach Zachodnich i Północnych: Praca zbiorowa* (Poznań: Instytut Zachodni, 1997); Zbigniew Mazur, *O adaptacji niemieckiego dziedzictwa kulturowego na Ziemiach Zachodnich i Północnych* (Poznań: Instytut Zachodni, 2001); Gregor Thum, *Die fremde Stadt: Breslau 1945* (Berlin: Siedler, 2003); Marek Zybura, *Pomniki niemieckiej przeszłości: Dziedzictwo kultury niemieckiej na Ziemiach Zachodnich i Północnych Polski* (Warsaw: Fundacja CSM, 1999). On historic preservation and its ties to national identity, see Susan Crane, *Collecting and Historical Consciousness in Early Nineteenth-Century Germany* (Ithaca, NY: Cornell University Press, 2000); Joshua Hagen, *Preservation, Tourism and Nationalism: The Jewel of the German Past* (Burlington, VT: Ashgate, 2006); Rudy Koshar, *Germany's Transient Pasts: Preservation and National Memory in the Twentieth Century* (Chapel Hill: University of North Carolina Press, 1998); Jerzy Frycz, *Restauracja i konserwacja zabytków architektury w Polsce w latach 1795–1918* (Warsaw: PWN, 1975); Winfried Speitkamp, *Die Verwaltung der Geschichte: Denkmalpflege und Staat in Deutschland, 1871–1933* (Göttingen: Vandenhoeck & Ruprecht, 1996). On national historic consciousness more broadly, see Celia Applegate, *A Nation of Provincials: The German Idea of Heimat* (Berkeley: University of California Press, 1990); Alon Confino, *The Nation as a Local Metaphor: Württemberg, Imperial Germany, and National Memory, 1871–1918* (Chapel Hill: University of North Carolina Press, 1997); Peter Fritzsche, *Stranded in the Present: Modern Time and the Melancholy of History* (Cambridge, MA: Harvard University Press, 2004).

5. Maurice Halbwachs, *The Collective Memory,* trans. Francis J. Ditter, Jr., and Vida Yazdi Ditter (New York: Harper & Row, 1980), 140.

6. "Die Einweihung der neuen Synagoge zu Essen," *Essener Volkszeitung,* September 27, 1913. See also Timo Saalmann, "Die Einweihung der Synagoge am Steeler Tor 1913: Bürgerliche Festkultur und Lebensführung der Essener Juden," *Essener Beiträge: Beiträge zur Geschichte der Stadt und Stift Essen* 119 (2006): 484.

7. Paul Mendes-Flohr, *German Jews: A Dual Identity* (New Haven, CT: Yale University Press, 1999), 1.

8. "Die Einweihung der neuen Synagoge zu Essen," 457–98.

9. "Edmund Körners Synagoge in Essen (Ruhr)," *Die Kirche* no. 12 (1915): 109.

10. Richard Klapheck, *Die neue Synagoge in Essen a. d. Ruhr, erbaut von Professor Edmund Körner* (Berlin: Ernst Wasmuth, 1914), 5–6.

11. Quoted in Michael Zimmermann, "Die 'Kristallnacht' 1938 in Essen," in *Entrechtung und Selbsthilfe: Zur Geschichte der Juden in Essen unter dem Nationalsozialismus* (Essen: Klartext, 1994), 69.

12. Klaus Wisotzky, "Die Jahre der Gewalt—Essen 1914 bis 1945," in *Essen: Geschichte einer Stadt,* ed. Ulrich Borsdorf (Bottrop/Essen: Pomp, 2002), 461–65.

13. Wilhelm Godde, "Wahrnehmung eines Monuments im Herzen der Stadt," in *Ein Haus, das bleibt: Aus Anlass 20 Jahre Alte Synagoge Essen* (Essen: Klartext, 2000), 33.

14. Wisotzky, "Jahre der Gewalt."

15. ESA, Sturm Kegel, "Das Zukunftsbild des Stadtkernes Essen. Erläuterungen zum Entwurfsplan vom 1. Februar 1941."

16. ESA, Neuordnungsplan von 1949; J. W. Hollatz, "Der Wiederaufbau Essens und seine wirtschaftliche und kulturelle Zielsetzung," *Der Bau und die Bauindustrie* no. 9 (1954): 208–15.

17. *Essen: Aus Trümmern und Schutt wächst eine neue Stadt: 10 Jahre Planung und Aufbau der Metropole an der Ruhr* (Essen: Die Stadt Essen, 1956), 29.

18. Andreas Benedict, "Das Amerika-Haus in Essen: Architektur der 50er Jahre zwischen Tradition und Moderne," *Essener Beiträge: Beiträge zur Geschichte der Stadt und Stift Essen* 105 (1993): 102–209.

19. *Essen: Trümmern,* 78.

20. Ibid., 36.

21. Wilhelm Lücke, "Die Zerstörung des Münsters am Hellweg," *Das Münster am Hellweg: Mitteilungsblatt des Vereins für die Erhaltung des Essener Münsters* 5 (1951): 44–46; Walther Zimmermann, *Das Münster zu Essen* (Essen: Fredebeul und Koenen, 1956).

22. ESA, Kegel, "Zukunftsbild," 48–49.

23. "Was wird aus der Synagoge?" *Rheinische Post,* May 19, 1948, in ESA, B4 (Zeitungsausschnitte).

24. Ibid.

25. "Beschädigung des Ehrenmals vor der Synagoge," *Stenografischer Bericht über die Sitzung des Rates der Stadt Essen,* April 29, 1949.

26. Quotes respectively from "Vor 17 Jahren brannte die Synagoge," *Ruhr-Nachrichten,* November 9, 1955; "Wird Synagoge aufgebaut?," *Essener Tageblatt,* May 3, 1953, in ESA, B4 (Zeitungsausschnitte).

27. "Ist die Essener Synagoge dem Verfall preisgegeben? Schild sagt: 'Einsturzgefahr!'—Jüdische Gemeinde macht Vorschläge," *NRZ,* June 18, 1955, in ESA, B4 (Zeitungsausschnitte).

28. "Ein Zaun soll Fußgänger schützen," *NRZ,* May 24, 1957.

29. "Ist die Essener Synagoge dem Verfall preisgegeben?," *NRZ,* June 18, 1955; "Problem Synagoge wird immer dringlicher," *WAZ,* August 23, 1956; "Was wird aus der Synagoge," *Rheinische Post,* May 19, 1948.

30. "Vor 17 Jahren brannte die Synagoge," *Ruhr-Nachrichten,* November 9, 1955.

31. ESA, 144, nr. 1571, court decision, July 10, 1953; ZA, B 1/7, nr. 56, memo on communal property in Essen, January 25, 1956.

32. ESA, 143, nr. 10798, JTC to Essen, June 14, 1956.

33. "Vor 17 Jahren brannte die Synagoge," *Ruhr-Nachrichten,* November 9, 1955; "Problem Synagoge wird immer dringlicher," *WAZ,* August 23, 1956; "Synagoge könnte Museum werden," *NRZ,* September 17, 1959; "Was macht die Stadt mit der angekauften Synagoge?," *Ruhr-Nachrichten,* September 15, 1959.

34. ESA, 1001, nr. 249, memo of chief municipal director, February 3, 1960.

35. ESA, 144, nr. 5543, memo, November 6, 1959; ESA, 1001, nr. 249, letter from Hundhausen to association members, February 16, 1960.

36. *Niederschrift über die Sitzung des Ältestenrates,* February 13, 1960.

37. ESA, 1001, nr. 249, Jewish Community to Essen, March 10, 1960.

38. ESA, 101, nr. 249, bishop to mayor, March 31, 1960 and city director to bishop, April 11, 1960. For other letters, see ESA, 1001, nr. 249; BAK, B 136, nr. 5864, Interior Ministry to Arbeitskreis Essen der Gesellschaft für christlich-jüdische Zusammenarbeit, May 19, 1960; Karl Johannes Heyer, "Die minimale Lösung," *Ruhrwort,* December 9, 1961.

39. Letters to the editor in *Ruhr-Nachrichten,* February 26, 1960; Gerhard Krupp, "Richtet ein Zeichen auf! Keine Profanierung des alten Gotteshauses," *Ruhr-Nachrichten,* February 26, 1960.

40. ESA, 1001, nr. 249, Landesverband to Haus Industrieform, November 7, 1960.

41. ESA, 1001, nr. 249, circular for board of directors, December 22, 1960.

42. Karl Marx, "Synagoge wird Ausstellungszentrum: Eine würdige Lösung für die ehemalige Große Essener Synagoge," *Allgemeine Wochenzeitung der Juden in Deutschland,* March 4, 1961.

43. "Die Kuppel ist verschwunden," *Ruhr-Nachrichten,* July 20, 1961, ESA, B4 (Zeitungsausschnitte).

44. ESA, 1001, nr. 249, Schütz to Hundhausen, August 9, 1961.

45. ESA, 143, nr. 10798, speech by Schütz, November 24, 1961.

46. "Bessere Lösung gab es nicht: Fast alle Besucherstimmen loben das neue Haus Industrieform," *NRZ,* August 21, 1963.

47. For example, *Generalstadtplan Essen* (Stuttgart: Mairs Geographisher Verlag, 1971); *Amtlicher Stadtplan Essen* (Essen: Stadtvermessungsamt, 1970).

48. Till van Rahden, *Juden und andere Breslauer: Die Beziehungen zwischen Juden, Protestanten und Katholiken in einer deutschen Großstadt von 1860 bis 1925* (Göttingen: Vandenhoeck & Ruprecht, 2000).

49. Carol Herselle Krinsky, *Synagogues of Europe: Architecture, History, Memory* (Cambridge, MA: MIT Press, 1985), 325–26.

50. Erläuterungsbericht Opplers, September 28, 1865, quoted in Harold Hammer-Schenk, *Synagogen in Deutschland: Geschichte einer Baugattung im 19. und 20. Jahrhundert* (Hamburg: Christians, 1981), 215.

51. "Mitteilungen über Bauprojekte und Bauausführungen," *Deutsche Bauzeitung* 1, no. 4 (1867): 29.

52. Walter Tausk, *Breslauer Tagebuch: 1933–1940* (Leipzig: Reclam, 1995), 165 and 172.

53. Leszek Ziątkowski, *Dzieje Żydów we Wrocławiu* (Wrocław: Wydawnictwo Dolnośląskie, 2000), 113.

54. *Niemcy w Polsce, 1945–1950,* vols. 1–4 (Warsaw: Neriton, 2000). See also Philipp Ther and Ana Siljak, eds., *Redrawing Nations: Ethnic Cleansing in East-Central Europe, 1944–1948* (New York: Oxford University Press, 2000); Stanisław Ciesielski, ed., *Przesiedlenie ludności polskiej z Kresów Wschodnich do Polski, 1944–1947* (Warsaw: PAN, 1999); Tomasz Szarota, *Osadnictwo miejskie na Dolnym Śląsku w latach 1945–1948* (Warsaw: PWN, 1969).

55. Flyer of the Central Committee for Resettlement, May 1945, reprinted in Szarota, *Osadnictwo*, 81.

56. Jakub Egit, "Rok życia żydowskiego na Dolnym Śląsku," *Nowe Życie,* July 15, 1946.

57. Bożena Szaynok, *Ludność żydowska na Dolnym Śląsku 1945–1950* (Wrocław: Wydawnictwo Uniwersytetu Wrocławskiego, 2000).

58. NA-College Park, RG 407/368/1518, report on Poland, August 2, 1946.

59. Numbers from Ewa Waszkiewicz, *Kongregacja Wyznania Mojżeszowego na Dolnym Śląsku na tle polityki wyznaniowej Polskiej Rzeczypospolitej Ludowej, 1945–1968* (Wrocław: Wydawnictwo Uniwersytetu Wrocławskiego, 1999), 32, 37, and 141; Szaynok, *Ludność,* 51 and 194.

60. Quoted in Padraic Kenney, *Rebuilding Poland: Workers and Communists, 1945–1950* (Ithaca, NY: Cornell University Press, 1997), 137–38. For a vivid analysis of the immediate postwar years, see ibid., chapter 3.

61. Kirył Sosnowski and Mieczysław Suchocki, eds., *Dolny Śląsk,* 2 vols. (Poznań: Instytut Zachodni, 1948); Wacław Długoborski, Józef Gierowski, and Karol Maleczyński, *Dzieje Wrocławia do roku 1807* (Warsaw: PWN, 1958). See Włodzimierz Borodziej, "'Ostforschung' aus der Sicht der polnischen Geschichtsschreibung," *Zeitschrift für Ostmitteleuropa-Forschung* 46, no. 3 (1997): 405–26; Jörg Hackmann, "Strukturen und Institutionen der polnischen Westforschung, 1918–1960," *Zeitschrift für Ostmitteleuropa-Forschung* 50, no. 2 (2001): 230–55.

62. Thum, *Stadt,* chapters 7 and 10. The following short discussion on the city's reconstruction comes from my research as well as information from these two excellent chapters.

63. Quoted in Marcin Bukowski, *Wrocław z lat 1945–1952: Zniszczenia i dzieło odbudowy* (Warsaw: PWN, 1985), 5.

64. Emil Kaliski, "Wrocław wrócił do Polski," *Skarpa Warszawska,* March 3, 1946.

65. APWr, 239, report on rebuilding activity for 1945–48. On the reconstruction of the old town, see Małgorzata Olechnowicz, "Architektura na obszarze

wrocławskiego starego miasta po 1945 roku, jej uzależnienie od planów zagospo-
darowania przestrzennego i przemian budownictwa" (PhD diss., University of
Wrocław, 1997). My thanks to Dr. Olechnowicz for kindly sending a copy of her
dissertation to me. See also Bukowski, *Wrocław;* Edmund Małachowicz, *Stare
miasto we Wrocławiu: Rozwój urbanistyczno-architektoniczny, zniszczenia wojenne
i odbudowa* (Warsaw: PWN, 1985); Edmund Małachowicz, *Wrocław na wyspach:
Rozwój urbanistyczny i architektoniczny* (Wrocław: Ossolineum, 1992); Thum,
Stadt, chapter 10.

66. Gwido Chmarzyński, "W aureoli gotyckich kościołów," in Sosnowski and
Suchowski, *Dolny Śląsk,* vol. 2, 67.

67. Richard Blanke, *Prussian Poland in the German Empire, 1871–1900* (New
York: Columbia University Press, 1981); Peter Brock, "Polish Nationalism," in
Nationalism in Eastern Europe, ed. Peter F. Sugar and Ivo John Lederer (Seattle:
University of Washington Press, 1994), 310–72; Brian Porter, *When Nationalism
Began to Hate: Imagining Modern Politics in Nineteenth-Century Poland* (New
York: Oxford University Press, 2000); Andrzej Walicki, "Intellectual Elites and
the Vicissitudes of 'Imagined Nation' in Poland," in *Intellectuals and the Articula-
tion of the Nation,* ed. Richard Grigor Suny and Michael D. Kennedy (Ann Arbor:
University of Michigan Press, 1999), 259–87; Marcin Zaremba, *Komunizm, legity-
mizacja, nacjonalizm: Nacjonalistyczna legitymizacja władzy komunistycznej w
Polsce* (Warsaw: Trio, 2001).

68. Speech of August 31, 1965, reprinted in *Die katholische Kirche und die
Völker-Vertreibung,* ed. Oskar Golombek (Cologne: Wienand, 1966), 244. On the
building projects, see Karol Maleczyński, Marian Morelowski, and Anna Ptaszycka, *Wrocław: Rozwój urbanistyczny* (Warsaw: Budownictwo i Architektura,
1956); Małachowicz, *Wrocław na wyspach;* Edmund Małachowicz, *Wrocławski
zamek książęcy i kolegiata św. Krzyża na Ostrowie* (Wrocław: Oficyna Wydawnicza
Politechniki Wrocławskiej, 1994); Thum, *Stadt,* chapter 10.

69. Kenney, *Rebuilding Poland,* 152.

70. Thum, *Stadt,* 475–88; Peter Oliver Loew, *Danzig und seine Vergangenheit:
Die Geschichtskultur einer Stadt zwischen Deutschland und Polen, 1793–1997* (Os-
nabrück: Fibre, 2003).

71. Długoborski, Gierowski, and Maleczyński, *Dzieje Wrocławia,* 10.

72. Ewa Maleczyńska, "Sedes regni principalis—projektowaną siedzibą rządu
narodowego (historia)," in Sosnowski and Suchocki, *Dolny Śląsk,* vol. 2, 20–43; Karol
Maleczyński and Anna Ptaszycka, "Miasto w XIX i XX w. pod panowaniem prus-
kim," in Karol Maleczyński, Marian Morelowski, and Anna Ptaszycka, *Wrocław:
Rozwój urbanistyczny* (Warsaw: Budownictwo i Architektura, 1956), 119–86.

73. Jan Harasimowicz, *Atlas architektury Wrocławia,* vol. 2 (Wrocław:
Wydawnictwo Dolnośląskie, 1997), 53. In 1947, a map had the square called "Plac
Żydowski," but it was changed sometime in 1947–48 to "Plac Bohaterów Getta."
See *Plan m. Wrocławia* (Kraków: Wydawnictwo Przełom, 1947); Thum, *Stadt,* 358.

74. Lublin is another prominent example where municipal authorities cleared away the town's historic Jewish district for the construction of socialist realist houses. See Jerzy Bojarski, ed., *Ścieżki pamięci: Żydowskie miasto w Lublinie— Losy, Miejsca, Historia* (Lublin: Rishon LeZion, 2002). The absence of Jewish sites is also notable in some of the essays and guides written about Wrocław's architectural past. See Maleczyński and Ptaszycka, "Miasto"; Krystyna Pilch and Józef Pilch, *Zabytki Dolnego Śląska* (Wrocław: Ossolineum, 1962), 172–91; Gwidon Król, *Przewodnik po zabytkach Wrocławia* (Wrocław: Polskie Towarzystwo Turystyczno-Krajoznawcze, 1957); Krzysztof Kwaśniewski, *Wrocław jakiego nie znamy* (Wrocław: Ossolineum, 1972). Finally, historic preservationists rarely discussed Jewish sites, with the exception of those who worked at the Jewish Historical Institute. See Anna Kubiak, "Żydowska architektura zabytkowa w Polsce," *Biuletyn ŻIH* nos. 2–3 (1953): 122–68. Another exception is Maria and Kazimierz Piechotka, *Wooden Synagogues* (Warsaw: Arkady, 1959). Thus, I am suggesting that the postwar neglect of Jewish sites is embedded in the longer history of Polish nationalism and its exclusion of "others." See Patrice M. Dabrowski, *Commemorations and the Shaping of Modern Poland* (Bloomington: Indiana University Press, 2004); Keely Stauter-Halsted, *The Nation in the Village: The Genesis of Peasant National Identity in Austrian Poland, 1848–1914* (Ithaca, NY: Cornell University Press, 2001); Porter, *Nationalism;* Timothy Snyder, *The Reconstruction of Nations: Poland, Ukraine, Lithuania, Belarus, 1569–1999* (New Haven, CT: Yale University Press, 2003); Andrzej Walicki, *Philosophy and Romantic Nationalism: The Case of Poland* (Notre Dame, IN: University of Notre Dame Press, 1982); Theodore R. Weeks, *From Assimilation to Antisemitism: The "Jewish Question" in Poland, 1850–1914* (DeKalb: Northern Illinois University Press, 2006).

75. Waszkiewicz, *Kongregacja,* 80–91 and 104–19.

76. Wrocław Jewish Congregation to ZRWM, July 5, 1963, quoted in Waszkiewicz, *Kongregacja,* 141; AAN, UdW, 131/513, memo on the Wrocław synagogue, undated but likely 1967.

77. Ibid. (memo).

78. AAN, UdW, 131/513, Jewish congregation to Wrocław mayor, March 28, 1967; ZRWM to UdW, December 5, 1967.

79. AAN, UdW, 131/514, ZRWM to UdW, February 18, 1974.

80. AAN, UdW, 22/431, TSKŻ to Ministry of Culture and Art, July 15, 1954, and UdW to TSKŻ, March 21, 1955.

81. AAN, UdW, 75/32, ZRWM to UdW, November 17, 1965. For an extensive documentation of Jewish cemeteries in early postwar Poland, see Kazimierz Urban, *Cmentarze żydowskie, synagogi i domy modlitwy w Polsce w latach 1944– 1966* (Kraków: Nomos, 2006).

82. Numerous letters in AAN, UdW, 131/505. The decree is *Dziennik Urzędowy Ministra Gospodarki Komunalnej,* Okólnik nr. 11, August 3, 1964. In 1966, the Jewish religious congregations had 51 cemeteries and the state 400. See IPN, MSW II 7150, memo of Ministry of Public Works (MGK), January 17, 1966.

83. IPN, MSW II 7443, memo on conversation with Morejno, November 22, 1965.

84. Audrey Kichelewski, "A Community under Pressure: Jews in Poland, 1957–1967," *POLIN: Studies in Polish Jewry* 21 (2008): 159–86.

85. AAN, UdW, 75/32, MGK to UdW, March 3, 1965, with enclosed draft letter.

86. AAN, UdW, 75/32, draft of MGK circular.

87. Christina Emmerich-Focke, *Stadtplanung in Potsdam, 1945–1990* (Potsdam: Stadt Werk, 1999); Campbell, "Resurrected from the Ruins," 49–60 and 203–23.

88. Alan Nothnagle, *Building the East German Myth: Historical Mythology and Youth Propaganda in the German Democratic Republic* (Ann Arbor: University of Michigan, 1999); Sigrid Meuschel, *Legitimation und Parteiherrschaft: Zum Paradox von Stabilität und Revolution in der DDR, 1945–1989* (Frankfurt am Main: Suhrkamp, 1992); Martin Sabrow, ed., *Verwaltete Vergangenheit: Geschichtskultur und Herrschaftslegitimitation in der DDR* (Leipzig: Akademische Verlagsanstalt, 1997); Eric D. Weitz, *Creating German Communism, 1890–1990: From Popular Protests to Socialist State* (Princeton, NJ: Princeton University Press, 1997), 357–86.

89. "Großzügiger Aufbau Potsdam," *MV*, November 14, 1959.

90. Hans-Jürgen Kluge, "Planung des Zentrums von Potsdam," *DA* no. 9 (1960): 542–47. On the centrality of the city center, see Werner Durth, Jörn Düwel, and Niels Gutschow, *Architektur und Städtebau der DDR* (Frankfurt am Main: Campus, 1999), 58–60 and 72–75.

91. BLHA, Rep. 530/1264, meeting of November 24, 1958.

92. "Großzügiger Aufbau Potsdam."

93. PSA, 382, city council decision, February 4, 1958.

94. Peter Scheib, "Offener Brief an den Herrn Oberbürgermeister," *MV*, January 11, 1949.

95. PSA, 480, city council protocol, January 31, 1949. A number of the letters are located in BLHA, Rep. 332. Some are also reprinted in Emmerich-Focke, *Stadtplanung*, 15–17.

96. BLHA, Rep. 530/1271, meeting on *Stadtschloss*, April 23, 1956.

97. BLHA, Rep. 530/1269, "Argumentation des Instituts für Denkmalpflege zur Wiederherstellung des Stadtschlosses in Potsdam." For extensive discussion, see Campbell, "Resurrected from the Ruins," 203–23, and Emmerich-Focke, *Stadtplanung*, 11–26.

98. PSA, 388, "Objektliste der künstlerischen und historischen Baudenkmale (Einzelobjekte)," Institut für Denkmalpflege, 1956.

99. PSA, 264, city to Cultural Ministry, December 27, 1966. First omission of the church in "Ideenwettbewerb zur sozialistischen Umgestaltung des Zentrums der Bezirkshauptstadt Potsdam 1960," *DA* no. 10 (1960): 534–41.

100. *MV*, April 14, 1951.

101. "Aufruf des SK der KPD vom 11. Juni 1945," reprinted in *Dokumente und Materialien zur Geschichte der deutschen Arbeiterbewegung* 3, no. 1 (Berlin, 1959), 15.

102. Jeffrey Herf, *Divided Memory: The Nazi Past in the Two Germanys* (Cambridge, MA: Harvard University Press, 1997), chapters 4–6.

103. PSA, 381, city council draft, June 25, 1956; PSA, 388, "Objektliste der künstlerischen Baudenkmale."

104. PSA, 381, chief architect to IfD, June 27, 1956.

105. "Der Wohnungsbau steht weiter im Vordergrund," *Brandenburgische Neuste Nachrichten,* February 2, 1958.

106. "Potsdam wird schöner denn je," *MV,* May 1, 1960. On the importance of the complex, see PSA, 381, Potsdam district decision, February 14, 1958; PSA, 382, "Erläuterungsbericht zum Bebauungsvorschlag für das Wohngebiet 'Zentrum Potsdam' am Platz der Einheit," April 1, 1958. For the plan, see Hans-Jürgen Kluge, Hellmut Schulz, and Paul Gebel, "Industrieller Wohnungsbau im Stadtkern von Potsdam," *DA* no. 12 (1959): 664–666.

107. Willi Nitschke, "Einige Bemerkungen zum Teilbebauungsplan für das Stadtzentrum von Potsdam," *DA* no. 5 (1960): 264.

108. "In Potsdam für Potsdam gebaut," *BNN,* March 10, 1957.

109. PSA, 388, "Objektliste."

110. PSA, 382, city council draft decision, February 4, 1958.

111. Quotations from E. Neuß, "Technische Denkmale," in *Einführung in die Heimatgeschichte,* ed. Hubert Mohr and Erik Hühns (Berlin: Deutscher Verlag der Wissenschaften, 1959), 80–84; BA (SAPMO), DO 4, nr. 883, memo on the preservation of churches, 1955.

112. PSA, 3553, meeting minutes, Institute for Historic Preservation, October 25, 1956. More broadly, see Nothnagle, *Building the East German Myth;* Jan Palmowski, "Building an East German Nation: Construction of a Socialist *Heimat,* 1945–1961," *CEH* 37, no. 3 (2004): 365–99.

113. Cathleen M. Giustino, *Tearing Down Prague's Jewish Town: Ghetto Clearance and the Legacy of Middle-Class Ethnic Politics* (Boulder, CO: East European Monograph Series, 2003); David Ira Snyder, "The Jewish Question and the Modern Metropolis: Urban Renewal in Prague and Warsaw, 1885–1950" (PhD diss., Princeton University, 2006). On Jewish architecture during the emancipation period, see Carol Herselle Krinsky, *Synagogues of Europe: Architecture, History, Meaning* (Cambridge, MA: MIT Press, 1985); Scott L. Lerner, "The Narrating Architecture of Emancipation," *JSS* 6, no. 3 (2000): 1–30; Saskia Coenen Snyder, "Acculturation and Particularism in the Modern City: Synagogue Building and Jewish Identity in Northern Europe" (PhD diss., University of Michigan, 2008).

114. Toni Morrison, *Beloved* (New York: Everyman's Library, 2006), 47. I came upon this quote when reading Marianne Hirsch and Leo Spitzer's fascinating

reflection on encountering the Jewish sites of prewar Czernowitz in present-day Chernivtsi. Marianne Hirsch and Leo Spitzer, *Ghosts of Home: The Afterlife of Czernowitz in Jewish Memory* (Berkeley: University of California Press, 2010), 138.

4. Restoring Jewish Ruins

1. Richard Kostelanetz, "A Lost World Interred in Berlin," *NYT,* November 8, 1987; Monika Krajewska, *Czas Kamieni* (Warsaw: Interpress, 1982), 1.

2. Ernst Bloch, *The Principle of Hope,* trans. Neville Plaice, Stephen Plaice, and Paul Knight (Cambridge, MA: MIT Press, 1986), 386. See also Alois Riegl, "The Modern Cult of Monuments: Its Character and Its Origin," trans. and ed. Kurt W. Forster and Diane Ghirardo, *Oppositions* no. 25 (Fall 1982): 21–51; Georg Simmel, "The Ruin," in *Georg Simmel, 1858–1918: A Collection of Essays,* ed. Kurt H. Wolff (Columbus: Ohio State University Press, 1959), 259–66. On the common dismissal of nostalgia, see Svetlana Boym, *The Future of Nostalgia* (New York: Basic Books, 2002), xiii–xix; David Lowenthal, "Nostalgia Tells It Like It Wasn't," in *The Imagined Past: History and Nostalgia,* ed. Christopher Shaw and Malcolm Chase (New York: Manchester University Press, 1989), 18–32; Tamara S. Wagner, *Longing: Narratives of Nostalgia in the British Novel, 1740–1890* (Lewisburg, PA: Bucknell University Press, 2004), 21–22. The most extensive historical study on nostalgia is Simon Bunke, *Heimweh: Studien zur Kultur- und Literaturgeschichte einer tödlichen Krankheit* (Freiburg: Rombach Verlag, 2009).

3. Michael S. Falser, *Zwischen Identität und Authentizität: Zur politischen Geschichte der Denkmalpflege in Deutschland* (Dresden: Thelem, 2007), 112–23. On the particularly interesting case of the United States, see Ned Kaufman, *Place, Race, and Story: Essays on the Past and Future of Historic Preservation* (New York: Routledge, 2009).

4. Atina Grossmann has captured this ritualistic quality in "The 'Goldhagen Effect': Memory, Repetition, and Responsibility in the New Germany," in *The "Goldhagen Effect": History, Memory, Nazism—Facing the German Past,* ed. Geoff Eley (Ann Arbor: University of Michigan Press, 2000), 89–129. More provocatively, see A. Dirk Moses, *German Intellectuals and the Nazi Past* (New York: Cambridge University Press, 2007), 239–45.

5. Teresa Torańska, *Jesteśmy* (Warsaw: Świat Książki, 2008), 23.

6. Maria Hirszowicz, *Pułapki zaangażowania: Intelektualiści w służbie komunizmu* (Warsaw: Scholar, 2001); Dariusz Jarosz, *Polacy a stalinizm, 1948–1956* (Warsaw: PAN, 2000); Padraic Kenney, *Rebuilding Poland: Workers and Communists, 1945–1950* (Ithaca, NY: Cornell University Press, 1997); Padraic Kenney, "After the Blank Spots Are Filled: Recent Perspectives on Modern Poland," *JMH* 79, no. 1 (March 2007), esp. 151–61; Czesław Miłosz, *The Captive Mind,* trans. Jane Zielonko (New York: Vintage, 1990); Marci Shore, *Caviar and Ashes: A Warsaw*

Generation's Life and Death in Marxism, 1918–1968 (New Haven, CT: Yale University Press, 2008).

7. Kenney, *Rebuilding Poland*.

8. Jerzy Eisler, *Polski rok 1968* (Warsaw: IPN, 2006); Leszek Gluchowski and Antony Polonsky, eds., *POLIN: Studies in Polish Jewry* 21 (2008); Anat Plocker, "Zionists to Dayan: The Anti-Zionist Campaign in Poland, 1967–1968" (PhD diss., Stanford University, 2009); Dariusz Stola, *Kampania antysyjonistyczna w Polsce 1967–1968* (Warsaw: Instytut Studiów Politycznych PAN, 2000).

9. Excerpts of Gomułka's speech in Stola, *Kampania*, 274.

10. Previous quote from "Do studentów Uniwersytetu Warszawskiego," *Słowo Powszechne*, March 11, 1968; numbers from Dariusz Stola, "Anti-Zionism as a Multipurpose Policy Instrument: The Anti-Zionist Campaign in Poland, 1967–1968," *Journal of Israeli History* 25, no. 1 (2006): 191.

11. Michał Głowiński, "Marcowe fabuły (Rzecz o propagandzie roku 1968)," in his *Pismak 1863 i inne szkice o różnych brzydkich rzeczach* (Warsaw: Open, 1995), 60–94; Piotr Osęka, *Syjoniści, inspiratorzy, wichrzyciele: Obraz wroga w propagandzie marca 1968* (Warsaw: ŻIH, 1999).

12. Quotes in respective order from "Do studentów"; "Wspólnicy antypolskiej histerii," *Sztandar Młodych*, April 4, 1968; Tadeusz Walichnowski, *Izrael a NRF* (Warsaw: Książka i Wiedza, 1968). For an extensive analysis, see Plocker, "Zionists," chapter 2. See also Jonathan Huener, *Auschwitz, Poland, and the Politics of Commemoration, 1945–1979* (Athens: Ohio University Press, 2003), 169–84; Jacek Leociak, "Instrumentalizacja Zagłady w dyskursie marcowym," *Kwartalnik Historii Żydów* no. 4 (2008): 447–58.

13. Natalia Aleksiun, "Polish Historiography of the Holocaust: Between Silence and Public Debate," *German History* 22, no. 3 (2004): 406–32. Poland appears exceptional compared to other Soviet bloc states. See Zvi Gitelman, "Politics and the Historiography of the Holocaust in the Soviet Union," in *Bitter Legacy: Confronting the Holocaust in the USSR*, ed. Zvi Gitelman (Bloomington: Indiana University Press, 1997), 14–42; David Shneer, "Picturing Grief: Soviet Holocaust Photography at the Intersection of History and Memory," *AHR* 115, no. 1 (2010): 28–52.

14. AAN, KC PZPR, 237/VIII/726, ZBoWiD to KC PZPR, October 27, 1962.

15. "Warsaw, 25 Years After," *NYT*, April 19, 1968. Little research exists on the post-1945 history of anti-Polish prejudice with a few exceptions on the post-1989 period: Zvi Gitelman, "Collective Memory and Contemporary Polish-Jewish Relations," in *Contested Memories: Poles and Jews during the Holocaust and Its Aftermath*, ed. Joshua D. Zimmerman (New Brunswick, NJ: Rutgers University Press, 2003), 271–90; Robert Cherry and Annamaria Orla-Bukowska, eds., *Rethinking Poles and Jews: Troubled Past, Brighter Future* (New York: Rowman & Littlefield, 2007), 23–79. On Holocaust memory, see Lawrence Baron, "The Holocaust and

American Public Memory, 1945–1960," *HGS* 17, no. 1 (2003): 62–88; Hasia R. Diner, *We Remember with Reverence and Love: American Jews and the Myth of Silence after the Holocaust, 1945–1962* (New York: New York University Press, 2008), 66–79; Daniel Levy and Natan Sznaider, *The Holocaust and Memory in the Global Age,* trans. Assenka Oksiloff (Philadelphia: Temple University Press, 2006); Dalia Ofer, "The Strength of Remembrance: Commemorating the Holocaust during the First Decade of Israel," *JSS* 6, no. 2 (2000): 24–55; Herbert Marcuse, *The Legacies of Dachau: The Uses and Abuses of a Concentration Camp, 1933–2001* (New York: Cambridge University Press, 2001), 199–220; Markus Meckl, *Helden und Märtyrer: Der Warschauer Ghettoaufstand in der Erinnerung* (Berlin: Metropol, 2000); Peter Novick, *The Holocaust in American Life* (New York: Houghton Mifflin, 1999).

16. "Obozy koncentracyjne Hitlerowskie," *Wielka Encyklopedia Powszechna* (Warsaw: PWN, 1966), 88 and 89.

17. Plocker, "Zionists," chapter 2.

18. CZA, C2/2032, WJC, Department of International Affairs, May 13, 1963.

19. IPN, BU MSW II 7251. See also Audrey Kichelewski, "A Community under Pressure: Jews in Poland, 1957–1967," *POLIN: Studies in Polish Jewry* 21 (2008): 178–81.

20. "Zbrojny czyn warszawskiego getta—integralną częścią ogólnopolskiej walki z okupantem," *Trybuna Ludu,* April 19, 1968.

21. On the flood of publications that emerged on Polish rescue of Jews in the 1960s, see Dariusz Libionka, "Polskie piśmiennictwo na temat zorganizowanej i indywidualnej pomocy Żydom (1945–2008)," *Zagłada Żydów* 4 (2008): 34–44.

22. Joanna Wawrzyniak, *ZBoWiD i pamięć drugiej wojny światowej, 1949–1969* (Warsaw: Trio, 2009), 105–299.

23. Michael C. Steinlauf, *Bondage to the Dead: Poland and the Memory of the Holocaust* (Syracuse, NY: Syracuse University Press, 1997); Iwona Irwin-Zarecka, *Neutralizing Memory: The Jew in Contemporary Poland* (New Brunswick, NJ: Transaction, 1989).

24. Antoni Gołubiew, "Tutejsi," *Znak* 22, no. 10 (1970): 1313; Jacek Trznadel, *Hańba domowa: Rozmowy z pisarzami* (Paris: Instytut Literacki, 1986), 191. See Christina Manetti, "Sign of the Times: The Znak Circle and Catholic Intellectual Engagement in Communist Poland, 1945–1976" (PhD diss., University of Washington, 1998).

25. Jerzy Turowicz, "Sprawa katolicyzmu," *TP*, June 11, 1945; Jerzy Turowicz, "1000," *TP,* April 10–17, 1966, reprinted in Jerzy Turowicz, *Kościół nie jest łodzią podwodną* (Kraków: Znak, 1990), 232 and 242.

26. Roman Dmowski, "Kościoł, naród i państwo," reprinted in *Roman Dmowski: Wybór Pism,* vol. 4 (New York: Instytut Romana Dmowskiego, 1988), 99.

27. Mikolaj Kunicki, "The Polish Crusader: The Life and Politics of Bolesław Piasecki, 1915–1979" (PhD diss., Stanford University, 2004).

28. Interpellation, June 8, 1967, reprinted in Andrzej Friszke, *Koło posłów "Znak" w Sejmie PRL 1957–1976* (Warsaw: Wydawnictwo Sejmowe, 2002), 475–77.

29. Interpellation, March 11, 1968, reprinted in Friszke, *Koło posłów "Znak,"* 488.

30. *Sprawozdanie stenograficzne z 19 posiedzenia Sejmu PRL,* April 9, 1968, 115.

31. Andrzej Friszke, "Trudny egzamin: Koło Posłów Znak w okresie Marca 68," in *Marzec 1968: Trzydzieści lat później,* ed. Marcin Kula, Piotr Osęka, and Marcin Zaremba (Warsaw: PWN, 1998), 192.

32. *Sprawozdanie stenograficzne z 19 posiedzenia Sejmu PRL,* April 9, 1968, 167.

33. Łubieński from ibid., April 11, 1968, 275; Zabłocki quoted in Friszke, "Trudny egzamin," 199–200.

34. Adam Michnik, "A New Evolutionism," in Adam Michnik, *Letters from Prison and Other Essays,* trans. Maya Latynski (Berkeley: University of California Press, 1985), 135–48. See David Ost, *Solidarity and the Politics of Anti-Politics: Opposition and Reform in Poland since 1968* (Philadelphia: Temple University Press, 1990).

35. Adam Michnik, *The Church and the Left,* trans. David Ost (Chicago: University of Chicago Press, 1993), 151 and 153.

36. Jan Józef Lipski, *Dwie ojczyzny—dwa patriotyzmy: Uwagi o megalomanii narodowej i ksenofobii polaków* (Warsaw: Niezależna Oficyna Wydawnicza, 1981).

37. Marcin Król, "Czy istnieje pokolenie marcowe?" *Więź* 31, no. 3 (1988): 7.

38. AAN, KIK, 212, undated description of "Week of Jewish Culture."

39. AAN, KIK, 212, "Dlaczego Tydzień Kultury Żydowskiej?," 1976.

40. Małgorzata Niezabitowska, "Polak, który próbuje być Żydem," *TP,* April 24, 1983; quote from uncensored interview in *Karta* no. 4 (1987): 56.

41. Małgorzata Niezabitowska, *Remnants: The Last Jews of Poland* (New York: Friendly Press, 1986), 241–42; selections were later published in *Karta* no. 4 (1987): 35–52.

42. "Remnants of the Last Jews of Poland," *National Geographic* 170, no. 3 (September 1986): 362–89.

43. "Żydzi i Polacy," *Biuletyn Dolnośląski* no. 11 (November 1980), 1.

44. *Arka,* no. 10 (1985): 102–33; *Aneks,* nos. 41–42 (1986): 3–133; *Krytyka* no. 15 (1983): 185–247.

45. Jan Józef Lipski, "Kwestia żydowska," in "Marzec 1968: Sesja na Uniwersytecie Warszawskim," *Zeszyty Edukacji Narodowej* no. 1 (1981): 46.

46. Jan Józef Lipski, "Polscy Żydzi," April 16, 1983; reprinted in *Kultura* 429, no. 6 (1983): 5.

47. Jan Józef Lipski, *Dwie ojczyzny i inne szkice* (Warsaw: Mysl, 1985), 35 and 37; Jan T. Gross, "Polish-Jewish Relations during the War: An Interpretation," *Dissent* (Winter 1987): 73–81.

48. Anna Sawisz, "Obraz Żydów i stosunków polsko-żydowskich w listach telewidzów po emisji filmu 'Shoah,'" in *Bliscy i Dalecy,* vol. 2, ed. Grażyna Gęsicka (Warsaw: Uniwersytet Warszawski Instytut Socjologii, 1992), 137–65.

49. Jerzy Turowicz, "'Shoah' w polskich oczach," *TP,* November 10, 1985, 1; Timothy Garton Ash response to Turowicz, *NYRB,* May 8, 1986.

50. Jan Błoński, "The Poor Poles Look at the Ghetto," in *My Brother's Keeper: Recent Polish Debates about the Holocaust,* ed. Antony Polonsky (New York: Routledge, 1990), 34–48.

51. Ewa Berberyusz, "Guilt by Neglect," in Polonsky, *My Brother's Keeper,* 69; Jerzy Turowicz, "Polish Reasons and Jewish Reasons," in ibid., 141; Władysław Siła-Nowicki, "A Reply to Jan Błoński," in ibid., 59; Kazimierz Kąkol, "The Eighty-First Blow," in ibid., 144–49. On the debate, see Ewa Koźmińska-Frejlak, "Świadkowie Zagłady—Holocaust jako zbiorowe doświadczenie Polaków," *Przegląd Socjologiczny* 49, no. 2 (2000): 181–206.

52. Zofia Wóycicka, "Zur Internationalität der Gedenkkultur: Die Gedenkstätte Auschwitz-Birkenau im Spannungsfeld zwischen Ost und West 1954–1978," *Archiv für Sozialgeschichte* 45 (2005): 269–92.

53. All quotes from AAN, UdW, 132/260, "Notatka dotycząca problematyki żydowskiej," undated but most likely 1979. See Marcin Zaremba, "Zorganizowane zapominanie o Holokauście w dekadzie Gierka: Trwanie i zmiana," *Kwartalnik Historii Żydów* no. 1 (2004): 216–24.

54. AAN, KC PZPR, Wydział Administracjny, 37, "Notatka z przebiegu narady w sprawie przeciwdziałań w związku z atakami zagranicznych środowisk żydowskich przeciwko Polsce," March 15, 1976. For discussion of this shift at Auschwitz, see Huener, *Auschwitz,* chapters 4–5.

55. AAN, UdW, 132/269, Kąkol to Łukasiewicz, March 13, 1978.

56. AAN, UdW, 132/268, Kąkol to UdW, November 11, 1976.

57. James Feron, "At the Wall in Warsaw: 30 Years Later," *NYT,* April 15, 1973.

58. AAN, UdW, 24/549, protocol, February 12, 1956; reprinted in Kazimierz Urban, *Cmentarze żydowskie, synagogi i domy modlitwy w Polsce w latach 1944–1966* (Kraków: Nomos, 2006), 499–501.

59. AAN, UdW, 45/464, ZRWM to Warsaw Public Utilities Division, January 15, 1962; AAN, KC PZPR, 237/XIV/149, TSKŻ to Secretary of PZPR, March 22, 1957.

60. AAN, UdW, 131/321, Jaroszewicz to Kąkol, August 29, 1979, Kąkol to Jaroszewicz, December 7, 1979.

61. AAN, UdW, 132/321, Kąkol to Gierek, May 29, 1979.

62. AAN, UdW, 132/321, decision nr. 17/82, June 17, 1982. On antisemitism in the 1980s, see "The Current Polish Crisis and the 1968 Antisemitic Campaign," *Research Report, Institute of Jewish Affairs* no. 3 (1980): 3–15; "Jewish Themes in Polish Crisis," *Research Report, Institute of Jewish Affairs* nos. 10 and 11 (1981): 1–19; "Poland's Jewish Policies under Martial Law," *Research Report, Institute of Jewish Affairs* no. 3 (1982): 1–16; "Antisemitism in Today's Poland," *Soviet Jewish Affairs* 12, no. 1 (1982): 55–65.

63. "40 rocznica powstania w Getcie Warszawskim: Uroczystość przekazania wiernym synagogi w Warszawie," *ŻW,* April 19, 1983.

64. AAN, UdW, 132/263, Nissenbaum to Łopatka, September 26, 1986 and memo on foundation, February 21, 1989.

65. "List otwarty Marka Edelmana," reprinted in Władysław Bartoszewski and Marek Edelman, *Los Żydów Warszawy, 1939–1943* (Lublin: Towarzystwo Naukowe Katolickiego Uniwersytetu Lubelskiego, 1993), 178.

66. IPN, BU MSW II 2400, Informacja nr. 12 dot. podsumowania imprez związanych z 40 rocznicą powstania w Getcie Warszawskim.

67. John Kifners, "Polish Police Bar March on Uprising," *NYT,* April 18, 1983.

68. Padraic Kenney, *A Carnival of Revolution: Central Europe 1989* (Princeton, NJ: Princeton University Press, 2002).

69. Jacek Kuroń, "My First Encounters with Jews and Ukrainians," *POLIN: Studies in Polish Jewry* 14 (2001): 241–42. See also Joanna B. Michlic, "Jacek Kuroń: The Last Romantic Politician Committed to the Struggle for the Rights of Minorities, 1934–2004," *POLIN: Studies in Polish Jewry* 19 (2006): 621–28.

70. The appeal and Kuroń's prediction in IPN, BU MSW 0236/346, t. 2, "Załącznik do informacji dziennej z dnia 1988-04-06."

71. IPN, BU MSW 0236/346, t. 2, "Załącznik do informacji dziennej z dnia 1988-04-18."

72. Mark Erlich, "Solidarity and the Warsaw Ghetto," *Tikkun* 3, no. 5 (1988): 26.

73. ANN, UdW, 131/513, memo on the Wrocław synagogue.

74. AAN, UdW, 132/323, Wrocław National Council to Wrocław Jewish Congregation, July 26, 1972; Wrocław Jewish congregation to Ministry of Public Utilities, July 31, 1972.

75. AMKZ, Synagogue File, District Office, Old Town to Wrocław Regional Government, April 9, 1985, and historic preservation decision, December 30, 1970.

76. Ibid., Wrocław Regional Government to City Director for Renovation, March 25, 1987, and Wrocław Regional Government to Center for Culture and Art, July 31, 1986. All plans located in AMKZ, Synagogue File.

77. "Szukam historii miasta," *Sztandar Młodych,* December 6, 1989.

78. "O starym cmentarzu żydowskim," *WW,* January 20, 1987; "Dzieje wrocławskiego cmentarza żydowskiego," *WW,* April 13, 1983; "Cmentarz żydowski," *WW,* October 31, 1986; "Wrocławscy Żydzi," *WW,* March 24–27, 1989; "Żydzi Wrocławscy 1850–1945," *Nowe Życie,* April 4, 1989.

79. Hugo Peer, "Wenn Steine reden: Der jüdische Friedhof in Breslau—einer der letzten Zeugen deutscher Kultur in Schlesiens Hauptstadt," *Der Staatsbürger: Beilage der Bayerischen Staatszeitung,* January 1988.

80. Klaus Reiff, "Ferdinand Lassalles Ruhestätte wird mit Akribie und Detail-Treue erneuert: Über viele Jahre hinweg schien sein Grab im heutigen Wrocław vergessen," *WAZ,* July 10, 1984.

81. Jürgen Wahl, "Breslaus überwachsene Davidsterne," *Rheinischer Merkur,* November 4, 1988.

82. Katherine Verdery, *The Political Lives of Dead Bodies: Reburial and Postsocialist Change* (New York: Columbia University Press, 1999), 106–10.

83. Ewa Berberyusz, "Dlaczego idą?" *Gazeta,* October 30, 1989.

84. Lothar Mertens, *Davidstern unter Hammer und Zirkel: Die jüdischen Gemeinden in der SBZ/DDR und ihre Behandlung durch Partei und Staat, 1945–1990* (Hildesheim: Olms, 1997); Ulrike Offenberg, *"Seid vorsichtig gegen die Machthaber": Die jüdischen Gemeinden in der SBZ und der DDR, 1945–1990* (Berlin: Aufbau-Verlag, 1998); Jutta Illichmann, *Die DDR und die Juden: Die deutschlandpolitische Instrumentalisierung von Juden und Judentum durch die Partei- und Staatsführung der SBZ/DDR von 1945 bis 1990* (Frankfurt am Main: Lang, 1997).

85. Walter Ulbricht, June 15, 1967, excerpts reprinted in Mario Keßler, *Die SED und die Juden—Zwischen Repression und Toleranz* (Berlin: Akademie Verlag, 1995), 173; *Berliner Zeitung,* July 14, 1967, reprinted in Thomas C. Fox, *Stated Memory: East Germany and the Holocaust* (Rochester, NY: Camden House, 1999), 19.

86. "Erklärung der Leitenden Geistlichen der Gliedkirchen des Bundes der Evangelischen Kirche in der Deutschen Demokratischen Republik vom 27. November 1975," reprinted in *Juden in der DDR: Geschichte, Probleme, Perspektiven* (Sachsenheim: Burg Verlag, 1988), 52.

87. Statement of the Conference of the Protestant Leadership, September 24, 1978, reprinted in *Die Kirchen und das Judentum: Dokumente von 1945 bis 1985,* ed. Rolf Rendtorff and Hans Hermann Henrix (Paderborn: Bonifatius Verlag, 1988), 589–90. See Irena Ostmeyer, *Zwischen Schuld und Sühne: Evangelische Kirche und Juden in SBZ und DDR, 1945–1990* (Berlin: Institut Kirche und Judentum, 2002).

88. EZA, 97/1010, invitation to event, 1978.

89. EZA, 97/879, Aktion Sühnezeichen bulletin, May–June 1986.

90. Interview with Irene Junge in Robin Ostow, *Jews in Contemporary East Germany: The Children of Moses in the Land of Marx* (New York: St. Martin's Press, 1989), 51.

91. Christine-Félice Röhrs, "Jüdin sein kam lange nicht in Frage," *Die Zeit,* March 2, 2000.

92. Heinz Knobloch, *Herr Moses in Berlin: Auf den Spuren eines Menschenfreundes* (Berlin: Buchverlag der Morgen, 1979); *Gedenke! Vergiß nie! 40. Jahrestag des faschistischen Kristallnacht-Pogroms* (Berlin: Union-Verlag, 1979). See Illichmann, *DDR,* 239–50; Mark A. Wolfgram, "The Holocaust through the Prism of East German Television: Collective Memory and Audience Perceptions," *HGS* 20, no. 1 (2006): 57–79.

93. PSA, 4508, City to Association of Jewish Communities, August 31, 1970, Potsdam Interior Department to GDR Cultural Ministry, May 31, 1978, and pastor to Potsdam Interior Department, May 8, 1983.

94. Ibid., Merkel to Potsdam Interior Department, May 31, 1983.

95. Ibid., Potsdam Interior Department to Merkel, June 7, 1983.

96. Herbert Lange, *MV,* November 1, 1989.

97. PSA 4508, letter to mayor, April 21, 1984.

98. Aron Hirt-Manheimer, "Ten Days in East Germany," *Reform Judaism* (February 1981): 8.

99. LAB, C Rep. 104, nr. 601, "Information zu einigen Problemen der jüdischen Gemeinde von Groß-Berlin," April 2, 1976; BA (SAPMO), DY 30 IV/B2 14/174, "Zu einigen Fragen der Situation, Struktur, usw. in den jüdischen Gemeinden in der DDR," August 19, 1975. See also LAB, C Rep. 104, nr. 382, report by Director of VP-Inspection, Prenzlauer Berg, February 19, 1975; LAB, C Rep. 104, nr. 382, notes on Jewish cemetery, March 11, 1975.

100. BA (SAPMO), DY 30/IV/B2/12/176, letter, July 6, 1986; Mertens, *Davidstern,* 267.

101. "Jüdischer Friedhof bedroht: Zerstörung eines Stücks Kulturgeschichte," *DT,* July 24, 1986; "Trasse durch jüdischen Friedhof?," *Volksblatt Berlin,* July 30, 1986; BA (SAPMO) DY 30/IV/B2/12/176, memo, July 31, 1986.

102. BA (SAPMO), DY 30/vorl. SED, 41910, Büro Jarowinsky, Galinski to Honecker, September 10, 1986, and Honecker to Galinski, October 1, 1986. On Hildebrandt's role, see Ostmeyer, *Schuld,* 151–59.

103. LAB, C Rep. 104, nr. 633, City to Minister of Church Affairs, February 24, 1989; LAB, C Rep. 104, nr. 593, Kirchner to Gysi, April 2, 1984; LAB, C Rep. 104, nr. 593, draft decision, June 21, 1984; "Was die Nazis übrigließen: Über die jüdischen Friedhöfe in Ost-Berlin," *Aufbau,* February 8, 1980.

104. BA (SAPMO), DY 30/IV B2/14, nr. 180, Offenberg to Gysi, July 29, 1985.

105. Ibid., "Zu Bauvorhaben auf einem Gelände am jüdischen Friedhof 'Adass-Jisroel.'"

106. Ibid., Offenberg to Honecker, October 28, 1985, and Honecker to Offenberg, November 6, 1985; "Adass-Jisroel-Friedhof in Berlin wieder der Öffentlichkeit übergeben," *Neues Deutschland,* June 27, 1986.

107. The four attempts are located in BA (SAPMO), DO 4, nr. 1337, LAB, C Rep. 131–12, nr. 27, and LAB, C Rep. 104, nr. 601; BA (SAPMO), DY 30/IV B2/14, nr.174, Salomea Genin, "Die Notwendigkeit, sich zur Festigung der Gesellschaft in der DDR mit der historischen Entwicklung des Judentums zu beschäftigen."

108. LAB, C Rep. 104, nr. 601, conception for the rebuilding of the New Synagogue in Berlin, December 1, 1986.

109. BStU, MfS HA XX/4, nr. 1389, internal memo, November 26, 1987.

110. Ostmeyer, *Schuld,* 176–81.

111. BStU, MfS HA XX/4, nr. 1368, "Politisch-operative Sicherung der Gedenkveranstaltungen anlässlich des 50. Jahrestages der faschistischen Pogromnacht vom 9.11.1938," November 25, 1988; leaflet quoted in Fred Kowasch, "Die Entwicklung der Opposition in Leipzig," in *Opposition in der DDR von den 70er*

Jahren bis zum Zusammenbruch der SED-Herrschaft, ed. Eberhard Kuhrt (Opladen: Leske and Budrich, 1999), 221.

112. BStU, MfS HA XX/4, nr. 1368, "Politisch-operative Sicherung der Gedenkveranstaltungen anlässlich des 50. Jahrestages der faschistischen Pogromnacht vom 9.11.1938," November 25, 1988.

113. BStU, MfA HA XX/4, nr. 2183, Bezirksverwaltung für Staatssicherheit Karl Marx Stadt, undated but probably November 9, 1988.

114. BStU, MfA HA XX/4, nr. 2183, Jewish Community to Gysi, May 12, 1988.

115. Ibid., information reports, November 8, 1988 and July 27, 1988; Annette Leo, *Umgestoßen: Provokation auf dem Jüdischen Friedhof in Berlin Prenzlauer Berg 1988* (Berlin: Metropol, 2005); Monika Schmidt, *Schändungen jüdischer Friedhöfe in der DDR: Eine Dokumentation* (Berlin: Metropol, 2007).

116. LAB, C Rep. 104, nr. 600, Gysi to Honecker, January 15, 1988, and Department of Finance to Office for the Legal Protection of Property, February 25, 1988.

117. BAK, B 106, nr. 21559, BMI to LMI, June 14, 1950; AAJDC-Jerusalem, Geneva IV, 9/1a, file 2, Katzenstein to Kagan, November 21, 1951.

118. BAK, B 136, nr. 5862, BMI to State Secretary of Federal Chancellery, January 13, 1956.

119. ZA, B 1/7, nr. 347, Schröder to van Dam, September 3, 1956.

120. Thea Altaras, *Synagogen in Hessen: Was geschah seit 1945?* (Königstein im Taunus: Langewiesche, 1988); Ina Lorenz, *Streitfall jüdischer Friedhof Ottensen 1663–1993,* 2 vols. (Hamburg: Dölling and Galitz, 1995); Joachim Hahn, *Synagogen in Baden-Württemberg* (Stuttgart: Theiss, 2007); Utz Jeggle, "Nachrede: Erinnerungen an die Dorfjuden heute," in *Jüdisches Leben auf dem Lande,* ed. Reinhard Rürup and Monika Richarz (Tübingen: Mohr Siebeck, 1997), 399–411; Susanne Schönborn, "The New Börneplatz Memorial and the Nazi Past in Frankfurt am Main," in *Beyond Berlin: Twelve German Cities Confront the Nazi Past,* ed. Gavriel Rosenfeld and Paul Jaskot (Ann Arbor: University of Michigan Press, 2008), 273–94.

121. Quotes from Michael Schmidtke, "The New German Left and National Socialism," in *Coping with the Nazi Past: West German Debates on Nazism and Generational Conflict, 1955–1975,* ed. Philipp Gassert and Alan E. Steinweis (New York: Berghahn, 2006), 176.

122. For criticisms of this whiggish argument, see David Art, *The Politics of the Nazi Past in Germany and Austria* (New York: Cambridge University Press, 2006); Gassert and Steinweis, *Coping with the Nazi Past*; Dagmar Herzog, *Sex after Fascism: Memory and Morality in Twentieth-Century Germany* (Princeton, NJ: Princeton University Press, 2005); Marcuse, *Legacies;* Moses, *German Intellectuals.*

123. Hermann Peter Piwitt, "Kristallnacht und Nebel," *Konkret,* December 1978; quoted in Herzog, *Sex,* 176.

124. Letter located in LAB, B 004, nr. 395. See Wolfgang Kraushaar, *Die Bombe im jüdischen Gemeindehaus* (Hamburg: Hamburger Edition, 2005). On antisemitism

among segments of the left, see Herzog, *Sex,* 171–83; Annette Vowinckel, "Der kurze Weg nach Entebbe oder die Verlängerung der deutschen Geschichte in den Nahen Osten," *Zeithistorische Forschungen/Studies in Contemporary History,* Online Edition 1, no. 2 (2004).

125. On the liberalization of West German society and politics more broadly, see Ulrich Herbert, ed., *Wandlungsprozesse in Westdeutschland: Belastung, Integration, Liberalisierung 1945–1980* (Göttingen: Wallstein, 2002); Axel Schildt, Detlef Siegfried, and Karl Christian Lammers, eds., *Dynamische Zeiten: Die 60er Jahre in den beiden deutschen Gesellschaften* (Hamburg: Christians Verlag, 2002).

126. Anthony D. Kauders, *Democratization and the Jews: Munich, 1945–1965* (Lincoln: University of Nebraska Press, 2004); Marcuse, *Legacies,* 199–220; Benjamin Pearson, "Faith and Democracy: Political Transformations at the German Protestant Kirchentag, 1949–1969" (PhD diss., University of North Carolina at Chapel Hill, 2007), chapter 7; Christian Staffa, "Die 'Aktion Sühnezeichen': Eine protestantische Initiative zu einer besonderen Art der Wiedergutmachung," in *Nach der Verfolgung: Wiedergutmachung nationalsozialistischen Unrechts in Deutschland?* ed. Hans Günter Hockerts and Christiane Kuller (Göttingen: Wallstein, 2003), 139–56.

127. Moses, *German Intellectuals,* chapter 9.

128. Moses brilliantly captures the verve of this conflict between right and left over the Nazi past in his *German Intellectuals.*

129. "Culture of contrition" from Art, *Politics of the Nazi Past,* chapter 3. See Saul Friedländer, *Memory, History, and the Extermination of the Jews of Europe* (Bloomington: Indiana University Press, 1993); Geoffrey H. Hartman, ed., *Bitburg in Moral and Political Perspective* (Bloomington: Indiana University Press, 1986); Ilya Levkov, ed., *Bitburg and Beyond: Encounters in American, German, and Jewish History* (New York: Shapolsky Publishers, 1987); Richard J. Evans, *In Hitler's Shadow: West German Historians and the Attempt to Escape from the Past* (New York: Pantheon Books, 1989); Charles Maier, *The Unmasterable Past: History, Holocaust, and German National Identity* (Cambridge, MA: Harvard University Press, 1988); H. Glenn Penny, "The Museum für Deutsche Geschichte and German National Identity," *CEH* 28, no. 3 (1995): 343–72.

130. But exactly how deep interest in the Holocaust ran is difficult to know. Indeed, even as Germans learn more about the Holocaust, they continue to recall family memories of victimization and resistance. See Olaf Jensen, *Geschichte machen: Strukturmerkmale des intergenerationellen Sprechens über die NS-Vergangenheit in deutschen Familien* (Tübingen: Edition Diskord, 2004); Harald Welzer, Sabine Moller, and Karoline Tschuggnall, *"Opa war kein Nazi:" Nationalsozialismus und Holocaust im Familiengedächtnis* (Frankfurt am Main: Fischer, 2002). On television, see Wulf Kansteiner, *In Pursuit of German Memory: History, Television, and Politics after Auschwitz* (Athens: Ohio University Press, 2006), chapters 6 and 7. On *Bild,* see Art, *Politics of the Nazi Past,* 68–69.

131. ESA, 143, nr. 10798, speech by Werner Schütz, November 24, 1961.

132. "Noch immer kein Denkmal?," *NRZ,* February 20, 1964.

133. "Erinnerung an Opfer muß wach bleiben," *NRZ,* February 22, 1964.

134. Karl Heinz Brokerhoff, "Westdeutschland braucht ein Museum für moderne Geschichte," *WAZ,* March 5, 1966.

135. "Geschichtsmuseum in die Synagoge bringen," *WAZ,* March 12, 1966.

136. RAES, Hans Lomberg and Ernst Schmidt to Karl Heinz Brokerhoff, March 17, 1966, quoted in Ernst Schmidt, "Alte Synagoge Essen: Der lange Weg zur Mahn- und Gedenkstätte," unpublished essay, 15; RAES, 19–606, box 1, Jewish Community to Karl Cervik, December 7, 1966.

137. *Ruhrbote,* February 27, 1960, quoted in Schmidt, "Alte Synagoge," 7.

138. Harald Schmid, *Erinnern an den "Tag der Schuld": Das Novemberpogrom von 1938 in der deutschen Geschichtspolitik* (Hamburg: Ergebnisse Verlag, 2001), chapter 6.

139. Johannes Gorlas, "Gedenktafel," *WAZ,* November 6, 1978; *NRZ,* September 26, 1978 and September 30, 1978.

140. "WAZ-Leser sprechen mit," *WAZ,* October 17, 1978.

141. RAES, protocol of "Alte Synagoge" working group, quoted in Schmidt, "Alte Synagoge," 26–27.

142. AAS, 10277, "Denkschrift zur Bildung eines Sondervermögens: Förderkreis Alte Synagoge," February 2, 1981.

143. RAES, 19–606, box 1, "Entwurf zur Konzeption einer Ausstellung 'Essen 1933–1945: Verfolgung und Widerstand,'" December 1978.

144. Schmidt, "Alte Synagoge," 40.

145. AAS, 10241, "Nutzungskonzeption Alte Synagoge," September 28, 1979.

146. "Widerstand und Verfolgung in Essen, 1933–1945," exhibition pamphlet, located in Essen Stadtbibliothek. See also *Widerstand und Verfolgung in Essen, 1933–1945* (Essen: Alte Synagoge, 1980).

147. "Synagoge Gedenkstätte für alle Gewaltopfer," *WAZ,* January 9, 1980.

148. "Widerstand und Verfolgung in Essen, 1933–1945," exhibition pamphlet. While more common in East Germany with Dresden, the bombed-out city also became an important element of West German cultural and communicative memories. See Gilad Margalit, *Guilt, Suffering, and Memory: Germany Remembers Its Dead of World War II,* trans. Haim Watzman (Bloomington: Indiana University Press, 2010), 147–85.

149. RAES, 19–606, box 1, speech by Horst Katzor, November 9, 1980.

150. *Synagogen in Berlin: Zur Geschichte einer zerstörten Architektur* (Berlin: Berlin Museum, 1983); *Wegweiser durch das jüdische Berlin* (Berlin: Nicolai, 1987); *Juden in Spandau: Vom Mittelalter bis 1945* (Berlin: Edition Heinrich, 1988); *Juden in Kreuzberg: Fundstücke, Fragmente, Erinnerungen* (Berlin: Edition Heinrich, 1991); *Berlin-Wilmersdorf—die Juden, Leben und Leiden* (Berlin: Berlin-Wilmersdorf Kunstamt, 1987).

151. AGTS, "Offener Ideenwettbewerb, Mahnen und Gedenken im Bayerischen Viertel," 39.

152. *Drucksachen der Bezirksverordnetenversammlung Schöneberg von Berlin,* Antrag der SPD, April 20, 1988.

153. Joachim Schlör, *Das Ich der Stadt: Debatten über Judentum und Urbanität, 1822–1938* (Göttingen: Vandenhoeck & Ruprecht, 2005), 110.

154. "13 November: Gedenken an die Judendeportationen: Wider das Vergessen," *Schöneberger Stadtsgespräch,* August 1988.

155. AGTS, "Kein vereinzelter Gedenkstein—sondern Steine des (Denk)-Anstoßes," Berliner Geschichtswerkstatt and Aktives Museum Faschismus und Widerstand in Berlin, 1988.

156. AGTS, "Offener Ideenwettbewerb," 1991.

157. AGTS, speech by Uwe Saager, November 6, 1993. For more on the memorial, see Caroline Wiedmer, *The Claims of Memory: Representations of the Holocaust in Contemporary Germany and France* (Ithaca, NY: Cornell University Press, 1999).

158. Alex Storozynski, "History of Poland's Jews to Go on Display," *The New York Sun,* November 28, 2005.

159. Jerzy Ficowski, *Odczytanie popiołów* (London: Association of Jews of Polish Origin in Great Britain, 1979), 24. Unpublished English translation by Madeline G. Levine.

160. David Lowenthal, *The Past Is a Foreign Country* (New York: Cambridge University Press, 1985), 240.

5. Reconstructing the Jewish Past

1. Marcin Kacprzak, *Midrasz* nos. 7–8 (November/December 1997): 4; Ruth Ellen Gruber, "Visiting the Vestiges of Jewish Poland," *NYT,* October 21, 1990.

2. Ruth Ellen Gruber, *Virtually Jewish: Reinventing Jewish Culture in Europe* (Berkeley: University of California Press, 2002). I am also referring to Pierre Nora's distinction between "real environments of memory" and "sites of memory." He considers the latter an inauthentic and nonspontaneous artifice of living memory, the "shells on the shore when the sea of living memory has receded." Pierre Nora, "Between Memory and History: Les Lieux de Mémoire," *Representations* 26 (Spring 1989): 12.

3. Barbara Kirshenblatt-Gimblett and Jonathan Karp, eds., *The Art of Being Jewish in Modern Times* (Philadelphia: University of Pennsylvania Press, 2008), 3; Erica Lehrer, "Bearing False Witness? 'Vicarious' Jewish Identity and the Politics of Affinity," in *Imaginary Neighbors: Mediating Polish-Jewish Relations after the Holocaust,* ed. Dorota Glowacka and Joanna Zylinska (Lincoln: University of Nebraska Press, 2007), 84–109.

4. Walter Benjamin, "The Work of Art in the Age of Its Technological Reproducibility," in *The Work of Art in the Age of Its Technological Reproducibility and Other Writings on Media,* ed. Michael W. Jennings, Brigid Doherty, and Thomas Y. Levin (Cambridge, MA: Harvard University Press, 2008).

5. Andreas Huyssen, "Nostalgia for Ruins," *Grey Room* 23 (Spring 2006): 11.

6. James E. Young, *At Memory's Edge: After-Images of the Holocaust in Contemporary Art and Architecture* (New Haven, CT: Yale University Press, 2000), 62; Jennifer A. Jordan, *Structures of Memory: Understanding Urban Change in Berlin and Beyond* (Stanford, CA: Stanford University Press, 2006), 14–19.

7. Deutscher Bundestag, 16. Wahlperiode, Antwort der Bundesregierung auf die kleine Anfrage der Fraktion Bündnis 90/Die Grünen, Drucksache 16/8716, April 4, 2008; "Neue Zahlen," *Zukunft,* October 28, 2005; *Ausländerzahlen* (Nürnberg: Bundesamt für Migration und Flüchtlinge, 2009), 7.

8. Jeffrey M. Peck, *Being Jewish in the New Germany* (New Brunswick, NJ: Rutgers University Press, 2006), chapter 3.

9. Alexander Jungmann, *Jüdisches Leben in Berlin: Der aktuelle Wandel in einer metropolitanen Diasporagemeinschaft* (Bielefeld: Transcript Verlag, 2007), 427–542; Peck, *Being Jewish,* 165–68.

10. Quoted in Claire Ann Rosenson, "Jewish Identity Construction in Contemporary Poland: Influences and Alternatives in Ethnic Renewal" (PhD diss., University of Michigan, 1997), 69.

11. Ibid., chapter 4.

12. Mariusz Gądek, ed., *Wokół Strachu: Dyskusja o Książce Jana T. Grossa* (Kraków: Znak, 2008); Monika Krawczyk, "Restytucja mienia gmin żydowskich w Polsce—stan rzeczy z perspektywy (prawie) 10 lat," *Midrasz* no. 1 (January 2006): 26–28; Antony Polonsky and Joanna B. Michlic, eds., *The Neighbors Respond: The Controversy of the Jedwabne Massacre in Poland* (Princeton, NJ: Princeton University Press, 2004); Stanisław Tyszka, "Holocaust Remembrance and Restitution of Jewish Property in the Czech Republic and Poland after 1989," in *A European Memory? Contested Histories and Politics of Remembrance,* ed. Małgorzata Pakier and Bo Sträth (New York: Berghahn Books, 2010), 175–90; Magdalena Waligórska, "Der Fiedler als Feigenblatt: Die Politisierung des Klezmer in Polen," *Osteuropa* 58, nos. 8–10 (2008): 395–408; Geneviève Zubrzycki, *The Crosses of Auschwitz: Nationalism and Religion in Post-Communist Poland* (Chicago: University of Chicago Press, 2006).

13. U.S. Public Law 99–83, Section 1303, August 8, 1985.

14. Theo Richmond, *Konin: A Quest* (New York: Pantheon Books, 1995). On post-Zionism, positive evaluations of diaspora, and new Jewish identities, see Aviv Caryn and David Shneer, *New Jews: The End of the Jewish Diaspora* (New York: New York University Press, 2005); Daniel Boyarin and Jonathan Boyarin, "Generation: The Ground of Jewish Identity," *Critical Inquiry* 19, no. 4 (1993): 693–725; Laurence Silberstein, *The Postzionism Debates: Knowledge and Power in Israeli Culture* (New York: Routledge, 1999).

15. The first major travel book appeared in 1962, and since 1958 the London *Jewish Chronicle* has published the *Jewish Travel Guide,* but these were the only main travel guides available that covered Jewish tourist sites in Europe until the

1980s (Bernard Postal and Samuel H. Abramson, *The Landmarks of a People: A Guide to Jewish Sites in Europe* [New York: Hill and Wang, 1962]). In 2003, a *NYT* reporter indicated that more than 100,000 Israeli and American Jews visit Poland every year (Peter S. Green, "Jewish Museum in Poland: More than a Memorial," *NYT,* January 9, 2003). I do not know of a similar estimate for Germany, but it is most likely lower because standard Jewish tours do not include Germany. The main exception is Berlin, which has become a major site of Jewish travel. Germany also gets a sizeable number of non-Jews who visit Holocaust sites (Poland does as well with many non-Jews visiting Auschwitz).

16. Eva Hoffman, *Shtetl: The History of a Small Town and an Extinguished World* (New York: Vintage, 1997), 1.

17. Jack Kugelmass and Jonathan Boyarin, *From a Ruined Garden: The Memorial Books of Polish Jewry* (Bloomington: Indiana University Press, 1998); Jeffrey Shandler, *Adventures in Yiddishland: Postvernacular Language and Culture* (Berkeley: University of California Press, 2006).

18. Hillel Halkin, "The Road to Naybikhov," *Commentary* (November 1998): 39.

19. David H. Lui, "A Return to Galicia: Shtetl Life at the Turn of the Twenty-First Century," *Avotaynu* 11, no. 4 (1995): 49. For similar narratives about Poland and Ukraine, see Roseanna Tendler Worth, "A Trip to the Shtetl of My Ancestors," *Avotaynu* 3, no. 4 (1987): 19–26; Gordon Cohn, "Traces of a Vanished World," *Avotaynu* 14, no. 4 (1998): 61–63; Ruth Rosenbloom, "A Trip to Ukraine," *Avotaynu* 14, no. 4 (1998): 51–53; Aharon Appelfeld, "Buried Homeland," *The New Yorker* (November 23, 1998): 48–61.

20. Jack Kugelmass, "The Rites of the Tribe: The Meaning of Poland for American Jewish Tourists," *YIVO Annual* 21 (1993): 419; Jackie Feldman, *Above the Death Pits, Beneath the Flag: Youth Voyages to Poland and the Performance of Israeli National Identity* (New York: Berghahn Books, 2008); Rona Sheramy, "From Auschwitz to Jerusalem: Re-enacting Jewish History on the March of the Living," *POLIN: Studies in Polish Jewry* 19 (2007): 307–26.

21. Director General's Circular, Ministry of Education, January 1991, quoted in Feldman, *Death Pits,* 58.

22. Greer Fay Cashman, "The March of the Living," *Jerusalem Post,* May 15, 1990.

23. Appelfeld, "Buried Homeland," 51, 61.

24. www.berlinseruv.com, created by Maya Escobar (accessed June 22, 2010).

25. Hugo Bettauer, *Die Stadt ohne Juden: Ein Roman von übermorgen* (Vienna: Gloriette-Verlag, 1922); Artur Landsberger, *Berlin ohne Juden* (Hannover: Paul Steegemann, 1925). See Scott Spector, "Modernism without Jews: A Counter-Historical Argument," *Modernism/Modernity* 13, no. 4 (2006): 615–33.

26. Harry Zohn, "Die Stadt ohne Juden," *Das Jüdische Echo,* 4, no. 5 (1956), quoted in *Stadt ohne Juden,* ed. Guntram Geser and Armin Loacker (Vienna: Filmarchiv Austria, 2000), 7; Bernt Engelmann, *Germany without Jews,* trans. D. J. Beer (New York: Bantam Books, 1984); Milan Kundera, "The Tragedy of Central Europe," *NYRB,* April 26, 1984, 35.

27. "In Worte gefasst," *DT,* March 16, 2008.

28. *Imagebefragung: Tourismusstandort Berlin in seiner bezirklichen Vielfalt* (Berlin: KOMBI Consult GmbH, 2006), 77–78.

29. Meike Wöhlert, "Der Hype um den Davidstern: Was als jüdisch gilt, ist schwer in Mode: Doch Normalität ist deshalb noch lange nicht eingekehrt," *Zitty,* July 30–August 12, 1998, 14–20.

30. Hartwig Dieser and Andreas Wilke, *Zwischenbilanz und Ausblick: Stadterneuerung in Berlin-Mitte, Sanierungsgebiet Spandauer Vorstadt* (Berlin: Bezirksamt von Mitte, 2005).

31. Joachim Schlör, *Das Ich der Stadt: Debatten über Judentum und Urbanität, 1822–1938* (Göttingen: Vandenhoeck & Ruprecht, 2005), 111–13.

32. Alexander Granach quoted in *Das Scheuenenviertel: Spuren eines verlorenen Berlins* (Berlin: Haude und Spencer, 1996), 63.

33. Quoted in Steven E. Aschheim, *Brothers and Strangers: The East European Jew in German and German-Jewish Consciousness, 1800–1923* (Madison: University of Wisconsin Press, 1982), 185.

34. Ibid., chapters 7 and 8.

35. Joachim Schlör, "Bilder Berlins als 'jüdischer Stadt': Ein Beitrag zur Wahrnehmungsgeschichte der deutschen Metropole," *Archiv für Sozialgeschichte* (1997): 207–29.

36. See Ruth Ellen Gruber, *Upon the Doorposts of Thy House: Jewish Life in East-Central Europe* (New York: Wiley, 1994); Claudio Magris, *Weit von wo: Die verlorene Welt des Ostjudentums* (Vienna: Europa-Verlag, 1974); Martin Pollack, *Nach Galizien: Von Chassiden, Huzulen, Polen und Ruthenen: Eine imaginäre Reise durch die verschwundene Welt Ostgaliziens und der Bukowina* (Vienna: C. Brandstätter, 1984); Michael A. Riff, *The Face of Survival: Jewish Life in Eastern Europe Past and Present* (London: Valentine Mitchell, 1992); Edward Serotta, *Out of the Shadows: A Photographic Portrait of Jewish Life in Central Europe since the Holocaust* (Secaucus, NJ: Carol Publishing Group, 1991); Mark Zborowski and Elizabeth Herzog, *Life Is with People: The Jewish Little Town of Eastern Europe* (New York: International Universities Press, 1952).

37. Kirsten Küppers, "Marketing mit Davidstern," *DT,* November 20, 2000; Andrew Roth and Michael Frajman, *The Goldapple Guide to Jewish Berlin* (Berlin: Goldapple, 1998); Bill Rebiger, *Jewish Berlin: Culture, Religion, and Daily Life Yesterday and Today* (Berlin: Jaron, 2005). See also Joachim Schlör, "From Remnants to Realities: Is There Something beyond a 'Jewish Disneyland' in Eastern Europe," *Journal of Modern Jewish Studies* 2, no. 2 (2003): 150–51; Joachim Schlör, "Auf der Suche nach dem Ort des Judentums," *Kritische Berichte: Zeitschrift für Kunst- und Kulturwissenschaften* 24, no. 3 (1996): 6–12.

38. Shimon Attie, "The Writing on the Wall, Berlin, 1992–1993: Projections in Berlin's Jewish Quarter," *Art Journal* 62, no. 3 (2003): 75.

39. Iris Weiss, "Jewish Disneyland—die Aneignung und Enteignung des 'Jüdischen,'" *Golem: Europäisch-jüdisches Magazin* nr. 3 (2000): 47.

40. Ibid.

41. *"Tuet auf die Pforten": Die Neue Synagoge 1866–1995* (Berlin: Stiftung Centrum Judaicum, 1995), 63–83.

42. "Trügerischer Schein eingedenk der 'Weltunordnung,'" *DT,* May 8, 1995.

43. Tomasz Urzykowski, "Nie z cegły i cementu, lecz z rurek i brezentu," *GW,* April 9, 2004.

44. Tomasz Markiewicz, "Próżna: Czas podsumowań," *GW,* March 19, 1999; Janusz Sujecki, *Próżna: Ocalona ulica żydowskiej Warszawy* (Warsaw: Ortis, 1993), 26–28.

45. "Próżna po staremu," *GW,* February 6, 1998.

46. Dariusz Bartoszewicz, "Próżna jak dawniej," *GW,* March 12, 1999.

47. Dariusz Bartoszewicz, "To nie będzie 'żydowski Disneyland,'" *GW,* March 12, 1999.

48. Tomasz Urzykowski, "Kto uratuje Próżną," *GW,* September 20, 2005.

49. Dorota Jarecka, "Kto uratuje żółte drzwi z Próżnej," *GW,* September 10, 2007.

50. "Czy ulica Próżna może być pełna?" June 6, 2008, in author's possession.

51. Joanna Woźniczko, "Święto żydowskiej kultury," *GW,* September 9, 2005; Karolina Błońska and Tomasz Urzykowski, "Singer wraca na Próżną," *GW,* October 14, 2004.

52. "Projekt Próżna 2007," *GW,* September 2–9, 2007 (a special insert for the festival).

53. Dorota Jarecka, "Pusta Próżna," *GW,* September 6, 2006.

54. www.otwartatwarda.pl, official website for the "Open Twarda" Jewish Festival organized by the Warsaw Jewish Community; www.stacjamuranow.art.pl, official website for the Internet project "Station Muranów;" www.chlodna25.blog .pl, official website for Café Chłodna 25 (all three accessed June 29, 2010).

55. "The Winner: The Never-Ending Dialogue Project," *Newsletter of the Museum of the History of Polish Jews* (Summer 2005): 9.

56. Quotes in "The Groundbreaking Ceremony," *Newsletter of the Museum of the History of Polish Jews* (Fall 2007): 5–6.

57. Adrian Wójcik, Michał Bilewicz, and Maria Lewicka, "Living on the Ashes: Collective Representations of Polish-Jewish History among People Living in the Former Warsaw Ghetto Area," *Cities* 27, no. 4 (2010): 195–203.

58. Joanna Podgórska, "Muzeum życia," *Polityka,* June 27, 2007; Tomasz Urzykowski, "Podróż w czasie," *GW,* January 31, 2005.

59. Andrzej Osęka, "Blizna pamięci," *Wprost,* July 10, 2005. See also Bartosz Marzec, "Przejdźmy się Nalewkami," *Rzeczpospolita,* July 18, 2002; "Wirtualne Nalewki," *GW,* April 20, 2001. On the exhibition contents, see Michael C. Steinlauf, "What Story to Tell? Shaping the Narrative of the Museum of the Holocaust of Polish Jews," *POLIN: Studies in Polish Jewry* 20 (2008): 318–23.

60. The Museum of the History of Polish Jews in Warsaw, International Design Competition, Competition Regulations, 3–4.

61. *Leistung und Schicksal: 300 Jahre Jüdische Gemeinde zu Berlin* (Berlin: Berlin Museum, 1971), 7.

62. Irmgard Wirth, "Die Jüdische Abteilung: Zur geplanten Neugründung des Berlin Museums," *Berlinische Notizen* nr. 1–2 (1975): 7–12.

63. Ibid., 10.

64. Eberhard Diepgen, November 26, 1986, printed in "Eröffnung neuer Schauräume für die Jüdische Abteilung des Berlin Museums im Martin-Gropius-Bau," *Berlinische Notizen* nr. 4 (1987): 132.

65. Gesellschaft für ein Jüdisches Museum in Berlin to Mayor Richard von Weizsäcker, June 10, 1983, reprinted in *Das Jüdische Museum im Stadtmuseum Berlin: Eine Dokumentation,* ed. Martina Weinland and Kurt Winkler (Berlin: Nicolai, 1997), 172–73.

66. *Realisierungswettbewerb Erweiterung Berlin Museum mit Abteilung Jüdisches Museum* (Berlin: Senat für Bau und Wohnungswesen, 1988), 15.

67. Katrin Pieper, *Die Musealisierung des Holocaust: Das Jüdische Museum Berlin und das U.S. Holocaust Memorial Museum in Washington D.C.* (Cologne: Böhlau, 2006), 225–32.

68. Quotes from "Daniel Libeskind: An Architectural Interview," *Architectural Design* 60 nos. 3–4 (1990): 17; Daniel Libeskind, *Traces of the Unborn* (Ann Arbor: University of Michigan College of Architecture and Urban Planning, 1995), 35. The picture of the Berlin museum as a "ruin" I discovered from George Steinmetz, "Colonial Melancholy and Fordist Nostalgia: The Ruinscapes of Namibia and Detroit," in *Ruins of Modernity,* ed. Julia Hell and Andreas Schönle (Durham, NC: Duke University Press, 2010), 302.

69. *Stories of an Exhibition: Two Millennia of German-Jewish History* (Berlin: Jewish Museum Berlin, 2001), 14. For discussion of the exhibition planning, see Pieper, *Musealisierung,* 250–302.

70. "Grußwort von Bundespräsident Johannes Rau bei der Eröffnung der ständigen Ausstellung des Jüdischen Museums Berlin," September 9, 2001, *Mitteilungen für die Presse: Bundespräsidialamt.*

71. www.wroclaw.pl, official website of Wrocław Municipality (accessed June 3, 2010).

72. Ibid.

73. Gregor Thum, "Wrocław and the Myth of the Multicultural Border City," *European Review* 13, no. 2 (2005): 227–35; Gregor Thum, "Wrocław's Search for a New Historical Narrative: From Polonocentrism to Postmodernism," in *Cities after the Fall of Communism: Reshaping Cultural Landscapes and European Identity,* ed. John Czaplicka, Nida Gelazis, and Blair A. Ruble (Washington, DC: Woodrow Wilson Center, 2009), 75–101.

74. Norman Davies and Roger Moorhouse, *Microcosm: A Portrait of a Central European City* (London: Jonathan Cape, 2002). On the concept of "Central Europe," see Peter Bugge, "The Use of the Middle: Mitteleuropa vs. Střední Evropa,"

European Review of History 6, no. 1 (1999): 15–35; Maciej Janowski, "Pitfalls and Opportunities: The Concept of East-Central Europe as a Tool of Historical Analysis," *European Review of History* 6, no. 1 (1999): 91–100; Lonnie R. Johnson, *Central Europe: Enemies, Neighbors, Friends* (New York: Oxford University Press, 1996); Tony Judt, "The Rediscovery of Central Europe," in *Eastern Europe— Central Europe—Europe,* ed. Stephen R. Graubard (Boulder, CO: Westview, 1991), 23–58; Iver B. Neumann, "Russia as Central Europe's Constituting Other," *EEPS* 7, no. 2 (1993): 349–69; Jacques Rupnik, "Central Europe or Mitteleuropa?" in *Eastern Europe,* ed. Graubard, 233–65; Gale Stokes, "Eastern Europe's Defining Fault Lines," in *Three Eras of Political Change in Eastern Europe,* ed. Gale Stokes (New York: Oxford University Press, 1997), 7–22; Jeno Szucs, "The Three Historical Regions of Europe," *Acta Historica Academiae Scientarium Hungaricae* 29, nos. 2–4 (1983): 131–84.

75. AMKZ, synagogue file, public letter, September 24, 1995. See also AMKZ, synagogue file, "Synagoga pod Białym Bocianem we Wrocławiu," undated; "Dzieje Synagogi pod Białym Bocianem," in *Biuletyn Informacyjny Gminy Wyznaniowej Żydowskiej we Wrocławiu* no. 3 (July 1999): 1–3.

76. "Ocalić wierzącym, uwierzyć ocalonym," *Gazeta Dolnośląska,* January 27, 1995.

77. "I spotkania z kulturą żydowską," *GW,* January 29, 1999; "Na pograniczu dwóch światów," *GW,* May 29, 2000. See also www.simcha.art.pl, a website devoted to Jewish culture in Wrocław sponsored by the Jewish Culture Festival SIMCHA.

78. Craig S. Smith, "In Poland, a Jewish Revival Thrives—Minus Jews," *NYT,* July 12, 2007.

79. Quote from first page of www.fbk.org.pl, the Bente Kahan Foundation website (accessed June 9, 2008).

80. Maciej Łagiewski, *Wrocławscy Żydzi 1850–1944* (Wrocław: Muzeum Historyczne, 1994); Leszek Ziątkowski, *Dzieje Żydów we Wrocławiu* (Wrocław: Wydawnictwo Dolnośląskie, 2000); "Wallstrasse dla Włodkowica," *GW,* March 20, 1999 and March 27, 1999; "Jak zostałem Żydem," *GW,* November 10, 2006, November 17, 2006, and November 24, 2006.

81. Kahan quote from www.fbk.org.pl, the Bente Kahan Foundation website (accessed June 9, 2008); mayor quoted in "Wrocław: Uroczystość otwarcia Synagogi pod Białym Bocianem," *Katolicka Agencja Informacyjna,* May 7, 2010, www.system.ekai.pl/kair (accessed May 27, 2010).

82. This becomes especially clear in comparison to Łódź. See Joanna Michlic, "Łódź in the Postcommunist Era: In Search of a New Identity," in Czaplicka, Gelazis, and Ruble, *Cities after the Fall of Communism,* 281–303.

83. John Arnold and Ute Stargardt, "The Wrocław Project," *Shofar: An Interdisciplinary Journal of Jewish Studies* 21, no. 4 (2003): 68.

84. RAES, 19–606, box 1, meeting protocols for March 18, 1980, November 26, 1981, and March 16, 1982; Wilhelm Godde, "Wahrnehmung eines Monuments

im Herzen der Stadt," in *Ein Haus, das bleibt: Aus Anlass 20 Jahre Alte Synagoge Essen* (Essen: Klartext, 2000), 52.

85. RAES, 19–606, box 1, meeting protocol for March 16, 1982; memo on meeting with Chief Rabbi Hochwald, November 27, 1984.

86. RAES, 19–606, box 1, notes on meeting, October 2, 1986.

87. *Gestern Synagoge—Alte Synagoge heute* (Essen: Alte Synagoge, 1999), 20.

88. "Werk eines Meisters," *WAZ,* November 5, 1988.

89. "Bauwerk der Erinnerung," *WAZ,* November 5, 1988.

90. "Nach 1945 wurde noch viel zerstört," *NRZ,* September 6, 1986.

91. RAES, 19–606, box 1, Godde to Gaudig, April 17, 1985.

92. RAES, 19–606, box 1, Schmidt to Drewel, September 17, 1987.

93. "Alte Synagoge in Essen wurde wiedereröffnet," *WAZ,* November 7, 1988; "Weiter wirken als Stein des Anstoßes," *WAZ,* November 7, 1988.

94. "Neukonzeption Alte Synagoge Essen," *Niederschrift über die Sitzung des Rates der Stadt,* February 27, 2008.

95. Reinhard Paß, "Neueröffnung der Alten Synagoge zum Haus jüdischer Kultur," July 13, 2010, from www.essen.de, the official website of the city of Essen (accessed July 21, 2010).

96. Marcus Schymiczek, "Ein Haus des Austauschs," *WAZ,* March 5, 2008.

97. Jordan, *Structures of Memory;* Karen E. Till, *The New Berlin: Memory, Politics, Place* (Minneapolis: University of Minnesota Press, 2005).

98. Both quotes from www.potsdam.de, the official website of the city of Potsdam (accessed June 10, 2008).

99. This number is for the Jewish Community of Potsdam (Jüdische Gemeinde Stadt Potsdam), which is the community recognized by the Central Council of Jews in Germany. Potsdam has two other communities: the Law-Abiding Jewish State Community (Gesetzestreue Jüdische Landesgemeinde; about 30 members) and the Synagogue Community (Synagogengemeinde; about 60 members). Numbers from www.zentralratdjuden.de, the Central Council of Jews' official website (accessed March 10, 2011), and "Land beteuert, es fördere jüdisches Leben in Potsdam," *MA,* January 11, 2011.

100. See Schoeps's opening editorial of the first issue, *Dialog* no. 1 (1998): 1.

101. Jürgen Zieher, "'Wer ein Haus baut, will bleiben': Synagogenbau in Dortmund, Düsseldorf, und Köln in den fünfziger Jahren," *Beiträge zur Geschichte Dortmunds und der Grafschaft Mark* 91 (2000): 203–43.

102. Thomas Kunze, "Aus einer Kirchenruine soll die Synagoge wachsen," *Berliner Zeitung,* April 6, 1995.

103. Werner van Bebber, "Neubau der Synagoge ist es noch weit," *DT,* March 10, 1998.

104. Thorsten Metzner, "Authentische Orte des Schreckens als Gedenkstätten," *DT,* October 30, 1998.

105. Volker Eckert, "Auf der Suche nach dem verlorenen Ort," *DT,* February 2, 2004.

106. Ildiko Röd, "Jüdische Gemeinde ohne Platz," *MA*, January 29, 2007.

107. Christoph Tanneberger, "Geld für neue Synagoge fehlt," *MA*, November 10, 2007.

108. "Potsdam verdient eine echte Synagoge," *PNN*, March 3, 2010; "Und das soll eine Synagoge sein?," *PNN*, March 25, 2010; "Ud Joffe Zugang zum Synagogenverein verwehrt," *PNN*, May 28, 2010; Olaf Glöckner, "Zu klein, zu hoch, zu unjüdisch," *Jüdische Allgemeine*, June 10, 2010; "Eine dritte Gemeinde in Potsdam," *Jüdische Allgemeine*, June 24, 2010.

109. Manuel Herz, "Institutionalized Experiment: The Politics of 'Jewish Architecture' in Germany," *JSS* 11, no. 3 (2005): 62.

110. Avraham Burg, *The Holocaust Is Over: We Must Rise from Its Ashes* (New York: Palgrave MacMillan, 2008), 14. Critical scholarly accounts of the Holocaust in American and Israeli life include Feldman, *Death Pits;* Ronit Lentin, *Israel and the Daughters of the Shoah: Reoccupying the Territories of Silence* (New York: Berghahn, 2000); Peter Novick, *The Holocaust in American Life* (New York: Houghton Mifflin, 1999); Idith Zertal, *Israel's Holocaust and the Politics of Nationhood*, trans. Chaya Galai (New York: Cambridge University Press, 2005).

111. Here my thinking has been influenced by A. Dirk Moses's highly insightful use of redemption to interpret German intellectual debates about the Nazi past in A. Dirk Moses, *German Intellectuals and the Nazi Past* (New York: Cambridge University Press, 2007). See also Ulrike Jureit, "Opferidentifikation und Erlösungshoffnung: Beobachtungen im erinnerungspolitischen Rampenlicht," in *Gefühlte Opfer: Illusionen der Vergangenheitsbewältigung*, Ulrike Jureit and Christian Schneider (Stuttgart: Klett-Cotta, 2010), 19–103. Although "redemption" by expelling or including Jews is one broad similarity with Saul Friedländer's redemptive antisemitism, I am not attempting to draw simplistic parallels between antisemitism and philosemitism. Rather, my point is to capture the redemptive effect that I see present in public, political discourses about Jewish sites.

112. Jürgen Habermas, *The Postnational Constellation: Political Essays*, trans. and ed. Max Pensky (Cambridge, MA: MIT Press, 2001).

113. Tadeusz Mazowiecki, "Questions to Ourselves," *Dialectics and Humanism* 17, no. 2 (1990): 13.

114. The right is stronger in Poland than in Germany despite similar causes— unemployment, dissatisfaction after 1989, and traditional anti-Jewish prejudices. One main difference is that Germany's political elite has reacted strongly against right-wing populism after a long postwar learning process. See Werner Bergmann, *Antisemitismus in öffentlichen Konflikten: Kollektives Lernen in der politischen Kultur der Bundesrepublik 1949–1989* (Frankfurt am Main: Campus Verlag, 1997). On the denigration of cosmopolitanism as "Jewish," see Geneviève Zubrzycki, "'Poles-Catholics' and 'Symbolic Jews:' Jewishness as Social Closure in Poland," *Studies in Contemporary Jewry* 21 (2005): 79–80.

115. Quoted in *Newsletter of the Museum of the History of Polish Jews* (Summer 2005): 17.

116. *Stories of an Exhibition,* 12–13.

117. Paß, "Neueröffnung."

118. Maciej Kozłowski, "Muzeum dla Żydów czy dla Polaków?," *Rzeczpospolita,* December 8, 2003.

119. Joschka Fischer, "A Second Chance? Germany and the Jewish Community Today," Annual Meeting of the American Jewish Committee, May 3, 2001, Washington, DC, published at www.germany.info, an information portal sponsored by the German embassy in the United States (accessed July 3, 2008).

120. I am indebted here to Wendy Brown for conceptualizing public displays of tolerance as a management strategy for regulating discomforting, abject parts of the collective self. I do, though, depart from her in seeing tolerance as redemptive in the case of cultural memory, in which restored memory posits resolution, completion, and rehabilitation in the present. Wendy Brown, *Regulating Aversion: Tolerance in the Age of Identity and Empire* (Princeton, NJ: Princeton University Press, 2006).

121. "Enlightened knowledge" from Michael Geyer, "The Politics of Memory in Contemporary Germany," in *Radical Evil,* ed. Joan Copjec (New York: Verso, 1996), 170; Mark Mazower, *Dark Continent: Europe's Twentieth Century* (New York: Vintage, 1999).

122. Ruth Mandel has made the same point in her *Cosmopolitan Anxieties: Turkish Challenges to Citizenship and Belonging in Germany* (Durham, NC: Duke University Press, 2008), 14. In the case of Italy, Jeffrey Feldman has noted a similar development. See Jeffrey D. Feldman, "Ghetto Association: Jewish Heritage, Heroin, and Racism in Bologna," *Identities* 8, no. 2 (2001): 247–282.

123. Klaus Bachmann, "Tolerancja kosztuje," *GW,* April 15, 2007. On immigration, see Rita Chin, *The Guest Worker Question in Postwar Germany* (New York: Cambridge University Press, 2007); Agata Górny et. al., eds., *Immigration to Poland: Policy, Employment, Integration* (Warsaw: Wydawnictwo Naukowe Scholar, 2010); Teresa Halik, *Migrancka społeczność Wietnamczyków w Polsce w świetle polityki państwa i ocen społecznych* (Poznań: Wydawnictwo Naukowe Uniwersytetu im. Adama Mickiewicza, 2006); Joan Wallach Scott, *The Politics of the Veil* (Princeton, NJ: Princeton University Press, 2007); John R. Bowen, *Why the French Don't Like Headscarves: Islam, the State, and Public Space* (Princeton, NJ: Princeton University Press, 2007).

Conclusion

1. Karel C. Berkhoff, *Harvest of Despair: Life and Death under Nazi Rule* (Cambridge, MA: Harvard University Press, 2004), 5; Timothy Snyder, *Bloodlands: Europe between Hitler and Stalin* (New York: Basic Books, 2010).

2. Sarah Farmer, *Martyred Village: Commemorating the 1944 Massacre at Oradour-sur-Glane* (Berkeley: University of California Press, 1999); Tony Judt, *Postwar: A History of Europe since 1945* (New York: Penguin, 2005), 803–31; Pieter Lagrou, *The Legacy of Nazi Occupation: Patriotic Memory and National Recovery*

in Western Europe, 1945–1965 (New York: Cambridge University Press, 2000); Henry Rousso, *The Vichy Syndrome: History and Memory in France since 1944,* trans. Arthur Goldhammer (Cambridge, MA: Harvard University Press, 1991); Joan B. Wolf, *Harnessing the Holocaust: The Politics of Memory in France* (Stanford, CA: Stanford University Press, 2004); Amir Weiner, *Making Sense of War: The Second World War and the Fate of the Bolshevik Revolution* (Princeton, NJ: Princeton University Press, 2001), chapter 4. On Eastern Europe, see the thirteen country overviews in *Osteuropa* 58, nos. 8–10 (2008): 353–497.

3. Judt, *Postwar,* 808.

4. Christine Bauhardt, *Stadtentwicklung und Verkehrspolitik: Eine Analyse aus feministischer Sicht* (Berlin: Birkhäuser, 1995); Michael Keith and Steve Pile, *Place and the Politics of Identity* (New York: Routledge, 1993); Henri Lefebvre, *The Production of Space,* trans. Donald Nicholson-Smith (Malden, MA: Blackwell, 1991); Doreen B. Massey, *For Space* (Thousand Oaks, CA: Sage, 2005); Karen M. Morin and Jeanne Kay Guelke, *Women, Religion, and Space: Global Perspectives on Gender and Faith* (Syracuse, NY: Syracuse University Press, 2007); Edward W. Soja, *Postmodern Geographies: The Reassertion of Space in Critical Social Theory* (New York: Verso, 1989).

5. On rebuilding "normal" lives in postwar Europe, see Richard Bessel and Dirk Schumann, eds., *Life after Death: Approaches to a Cultural and Social History of Europe during the 1940s and 1950s* (New York: Cambridge University Press, 2003); Dagmar Herzog, *Sex after Fascism: Memory and Morality in Twentieth-Century Germany* (Princeton, NJ: Princeton University Press, 2005).

6. Svetlana Boym, *The Future of Nostalgia* (New York: Basic Books, 2002), xiii.

7. Rory Boland, "In Poland, Lamp of Jewish Culture Shines Anew," *Boston Globe,* September 30, 2007.

8. I have been influenced by the work of a number of historians on the GDR, PPR, and Soviet Union who have moved beyond the "totalitarian" view of Communist societies. My work enriches our understanding of the interactive relationship between state and society, uncovering not just moments of friction but also those when the regime reflected and was shaped by broader social demands, desires, and prejudices vis-à-vis encounters with the past. See Padraic Kenney, *Rebuilding Poland: Workers and Communists, 1945–1950* (Ithaca, NY: Cornell University Press, 1997); Corey Ross, *The East German Dictatorship: Problems and Perspectives in the Interpretation of the GDR* (New York: Arnold, 2002); Weiner, *Making Sense of War.* For a recent evaluation of the totalitarian model, see Michael Geyer and Sheila Fitzpatrick, eds., *Beyond Totalitarianism: Stalinism and Nazism Compared* (New York: Cambridge University Press, 2009).

9. Transcript at www.pbs.org/wgbh/pages/frontline/shows/germans, the PBS website for this *Frontline* program (accessed June 25, 2008).

10. Ibid.

11. Rita Chin et al., *After the Racial State: Difference and Democracy in Germany and Europe* (Ann Arbor: University of Michigan Press, 2009); Heide Fehrenbach, *Race after Hitler: Black Occupation Children in Postwar Germany and America* (Princeton, NJ: Princeton University Press, 2005); Grzegorz Janusz, *Raport o sytuacji osób należących do mniejszości narodowych i etnicznych w Polsce* (Warsaw: Helsińska Fundacja Praw Człowieka, 1994); Ireneusz Krzemiński, *Czy Polacy są antysemitami?* (Warsaw: Oficyna Naukowa, 1996); Robert G. Moeller, "Germans as Victims? Thoughts on a Post–Cold War History of World War II's Legacies," *History & Memory* 17, nos. 1–2 (2005): 147–94; Gilad Margalit, *Guilt, Suffering, and Memory: Germany Remembers Its Dead of World War II,* trans. Haim Watzman (Bloomington: Indiana University Press, 2010); Harald Welzer, Sabine Moller, and Karoline Tschuggnall, *"Opa war kein Nazi:" Nationalsozialismus und Holocaust im Familiengedächtnis* (Frankfurt am Main: Fischer, 2002); Geneviève Zubrzycki, *The Crosses of Auschwitz: Nationalism and Religion in Post-Communist Poland* (Chicago: University of Chicago Press, 2006). On the vandalization of Jewish property (often cemeteries), see Adolf Diamant, *Geschändete jüdische Friedhöfe in Deutschland, 1945 bis 1999* (Potsdam: Verlag für Berlin-Brandenburg, 2000); FODZ's antisemitic reports since 2003 at www.fodz.pl, the foundation's website (accessed August 24, 2010).

12. Frederic M. Biddle, "Jewish Americans Return to Still Divided 'Shtetl,'" *Boston Globe,* April 17, 1996.

13. Hermeneutics of suspicion from Anthony Kauders, "History as Censure: 'Repression' and 'Philosemitism' in Postwar Germany," *History and Memory* 15, no. 1 (2003): 97–122.

14. Thilo Sarrazin, *Deutschland schafft sich ab: Wie wir unser Land aufs Spiel setzen* (Munich: Deutsche Verlags-Anstalt, 2010), 9. For selections of the debate, see *Sarrazin—Eine Deutsche Debatte* (Munich: Pieper, 2010); *Die Sarrazin Debatte* (Hamburg: Die Zeit, 2010).

15. Sarrazin, *Deutschland schafft sich ab*, 353.

16. "Es gibt viele Sarrazins," *Der Spiegel* no. 36 (2010): 23. The book's success stems partly from the rise in anti-immigrant sentiment in Germany and throughout Europe, as four recent surveys of public opinion have shown. See Wilhelm Heitmeyer, *Deutsche Zustände*, vol. 9 (Berlin: Suhrkamp, 2010); *Die Mitte in der Krise: Rechtsextreme Einstellungen in Deutschland 2010* (Berlin: Friedrich-Ebert-Stiftung, 2010); Detlef Pollack, "Wahrnehmung und Akzeptanz religiöser Vielfalt," published at www.uni-muenster.de/Religion-und-Politik, Pollack's official university website (accessed February 26, 2011); *Sozialreport: Daten und Fakten zur sozialen Lage 20 Jahre nach der Vereinigung* (Berlin: Sozialwissenschaftliches Forschungszentrum Berlin-Brandenburg e.V. im Auftrag der Volkssolidarität Bundesverband e.V., 2010).

17. Starting points for comparative analysis are Allan Pred, *Even in Sweden: Racisms, Racialized Spaces, and the Popular Geographical Imagination* (Berkeley,

CA: University of California Press, 2000); Gallya Lahav, *Immigration and Politics in the New Europe* (New York: Cambridge University Press, 2004); John E. Roemer, Woojin Lee, and Karine Van der Straeten, *Racism, Xenophobia, and Distribution: Multi-Issue Politics in Advanced Democracies* (Cambridge, MA: Harvard University Press, 2007); Steven Vertovec and Susanne Wessendorf, eds., *The Multicultural Backlash: European Discourses, Policies, and Practices* (New York: Routledge, 2009).

18. Chin et al., *After the Nazi Racial State*; Michael Meng, "Sarrazin and Redemptive Cosmopolitanism in Contemporary Germany" (paper presented at the Thirty-Fifth Annual Meeting of the German Studies Association, Louisville, KY, September 2011).

19. On the centrality of Holocaust memory to Habermas's "redemptive republicanism," see A. Dirk Moses, *German Intellectuals and the Nazi Past* (New York: Cambridge University Press, 2007).

20. First appearing in the 1880s, the term "Judeo-Christian"—as a defining value of democracy and the "West"—has had a long, complex career, advanced by progressives and conservatives alike. The secondary literature is richest for the U.S. case. See Douglas Hartmann, Xuefeng Zhang, and William Wischstadt, "One (Multicultural) Nation Under God? Changing Uses and Meanings of the Term 'Judeo-Christian' in the American Media," *Journal of Media and Religion* 4, no. 4 (2005): 207–234; Deborah Dash Moore, "Jewish GIs and the Creation of the Judeo-Christian Tradition," *Religion and American Culture* 8, no. 1 (1998): 31–53; Mark Silk, "Notes on the Judeo-Christian Tradition in America," *American Quarterly* 36, no. 1 (1984): 65–85.

21. Jürgen Habermas, "Leadership and Leitkultur," *NYT,* October 28, 2010.

22. Craig Calhoun, "The Class Consciousness of Frequent Travelers: Toward a Critique of Actually Existing Cosmopolitanism," *South Atlantic Quarterly* 101, no. 4 (2002): 869–897.

23. Paul Gilroy, *Postcolonial Melancholia* (New York: Columbia University Press, 2006), 4.

24. Seyla Benhabib, *The Rights of Others: Aliens, Residents, and Citizens* (New York: Cambridge University Press, 2004), 18.

25. Martha Nussbaum, *For Love of Country: Debating the Limits of Patriotism* (Boston: Beacon Press, 1996), 4.

26. Kwame Anthony Appiah, *Cosmopolitanism: Ethics in a World of Strangers* (New York: W. W. Norton, 2006), xv; Kwame Anthony Appiah, *The Ethics of Identity* (Princeton, NJ: Princeton University Press, 2005), chapter 6.

27. Judith Butler, *Precarious Life: The Powers of Mourning and Violence* (New York: Verso, 2004); B. Venkat Mani, *Cosmopolitical Claims: Turkish-German Literatures from Nadolny to Pamuk* (Iowa City: University of Iowa Press, 2007). Additional discussions of cosmopolitanism include Carol A. Breckenridge et al., eds., *Cosmopolitanism* (Durham, NC: Duke University Press, 2002); Pheng Cheah

and Bruce Robbins, eds., *Cosmopolitics: Thinking and Feeling beyond the Nation* (Minneapolis: University of Minnesota Press, 1998); David Inglis and Gerard Delanty, *Cosmopolitanism,* 4 vols. (New York: Routledge, 2010); Steven Vertovec and Robin Cohen, eds., *Conceiving Cosmopolitanism: Theory, Context, and Practice* (New York: Oxford University Press, 2002); John Tomlinson, *Globalization and Culture* (Chicago: University of Chicago Press, 1999).

28. In advocating for an activist, historically conscious cosmopolitanism in which we challenge our own identifications and think deeply about our pasts I am at once drawing on and departing from Appiah's "cosmopolitan patriotism." While I appreciate his key insight that cosmopolitanism can be deeply rooted in a particular national or local context, I disagree with his seamless joining of cosmopolitanism with patriotism. Cosmopolitanism demands critique of patriotism in a number of circumstances if it is to be more than just a word, and in order for it to develop such a critique, it must rest on a critical understanding of the past. For a fuller articulation of the dilemmas of patriotic and cosmopolitan commitments, see Bruce Robbins, "Cosmopolitanism: New and Newer," *Boundary 2* 34, no. 3 (2007): 47–60.

29. Philip J. Deloria, *Playing Indian* (New Haven, CT: Yale University Press, 1999).

30. Erica Lehrer, "Bearing False Witness? 'Vicarious' Jewish Identity and the Politics of Affinity," in *Imaginary Neighbors: Mediating Polish-Jewish Relations after the Holocaust,* ed. Dorota Glowacka and Joanna Zylinska (Lincoln: University of Nebraska Press, 2007), 84–109; Erica Lehrer, *Jewish Heritage Tourism in Poland* (Bloomington: Indiana University Press, forthcoming). On the ethical potential of non-Jews becoming Jews, see Paul Eisenstein, *Traumatic Encounters: Holocaust Representation and the Hegelian Subject* (Albany: State University of New York Press, 2003), 192.

31. Marcin Kacprzak, *Midrasz* nos. 7–8 (November/December 1997): 4.

32. "Edna Brocke: 'Wir müssen unbefangen miteinander umgehen," *WAZ,* November 7, 2008.

33. Diana Pinto, "Fifty Years after the Holocaust: Building a New Jewish and Polish Memory," *East European Jewish Affairs* 26, no. 2 (1996): 80–81; Diana Pinto, "The Jewish Challenge in the New Europe," in *Challenging Ethnic Citizenship: German and Israeli Perspectives on Immigration,* ed. Daniel Levy and Yfaat Weiss (New York: Berghahn, 2002), 251.

34. I first came upon this quote in a compelling piece by Tony Judt, who argues similarly to what I am suggesting. Tony Judt, "The 'Problem of Evil' in Postwar Europe," *NYRB,* February 14, 2008. Hannah Arendt, *Essays in Understanding, 1930–1954* (New York: Harcourt Brace & Company, 1994), 271–72.

35. Daniel Levy and Natan Sznaider, *The Holocaust and Memory in the Global Age,* trans. Assenka Oksiloff (Philadelphia: Temple University Press, 2006), 197. My understanding of cosmopolitan remembrance mirrors more closely Michael

Rothberg's concept of "multidirectionality" in his *Multidirectional Memory: Remembering the Holocaust in the Age of Decolonization* (Stanford, CA: Stanford University Press, 2009).

36. Ruth Klüger, *Von hoher und niedriger Literatur* (Göttingen: Wallstein Verlag, 1996), 33.

Acknowledgments

Over nearly the decade of working on this book, I have relied on the support of dozens of colleagues, librarians, archivists, institutions, and organizations. A good deal of what I know about history and writing still goes back to my under-graduate years at Boston College in the history, German, and philosophy depart-ments. John Heineman, David Quigley, Michael Resler, and Larry Wolff deserve my thanks for their excellent teaching. At the University of North Carolina at Chapel Hill, Christopher Browning has supported my career at every stage, read-ing drafts, writing letters, listening to my ideas, and responding to endless emails. Konrad Jarausch shaped this project with his intellectual rigor and ability to pin-point exactly how to tighten an argument. Chad Bryant offered detailed com-ments on each chapter that I know made them stronger. Madeline G. Levine, who spent countless hours with me in her office honing my Polish skills and discussing Polish-Jewish relations, is one of the most generous people I know.

A number of colleagues and friends—Winson Chu, Adam Fuss, Erica Lehrer, Jeffry Diefendorf, Jay Geller, Jürgen Lillteicher, Thomas Pegelow-Kaplan, and Jon-athan Zatlin—provided feedback on chapters of this book. Gavriel Rosenfeld commented on the entire manuscript and has been encouraging from the begin-ning when I first emailed him now almost a decade ago. Other colleagues have responded to my work with advice as commentators and participants at confer-ences. I would like to thank Natalia Aleksiun, Doris Bergen, Daniel Blatman, Roger Chickering, David Engel, Jan Gross, Malachi Haim Hacohen, Jeffrey Herf, Jonathan Huener, Paul Jaskot, Catherine Epstein, Heide Fehrenbach, Audrey Kichelewski, Claudia Koonz, Piotr Kosicki, Tom Lekan, Joanna Michlic, Jennifer Miller, Monika Murzyn-Kupisz, Robin Ostow, Anat Plocker, Antony Polonsky, Martin Sabrow, Adam Seipp, Michael Steinlauf, Dariusz Stola, Magdalena Waligórska, and Richard Wetzell. In Germany and Poland, Gertrud Pickhan, Heinz Reif, Jerzy Tomasze-wski, and Philipp Ther kindly invited me to present my research in their graduate seminars.

I took part in three superb workshops, all coincidentally located in Washing-ton, DC, that deepened my thinking about shattered spaces in postwar Europe: the Transatlantic Doctoral Seminar of the German Historical Institute organized by Roger Chickering and Richard Wetzell; a two-week workshop on the Holocaust in Poland led by David Engel and Daniel Blatman at the Center for Advanced Holocaust Studies (CAHS); and a two-week workshop at CAHS on Jewish sites in contemporary Poland organized by myself and Erica Lehrer. A special thanks goes to Erica, whose novel ethnographic research on contemporary Kraków I have learned much from, for being such an enthusiastic co-organizer and colleague.

In Warsaw, Barbara Engelking, Konstanty Gebert, Jan Jagielski, Jolanta Żyndul, and Dariusz Stola took time from their busy schedules to discuss my research. Jacek Leociak met with me on several occasions to talk about our shared interests in the rebuilding of Warsaw. Eleonora Bergman welcomed me to the Jewish Historical Institute and assisted me throughout my time in Warsaw. Fellow graduate students at the time Zofia Wóycicka, Anat Plocker, and Audrey Kichelewski helped me get through a dark, cold Warsaw winter with many good conversations, lunches, and coffee breaks. In Berlin, I gained much from the yearlong interdisciplinary research seminar of the Berlin Program at the Free University, and I enjoyed the good company of Winson Chu, Karolina May-Chu, Greg Eghigian, Jennifer Miller, Greg Witkowski, and Yves Winter.

I wrote this book in Chapel Hill, revised it in Minneapolis, Davidson, NC and Washington, DC, and completed it in Greenville, SC. Along the way, I have been fortunate to have great colleagues at several institutions. At the University of Minnesota, Daniel Schroeter, Leslie Morris, and Gary Cohen provided useful advice about crafting the book. Mary Jo Maynes deserves special thanks for her kindness, support, advice, and grace—she warmly welcomed me into the intellectual life of the department, which she chaired during my year in Minneapolis. Sally McMillen, Michael Guasco, John Wertheimer, LaKisha Simmons, Patricia Tilburg, and Scott Denham made my year at Davidson College exceptionally pleasant and productive. In Washington, DC, I was lucky to spend two summers at CAHS. The staff at the center helped enormously, and I could not have asked for more generous colleagues than Emily Greble, Maggie Paxson, and Dirk Rubnow. At Clemson University, I thank my chair, Thomas Kuehn, for giving me time off from teaching to finish. Beth Carney, Steve Marks, Stephanie Barczewski, James Burns, and Michael Silvestri have made Clemson the collegial and welcoming place that it is. At Harvard University Press, Kathleen McDermott provided me with excellent advice at an early stage about constructing the book's narrative to reach both an academic and a broader audience. She also solicited two outside readers whose comments pushed me to develop my arguments further and refine several key parts of the book. I thank both readers for their stimulating thoughts.

During all of these years of writing, thinking, and research, Kristin Knight has lived with this project from the moment it began in late 2001 in Potsdam, and has read far more drafts than any one single person should. I am grateful for her support and encouragement.

The advice and support of editors, colleagues, friends, and family are crucial, but without libraries, archives, and grant organizations, historians could never even try to reconstruct the past. I want to thank the staffs of the numerous institutions that I visited in Germany, Poland, Israel, and the United States for their assistance. Finally, I owe a special thanks to the organizations that supported my research. This project began during a wonderful year when I was a Fulbright scholar just after my undergraduate studies. The Berlin Program for Advanced German and European Studies at the Free University of Berlin and the German Marshall Fund supported my research in Germany and Poland. The Holocaust Education Foundation enabled me to conduct research in Israel. Foreign Language and Area Studies and the American Council of Learned Societies (ACLS) funded my study of Polish. A Charles H. Revson Foundation Fellowship from CAHS made my research in Washington, DC, possible, and a Dr. Richard M. Hunt Fellowship for the Study of German Politics, Society, and Culture of the American Council on Germany funded one final push of research in Berlin and Essen. An ACLS East European Postdoctoral Fellowship gave me what every writer needs most but never seems to have enough of—time to think, read, write, revise, and finish. A Production and Presentation Grant from the Graham Foundation for Advanced Studies in the Fine Arts defrayed costs for the images, maps, and index. I am grateful to the Friends of the German Historical Institute in Washington, DC for their support and recognition in awarding me the Fritz Stern Prize.

Finally, I thank the University of Michigan Press for granting me permission to reprint some material that appears in Chapter 3, which was originally published in Gavriel Rosenfeld and Paul Jaskot's *Beyond Berlin: Twelve German Cities Confront the Nazi Past* (Ann Arbor, MI: University of Michigan Press, 2008).

Index